THE MEXICANS

THE
MEXICANS

A Personal
Portrait of a People

PATRICK OSTER

PERENNIAL LIBRARY

Harper & Row, Publishers, New York
Grand Rapids, Philadelphia, St. Louis, San Francisco
London, Singapore, Sydney, Tokyo, Toronto

To Sally and Alex

A hardcover edition of this book was originally published in 1989 by William Morrow and Company, Inc. It is here reprinted by arrangement with William Morrow and Company, Inc.

First PERENNIAL LIBRARY edition published 1990.

Library of Congress Cataloging-in-Publication Data

Oster, Patrick.
    The Mexicans : a personal portrait of a people / Patrick Oster. —
1st Perennial Library ed.
        p.   cm.
    Includes bibliographical references.
    ISBN 0-06-097310-2
        1. National characteristics, Mexican.   2. Mexico—Social
conditions—1970–   3. Mexico—Economic conditions—1970–   4. Mexico—
Politics and government—1970–   5. Mexico—Moral conditions.
I. Title.
F1210.O84   1990   89-45843
972.08'34—dc20

99 RRD-H 20 19 18 17 16 15 14

· Acknowledgments ·

When Alan Riding's book, *Distant Neighbors: A Portrait of the Mexicans,* was published, many of the people he thanked in his acknowledgments had to run for cover. The Mexican government often equates critical comments made by Mexicans about Mexico with treason. Officials make nasty calls even to Mexicans who live in the United States. They question their patriotism and tell them to shut up. Under such pressure, some of the people whom Riding thanked for help with his book publicly denied that they had given him any aid at all. With this in mind, I hesitantly thank a small group of people whose observations or writings helped me get a better handle on how Mexico works, or doesn't. I did not agree with all of what these people told me. In some cases, as the ideological range of the names listed below should make clear, I violently disagreed with them. But I thank them anyway for making me think about whether I was right or wrong in my opinions. That said, thanks to Reardon Roett, Luis Rubio, José Manuel Suárez Mier, Manuel Alonso, Soledad Loaeza, Sidney Weintraub, Clark Reynolds, Jorge Bustamante, Octavio Paz, Carlos Monsiváis, Carlos Fuentes, Gabriel Zaid, John Walsh, Manuel Compean, Sam Taylor, Rogelio Ramírez de la O, Jack Sweeney, Lieutenant Colonel Steve Wager, Martin Needler, Enrique Krause, Ed Heath, George Grayson, John Bailey, Gabriel Szekeley, Adolfo

Aguilar Zinser, Guadalupe Loaeza, Lorenzo Meyer, Rosario Ibarra de la Piedra, José González González, and hundreds of Mexicans I met in the streets of Mexico City or in the small towns of the countryside.

Special thanks to Octavio Paz, Vince Hovanec, Arturo Montaña, Froylán López Narváez, Jorge Castañeda, Richard Beene, Dianne Klein, Richard Millett, Clint Smith, Susan Kaufman Purcell, and Sally Shelton Colby, who read all or parts of my manuscript to help me weed out unfair comments and keep errors to a minimum. For anything they missed, blame only me.

This book is my first, so I'm invoking author's privilege to thank a few people who helped me get to the point where I could write one. Jim Hoge, now publisher of the New York Daily News, was brave enough to give a young, bored lawyer with no journalism experience his first reporting job when all the other editors in Chicago thought a move from the courtroom to the newsroom was financial madness. Those early years in the burly world of Chicago journalism gave me the chance to sit next to some great writers. Some, such as Mike Royko, Roger Simon, Bill Granger, and Bob Greene, were or have become famous columnists and book writers in their own right. Others, such as M. K. Newman and the late Hugh Hough, remain less famous outside Chicago but were no less talented. It was an excellent training ground for a beginner. I peeked over their shoulders shamelessly, cribbing bits of style that I hope have stuck. Roger Simon in particular, a sensitive writer of eloquence and wit, showed a newcomer the ropes.

I thank my wife, Sally, most of all. She was a reporter before I was. If you ask her, she will jokingly tell you that I stole the idea of being a reporter from her. I can't deny it. But I'm glad she was there for me to steal from. I've never had so much fun.

Thanks to Jim Anderson, who kept me up-to-date on Mexico after I left. Thanks too to my agent, Elaine Markson, who took a book idea that others said would be a hard sell because, supposedly, no one wants to read about Latin America. She sold it in less than a month. Lisa Drew, my editor at William Morrow, offered me intelligent suggestions on how to improve my material. At the beginning of the project, she knew little about Mexico. Now she tells me she has become fascinated with the country because of the people she has met in the chapters that follow. No one could have paid me a nicer compliment.

· Contents ·

III   Values

Conclusion

· Introduction ·

I grew up a Midwesterner, so perhaps it was natural that Mexico was not part of my world. I never tried to avoid it. It just seems that most of my life I voyaged around it.

My influences were the Irish, Dutch, and German traditions of Chicago, the influences of my parents. In my insularity, only belatedly did I come to realize that there were people called Mexicans whose land began in a young boy's netherworld called the border. Other Mexicans, I remember hearing, lived a bit closer, in Chicago neighborhoods such as Pilsen. But for whatever reason, I never got there. Even when I became a reporter for the *Chicago Sun-Times* in 1973 and set out fresh-faced and eager, to discover all the secret, obscure aspects of the Second City, I never made it to these Mexican realms. They and all things Mexican remained terra incognita.

Although Mexico would later become very important to me—the land of my adopted son—I thought very little about it as my career in journalism progressed. Even when I began covering foreign affairs from Washington, D.C., for the *Sun-Times* in 1978, Mexico was hardly ever what the diplomats call a front-burner issue. It seemed—or so I thought at the time—that it would remain in the penumbra of my thoughts.

I did not make my first trip to Mexico until 1979. The details of it remain mostly a blur. I was part of the White House press corps accompanying President Jimmy Carter on a state visit there. It was a quick, in-and-out trip. I learned little of the country. We traveled in a presidential cocoon, protected from the unpleasant reality of Mexico City. The normally clogged streets and highways of the capital were rudely cleared of traffic by officious police to ease the way for our motorcade. We stayed at the best hotel in town, ate at the best restaurants. My experience was not unlike that of most of the four million U.S. tourists who visit the country each year and come away with the impression that Mexico is mostly colonial costumes, mariachi bands, sunny beaches, spicy food, and impure water.

I came back to Mexico in 1981 with President Ronald Reagan to report on a summit meeting of Third World nations that he had agreed to attend. The meeting was held in the Caribbean resort of Cancún, which did little to improve my knowledge of the country. Finally, in 1982, I returned on my own to cover the beginning of the economic crisis that still grips Mexico today. Only then did I begin to get a glimmer of the importance and complexity of the country. It was only a two-week visit, though, nothing more than an interesting diversion from what seemed the important issues of the day: arms control, tensions in the Middle East, and the war in El Salvador. I still had no inkling that my fate and Mexico's would soon be linked. In fact, after experiencing Mexico City's horrendous pollution, uncooperative bureaucrats, unworkable phones, and gridlocked traffic, I remember telling my wife upon returning home: "I hope I never have to go back there again!" In early 1984, however, Australian media magnate Rupert Murdoch bought the *Sun-Times,* and I found myself looking for a new job. Mentally, I was heading east, hoping for an overseas post in Lebanon, which was red-hot at the time. But something was pulling me south. And I wound up in Mexico.

In July 1984, shortly before I left Washington to become the Mexico City bureau chief for the Knight-Ridder newspaper chain, I met author David McCullough, who told me that I should consider my new post a wonderful opportunity, even though it might not seem to be where the action was.

"I envy you," said McCullough, who had just spent a lot of time in Latin America researching *The Path Between the Seas,* his fine history of the Panama Canal. "A person who knows about Mexico will be worth something."

Inspired partly by that chat, I threw myself into my new beat, delving into every aspect of Mexican life that I found new, interesting, or weird. By the fall of 1986, after more than two years on the job, I was feeling that I was getting to know this hard-to-fathom beast called Mexico. Then a strange thing happened. I found myself rummaging through the still pervasive rubble of the twin earthquakes that had struck Mexico City in the fall of 1985. I wanted to see why reconstruction efforts were taking so long. One of the areas I visited was Tepito, a gritty, center-city neighborhood famous for black-market operations. I met a man whose house had just been bulldozed as part of frantic city efforts to clean up damaged areas as the government prepared to report on the quakes' one-year anniversary.

"I'm one of the Children of Sánchez," the short, gregarious man told me.

By chance I had met Manuel Sánchez, whose family had become an eponym for Latin American poverty thanks to Oscar Lewis's classic 1961 work, *The Children of Sánchez.* Like many who come to Mexico, I had heard of Lewis's book but had not read it. Before leaving Washington, I had purchased a copy for my office library. But there it had stayed, victim of seemingly more pressing projects. I knew enough about the importance of the book, however, not to let the mythic Mr. Sánchez slip through my fingers.

"I'd like to talk to you in a few weeks," I told him. "I'd like to write about what's happened to your family since the book was published."

Including a stop-everything, note-taking reading of Lewis's book, I spent more time reporting that story than any other during my tour in Mexico. I wrote more about the Sánchez family than I did about any other topic. More important, I learned more about Mexico in the weeks I spent with the Sánchezes than I had on any other reporting assignment. Many have said that daily journalism is a rough draft of history. I hadn't realized just how rough that draft was until I saw the rich detail and insights I gleaned from the time I spent with the Sánchezes.

By the time I met Manuel Sánchez, I had reported from twenty-six of Mexico's thirty-one states. I had covered Mexico's worst natural disaster, its worst plane crash, its worst industrial accident, and its worst economic crisis. I had reported on crooked elections and blatant police corruption. I had experienced the world's worst pollution and some of its worst traffic. I had seen poverty so bleak that it made life in the West and South Side ghettos of Chicago seem almost bearable. But I came to realize that the reporting required to write my usual stories on such topics just scratched the surface of Mexico's complicated truth. I began to think about all the things I wasn't learning or writing about because journalism's deadline pressures wouldn't permit me to spend more time on other Mexicans' stories. I began thinking about this book.

The Mexicans is a collection of stories about people I met during that unexpected voyage I found myself taking through Mexico. It's about people, such as Sánchez, who have taught me about Mexico as they see it. Some of their views are conflicting, as would be those of the same number of Americans I might choose to talk about the United States. But I have not picked my subjects haphazardly. I have selected Mexicans whose lives tell something important about Mexico. Adelaida Bollo's story tells how millions of Mexicans live on the minimum wage of three dollars a day, a salary the poorest American can earn in an hour. Miguel Tostado's tale explains why Mexicans risk injury, robbery, rape, and even death to go to the United States in search of work. Manuel Sánchez's story, one about a contraband dealer, tells why Mexico's economy got so out of whack and what's being done to remedy it. Along the way, readers will also meet a garbage picker, a cop, a politician, a movie star, an expatriate, and a homosexual, among others. These are not the Mexicans one would meet during a week's vacation in Acapulco. But they are real Mexicans all.

Even if readers don't care about the important messages embedded in each of these stories, the tale of each person's life, I think, stands alone in human terms. If readers do no more than soak up the drama or humor of these characters, I'll consider my effort a success, for in knowing these Mexicans, readers will come to know all Mexicans a little better. But I hope that some readers will get beyond the stories that sugarcoat the important issues and think about the issues themselves.

It's often said in jest that Americans will do anything about

Latin America except read about it. After four years in Mexico, I find that fact a lot more worrisome than I used to. It's particularly disturbing that Americans don't pay attention to Mexico, as I once didn't. If one takes a look at the numbers, it just doesn't make any sense. The most startling thing about Mexico is that it shares an unguarded, two-thousand-mile border with the United States. Note that word "unguarded." Under present circumstances, I don't think Mexico is likely to become a Communist nation, as some U.S. conservatives warn. But with a few unexpected twists and turns, that's not an impossible development. For those who think U.S. defense costs are already too much of a tax burden, it ought to send shivers down the spine to calculate what it would cost to establish border defenses along a two-thousand-mile expanse should Mexico become more hostile to the United States than it already is.

That threat aside, Americans ought to be thinking about Mexicans if for no other reason than there are so many of them. Mexico has about 85 million people, more than France, West Germany, or the United Kingdom—and three times as many as the United States' northern neighbor, Canada. It is the eleventh most populous country in the world. Half its people are under the age of fifteen. At current birth rates, it could have 115 million by the year 2000. Mexico City alone, already the world's largest metropolitan area, could have 27 million people by then.

Mexico is the world's fifth largest producer of oil, with about forty-eight billion known barrels of petroleum in the ground. It's a key supplier of U.S. imported oil, sometimes ranking no. 1. And it's a much more secure source than any of our Persian Gulf providers.

Mexico is the no. 3 market for the United States (after Canada and Japan). It will grow in importance as its middle class and business sector mature. More than 200,000 Americans already owe their jobs to Mexico's continued ability to buy exports from us. About two thirds of all Mexico's imports come from the United States. Conversely, the United States is Mexico's no. 1 market. Two-way trade is generally about thirty billion dollars, with Mexico selling us several billion dollars more in goods than we do them.

Mexico is also the no. 1 U.S. source of some illegal goods— drugs. A third of the marijuana, heroin, and cocaine that comes to the United States comes from Mexico (either as grower or transshipper). Even with the 1986 Simpson-Rodino immigration law, Mexico remains the no. 1 source of millions of undocumented U.S. workers. And as the effects of zero-population growth increasingly take hold in the United States, it will become a key source of needed, legal labor for U.S. factories, offices, and fields.

Mexico is the cultural homeland for the fastest growing political force in the United States—Mexican-Americans. Readers who don't care about what goes on inside Mexico may still have to deal with Mexican culture, habits, demands, and sensitivities at home, especially if they live in California, Arizona, New Mexico, or Texas, or in key Mexican-American towns such as Chicago or Denver.

As residents of border towns will tell you, Americans also can't afford to ignore the cross-border pollution problems that Mexico can create for the United States (which does some cross-border polluting of its own). The joke goes that when someone flushes a toilet in Tijuana, the second most populous city on the West Coast after Los Angeles, it's sometimes a very unpleasant day in San Diego. Texans also found out in 1979 what an oil spill from a Mexican offshore oil rig can do to local beaches. And if you thought Chernobyl was fun, think of Mexico, a country that has shown only a passing interest in industrial safety, now that its first nuclear power plant, Laguna Verde, is coming on line.

The list goes on. Mexico City, the spy capital of Latin America, is the key springboard for Soviet-inspired espionage against U.S. high-technology sites. Mexico's anti-U.S. votes in the United Nations sometimes rival those of Iran. And as Mexico's pro-Nicaraguan participation in Central American diplomacy shows, even with a comic-opera army, Mexico can gum things up for the United States on the world stage.

Some foreign-policy experts seem to be increasingly appreciative of the fact that Mexico is a country Americans will soon have to reckon with, as the debates in the 1988 U.S. presidential race made clear. Asked recently what was the sleeper foreign-policy issue for the rest of the century, former secretary of state Henry Kissinger said simply: "Mexico." In contrast, most Americans remain asleep about Mexico, even though their government makes important policy decisions about it all the time. Certainly, not too many were thinking about it in late 1986 when the U.S. Congress passed the Simpson-Rodino immigration law, which enables hundreds of thousands of Mexicans to work in the United States legally and made millions eligible to become permanent U.S. residents or citizens. And when President Reagan launched his controversial "contra" policy against Nicaragua, how many Americans asked if the ultimate threat it was designed to thwart—a communist takeover in Mexico—was really a likely occurrence? Reagan himself would have had a hard time getting his diplomats to answer that question. In the last years of Reagan's second term, the U.S. State Department, by its own admission, had no resident expert on Mexico in Washington, D.C.

One way or another, Americans are going to have to stop this head-in-the-sand approach. And if we are to deal with Mexicans, we had better know what makes them tick, for they are as different from us as a chili pepper is from apple pie. For some, I hope, this book will be a first step toward that needed understanding.

Patrick Oster
Mexico City

· I ·
Conditions

· 1 ·

The *Muchacha*

In the Zapotec villages of Oaxaca, one can still hear the three-thousand-year-old tale of the Binniguendas. The Zapotecs once believed that the Binniguendas, a race of demigods, would come from the sky to build giant palaces and bring prosperity. But the Zapotecs, like millions of Indians in the economically depressed southern states of Mexico, eventually got tired of waiting for celestial help to relieve their misery. They turned instead to more earthbound saviors.

About three decades ago, millions of Mexican Indians began fleeing the poverty of Oaxaca, Chiapas, and other poor states for the evanescent promise of wealth in Mexico City, their new Zion. They fled primitive housing, malnutrition, alcoholism, robbery, rape, incest, and illiteracy. But most of all they fled unemployment. They came with unbridled hope and little money to the soft-soiled, mountain-ringed valley in which the capital sits. Those with friends or family often lived temporarily on the roofs of one-room shacks of those who had come before them. They used sheets of plastic to shield themselves from the high-plateau rains and the chilling dew of daybreak. More aggressive newcomers squatted on land that no one seemed to want, especially in the uninhabited expanses east of Mexico City. Long ago this land had been the bed of Lake Texcoco, the once-vast body of water that had protected the magic Aztec city of Tenochtitlán. By the time these hopeful settlers arrived, however, the lake had become an evaporating cesspool. These days, it throws up dried fecal matter when the arid winds of late winter and early spring rip across the valley.

The newcomers begged, borrowed, and scrimped to get cinder blocks or flattened oil drums to construct their new dwellings. In the beginning, they often lived for months with only two or three walls and little that could be called a roof. As their numbers grew, they created impoverished metropolises, such as Nezahualcóyotl, whose three million residents claim it is the world's largest slum. Mexicans call these slums of open sewers and unpaved roads *ciudades perdidas,* or "lost cities." One of them is Ayotla, home of Adelaida Bollo Andrade, one of the millions of Zapotecs who migrated from Oaxaca.

From the day Adelaida came to the Valley of Mexico in 1980, she has taken whatever work she could get. A squat, leathery-skinned woman in her forties, she looks ten years older than she is. She has been a door-to-door laundress. She has hauled cement bags at construction sites. But most of all, she has been a maid. Maids (*"muchachas de casa"* in Spanish) are at the lowest rung of the social and economic ladder of Mexican society. Even poor families often have maids, who, in Mexico, are a necessity, not a luxury. If you want to have your garbage picked up, or your mail delivered, or your house protected from burglars while you're away, you get a maid. Things don't work without them.

One reason why so many can afford maids is that they are paid so little—typically, the minimum wage of about three dollars a day. They are not alone in this respect. About half the Mexican work force makes the same or less—what the poorest, least-educated American can make in an hour. Imagine what kind of society the United States would be if half its workers made the wages of a McDonald's cashier, a restaurant dishwasher, a parking-lot attendant, or a field hand. Who would buy automobiles, appliances, homes, and the other big-ticket items that make the enviable American economy what it is? Who would have the money to go to college, or even high school? With an uneducated middle class, what kind of culture or government would there be? How many people would be able to afford even the nutritious food, adequate health insurance, or other things that Americans take for granted as the basics of a developed society? The answer to those questions are at the heart of Adelaida's story, the story of a typical worker in a proud nation that somehow hasn't become developed, even though it has achieved the world's thirteenth largest economy.

The minimum wage was what Adelaida was making when I first met her in 1986. My wife and I hired her through an agency to fill in for two weeks while our regular maid went on vacation. Later, when it became necessary to replace our first maid, we hired Adelaida. Americans in Mexico often feel uncomfortable about having a maid. Many prefer to call them housekeepers. Perhaps that discomfort explains why we paid Adelaida about three times the normal wage for maids in Mexico City. But she and we knew that her short time with us would be a financial aberration. When we left Mexico, her salary would revert to what it had always been.

The Mexican constitution guarantees an adequate living wage to all Mexicans. But, as labor officials often tell the government's National Minimum Wage Commission, not even half the basic needs of a typical family are usually met by the prevailing minimum pay. To understand what that means, one need only look at where and how a minimum-wage earner lives, as we eventually did with Adelaida. The impressions we gained from those visits to her home are some of the strongest we retain of Mexico. It's not that the poverty was so overwhelming. Ayotla isn't the poorest place in the world, although a visit there or to any of Mexico City's slums would make any but the most unfeeling American appreciate how fortunate he or she is. My wife, Sally, and I had seen worse poverty in Central America, Africa, and Southeast Asia. We had both visited Nezahualcóyotl and other Mexican slums. But that was all abstract poverty. We dealt with its surfaces: flimsy housing materials, inadequate hygiene, tattered clothing, substandard food, rampant disease. Ayotla presented the poverty of someone we knew and lived with. It would not go away when the visit was over. It was poverty we were forced to think about.

There is a calculus to poverty that a casual visitor to Mexico or any poor country normally doesn't get into. It doesn't intrude as the waiter serves piña coladas on the veranda. It doesn't penetrate the sound of surf slapping against the hard-packed sand of a Mexican resort. But the mathematical truth is there just the same. It is a truth of what money can buy and what it can't. One can tote up the pesos to see what will be available for a family's housing, food, or transportation. But that only tells what physical needs can be met. It reveals nothing of dreams and aspirations beyond one's budget.

The minutiae of Adelaida's poverty begins with the trip from her house in the far-eastern reaches of the Valley of Mexico to our house in Bosques de las Lomas, a rich neighborhood in far-western Mexico City. Adelaida's commute started early. In bed by ten, she was up by five so she could catch a six o'clock bus for the three-hour trip to the other side of the city. The trip began with a twenty-minute walk from her one-room house, down the hilly, rutted, dirt streets of Ayotla, to the old Puebla Highway. There, if she could find a city bus with room in it, she would pay 250 pesos (about fifteen cents at the time) to be taken to the eastern end of one of Mexico City's subway lines. More often than not, however, the bus would be full—so full, in fact, that laughing young Mexican men, weaned on machismo, would be hanging out the front door, their feet flapping in the air, as the dilapidated vehicle cruelly zoomed past her stop. A full bus meant Adelaida would have to take a private minibus instead. It cost six times as much, even though it moved no faster in the gridlocked morning traffic.

All over the Mexico City area the scene would be the same: dense traffic and large clumps of commuters fighting for buses and subways that could accommodate only half of those who needed them. Commuters make twenty-one million passenger-trips a day in Mexico City. The subways are particularly jammed. Those lucky enough to get on are met with sweltering heat. Until a few years ago, women also had to endure the fanny pinchings and worse molestations of Mexican men or boys who used the sardine-can atmosphere of the subway trains to hide their nefarious deeds. Now there are women-only cars during rush hour. With fear of molestation out of the way, all Adelaida had to worry about was whether the fickle subway would run on time, or whether she would be robbed.

The fare for the subway, fifty pesos a day, was cheap by U.S. standards—about three cents. But it had increased fiftyfold in less ᵗⁿ a year due to triple-digit inflation and government efforts to

cut its whopping budget deficits by reducing transportation subsidies. The fifteen-day ticket required to get the fifty-peso fare
also provided unlimited free rides on special connecting Route
100 buses that took Adelaida from the subway's Chapultepec Park
station to within a block of our house. But, typically, she encountered the same overcrowded conditions on that route that she did
on the Puebla Highway. More often than not she had to pay 600
pesos extra for another private minibus to get to work on time.
Thus, on a bad day, Adelaida's round-trip fare could run 4,300
pesos, or about half her above-average salary.

Even though Adelaida worked like a packhorse, we had been
hesitant to hire her. We thought a job so far from Ayotla would
be inconvenient. But she begged us to let her have the job, because she could find no other. There was a small maid's room in
our house. Adelaida could have lived in, as many maids in Bosques do. But she said she preferred to live in Ayotla with her
husband, Félix, and four of her five children. (One grown daughter, Acacia, had already moved out.) Later, when Félix was laid
off from his job as a construction worker on the ever-expanding
subway system, Adelaida did move in for a while to save on transportation costs. But even with regular raises from us, she never
seemed able to make ends meet.

Most Mexicans had the same problem. After Mexico's economic crisis struck in 1982, the country experienced double- and
triple-digit inflation that made a mess of family budgets. The government, which regularly increased the minimum wage a couple
of times a year, insisted it was trying to keep workers even with
inflation. But even the pro-government Confederation of Mexican
Workers (CTM) complained that, in real terms, workers in the
1980s were being paid wages of the 1960s. In the first five years
of the administration of President Miguel de la Madrid Hurtado
(1982–88), average Mexicans lost about a third of their purchasing power due to the effects of inflation, according to the CTM.
Others calculated it was more.

With only two years of grammar school, Adelaida didn't know
much about inflation. She just knew her wages weren't going as
far, even though she was making more. She knew she and Félix,
who averaged less than the minimum wage from his off-again,
on-again work at the subway, could only afford to buy meat once
a week for their children, less than they once could. Eighty per-

cent of Mexicans couldn't afford to eat meat at all anymore, according to some studies. Lard had replaced oil in many kitchens. Jelly had replaced fruit. Mexicans were drinking 75 percent less milk because it cost too much. Even if meat and milk hadn't become too expensive for Adelaida, there was the problem of the refrigerator. There was none. In fact, the only kitchen appliance Adelaida had in her fifteen-by-twenty-four-foot cinder-block home was a portable, three-burner gas stove. With no refrigerator, meat and milk spoiled quickly as the strong afternoon sun beat down on Adelaida's corrugated asbestos roof, making a furnace of the house. Vegetables wouldn't keep more than a day. That meant Adelaida had to go to the market every day, an hour's round trip to add to her six hours of travel, seven hours of sleep, and eight hours of work. That left her two hours to clean the house, wash up, dress the children for school, and relax.

Relaxation meant watching television, for there were no newspapers, magazines, books, games, or other diversions in Adelaida's house. In fact, there was not much of anything. A small bed sat in one corner, where her four youngest children slept. Adelaida and Félix curled up on the rugless concrete floor next to Cuaxi, a mongrel German shepherd who was a gift from a neighbor. Across the room was a battered kitchen table that sat six. The portable stove was in another corner, separated from the television by the house's only window. The only other items to be seen were a small pile of blankets and clothes and a bare twenty-five-watt light bulb hanging from the center of the ceiling.

There wouldn't even have been a television if it hadn't been for a kindly doctor. He was treating Adelaida's ten-year-old daughter, Carmela, for severe depression in 1985. He said Carmela needed something to entertain her, such as a television. As he put it: "She has no fun in her life." Adelaida couldn't afford a television, so the doctor scrounged up an old black-and-white one out of his garage. It quickly became the center of family life.

When Adelaida told me this story, our adopted son, Alex, had just turned ten months old. He had blossomed since we brought him home, skinny and shy, from the adoption agency six months before. Like most doting parents, my wife and I were enthusiastic about his intellectual future, even though, at the time, his vocabulary was limited to "Da-da," "Ma-ma," and a few other words gaga new parents can decipher. Sally and I make our livings writing, so perhaps it wasn't so strange that Alex already had Mother Goose, a two-volume set of the Brothers Grimm, a three-volume set of Hans Christian Andersen, E. B. White's *Charlotte's Web* and *Stuart Little,* and about twenty-five other books in his bedroom library, even though he couldn't yet read a word. If I hadn't been so wound up in thinking about all the good books I hoped Alex would read, I might never have asked what Carmela's favorite books were. It took a little while for Adelaida's startling answer to sink in. Aside from books Carmela had to buy for school, she had never read a real book. None of Adelaida's children had. In fact, they had no fantasy life to speak of. Adelaida had little time to tell her kids what she remembered of the Zapotec bedtime stories that her parents had told her. In a world where many children grow up on the magic tales of Cinderella, Snow White, Bambi, Jack and the Beanstalk, and Puss-in-Boots, Adelaida's kids had to settle for G.I. Joe, He-Man, and the other one-dimensional cartoon characters they could see on their black-and-white television. Fantasies were beyond Adelaida's budget.

With little money for any kind of fun, Christmas was rarely a special event. Nonetheless, Adelaida's three youngest children, ages four through ten, all continued to write letters to Santa Claus. They asked him, as kids will, for the moon. Hopefully they hung up stockings on Christmas Eve. But Adelaida and Félix rarely could afford to put much in them.

"They'd ask for a doll or a bicycle," said Adelaida. "But I couldn't buy anything. I had some money for Christmas last year. But there was an accident in the family. I had to spend it on that. The children cried."

What made things worse for Adelaida was that her neighbors, with a boy about her son Antonio's age, were always able to afford the presents she never could. Her neighbors had relatives who worked illegally in the United States and sent back money regularly. Two years before Adelaida came to work for us, Antonio, then age four, had asked Santa for a bicycle that he had seen on the newly acquired television. All Adelaida and Félix could afford that year was a small wooden horse that cost a few pesos. Antonio was crestfallen. Matters were only made worse when the neighbor's young boy came by to show off his Christmas treasures. After the young visitor left, Antonio, quiet for a long while, finally said, "Doesn't Santa Claus love me, Mama?"

Accidents or emergencies, it seemed, were always popping up in Adelaida's life. They were usually very basic things, but not basic in an American sense. Middle-class American families feel the pinch when it's suddenly time to buy new tires for the family jalopy, or when the old fridge finally gives out. Adelaida wouldn't know about such matters. They are problems of what she calls the rich. For Adelaida, a problem was when one of Mexico City's violent rainstorms destroyed her flimsy roof and she needed about a hundred dollars to repair it. That happened twice in 1987. On a more mundane level, Adelaida and Félix were frequently being robbed. Once, on the day one of her daughters was confirmed as a Catholic, Adelaida had her pocket picked in church during the ceremony. She lost fourteen thousand pesos, all the money she had in the world that day. Another time, Félix was beaten senseless on his way home from work by muggers who were angry that he didn't have enough on him to justify their criminal effort. He lost the use of his arms for months and was laid off from his subway job.

Adelaida never had very much saved in a lump sum—certainly not a hundred dollars for a new roof. In fact, she has never had a savings or checking account. "Savings" were usually a few thousand pesos she hid around the house in case something came up, as it always did. Bank loans were out of the question. The Mexican government, which nationalized the banks in 1982, typically took about three quarters of the available credit to finance its budget deficits and other government activities. It doled out the paltry remainder to politically connected friends. But even if money had been available, Adelaida had no collateral and, as far as bankers were concerned, no future. Instead of banks, the government provides the poor with a chain of state-owned pawnshops. At almost any time of year, but especially around Christmas or Easter, when families want to make trips to their hometowns, one can see lines of people snaking out of the branches of the Monte de Piedad (the "Mountain of Pity"), as the chain is called in Spanish. People come with old televisions, watches, and even appliances in hopes of getting some small percentage of their value. The government tries to keep interest charges on such pawns at rates less than inflation. But during the years of economic crisis, many Mexicans, saddled with dwindling real salaries, lost their property to the Monte anyway.

The average person borrows only ten dollars from the *Monte*. But Adelaida never used pawnshops. She had nothing to pawn. Without a nest egg to fall back on, she did what many minimum-wage earners do when a problem such as a leaky roof comes up. She borrowed from her *patrón* or "boss." In Adelaida's case, this was the most natural thing to do. Zapotecs have a tradition called *guelaguetza* by which members of the village collectively help those who suddenly develop a need. As millions of Zapotecs moved to the city, the employer took the place of the village. Interest-free loans became an unofficial fringe benefit, as did paid health care when medical emergencies arose. Given the primitive sanitary conditions in Ayotla, medical emergencies often did arise. In the days when Adelaida was a door-to-door laundress, there was no regular *patrón,* so she had to absorb the costs for medical treatment herself. Kitchen burns and other household accidents went untreated. Alcohol mixed with an egg was often the only remedy she could afford for the diarrhea, vomiting, and fevers her children regularly contracted from Ayotla's contaminated water supply.

The water was impure because it did not come from a regular city system. In the beginning, residents of Ayotla had to depend on municipal trucks to bring them water to bathe and cook each day. Eventually, as happens in squatter slums all over Mexico, Ayotla's residents tapped into city hydrants and underground pipes, using a dizzying network of interconnected garden hoses to bring cold water to their homes. In 1987, city authorities finally demanded that Ayotla residents pay 150,000 pesos each (more than a hundred dollars at the time) for a new, piped-in system of faucets right outside the door. If residents didn't pay, they were told, authorities would confiscate all the hoses. For Adelaida, who had paid only about three hundred dollars for her house some four years before, 150,000 pesos was a fortune. To pay it would mean weeks of having to serve an even more meager fare than the tortillas, beans, rice, and coffee that were the regular family menu. But not to pay would have meant no water, so Adelaida borrowed the money from us and paid.

Other services in Ayotla were equally abysmal. One reason was that all the land claims of Ayotla's residents were only semirecognized by local authorities, a problem one could encounter across the valley. In Mexico City alone, officials admit, there are at least 700,000 real-estate parcels that aren't on title books. This real-estate anarchy has led to an interesting situation. Millions of Mexican peasants have come to Mexico City and other large Mexican cities, seizing unused land that they claim is part of their birthright under the revolutionary land-reform articles of the Mexican constitution. Officials of the ruling Institutional Revolutionary Party, known as the PRI, hem and haw about the legality of such seizures. But periodically—usually just before an election, when the votes of the poor are needed—the government regularizes thousands of suspect titles at a time. In nonelection years, unlucky squatters just get thrown violently off the land.

Adelaida, who bought her small plot of land and home from her sister, didn't have a formal title either. In fact, she didn't even have an official address. She lived on Pensamiento Street, near the corner of another street with no name, but her house had been assigned no number. Maybe there was no point to having an address, because there was no mail service. If she needed to send mail home to her *pueblo* ("hometown"), she just waited a few weeks for a neighbor traveling back to Oaxaca to carry it for her. Likewise, mail that came from relatives in Oaxaca was held for travelers going to Ayotla. Even if she had mail service, it probably wouldn't have amounted to much. Mail carriers, like police officers and many civil servants, make the minimum wage, too. Their insouciant delivery habits reflect their low pay. What isn't stolen by carriers is delivered late. Christmas cards can arrive in March. Mail from abroad may never arrive at all. Mail is so unreliable that the government set up a payment system at banks so that people could pay their utility bills on time. Anyone who pays an electric or phone bill by mail is just asking to have service cut off.

Adelaida didn't have problems paying such bills. But it wasn't because she went to the bank. She didn't have to pay most utility bills because she had no regular electric service and no telephone. As most of her neighbors did, she stole electricity from a nearby public power pole. She tapped into city mains with makeshift wires and cables that she ran from the pole to her house. Thousands of these bootlegging wires were strung from rooftop to rooftop in Ayotla, standing out against the polluted gray sky like tossed spaghetti frozen in air. It was an open secret. As long as residents voted for the ruling party's candidates, the authorities would pretend not to notice the wires.

As for the phone, not having one wasn't such a rare thing. There are only about eight million private phones in Mexico. Only one house in five has one. Few of the lucky ones, however, lived in Ayotla. One reason why Mexico has so few phones is its crippling one-hundred-billion-dollar foreign debt. Debt payments, combined with the drag of the government's budget deficit, didn't leave the government much for installation of new phones. If economic conditions permit in the future, the government has ambitious plans to boost the number of phones. But even if Telmex could offer everyone service, most of Mexico's poor can't afford Telmex's hefty hookup charges. As a result, minimum-wage earners typically use public phones, which almost always have knots of people gathered around them. Private phones are bad enough. It often takes ten dialings to reach the right party. There's a saying that the easiest way to meet a stranger in Mexico is to dial a friend. But public phones, which the government made free after thousands of phones were damaged in the 1985 Mexico City earthquakes, often don't work at all. When they do, they frequently deliver inaudible connections and then cut the caller off after three minutes.

Ayotla was so poor it didn't have its own public phone. Adelaida had to learn to do without one. If Antonio cut his foot on a piece of broken glass, as he did shortly after she came to work for us, she had no way of calling the doctor to come to stitch up the wound. She had no way of calling us to say she would be late for work because she had to go to the hospital. In emergencies, she had no way of contacting Félix, who worked nights.

Ayotla also had no sewers. That made things particularly interesting during the floods of the six-month rainy season. But, most important, no sewers meant Adelaida had no bathroom, not even a toilet. What she had was a hole in the ground, outside, out of sight. Such housing conditions, though lamentable, were hardly extraordinary. At least she had a house. Though the Mexican constitution guarantees citizens a decent and comfortable house, there is a shortage of 4.5 million housing units in Mexico, equal to a third of all existing homes. Forty percent of Mexico's homes have no in-the-home water service. Forty percent have no indoor plumbing. More than 10 percent have no electricity. A quarter have dirt floors. Central heating, even at the chilly, high altitudes of places such as Mexico City, is rare. Faced with such conditions, one might suspect, as many U.S. conservatives do, that Adelaida and millions like her are ripe for conversion by Mexico's leftist political parties, or by Communists, should the revolutions of Central America spread to Mexico. This doesn't seem to be the case, however. In her soul, Adelaida has the instincts of a chairman of an multinational conglomerate. Simply put, she is a dyed-in-the-wool capitalist. She was always looking for ways to make more money for what Communists might call bourgeois purposes. Once we hired a professional cleaning company to lift about ten years of wax from the tile floors of our rented house. After it took two days just to clean the dining-room floor, the company's exhausted workers begged off on the rest of the house. It was too hard, they said. Adelaida, however, quickly offered to bring in this cousin and that sister-in-law to do the job. She promised her team would clean the floors brick by brick, if necessary. All they would ask, she said, was the minimum wage. When we decided to forget the whole thing, Adelaida began the painstaking work herself, perhaps hoping for a little bonus, which she ultimately got. When no such opportunities appeared, Adelaida would rummage through our garbage cans. She sorted out items that we thought had no value. She knew they would bring in a few pesos as scrap.

What little she could save from her salary and extra earnings went toward Adelaida's goals of a better job, a good education for her kids, and a nicer home. Perhaps as a result of viewing two years of dubbed American television programs on her black-and-white set, she had developed a limited version of the American dream. Whatever the source of her ambitions, it was not communism. In fact, when I asked her what she thought of communism, she said she had never heard of it—or the Soviet Union either. She had only a vague idea of what was going on in Nicaragua.

"I have seen something about Nicaragua [on the television]," she said. "There's fighting there. People are killing their countrymen."

Adelaida's ism is pragmatism. She and Félix have joined the PRI, even though they don't believe Mexico's ruling party is really as concerned about the poor as its officials say it is. The reason was simple. The PRI can provide the services that she and Félix want for their family. The opposition parties can't. With their water service finally regularized and new sidewalks almost installed,

Adelaida and Félix are hoping for paved streets, and maybe regular electric service next. But they know they may have to wait for an election.

Above all, Adelaida is a realist. Having been kept down most of her life by people and forces over which she has little control, she recognizes that she may never see her dreams fulfilled. She has set her own sights low, not wanting to be any more disappointed than she already is. For her, a factory job would be a dream come true. There's a textile plant not too far from Ayotla that she has in mind. Her commute to it would be minutes rather than hours. But factory work, like a lot of work in Mexico, a country of red tape and officious bureaucrats, requires certain documents. Among other things, it requires a birth certificate. Adelaida doesn't have one. As best she can tell, she was born on Valentine's Day of 1945 or 1946. Her parents, Marcelino and Margarita, both poor, uneducated Zapotecs, put little importance in recording her birth with the Spanish-speaking authorities in San Juanito, the small village where she was born and grew up. For the first five years she and Félix lived together, she didn't have a marriage certificate either. They couldn't afford the fee to get married. By chance, when Félix was working in the oil fields of Minatitlán in 1970, local PRI officials offered workers free marriage certificates—just before an election. Félix and Adelaida seized the opportunity to marry—five years after the birth of their daughter Acacia. Adelaida has had no such luck in getting a birth certificate, which would require testimony of friends, a baptismal certificate, and a bribe to the issuing official. She'd also need money for the trip back to Oaxaca, where the birth-certificate office is located. Every once in a while, Adelaida accumulates roughly the amount she needs, but something else always comes up that requires her to spend the money on it instead.

"I tried to do it by mail," she said. "But they always had excuses."

Adelaida has no illusions about completing her own education. She has no time and less money. But she is bent on making sure that her children at least finish grammar school, which ends at the sixth grade in Mexico. Only 50 percent of Mexicans have gotten that far, although more and more young Mexicans finish grammar school, and even junior high and high school, these days. Adelaida wants her kids to go to high school, too, so "they can have an easier job than we do." But the only way she'll be able to afford that is if her kids quit school and work for a while or work part-time while they attend. School tuition is nominal in Mexico. But the cost of books and supplies puts school beyond many poor Mexican families. Such costs averaged twenty-five thousand pesos per pupil in 1987, about half Adelaida's already strained weekly salary.

Félix's dreams are even more restricted. Abandoned at age four by his father after his mother died and his father remarried, Félix got no education at all. Now a wiry, well-tanned man in his mid-fifties, he grew up tending livestock in a town not far from Adelaida's *pueblo*. He met her there while looking for work. He doesn't have a birth certificate either. He has had to take low-paying jobs all his life, jobs that don't require documentation. He has never worked a full twelve months on such jobs in Mexico City. Each December, Félix's employer lays him off so that he doesn't have to pay Félix an *aguinaldo*, the mandatory "thirteenth month" bonus for those who have worked the full year. But Félix thinks that eleven months of minimum-wage work is better than no work at all, the fate of some of his friends. Eventually, he realizes, the subway work will end and he will have to find other employment. He knows he'll probably have to work all his life, given Mexico's extremely limited social-security system. Most Mexicans over the age of sixty still work, largely because those eligible for pensions can receive as little as a dollar a day.

"When he's older," said Adelaida, "he'll have to wash the streets or do something simple that doesn't require a birth certificate."

Félix doesn't really imagine that he'll be able to get that birth certificate one day, as Adelaida hopes. He'd settle for something more basic.

"I would like to be able to read and write," he said. "I would have liked to have had more education. I wasn't able to study anything. My life has been very sad."

Mexico has made great strides in reducing illiteracy, which afflicts only 6 percent of its people, half the rate in 1982. But the government's widespread literacy campaign hasn't reached Ayotla yet. And Félix isn't sure when he'd have time to take advantage of it anyway, given his work hours.

Because Félix and Adelaida have had little education in Spanish, both feel more comfortable speaking Zapotec, a language with a Scandinavian lilt to it. Zapotec is what they speak to their children, who did not get their first serious instruction in Spanish until they entered first grade. As a result, Ihilvia, their thirteen-year-old, had trouble adjusting and was held back a grade, as was Antonio. Even if more at-home instruction could have made her children's Spanish more fluent, Adelaida said she'd still have wanted to teach her kids Zapotec so they would know something of their Indian heritage. Adelaida, whose long hair, shiny as coal-black corn silk, hangs free to the waist, Indian style, feels her kids should know something of the Zapotecs even though being Indian in Mexico is not something one is made to feel proud of.

"It's something to hide," she said. "You pay a penalty if you're Indian."

•　　　•　　　•

In late 1987, a little good fortune crept into Adelaida's life. With a loan from us, she bought her brother's one-room house, which sits right behind hers. The family has more space now. Adelaida and Félix have their first sexual privacy since moving to the Mexico City area. Adelaida also got some help from some of my readers who wrote with offers of money and clothes after I did a story on her in late 1987. One letter from Kathy Vierra, of San Jose, California, typifies the response. She wrote: "I would like to find a way to contact Mrs. [Adelaida Bollo] Andrade to see if I can help her. . . . Tho I am not rich I am also not so poor that I have to sleep on cold cement. Something must be done about these dreadful living conditions." Another reader, Irene Kopel, of Redwood City, California, sent Adelaida about a hundred dollars when fierce winds destroyed Adelaida's roof a second time in 1987.

Carmela got Spanish versions of Cinderella, Snow White, and Puss-in-Boots after my wife and I did a little shopping one day in a children's bookstore. That last Christmas before we left Mexico, we also bought Adelaida a small refrigerator. Milk and meat have become more common at the dinner table. Santa Claus finally came, too. He left a few things for Adelaida's children at our house by mistake. We made sure they got to Ayotla. On the last day we saw her, we gave Adelaida and Félix the money to get their birth certificates. We wished them *buena suerte* ("good luck"). I kept thinking they were going to need it.

· 2 ·

The *Junior*

That Saturday night, the sports cars and expensive sedans began to cluster early around Histeria, one of Mexico City's newest and kickiest nightclubs. Histeria's young clients parked willy-nilly on sidewalks and private lawns in the residential neighborhood and two deep at the curb. They showed no concern for the traffic they backed up on Masarik Avenue.

Histeria is an exclusive club, its rules of entrance having been borrowed shamelessly from New York City's defunct Studio 54. The club's beefy doormen scanned the crowd of hopefuls to see who might add something to the ambiance of the still-young night inside. As he approached the chain that blocked the club's entrance, Gerardo Dagdug Marcos showed no sign of anxiety about being admitted. With a knowing nod from the head bouncer, he and his party pushed past less fortunate nighthawks and prepared to taste the club's rare fruit.

The club was done in high tech, a decor that remains au courant in haute Mexico City, though already passé in chic boîtes north of the border. Incandescent downlights gave Histeria, once a private residence, an intimate look. Their warm glow flattered the troublesome skin of the club's young clients. Histeria has no dance floor, no tables, no chairs. It is a place where people come mainly to see and be seen. They stand, iced drinks in hand, behind pipe railings that rise out of stair-step platforms. The railings create a stadium effect. Those positioned at the highest railings can see the most. Those at the lowest can be seen the most. Gerardo and his friends grabbed a spot at the lowest.

"Isn't it fabulous?" beamed Gerardo. "It's just like the States. Isn't it?"

Anything from "the States" or abroad is held in high regard by this crowd, who drop English phrases and swear words like natives. They disdain the poor quality of Mexican manufactured goods, which hold no cachet for their set. Histeria's richest clients, who think nothing of jetting up to Houston, Los Angeles, or New York for a little weekend shopping, wear fashions by Calvin Klein, Georges Marciano, Ralph Lauren, and Halston. Their poorer cousins settle for made-in-Mexico versions of the same labels. Histeria's clients dote on pricey imported booze, too. Behind the bar were bottles of Chivas Regal, Hennessy, Johnnie Walker, and other well-known international brands that most Mexicans never get to experience. A round of drinks for Gerardo's party cost fifty-five thousand pesos with tip—about six dollars a person, or twice what the average Mexican makes in a day.

Through the air, over the high-decibel rock music of Histeria's expensive sound system, one could hear the patois of this privileged crowd. "¿Qué onda, mano?" asked Gerardo of a friend he hadn't seen in a while. It was his hip way of asking, "What's shakin', brother?" Another Histeria devotee, a zaftig teenager in iridescent makeup and spiky punk hairdo, gushed about a friend's black-leather pants suit: "¡Qué padre! ["How fantastic!"] It's not from here [Mexico], is it?"

As he waited for another drink order to come, Gerardo, a bulky six-footer in his mid-twenties, engaged unashamedly in what Histeria's clients enjoy most—watching. Carolina, his nineteen-year-old chava ("girlfriend"), did the same. The uniform of the night was expensive casual. Few clients wore suits, sport coats, or cocktail dresses. Gerardo, a body builder and full-contact-karate enthusiast, wore high-top, black-leather aerobic shoes, black men's harem pants, and a beige polo shirt that set off his well-tanned, heavily muscled arms. His brother Emilio, who also pumps iron, had on tailored slacks and a long-sleeved white shirt, with cuffs rolled up to the middle of his bulging biceps. The shirt was unbuttoned to the waist to display several gold chains that hung from his thick neck.

Though legally one must be sixteen, if a girl, or eighteen, if a boy, to drink alcohol in Histeria, Gerardo found that the "action" that night included kids as young as twelve. Dressed to the nines, they eye-flirted with the best of them.

"It doesn't matter how old you are," explained Gerardo as to why the doormen let such youngsters in. "It's who you are. These girls are from good families."

For more than two hours, Gerardo and his *cuates* ("buddies") soaked up the joking, drinking, teasing, and flirting that is Histeria's regular fare. Then, close to midnight, one of his crowd suggested they all go dancing at El News. If Histeria was the place to be early that Saturday night, El News, a trendy discotheque just over the city line in the State of Mexico suburbs, was where one wanted to be as Sunday began. Gerardo lost no time in getting there. As is his wont when driving his Renault 18 almost anywhere in Mexico, Gerardo ran every red light on the way over, laughing toward Carolina as he did. On arrival at the disco, Gerardo was told by the parking attendant that there was no more room in El News's lot. Undeterred, Gerardo left his car, door ajar, in the middle of the street, tossed the attendant his keys and a few thousand pesos, and swaggered toward the club entrance.

"I'm a client, man!" he yelled back over his shoulder to the attendant, who looked around helplessly for some place to stash Gerardo's car until he came out.

At the door, the procedure for getting in was nearly the same as at Histeria. Doormen snubbed the unexceptional rich, while letting Gerardo and company in without a hitch. Inside, security men in expensive suits ran hand-held metal detectors over clients' clothes before the cashier would take their money or a credit card for the hefty cover charge.

"They've had a problem with guns," explained Gerardo. "Some of the clients have brought theirs in."

El News, which can hold about two thousand customers, was already nearly full. The dance floor pulsed to a number by Whitney Houston as clients tried to lose themselves in the music. Gerardo scanned the raised area surrounding the dance floor for a good table. Most seemed to be full. Gerardo huddled with the maître d' for a moment and then, smilingly, told us a table had been found. It was, it turned out, the owner's table, a point Gerardo didn't want us to miss.

"You have to spend a lot of money here," he explained of our good fortune. "Then they take care of you. That's why we got this table."

El News's clients were indistinguishable from Histeria's: young, well-dressed Mexicans, looking fit and rich and trying to be cool.

"All the rich of Mexico are here," said Gerardo. "Lebanese, Jews, everyone!"

Outside El News one could encounter Mexico's troubles in the 1980s: inflation, unemployment, pollution, crime, corruption. But inside, these rich kids had found a pleasure-garden refuge from such harshness, a Xanadu of television monitors, rock videos, strobe lights, and mirrors. Gerardo said it best: "Isn't it fabulous? Here there is no crisis. We just spend money, get drunk, have fun, and forget about everything."

•   •   •

It would have been easy to dislike Gerardo. He was brash, boastful, inconsiderate, rude, and ignorant. His hobbies were sports, discos, and women. He had an ebullience for life, but he wasted it on frivolity at a time when his country needed more serious attention to its problems by its future generation of leaders. I thought about asking Gerardo if he saw any parallels between his life and Nero's. But Gerardo, a college dropout, read no books except nutrition texts, rarely bought a newspaper, and hardly watched television news. He had enough trouble with current events, let alone ancient history. I don't think he would have realized I was tweaking him about fiddling while Mexico burned.

"I don't want to know that there are wars or what's happening," said Gerardo, who, despite daily headlines about his government's involvement in the Contadora peace process, didn't know who Nicaragua's Sandinistas were.

In the end, I think I found Gerardo more amusing than obnoxious because he was such a caricature of his tiny class. I had met many wealthy young Mexicans like him, in the capital and other big cities. The ones from old-money families lived in understated but lavish homes in the west or south of Mexico City, or in swanky neighborhoods in Monterrey, Guadalajara, or Chihuahua. New-money types, whose families had made their fortunes during

Mexico's oil boom of the 1970s, lived in fabulous mansions or tasteless castles that their parents had built in my neighborhood and other realms of the *"naco,"* a nasty Mexican slang word for nouveau riche. I saw these rich youngsters on Saturday mornings in jodhpurs and riding boots or fresh tennis whites. During their frequent weekends in Acapulco, Cancún, or other Mexican resorts, they switched to beach wear by Aca Joe or Fiorucci. Those who couldn't make it to the beach spent weekends at bachelor hideaways in out-of-the-way neighborhoods watching imported X-rated films. Those whom I remember talked loudly as they moved down the sidewalk, wearing their disdain for the rest of society like a badge. They mocked others' poverty. *"¿Tienes coche o Volkswagen?"* one could hear them say in perfect, drop-dead fashion—"Do you have a car or a Volkswagen?"—a putdown by those with expensive cars of those who owned the most common automobile on the road in Mexico. In a society where police corruption is endemic, they did what they wanted, knowing that their or their parents' money would get them out of any jam. They drove wildly, ignoring traffic rules even more than most Mexicans. They parked in people's driveways because they couldn't be bothered to look for a legal parking space. They spoke in a bubbleheaded dialogue. In restaurants and at dinner parties they complained that it was such "un down" that they had to travel coach to Europe, now that the Concorde had become so expensive in peso terms. In beauty salons, they discussed which cosmetic surgeon did the best nose jobs and who was good for cellulite.

Journalist Guadalupe Loaeza wickedly chronicled the female member of this species, calling them *"Las Niñas Bien"* (The Well-to-do Children) in her 1987 best-seller of the same name. For all their dippy conversation that she recorded she might have called them Valley (of Mexico) Girls. But most Mexicans call these spoiled young people "juniors," an insulting nickname for those whose key worth in life comes from the power or money of their parents. Loaeza facetiously created subspecies of juniors in her chronicle. For example, she divided those who can still shop in Paris, notwithstanding the drop in the peso's value that accompanied the 1982 economic crisis, from those who now have to settle for ersatz designer goods at Mexico City's best department stores, Liverpool and Palacio de Hierro. She distinguished political juniors from business juniors. Carlos Salinas de Gotari, who was elected president of Mexico in July 1988, is a political junior. He got his start in politics because his father was a powerful government official. His technocrat background and lack of political experience was lamented by the old guard of the ruling Institutional Revolutionary Party. But he was nominated and elected nonetheless. Gerardo and his brothers are business juniors—or so I argued one day over a lunch of fresh seafood at the restaurant Gerardo owns in Polanco, Mexico City's closest thing to an Upper East Side. Gerardo got his start in business by being made a partner in a T-shirt factory that his father owned. With profits he made from the sale of that venture, he opened the restaurant and became a partner with his brother Emilio in an Acapulco disco that offered the first Chippendale's-style male striptease acts in Mexico. Nonetheless, Gerardo bristles at the term.

"The word 'junior' sounds like someone who's not going anywhere," said Gerardo. "I don't think it's a fair word—not for me."

In his own mind, Gerardo works hard. He thinks of the future. He has plans to expand his restaurant ventures soon to Cancún, his favorite place in Mexico, and perhaps to the United States, a country he thinks "is right in almost everything." He has a disciplined week. He's up around six Monday through Friday so he can work out for two hours at karate before getting to his restaurant a little before ten. He usually stays at the restaurant until about seven, when he leaves to work out for another two hours before turning in by ten or so. Twice during the week, Gerardo slips out in the afternoon from work for an hour or two to play golf, his passion. A scratch player, Gerardo hopes one day to join the P.G.A. tour in the United States, his main ambition in life.

"I'm one of the best golfers in Mexico right now," he said.

Gerardo also plays at least eighteen holes of golf each Saturday and Sunday. He belongs to the Club Chapultepec, which he described as "the most expensive in Mexico." A health fanatic, he nonetheless does a little steam-blowing on weekends. Every Friday night, he dines out with friends, staying up until about one. Saturday is his night to howl. He usually starts the evening at a bar such as Histeria and then stops at video bars, or goes disco hopping at places such as El News or its neighbor, El Magic.

"I party until I can't walk to a disco!" said Gerardo in describing his Saturday routine.

Gerardo lives at home, as do many young adults in housing-short Mexico. The Dagdug house is located in the Lomas de Chapultepec neighborhood in western Mexico City. It's a tranquil, wooded area of large homes owned by Mexico's elite or rented by top diplomats. With four bedrooms and quarters for two maids, Gerardo's two-story, glass-and-cement house is not the largest or most expensive home in the area. But it measures up well to its neighbors. Outside, there is room for a dozen cars in the partially covered carport. But that's not enough space for his father's twenty-automobile, vintage-car collection. For everyday use, his father, Edmundo, drives a Mercedes-Benz 450SL coupe. Inside the house, the floors of the living room–dining room are marble, covered here and there with Oriental carpets. The dining-room table, with a painting of a Roman chariot race behind it, seats twelve. A crystal light fixture hangs overhead. Expensive ceramics are displayed throughout the area, which is furnished in a French Provincial style. Snuggled in one corner of the living room is a baby grand piano, with oil portraits of Gerardo and his brothers and sisters on the wall behind it. The kitchen is stocked with electric appliances. Throughout the house are the trappings of wealth: videocassette recorders, rock videos, personal stereos, designer fashions, color televisions.

Mexico has its own rock stars, such as Lucia Méndez, Yuri, Luis Miguel, and Juan Gabriel. But Gerardo, like so many of his friends, eschews national singers. They listen instead to the growing number of Mexico City FM stations that have adopted an American sound, with exclusively U.S. and European rock music and disc jockeys who do a lot of patter and promotions in English. They stock their cassette, compact disc, and rock-video libraries with American and British rock music, which they buy during shopping sprees in the United States. Gerardo's favorite singers are Mick Jagger, Sade, and Phil Collins. Even his favorite television show is American: *Miami Vice*. Gerardo watches Crockett and Tubbs in the original English version—two seasons before the programs get to Mexico in dubbed versions. His family is one of about 350,000 subscribers to Cablevision, a cable service of Mexico's largest television network, Televisa. Cablevision provides programs of the three major U.S. networks, PBS, ESPN, and a movie channel. Other Mexican *ricos* ("rich"), an estimated hundred thousand of them, have satellite dishes and decoders that enable them to get the Playboy Channel, HBO, the Movie Channel, Cinemax, CNN, and MTV, as well as local news from the U.S. border cities they often visit.

Gerardo takes about six weeks of vacation a year, not including the time he spends in Acapulco looking after his business interests. He has traveled to the United States, visiting San Diego, La Jolla, Los Angeles, Las Vegas, Vail, and other haunts popular with rich Mexicans. At a time when millions of Mexicans are forced to enter the United States illegally each year in search of work, Gerardo slips in and out with little fuss. With established businesses in Mexico, he had no trouble getting a tourist visa three years ago, good for unlimited visits. He hasn't been to Europe yet. But he plans to do so soon, part of his dream to "travel everywhere" in the world.

I asked Gerardo what dreams he had besides world travel and joining the P.G.A. tour. "Having all the money in the world," he said. He quickly realized how this sounded and tried to play down the importance of money to him. But money is what Gerardo kept coming back to in our conversations. What was particularly sad was what he had chosen to do with it. With more money than most in Mexico, Gerardo could have had all the education he wanted, but he chose to drop out after two years at Anáhuac University, a college for Mexican yuppies in the suburbs of the capital.

"Here in Mexico, titles are of no use; neither are careers," he explained of his decision not to pursue a college degree in a country where the title Licenciado ("holder of a university degree") is regarded by many as the highest accolade. "What you have to have is money."

In this respect, Gerardo knows he's lucky. The best thing that ever happened to him was being born "the son of my father," he said. "In Mexico, if you don't have money, it's hard to do anything. If you begin with nothing, it's hard to succeed."

There are a few Horatio Alger success stories in Mexico, such as that of Manuel Espinosa Yglesias, whose first job paid only a few pesos a month but who, through banking and other ventures, accumulated perhaps the greatest fortune in Mexico. But many stories of wealth in Mexico are stories of wealth coming from wealth—the junior syndrome. The Fortune 500 of wealthy Mexican families is dotted with wealthy sons—the Alemáns, the Azcárragas, the Legorretas. Moreover, the government's statistics show that in the last forty years, Mexico's rich have remained rich while the poor got poorer, a socially destabilizing trend. In 1983, the richest 20 percent of Mexican households earned more than half the income in Mexico, just a touch below their share four decades ago. The poorest 20 percent earned only 4 percent of the country's income in 1983, a third less than their share in 1950.

Gerardo is aware of such differences, of the privileged status he has in Mexico. He is aware, and a little worried. A self-described "100 percent capitalist" and "a total rightist" in a country run by a pseudo-Socialist government, he complains how the government always blames business or the rich for what ails Mexico. As Gerardo sees it, it is corrupt government officials who have brought Mexico to its knees economically by stealing so much from the public till. Gerardo has had some personal experience in this respect. He had to pay bribes to get all the licenses for his restaurant. Whatever the merits of the who-is-to-blame debate, Gerardo worries that the government's antibusiness, antirich propaganda may be persuading Mexico's poor—the majority of Mexicans—that Gerardo and his class are their enemy. That could prove sticky if another revolution comes to Mexico, as some U.S. conservatives warn. Gerardo thinks an upheaval like the 1910 Revolution could happen again. But he doesn't think the United States would allow any Marxist takeover of the country. But just in case, his father, a Lebanese-Mexican who made his money in plastics, has set up bank accounts for himself, his wife, and his children in the United States to facilitate any hasty exit.

Gerardo's best friend already had to leave the country quickly, under slightly different circumstances. Francisco Durazo, son of Arturo Durazo, the former police chief of Mexico City, fled Mexico on foot after his father was accused of drug trafficking, murder, and extorting millions of dollars from his underlings as the price for their jobs and promotions. "Paco" Durazo moved to Canada, one of the countries in which, the Mexican government says, his father established multimillion-dollar bank accounts. I asked Gerardo if he felt sorry for Paco, who now had to live in exile.

"No," replied Gerardo, laughing. "He went with a lot of money. He lives well."

Gerardo recognized that the poor don't have all they need. In fact, he acknowledged, "the poor are getting poorer all the time. But it's not their fault. They were born without money. In Mexico you can't do anything without money. That's the truth. With the minimum salary, you can't do anything. You have to steal to survive. It's not their fault. But a lot of them are bad people. They threaten. They rob. And they don't like to work."

·   ·   ·

I left Gerardo early that Sunday morning at El News. I told him he'd have to do El Magic and the video bars without me. I fled the deafening din of the club's music and looked back at the artificial world El News had created for Mexico's young elite. What would my maid, Adelaida, think of this place if I could get her past the bouncers to see it, I wondered. For an instant I thought of how delicious it might be to bring Adelaida to Gerardo's restaurant and ask him to have lunch with us. But that instant quickly passed. What, after all, I thought, would they have to talk about?

· 3 ·

The *Tragafuego*

Back in July of 1984, when I first arrived in Mexico, the only out-of-work people who caught the eye were the women beggars in Mexico City's fashionable Zona Rosa neighborhood. They sat on sidewalks in front of posh hotels and shops, shooing their raga-muffin sons or daughters forward to panhandle tourists. As Mexico's unemployment rate spiraled upward, however, others appeared, spreading like an economic contagion.

In Cuernavaca, I began to see *limpiaparabrisas*, street urchins who washed road dust from windshields for a handout while the light was red. At the foot of car-clogged international bridges in Ciudad Juárez and Tijuana, hawkers of fruit, candy, and cheap trinkets became common.

Most of all, I remember the explosion of street sellers and performers that occurred along the capital's famed Reforma Avenue. The vendors sold an astounding number of things. From my car, I could buy fresh-cut flowers, chewing gum, car floor mats, rubber windshield-wiper refills, matches, tools, books of transit regulations, city maps, stuffed animals, toy blackboards, lottery tickets, deeley-bopper headgear, rabbits, birds, and even crystal chandeliers.

Economists might argue that these people were merely "underemployed," doing work beneath their training. But to these people, most of whom had no training at all, underemployment was just highfalutin' talk for not having a regular job. Mexico has no system of unemployment compensation, so these Mexicans had two choices. They could flee to the United States to earn a living, as millions of their compatriots had done. Or they could make up a job to eke out a living. Crossing the border was dangerous, usually requiring a guide who cost $300 or $400. One needed friends or relatives in the States to show you the ropes on how to get a job. These people had neither, so they chose to stay in Mexico, living by their wits.

I marveled at the imagination of some of these peddlers. They were always looking for a new item to entice buyers. Once a man even tried to sell me a live owl! What heights human optimism must have reached that day when he decided that his molting mate might be his meal ticket. The unflappable selling the inedible.

My real favorites, however, were the street performers—the clowns, the jugglers, the tumblers who sometimes did circus-quality work for a lot less than center-ring pay. Other street people sold goods. The performers sold themselves. I remember in particular a Charlie Chaplin lookalike who worked the corner of Reforma and Niza, at the edge of the Zona Rosa. Cane in hand, he did the Little Tramp's trademark waddle and mugging face in hopes of getting a few hundred pesos from appreciative motorists.

The most memorable performers of all, however, were the *tragafuegos*. As best I could tell, they made more than anyone else. Street people were lucky if their handouts equaled the minimum wage of three dollars a day. *Tragafuegos* could make three and four times that. But while they earned more, they paid more, too. In Mexican slang, *tragafeugos* are firebreathers. They make a living by putting kerosene, gasoline, or some other flammable liquid in their mouths and spitting it toward a lit torch. Using audiences of stopped motorists at busy intersections, they become human blowtorches dozens of times a day.

I was both appalled and fascinated by *tragafuegos*. One could applaud their bravery, but it didn't take long to figure out they had short careers ahead of them. When they first started appearing on Mexico City streets in number, around the end of 1984, medical experts from the national university began to study the effects of the sustained presence of corrosive petroleum fluids in a person's mouth. The experts found that *tragafuegos* were losing their sense of taste and, eventually, all feeling in their mouths. Their teeth fell out. Ulcers began to appear on the mucous linings next to their tongues. Brain damage was not uncommon. The adjective that came to mind when one thought of them was "punch-drunk."

That's what José Guadalupe Rivas was when I first met him in 1987. José worked Mexico City's busy intersection of Reforma and Juárez avenues, usually grabbing the south side of the crossing early in the morning before someone else did. He stayed until seven or eight at night, doing his act every three or four minutes. It never changed. As the light was about to turn red, he filled his mouth with diesel fuel from a plastic gallon jug. He lit his makeshift torch, a bent coat hanger with a soaked rag knotted on the end. He strode towards the front of the three rows of traffic waiting at the light, stared at the crowd of drivers before him, stopped for dramatic effect, and, with all the force he could manage, spit the combustible liquid toward the waiting flame at the end of his outstretched arm. An orangey burst of fire spread before him, ten or fifteen feet wide. Even jaded motorists had to take notice, for the heat of this inferno could be felt three and four cars back. When done, José strutted among his curbside audience looking for his prize, like a matador who had just delivered a brilliant coup de grâce. He had been macho in a country where machismo is valued highly. But instead of two ears and a tail, José usually got a handful of fifty- or hundred-peso coins, small change for a man who was slowly killing himself to amuse others.

José was only twenty-three years old. But already he had been a *tragafuego* for eight years. He was pushing the envelope. When pressed, he would admit that he knew it. His speech was slurred. He had a tough time focusing on the meaning of my questions. He had lost most of his sense of taste and had visible facial and arm burns. The burns were from earlier days when, as a novice, he had used cooking oil and even gasoline in his act, instead of kerosene. Both, he told me, tend to stick to the skin and catch fire if one doesn't spit them out hard enough.

"I can't find anything that pays me more," was José's explanation as to why he engaged in what many regarded as suicidal work.

On a good day, José told me, he made about eight thousand pesos, about twice the minimum wage of that time. With his six years of grammar school—the median level of education for Mexicans—he might have made as much in a real job. But there were no real jobs to be had, he told me. There weren't as many "good days" any more, either.

The government had been cracking down on street performers and sellers. Officials complained street people had no licenses to perform their activities and paid no taxes. With all the hassling that resulted, José was taking in only five thousand pesos a day. From that, he had to pay two thousand pesos a day for the room he shared at a dive over near the airport. That didn't leave him much for eating, clothes, and, most important, kerosene.

While taxes and licenses were the official explanation for the crackdown, what the government really wanted to do was get the "underemployed" off the streets. Street people were an embarrassing reminder that the Mexican economy was in crisis, and that unemployment in particular was in a chronic state. It wasn't the first crackdown either. In 1985, as the first stories appeared about the horrific side effects of the firebreathers' trade, the government instituted a flying squad of social workers who roamed Mexico City in search of wayward firebreathers to counsel. Government trucks took *tragafuegos* to detoxification clinics, where they were treated medically and trained for jobs that did not exist. *Tragafuegos,* like many street people in the United States, often did not want such help. Sometimes they resisted violently. José had dodged the flying squad more than once. He just wanted to be left alone, he said.

Frustrated at this attitude, the government intensified its discouragement of street performers and sellers in 1987. The approach of the 1988 presidential campaign may have had something to do with it, cynics suggested. Threats of punitive action were made. Police turned violent, bashing quite a few heads as they cleared key streets of unlicensed vendors. Most important to José, traffic cops began refusing the "tips" that street sellers and performers had been paying them every day for several years for the privilege of working lucrative intersections. Rousting became a way of life.

There wasn't always a regular traffic policeman at José's corner, so even after the crackdown he was able to ply his trade part of the day. But he always had to be looking over his shoulder. José's roommate of three months, Noe García González, who worked alongside him, did the same. Noe had been a fire-breather, too. But for the last three years José's sixteen-year-old pal had mostly been a clown. To enhance his act, he'd taught himself juggling. When I met him, however, Noe was a book-seller, a minion in yet another government program designed to obscure the grim reality of Mexico's high unemployment. In mid-1987, the Ministry of Education began providing plastic-wrapped packages of the classics to a few hundred youths who would agree to give up juggling, firebreathing, or other embarrassing activities to sell books. Enticed by what looked like a steady job, Noe joined up. Each morning he would go to a ministry office to buy an armful of book packages. Decked out in a snappy fuchsia vest stamped with the logo of the Education Ministry, Noe would try to sell the packages for two thousand pesos each. That was twice what he had paid for them. But even with a 100 percent profit, Noe was only making about two thousand pesos each day. What the program seemed to ignore was that Mexicans, hurt by low levels of education and low incomes, aren't exactly avid readers of Aristotle, Plato, Carlos Fuentes, or the other famous writers whose books the Education Ministry provided. In fact, Mexicans buy more comic books each week than newspapers. But, if the truth be told, the program was aimed at image, not results. Natty sellers of great books looked better to foreigners and potential voters than unseemly firebreathers and jugglers. That's what counted.

Imagery, however, didn't pay the rent. Noe's share of the hotel room cost him as much as he was clearing each day as a book-seller. As a result, when the police weren't looking, he reverted to juggling to augment his income. Under his spiffy bookseller's vest, he wore a homemade clown suit. Nearby, he kept a box of makeup. When the time was right, he'd quickly apply the makeup, rip off the vest, and pick up the fruit or balls he was using that day as his props. As a full-time clown he had grossed ten thousand pesos a day. With the crackdown, he made much less. But at least he had enough to eat.

Like a lot of government programs, the crackdown was unevenly applied. For example, when I went to talk to Education Ministry officials about the program, I found David Jiménez performing as a clown right outside the ministry's front door. He was earning fifteen thousand pesos a day, nearly four times the minimum wage. Likewise, the government, never intimidated by inconsistency, backed a program that encouraged out-of-work Mexicans to *"¡Empléate tú mismo!"* ("Employ yourself!"). Unstated was the message that they just couldn't do it in the most natural of places, the street.

The government was equally ineffective at hiding the real extent of national unemployment. The authoritative reports of the central bank gave unemployment rates that seemed astoundingly low to anyone familiar with the Mexican economic situation. One reason was the highly restrictive definition of "unemployed" that the government used. To be considered employed, one had only to have worked for pay or profit in the week before unemployment rates were calculated. Even if you worked only a few minutes, that was enough for the government to count you as employed. Unpaid family workers were counted as employed too, as were those seeking work for the first time. If one believed government figures, open unemployment in Mexico ranged from 4 percent to 6 percent of the active work force during most of the 1980s.

Using more traditional definitions of unemployment, private Mexican economists and international economic groups (and occasional government agencies) estimated that Mexico's real unemployment rate moved into double digits in the early 1980s, reaching 18 percent in 1987. That was twice the rate in 1982, when Mexico's economic crisis began. Underemployment was even more mind-boggling, sticking stubbornly at about 40 percent of the active work force for most of the 1980s.

Mexico's definition of the active work force was a bit startling, too. Anyone twelve years of age or older was counted. That was a tacit admission that many families, in need of extra income, couldn't afford to let their children stay in school much longer than that. They sent them out to work.

No matter how hard the government tried to paper over the magnitude of the unemployment problem, their task got only harder. It won't get any easier for the rest of the century because of what population experts call a demographic echo.

Demographics aren't something the street people talk much about. Most of them don't even know what the word means. José didn't when I asked him if he knew why he and so many other

Mexicans had to turn to the streets for work. *"El pinche gobierno"* was his salty response. Roughly translated, that means "the fucking government." In his own direct way, José came up with the right answer. But he didn't really know the details of how the government had screwed up.

What had caused the unmanageable number of workers entering the Mexico work force in the 1980s were the shortsighted government population policies of the 1960s and '70s. They had encouraged a birth rate that brought about a million new workers into the work force each year in the 1980s and will continue to do so in similar numbers for the rest of the century. The battered Mexican economy must grow sufficiently each year to create a million new jobs to absorb this influx. If it doesn't, a million new people will be taking to the streets—or migrating to the United States—in search of what work they can find.

The government's record of job creation wasn't exactly awe-inspiring in the period immediately following the beginning of Mexico's economic crisis. Even pro-government labor unions estimated that Mexico was not creating enough jobs for new workers. In fact, it was losing some of the ones it had. The Ministry of Planning and Budget said in 1986 that about 30 percent of Mexico's unemployment had been caused by layoffs. Some Mexican companies had gone bankrupt as the crisis caused the economy to contract. Others, prompted by the government's 1986 decision to join the free-trade–oriented General Agreement on Tariffs and Trade (GATT), became more efficient (read less labor-intensive) in anticipation of increased foreign competition. The government itself, in attempts to cut its huge budget deficit, closed down unprofitable state-owned enterprises. That put thousands into the streets. By some estimates, the closing of the state-owned Fundidora steel plant in Monterrey put forty thousand people out of work.

The government also wound up taking most of the available credit from Mexico's state-owned banks because it needed so much to finance its budget deficits. Precious little remained for business owners who wanted loans to finance expansion—and create more jobs. To make matters worse, skittish Mexicans sent billions in bank savings out of the country to the United States and other safer financial havens, exacerbating the credit crunch. To offset some of this, the government might have created quite a few new jobs itself with all the money it earned from oil imports. But payments on a hundred-billion-dollar foreign debt that it had foolishly incurred soaked up much of what Mexico earned from oil.

To be fair to the government, one might argue that Mexico's unemployment crisis can be traced back to the Spanish conquistadors, whom the government blames for a lot of other things. When Hernán Cortés arrived in Mexico in 1519, there were about twenty million indigenous Mexicans. Through bloody campaigns of conquest, and by spread of European diseases to which the descendants of the Aztecs and Mayas had no immunity, the Spanish rulers slashed that number to one million by 1605. Mexico's Spanish rulers, however, found they needed workers for their new colony. They adopted a pro-growth population policy that persisted until the 1970s, notwithstanding independence, changes of government, a few wars, and the murderous 1910 Mexican Revolution. In 1954, Mexico became the most populous Spanish-speaking country in the world. In 1980 it became the eleventh most populous country.

As late as 1970—six years after José was born—then-presidential candidate Luis Echeverría Alvarez was still urging Mexican women to have more children so Mexico could be bigger and better. On the average, Mexican women were having about five children each at the time, a figure surpassed by both José's and Noe's mothers. The government even awarded medals to the most prolific of mothers, not unlike the "hero mothers" whom the Soviet Union rewards for helping to solve its demographic problems. When Echeverría became president, however, his advisers suddenly discovered the population time bomb that past pro-growth policies had created. Without change, Mexico's population would double every twenty-five years, they concluded. Even the most chauvinistic Mexican politicians did not argue that Mexico, short of arable land and water, had the resources to sustain that kind of growth.

With his administration's efforts at family planning, Echeverría managed to reduce population growth from 3.5 percent to 3.2 percent during his administration (1970–76). Birth control got going in earnest during the time of President José López Portillo (1976–82), with the opening of many family-planning clinics and state-financed programs of sterilization. Mass-media campaigns

and not-so-subtle story lines on popular Mexican soap operas proclaimed the message of the day: *"La familia pequena vive mejor"*
("The small family lives better").

By the time President de la Madrid left office in December 1988,
population growth was down below 2 percent. Mexican women
were having three children instead of five. But the damage had
been done. Forty-five percent of the population was less than fifteen years old in 1980. The work force for the next thirty years
had been born. Their numbers would ripple through the population for years, having a profound impact both in Mexico and in
the United States, where many would seek work.

The population onslaught was being made worse by advances
in health care. Mexicans were living longer. More were staying
on the job later, opening up fewer spots for youngsters entering
the job market. Life expectancy for Mexicans jumped from fifty-
eight years for those born in 1960 to sixty-eight years for those
born in 1980, according to census figures. The average Mexican
born now will live into his seventies. To compound matters, more
Mexicans were around to grow that old because fewer were dying
in infancy. Infant mortality remains shamefully high, but nowhere near the cataclysmic levels of just a few decades ago.

On the first story I reported from Mexico, I found that some
politicians still hadn't grasped the threat of overpopulation. During the World Population Conference held in Mexico City in July
1984, leaders of left-wing opposition parties in Mexico were
spreading stories that the government, as part of its birth-control
programs, was sterilizing peasant women involuntarily, or at least
without proper notification about the difficulty of reversing sterilization. To check out the charges, I visited several family-planning clinics in the poor slums that ring Mexico City. What I found
was quite different from the politicians' charges. Indeed, sterilization had become the foremost form of birth control in Mexico.
But the reason was less sinister than the leftists would have had
me believe. Woman after woman, many with six or more children, told me that she had chosen sterilization because it was
certain. With not enough money to rear the children they had,
certainty was very important to these women. The pill wasn't safe
enough for them. One might forget to take it, several told me.
Condoms were out of the question, because their husbands or
lovers thought them unmanly. In macho Mexico, vasectomies

weren't even a topic of discussion. Besides, in a nominally Catholic country like Mexico, sterilization was the lesser of several moral evils.

"To take the pill is a sin every time," said one *campesino* woman in an explanation that might have impressed Thomas Aquinas. "Sterilization is a sin only once."

Confronted with these responses, one leftist politician I talked to admitted that he too had heard such answers. After a long dinner and a lot of drinking of wine, he told me that it was the policy of his tiny party to keep population pressures close to the boiling point because that made it more likely his party would grow in popularity.

Mexico has one other thing going against it in terms of the population bubble's pressure on the work force. On top of all else, the number of youngsters entering the work force gets even larger some years because so many kids drop out of grammar or high school. Parents toss children out of the house with astounding regularity because they can't afford to keep them. Others just demand that their kids go to work rather than school so the family will have enough to eat.

Not far from Los Pinos, where the president of Mexico lives, I met one of these kids. Alejandra, age five, should have been in kindergarten. But she was selling chewing gum along Reforma, as scores of people do each day. She said she couldn't give me her last name because her father had told her not to. She did say she made a few thousand pesos a day selling gum, which she gave to her father. He was a few hundred yards down the street selling flowers. At the time, there were about 2.5 million kids like Alejandra working Mexico City streets.

Noe was one of these kids when he started his clown career at the age of thirteen. His family back in Guerrero state had told him they couldn't afford to keep him. I asked Noe if he wouldn't have preferred to stay in school, rather than work. He replied: "When you don't have enough to eat, school is a luxury."

•   •   •

In early 1988, I went back to José's and Noe's corner to see how they were doing. They weren't there anymore, though. The two booksellers who had taken over their corner had never heard of them.

I drove out to the Hotel Morelos, where the two told me they had been staying. It's not much of a hotel—a flophouse, really. On top of the three-story white structure, there is a sign that says merely Hotel. Inside, there is no real lobby, just a long hallway carpeted in an ugly burnt orange. The reception desk is a mirrored, bullet-proof glass affair that permits one to hear the desk clerk but not to see him. The clerk checked the register to see if he had José or Noe listed. He didn't, I heard a faceless voice say. Did he know where they had gone, I asked. "No," he said. "We only keep records for a week. We don't ask for forwarding addresses."

I poked around the halls looking for someone who might know where the two had gone. A grubbily dressed man in his fifties said he remembered José, after I described the burns on his face.

"I remember he wasn't feeling well," he said. "Then he disappeared."

· 4 ·

The *Pollo*

It all happened so fast that it's hard to pinpoint just where things went wrong for Miguel Tostado. Maybe it was when María became pregnant. Surely that changed everything.

Miguel was finishing high school, something most Mexicans never do. A part-time job in hand, he was thinking about college and what courses to study. He had, as they say, possibilities. Then the news from María came. Miguel, a short, intense, handsome youth with a strong sense of obligation, "did the right thing." He married María, quit school, and took a full-time job as a machine operator at the only factory in his tiny village, Pabellón de Arteaga, an agricultural outpost in the fertile mountain plateau that runs north and south through the center of Mexico.

"When we started, I didn't have furniture, a house—nothing," said Miguel, who in the summer of 1987 would become the center of attention in a ghastly loss of life that would rivet the world's attention. "My wife was pregnant. We had a child coming. I was seventeen."

There was little room for his new family at the home on dusty Miguel Hidalgo street where he had been born and grown up as the fourth oldest of eleven children. As many new Mexican husbands do, he started to build a home of his own, cobbling a crude structure of bricks and cement in his spare time.

Unemployment was high in Pabellón. Miguel felt lucky to get the machine operator's job, even though it paid only the minimum wage of three dollars a day. In hopes that it might help him get a better paying job, he joined the ruling Institutional Revolutionary Party, even though privately he felt the party had done little to help Pabellón, a hardscrabble town of about fifteen thousand people. Party clout, however, brought no improvement. Miguel soon found that three dollars a day wasn't enough to meet the needs of a new and growing family. Every week he seemed to get more behind.

"I was more dead than alive," Miguel recalled of the depression he felt because of the inadequacy of his pay. "I was just waiting for death."

The scarcity of good jobs was just a sign of the times. Mexico's economic crisis had begun in earnest in August 1982. The administration of President de la Madrid decided that austerity was the road to economic recovery. In practical terms, that meant that prices were allowed to go up faster than wages. Every month it became more noticeable.

What Miguel also noticed was that his oldest brother, José Luis, who was working illegally as a dishwasher in Dallas, was able to send back fifty dollars or so every month to Miguel's father, Agustín, an employee of the Agriculture Ministry who also earned the minimum wage. Fifty dollars was the equivalent of three weeks' extra pay for Miguel, Agustín, or almost any worker in Pabellón.

Miguel noticed too the things that started popping up in his father's cramped, one-story home as a result of the money from José Luis. Miguel's father bought a new stereo system with immense speakers. It sits in the place of honor in the Tostado living room, visible to all who walk by the house's front windows. José Luis also sent his brother and sisters new clothes. They were well-made clothes, not the cheap polyester kind that one found in Pabellón's simple shops.

Eventually, at nighttime sessions in Pabellón's cantinas, an idea began to develop among Miguel and his friends about how they might improve their lives. Like so many millions before them, they decided they would go to the United States in search of work. With no high-paying job or established business, Miguel and his friends knew they could not qualify for a U. S. visa. They decided to enter illegally.

"Wetbacks" are what many Americans call Mexicans, such as Miguel, who cross the two-thousand-mile U.S.-Mexican border to find jobs on the U.S. side. But bodies of water such as the Rio Grande divide only a part of the U.S.-Mexican frontier. Hundreds of thousands of undocumented workers cross the frontier completely dry, some traversing the scorching desert terrain of Arizona and New Mexico. The more apt name for such illegal crossers is the one Mexicans use—*pollos*. To Mexicans, what is significant about the crossing is not that one gets wet. It's that one faces danger and even death, like a chicken thrown among coyotes. Thus the name *pollo*, which in Spanish means "chicken."

Many Mexicans are veterans of illegal crossings. They know the spots where the U.S. Border Patrol is spread thinly in its thankless, hopeless task of keeping hordes of illegal workers, mostly Mexicans, out of the country. In heavily patrolled areas, such as San Ysidro, across from Tijuana, and El Paso, across from Ciudad Juárez, the old-timers know when the border-patrol shifts change and when a window opens.

They know, too, the dangers. In Tijuana, for example, where a rugged, snake-infested, no-man's-land of canyons and gulches separates Mexico from Southern California, illegals not only have to worry about being caught by the border patrol but also are in danger of being robbed, raped, or even murdered by their own people. Gangs of thugs from Tijuana, armed with knives, machetes, and guns, regularly prey on the *pollos* who cross from Tijuana's La Libertad and other close-in neighborhoods just after dark. As I found out after spending a night in that no-man's-land with the border patrol in January 1986, even the Tijuana police get a piece of the action. Some demand bribes to let illegals make their passage. Others join in the robbing and raping themselves.

Miguel and his friends knew none of this. They did know that an inexperienced crosser often hires a "coyote," a sometimes swindling fixer, who, for a price, promises a successful crossing. But that first time, in February of 1983, no one in Miguel's group had the three hundred dollars that was the going rate for a coyote's services. Miguel and his buddies just jumped in the Rio Grande at a little border town called Ciudad Cuna and swam for the other side. As one might expect, some got caught, including Miguel's best friend, Mario García, who seemed to experience bad luck throughout his short, tragic life. But Miguel made it through. Though he spoke no English, he hopped a ride to Dallas, where he hoped his brother would be able to find him a job. Miguel got a job washing dishes in a restaurant, just like his brother. The pay was $3.35 an hour, as much as he had made in Pabellón in a day.

Those who hire workers such as Miguel argue it's justified because they can't find Americans who will do greasy kitchen work in Texas, or hard field work under the fiery California sun. Labor activists counter that illegals keep the pay of such jobs artificially low, shoving U.S. citizens out of the market. Economists say that's true, but low pay also knocks a dollar or two off everybody's restaurant bill. Miguel thought about none of this. All he wanted was a good job. He didn't care how he got it.

Though Miguel made more in Dallas, he found expenses were higher. He managed to keep costs down by sharing his brother's apartment and beat-up car. Like his brother, he managed to save fifty dollars a month to send home. Sometimes it was a hundred dollars when the overtime was good. The money went to his wife by postal money order, part of an estimated one billion dollars that illegals in the United States send back to relatives in Mexico each year. Such remittances are vital to the battered Mexican economy, rivaling tourism as a source of hard currency. The money Miguel sent back was vital to his family, too. With it, his still-unfinished house in Pabellón began to take shape. His wife bought a crib for their new baby, a daughter, whose birth Miguel missed because he was toiling a thousand miles away. Next came a dresser, a dining-room table and chairs, a stove, and some clothes for the baby, who was named Jessica.

Miguel got into a routine. Like a long-distance commuter, he'd stay in Dallas for ten or eleven months, working six days a week. Then he'd head home to spend a month reacquainting himself with his young bride and getting to know his daughter and, later, his second child, Miguel.

Miguel had had beginner's luck with his first successful crossing at Ciudad Cuna. But his luck turned worse with successive crossings. The second time, while crossing near Piedras Negras, just across from Eagle Pass, Texas, Miguel and his friends were robbed by *rateros*, the hyenas who make a profession of preying on illegal workers not only in Tijuana but all along the U.S.-Mexican border. The third time, in hopes of avoiding another robbery, he hired a coyote for protection. But the coyote took the money and ran, the fate of all too many *pollos*. On his fourth crossing, Miguel hired another coyote, who identified himself only as El Mosco ("The Fly"). El Mosco said he'd wait until he delivered Miguel and other workers to Dallas before he collected payment of $350. The crossing was successful. The trip to Dallas was uneventful and even fast. El Mosco put Miguel and others on a outbound train in the railyards of El Paso. Before long the group pulled into Big D. Miguel, at last, felt confident he had found a secure way to make his yearly crossing into the States.

El Mosco arranged Miguel's fifth trip to the United States, too, traveling to Pabellón to work the cantinas to see if he could persuade others to join Miguel. This time the fee was four hundred dollars. Miguel helped out, regaling the gathered with tales of money to be made on *el otro lado* ("the other side"), as Mexicans call the United States. His fifth trip began in late June of 1987. The group traveled by bus to Ciudad Juárez and stayed the night in a hotel on the Mexican side. El Mosco took care that the group avoided the Juárez police, who, like Tijuana cops, often extract bribes from outbound Mexicans for the privilege of crossing the border. Under Mexican law, it's not illegal to make a crossing to the U.S. side without proper U.S. documents. But Mexican police often make up the law as they go along.

On the night of June 30, Miguel and his group crossed the Rio Grande. But some of them, including Miguel, were caught. Miguel soon learned, however, that this was not the end of things. In fact, it was no more than a slight inconvenience. The border patrol and the U.S. Immigration and Naturalization Service don't have the staff to conduct court-supervised deportation proceedings against the millions of illegals they catch each year. They have worked out a process called voluntary return by which the apprehended illegal spends a few hours in a border-patrol lockup, waives his rights to a deportation hearing, and then is pushed back across the border, often through the same hole in the fence he crawled through. On any given night, the same illegal is likely to try to cross again, often making it through on the second or third try. It's a dirty little secret. But it makes things work.

In Miguel's case, he waited until the next day, Wednesday, July 1, to try again. All looked very good. El Mosco had scouted out a Missouri Pacific freight train that would take Miguel and his friends and another group of illegal workers to Dallas. But Miguel would

find out, to his horror, that El Mosco and his sidekick, El Chapulín ("The Grasshopper"), hadn't done all the homework they
should have. At the beginning, El Mosco's plan looked very clever.
He had picked a train scheduled to depart El Paso around sundown,
when dim light and shadows would hide his *pollos'* movements.
He waited for the regular check of empty boxcars by border-patrol agents, which occurs shortly before a train pulls out. With
that danger of discovery behind him, El Mosco's idea was that it
would be smooth sailing to Dallas once the train left El Paso—
unless other border-patrol agents pulled a surprise inspection down
the line at Sierra Blanca, as they sometimes did. Perhaps fear of
such an inspection explains why El Chapulín, at the last minute,
slid the boxcar door shut and locked Miguel and his companions
inside. Perhaps El Chapulín, who had an accomplice waiting to
meet the train in Dallas, figured a locked car was less likely to
attract notice. Whatever his reason, his closing the door frightened the bejesus out of Miguel and the other illegals inside.

"I didn't expect the door to close; I thought it was a mistake,"
Miguel told reporters a few days later in describing his state of
mind at the beginning of a tragedy that would grab headlines in
the days before the Fourth of July holiday. "If I had known [they
would close the door], I wouldn't have gotten in."

What El Mosco and El Chapulín apparently hadn't realized was
that they had not picked just any boxcar for the group. It was a
beer-storage car that sealed hermetically when the door was closed.
The car was designed to assume and retain the temperature of
the loading zone around it. In a beer factory, that would mean
refrigerated air. But the temperature in the railyards that July
night, in the high desert air of El Paso, was still about 100 degrees Fahrenheit. Moreover, the train El Mosco had picked was
using the right-of-way of another rail line. It had a low priority in
terms of when it could proceed in the face of other train traffic.
In fact, for the first three-and-a half hours of what would become
the worst ordeal of Miguel's life, the train just sat where Miguel
and his group had boarded it. The temperature inside, fueled
by the body heat of nineteen unexpected passengers, began to
climb.

As an afterthought, El Chapulín had tossed two blunt-tipped
railroad spikes into the car just before he slammed the boxcar
door shut. A few hours after the group had been sealed inside,
two of El Mosco's and El Chapulín's pals, who were making the

boxcar trip to Dallas, began using the spikes to hack a hole in the hardwood floor to let some air in. The going was slow, most of it done in the dark. Matches and candles threw light on the work sometimes. But their hungry flames also used up oxygen, a precious commodity which all began to worry about.

"After a few hours, the air and the oxygen ran out," said Miguel. "Things got very desperate."

Purely by chance, things weren't as desperate for Miguel. When he climbed into the boxcar, he had taken a spot next to the far wall where wear and tear had made a tiny crack next to the flooring. When the train finally pulled out that night, a little after nine, Miguel noticed a feeble breeze entering through the slit. He pressed his mouth to it for some relief from the suffocating, superheated air inside.

The men with the spikes worked furiously on carving out the air hole. They worked as if their lives depended on it. As it turned out, they did. After a while, the men became exhausted, and two others tried their luck at the stubborn floorboards. It might not have made any difference whether they had been able to punch a hole in the floor quickly if the train had left on time, or if it had not been ordered to spend a few more hours at a siding just outside El Paso to allow another train to pass. The border patrol, on alert more than ever since the May 1987 implementation of the stringent Simpson-Rodino immigration law, was indeed waiting at Sierra Blanca. They surely would have heard the frantic pounding of the spikes against the boxcar floor as the train stopped for inspection. But in all, the normally short trip from El Paso to Sierra Blanca, a mere seventy-five miles away, took some fourteen hours. It was too much for most of the group. In fact, it was too much for everyone except Miguel.

When border-patrol supervisor Melvin Dudley opened the boxcar that Thursday morning, he was not prepared for the ghastly sight before him. Corpses were everywhere. Blood, spewed from body cavities and organs exploded by intense heat, was splashed across the floor. Only Miguel, dehydrated to the point of danger, had survived what must have been a hell on earth. Eighteen men had been virtually cooked to death.

Hell and heaven apparently were on the minds of all in the boxcar before the end came. Miguel, at a press conference the next day, told reporters that many of his companions had cried out for help to the Almighty, men who in normal lives gave only lip service to the Catholic faith into which they had been baptized as infants. In their frenzy to get cool and stay alive, most had also ripped off their clothes, down to their cheap underwear. Some senselessly fought with each other, blindly flailing with their fists at anyone nearby in apparent frustration to punish someone, anyone, for their terrible fate.

Miguel, too, thought he was going to die. Just before the train pulled into Sierra Blanca, he noticed there were no sounds at all in the car. He called out to his best friend, unlucky Mario García. But there was no answer. Eventually he heard some other voices, maybe two or three, pitifully weak and incoherent. What he could not hear was the hacking and clawing at the air hole that had been a steady din since the El Paso yards. Miguel moved toward the air hole to see what he could do. The previous workers had managed to make an opening to the outside of a few inches. Now they all lay silently around him. Miguel picked up a spike and, slowly but steadily, worked at enlarging the hole. By the time the train pulled into Sierra Blanca, he was lying face down over it, sucking in the still-warm morning air. When the train jerked to a stop, he heard the sounds of border-patrol agents talking as they opened and shut boxcar doors down the line. He cried out for help.

Border-patrol agent Stanley Saathoff was first to discover Miguel's boxcar. He immediately called for Dudley, his supervisor, to come over.

"When I heard his footsteps," Miguel said, "I knew that I had made it."

When Miguel appeared before reporters on Friday, dressed in a clean sweatshirt, jeans, and red high-top sneakers, he was still visibly shaken. On the crucial details of the event, the details reporters always press to get, he could barely talk. The border patrol put Miguel under wraps for months after the disaster. He was a material witness to a possible homicide. Police in the United States and Mexico sought El Mosco and El Chapulín, whose identities were tentatively established. I tried several times to talk with Miguel after that. Always the response from the border patrol and Miguel was no. Miguel's mental condition, they told me, was too delicate for any more interviews. Then, around Christmas of 1987, Miguel suddenly decided he wanted to talk.

As it turned out, Miguel was hiding out in a very obvious place. The border patrol, rather than put him up in a hotel for months on end during the investigation, had let Miguel go back to work at his old job at Mother Mesquite's Cantina in Dallas. He was staying in his old apartment. With immigration authorities' help, Miguel's wife and children had even been allowed to join him.

Miguel was happy to have his family with him, although his wife missed her parents and friends in Pabellón terribly. Miguel's salary had gone up to $6.50 an hour. But, like a proud parent, he was spending all he earned on clothes, food, and toys for his family. His pay was scheduled to rise to $7.50 an hour as his responsibilities with the restaurant increased. But with a $420-a-month rent, even his six-day work week wouldn't produce much for savings as he waited for the investigation to wind down. Miguel told me he was worried that when the investigation was over, he would be sent back to Pabellón no better off than when he had made his first crossing to the United States.

Make no mistake. Miguel did want to go home. He had come to like the life he found in Dallas. The salaries were enough to buy nutritious food. The police were honest, not always demanding bribes like the cops in Mexico. Health services were good. And he felt he got something for the U.S. and Texas taxes he paid. He didn't even mind paying Social Security, though he knew, as a Mexican, he'd never get a dime in benefits. He had encountered real democracy. He liked what he saw. Although all these things had changed him—made him more critical of Mexico, more demanding about its future—he nonetheless wanted to go home. At least eventually.

It will probably come as a surprise to many Americans, but the majority of undocumented workers from Mexico do not want to stay in the United States. They do not want to become Americans.

"I am Mexican a hundred percent," said Miguel. "In my soul, I am a Mexican. I want to go back to Pabellón. It is so peaceful, so calm there. It is what I am used to. It is my home."

One of Miguel's fallen boxcar companions had similar sentiments. An amateur poet, he penned these words, which were found in a flimsy notebook among the debris on the bloody train floor:

> How beautiful is the United States.
> Illinois, California and Tennessee.
> But over in my country,
> A piece of the sky belongs to me.

Goodbye, Laredo, Weslaco and San Antonio.
Houston and Dallas are in my song.
Goodbye, El Paso. I am back Chamizal.
Your friend, the illegal, has returned.

That Christmas, there was every possibility that U.S. officials
would send Miguel home. His immigration status was shaky. He
had a temporary work permit that allowed him to stay in the United
States as long as he was needed as a material witness in the deaths
of the other eighteen boxcar passengers. In the six months that
had passed since the investigation had been opened, the border
patrol had no solid leads on the whereabouts of El Mosco and El
Chapulín. If the truth be told, Miguel wasn't really needed anymore. But no one—at least no one who knew plucky Miguel—
wanted to send him home.

Miguel wasn't asking to remain in the United States permanently. He just wanted to work long enough—maybe a few years—
to save up a grubstake to start a business in Pabellón that would
give him a decent income for him and his family.

"It doesn't have to be something big," he told me. "I'd settle for
something small. I don't make much now. But I can do things
for my family. I can do my part as a husband, as a father. At last,
I have pride."

As the new year approached, Miguel's best chance to stay in
the United States was to get a local member of the U.S. Congress
to get a private bill passed, authorizing his presence. That was
what his boss, Larry Richardson, said. But a private bill wasn't
much of a chance, Richardson admitted.

If Miguel had started to work in the United States about a year
earlier, he might have qualified for amnesty and permanent U.S.
residency under the Simpson-Rodino immigration law, which went
into effect earlier in the year. But because Miguel had not lived
continuously in the United States since before January 1, 1982,
he was not one of the millions eligible.

When Miguel met with reporters in July, I asked him if he
planned to try to reenter the United States illegally, given his
close call with death. Just a day after Miguel had been rescued,
another eleven illegals had been found near death in an over-
heated boxcar not far from where Miguel's eighteen companions
had died. Another group had been found near San Clemente, Cal-

ifornia, all unconscious, in a sealed truck. Apparently other people weren't being scared off by the experience Miguel had been through—or by the stiff sanctions of the new Simpson-Rodino immigration law. That's what had prompted my question.

"I think I'll stay in my own country from now on," Miguel responded to my question. But when I asked him the same thing again that Christmas in Dallas, his answer was different, more resigned. Miguel said that if he couldn't provide for his family with low-paying jobs in Mexico, or if he couldn't get any work at all (unemployment was about 18 percent at the time), he'd be coming back.

"*Ni modo*," he said, using a Mexican slang expression that roughly means, "What choice do I have?"

His father, Agustín, had the same response when I asked him the same question a few days later in Pabellón.

"People leave Pabellón because there is not enough work," said Agustín. "There is not enough of anything."

That wasn't always the case. Pabellón sits in the middle of rich farm country in Aguascalientes, Mexico's smallest state. Once this area provided good agricultural jobs, not jobs that would make a man rich but jobs that at least put what was needed on the table. Foolish government agricultural policies and an unprecedented economic crisis had changed all that.

Even though Pabellón's economic outlook was gloomy, I got some sense of why Miguel wanted to come back. Pabellón sits in the midst of magnificent countryside. Out on Route 45, the main thoroughfare that leads from the state capital to Pabellón, one can see for miles the verdant tableau of trapezoidal and rectangular bean and corn fields that have been hewn into the soil with the precision of a Mondrian. All around are the matte black peaks of Mexico's Sierra Madre Occidental mountains.

It's an idyllic spot in many ways. Thirties-style tractors ply the roads in numbers, their straw-hatted drivers in no hurry to move traffic along. On intersecting side roads, burro-drawn carts are about their business, clip-clopping their way to market. Below this idyllic surface, however, is misery and, most of all, unemployment. Agustín estimated that as many as 80 percent of Pabellón's able-bodied male workers were away from home, working in the United States, at any given time. It is the same in hundreds of tiny towns throughout central and southern Mexico. The exodus from Pabellón was not even the worst I had encountered. In the tiny, flyblown town of La Ermita de los Correa, in neighboring Zacatecas state, I found a village populated almost exclusively with women and children when I visited it in mid-1987. During picking time in Southern California, I was told, almost all La Ermita's able-bodied men lived in Riverside, California, and neighboring suburbs of Los Angeles.

The numbers didn't make it seem the future would be any different. Past government policies had encouraged outsized birth rates in the 1960s and 1970s. Those babies were coming into the work force, a million strong each year countrywide. A hundred-billion-dollar foreign debt and massive budget deficits made it unlikely that the economy would grow enough to create sufficient jobs for such youths.

Would things, I wondered, be even worse in Pabellón, which had lost several of its sons in the boxcar disaster? Scarred by the tragedy, would the fathers and mothers of Pabellón keep their sons home, safe from more boxcar disasters, even if it meant a life of penury?

I asked Miguel's nine-year-old brother, Ernesto, to show me the house of the mother of luckless Mario García, Miguel's best friend. Aurora met me at the door, dressed all in black. Like many Mexican women, she took her mourning seriously. Mario's death had left an empty pain, she said. But she had the consolation of knowing that she had escaped mourning for two. One of her sons, Pedro, had planned to make the trip in June with Mario, Miguel, and the others from Pabellón. But at the last moment, Aurora, fearful of the dangers of such trips, had forbidden Pedro to accompany the others.

"God or something told me to keep him at home," she said.

After the boxcar disaster, Aurora asked her two boys not to go to the United States, at least for a while. There were no jobs in Pabellón for Pedro and her other son, Ramón. Aurora admitted that in a year or so, she knew her boys would probably pressure her to let them go anyway. Given the economic prospects of Mexico, she said, she would probably have to let them go.

As I was leaving, she took down a small Polaroid photo from the wall, a keepsake she had of Mario. In the photo, he was sitting beneath a tree in a Dallas park. His sweatshirt, jeans, and sneakers made him look like one of the millions of Mexican-

American kids one can find in Texas, California, or other U.S. Hispanic strongholds. I handed back the photo. For the longest time she just stared at it. As I said good-bye, I noticed that tears had begun to flow freely from her dark-brown eyes.

Ernesto showed me the way back to my car. He had been quiet throughout the interview with Aurora. Now he had questions. What was life like in the United States? How was his big brother Miguel? How much could you earn in Dallas? What could you buy?

As I looked at Ernesto's face, I couldn't help thinking of Miguel, whose features must have been very similar at the same age. "What plans did you have?" I asked Ernesto. "Do you know what you want to be when you grow up?" Like many nine-year-olds, Ernesto was a little fuzzy on what he'd be doing ten years hence. I asked him finally: "What will you do if you grow up and can't get a job in Pabellón?"

Ernesto thought for a while as he dragged a stick along the dusty, unpaved street, now and then making sclaffing strokes at an imaginary ball.

"If I can't find work," he said, "then I guess I'll have to go to the United States."

· 5 ·

The *Médico*

The story of Enrique López Hernández is sort of a Mexican Horatio Alger tale. Enrique grew up on the mean streets of Mexico City, the product of a broken home. His father ran out on his mother, an all-too-common fate of poor Mexican children. To help his mother make ends meet, Enrique sold gum and gelatin at street corners to passing motorists. Pressure for money was so great at one point that he agreed to be a runner for local marijuana dealers who used children to fool the police. That might have led him down the wrong path, as it did some of his pals. But a mother's determination helped Enrique escape the streets and make it through college. In fact, he did even better. In a country where the average person never gets beyond the sixth grade, Enrique became a doctor.

In medical school, Enrique thought about specializing and working in a rich neighborhood. As medical students will do, he and his friends talked about the money they might make. But he chose instead to return to his roots. He became a general practitioner in the slums of Mexico.

"My mother made many sacrifices for me" said Enrique, now Dr. Enrique López Hernández, an intense, thoughtful man of thirty-six whose dark, full chin whiskers make him look a bit like a Quaker. "She wanted me to show that our people, *morenos* [dark-skinned Mexicans], are not animals. I felt I had a debt to these people."

Out on the east end of Chimalhuacán Avenue, amid the auto-parts stores and chicken take-out shops, Enrique is paying that debt back. He has a tiny consulting clinic that caters to local residents. It's not much of a place, but then neither is the city in which it's located, Nezahualcóyotl.

"This clinic is nothing," he said as he surveyed its surroundings. "It's miserable, but it's mine."

The clinic is not what many foreigners would be used to. The entire building is a concrete-walled structure, twelve feet by twenty feet. Enrique has put a thin wall down the middle so he has a ten-by-twelve-foot space for examining patients, and a ten-by-twelve-foot waiting room. The waiting room is Spartan, furnished only with twelve one-piece plastic chairs. There are no magazines for patients to read, no music piped in.

The consulting room is austere, too. Enrique sits behind a small, beat-up desk. There is a chair for one patient and a short examination table to Enrique's left. A white cabinet holds medicine and a few books. Up top is a plastic box that has all the clinic's medical files. There is a scale, a wastebasket, a long fluorescent light overhead, a few city licenses tacked on the wall, and nothing else.

"I could use a few things," Enrique said sardonically when I asked him what he might buy for the clinic if money were no object. He had a wish list ready. It was obviously something he had thought about. To begin, he said, he could use a phone. Phones are scarce in Mexico. There's a waiting list to get one; they cost a lot to install. Without a phone, patients can't call Enrique's office in an emergency or even to make an appointment. They can't call him at home either. He has no phone there. They can't even write him a letter, because there is no mail service yet in Tultitlán, where he lives.

A car would be nice, Enrique added, even a very old one. Without a car, Enrique has to take a bus to the clinic, spending two hours each way. With a car, he said, he'd be able to visit a few of his bedridden patients who live where there is no public transportation.

Enrique said he could also use some items that one finds in any American doctor's bag. For starters, Enrique said, he could use a doctor's bag. The one he has is just a light-blue woman's clutch purse made of plastic. In it, he carries a well-used stethoscope, a blood-pressure gauge, a rubber tube for tourniquets, some clamps and probes, a basal and an oral thermometer, and rubber gloves. That's it. The gloves are not the disposable type. Enrique can't afford the luxury of disposable equipment. He has no sterilizer—another item for the wish list—so he uses rubber gloves that he washes after each use. He has no ophthalmoscope, that tubular gadget with a green pointy cone at the top that doctors use to look into patients' eyes. An ophthalmoscope would be handy, Enrique said. The pollution in the Valley of Mexico, where Nezahualcóyotl and Mexico City are located, is considered the worst in the world and often creates eye infections. The list went on. A typewriter would improve record-keeping. A filing cabinet would replace the overflowing plastic box. A nurse would help.

If Enrique had the money, he could buy all those things. But, of course, he did not have the money. His is not a country-club practice. It is not even the practice of a struggling small-town physician. Enrique practices on the cusp of medicine. He calls it *medicina salvaje,* "savage medicine." When a doctor doesn't make much, medicine can be pretty inelegant. And Enrique certainly doesn't make much. In 1987, he had a net average income of ten thousand pesos a day. By the end of the year he was doing a bit better, averaging thirteen thousand pesos a day (less than six dollars). But he wasn't keeping pace with the 160 percent inflation that Mexico suffered that year.

"A skilled worker makes that," said Enrique, who keeps meticulous records in a well-thumbed notebook of graph paper. "A *curandero* ["herb healer"] makes that. I think even a *bruja* ["witch"] makes that."

Maybe that was fitting. Enrique often has to play the role of herb healer or witch doctor with his poor clients, many of whom have moved to Nezahualcóyotl and neighboring Chimalhuacán from primitive Indian villages in Oaxaca, Chiapas, and other impoverished areas in the south of Mexico. Many of his clients had never seen a doctor before they came to his clinic. They had always used herb healers and witches for what ailed them. They only came to Enrique, he surmised, because others had told them he knew the ways of magic.

Enrique knew about magic because he grew up in a household

that believed in such things. To illustrate, Enrique told me about an incident involving the birth of his nephew. Shortly after the baby was brought home from the hospital, a big, fat butterfly, almost the size of a bat, flew in the window. Enrique's mother and aunt became hysterical. They were convinced the butterfly was a messenger of death. It had come to steal the young baby's soul, they said. Frenetically they chased it around the house, trying to kill it. If they failed, they said, the child would die.

"That was the atmosphere of my childhood," said Enrique, "so I know something about how these people think."

Enrique's patients didn't need the medical mumbo jumbo they got from herb healers and witches, many of whom had moved to the Mexico City area with them. Their ailments were all too real, and often fatal. But sometimes Enrique had to enlist the help of such quacks so his patients, so accustomed to such people, would take their medicine or follow his prescription. Other times, it was enough for him to dream up some "magic" ceremony, part of which was the taking of a pill.

I had first met Enrique around Christmas of 1985. I was doing a story on how diarrhea was the no. 1 cause of death in Mexico. Diarrhea is an inconvenience to most foreigners who visit the country, something to be treated with Pepto-Bismol or Lomotil. But for millions of Mexicans, diarrhea and the dehydration it causes is a killer. It especially kills children under the age of four. The fact that its deadly effects could easily be avoided with a little education about boiling the water makes its deadly impact all the more dreadful. Those children that diarrhea doesn't kill it often retards. Enrique had treated some one-year-olds who weighed less than ten pounds due to the ravages of the desiccating malady.

When I went back to visit Enrique in February 1988, diarrhea was still topping the charts as a cause of death in Mexico. It was a leading cause of hospitalization and medical treatment, too. But respiratory ailments were the most common problem that Enrique and other area doctors saw, due to ever-worsening thermal inversions and the tons of pollution pumped into the valley's air from thousands of factories and millions of cars.

In the two previous months, Enrique had seen 256 patients, about five a day during his six-day work week. Typically, they were women or small children, but a few men overcame the anti-doctor constraints of machismo and dragged themselves in, too.

Ninety-one people, or about 36 percent, had upper-respiratory ailments, such as influenza, laryngitis, or what Mexicans call *la gripe,* a catchall term that generally means a serious cold. Twenty-six people had acute diarrhea problems, sixteen of them children under two years of age. Twenty-four people were suffering from the stress associated with living in the most polluted, most populous valley in the world.

"I don't include malnutrition as a disease," Enrique said in explaining his statistics. "It's endemic. Three to four of every five patients I see are malnourished."

The government doesn't count malnutrition as an official disease either. But it is nonetheless an acute problem in Mexico. Just like Enrique's patients, four out of five Mexicans are malnourished. Malnourished babies are a particular problem. The tragedy is that there is enough food to feed them. But ignorant parents don't always know what food is best for their children. Even if they do, diarrhea can undo good food's effects. Many parents foolishly buy coffee or soft drinks for their babies. Sometimes, according to nutrition experts, the difference between a well-nourished and a malnourished infant can be as little as one hundred to three hundred calories a day.

Even if babies do survive underfeeding, diarrhea, and acute pollution, they may still suffer stunted if not retarded physical and mental development. In 1986, the Pan-American Health Organization reported that one hundred thousand of the two million Mexican babies who were being born each year died before the age of five. Of those who survived, about half—or some one million—suffered physical or mental defects due to malnutrition.

Enrique's patients were a reflection of Mexico's other social problems, too. Seven out of ten Mexicans live in metropolises like the Mexico City area. They are products of a once-explosive birth rate and a misguided search by peasants for scarce city jobs. Some eighteen million people call Mexico City and other towns in the Valley of Mexico home—about one Mexican in five. They drive two-and-a-half-million cars, many of them badly tuned, few with catalytic converters. They ride in hundreds of thousands of polluting buses and trucks, many without mufflers. One in five has no real job. Kids drop out of school to help their parents get by, just as Enrique had three decades before. With jobs scarce, crime is on the rise, especially among the young. Youth gangs proliferate. Garbage piles up in the streets because Mexico's debt-strapped, deficit-burdened government can't afford to pay enough people to pick or sweep it up. Millions of wild dogs roam the streets, spreading disease. Rats outnumber dogs. Housing conditions are horrendous. Many homes have no electricity, water, or inside plumbing. With nowhere to go, people urinate and defecate in the streets. When the winter winds blow, their discarded fecal matter flies freely into lungs and eyes as well as into water and food supplies. Kids drink contaminated water and eat spoiled food. They get sick or die.

Enrique's patients—those with respiratory ailments, diarrhea, or stress—were a sample of the ailments that such conditions produced. Though Mexico has the thirteenth largest economy and can boast of world-class beach resorts, steel-and-glass high-rises, training grounds for Olympic equestrian teams, satellite communication systems, and lavish neighborhoods for the rich, it has a medical profile of a dirt-poor Third World country. People die of intestinal ailments and lung diseases. The afflictions of developed countries—heart disease, cancer, auto accidents—hardly make the charts. There's one exception: stress, particularly big-city stress. Poor people feel pressure as much as rich folks, if not more. Similarly, the reasons why Mexicans are hospitalized are very Third World: acute respiratory infections, enteritis, diarrhea, parasites, amoebas, and influenza. As one might expect, those Mexicans who survive all this disease don't live as long as people in better-off countries. Mexicans born in the 1980s can expect to live until they are sixty-nine, about five years less than Americans. Twenty-three out of every thousand newborns die in infancy, a rate twice that of the United States.

Enrique's income reflected conditions in Mexico, too. A clinic visit cost four thousand pesos, less than two dollars. He had thought about charging more, but his typical patient made little more than that a day. Upping his price would have meant that fewer patients would have come. Too many who needed help already stayed away as it was. More and more had gone back to herb healers and witches as Mexico's economic crisis put regular medical treatment out of reach. Worse, many people in the area treated themselves, buying medicine that a friend with a similar ailment had told them about. Mexico's hand-to-mouth pharmacies were only too eager to sell clients medicine without a doctor's prescription. Pill boxes never stated a recommended dosage. They just said, "As the doctor prescribes." People guessed what that might be. Often they guessed wrong, with tragic results.

Enrique could have made more money selling pills, ointments, and medical solutions, as many doctors do. But there was the problem of the bribes. City officials, Ministry of Health officials, Finance Ministry officials—everyone, it seemed—had a hand out, demanding some of Enrique's pitiful income. There was the bribe for the sign, for example. Out front, above the clinic's glass front door, Enrique had a two-sided, vertical white sign that said *Médico* ("Doctor") on each side in dark letters. The idea was that people would notice the clinic whether they traveled east or west on Chimalhuacán Avenue. That was the problem, Enrique was told. Enrique had paid for a license that authorized a sign with only one face, a city inspector had argued, even though nothing on the license mentioned this limitation. Enrique had seen this type of bloodsucker before. Inspectors were always coming in to say Enrique needed a fresh coat of paint on his walls, or a new tile floor to satisfy the building code. Even when nothing was wrong, as when a Finance Ministry auditor had checked Enrique's books two years before, such officials asked for a "tip," or money for gasoline, as the auditor had. Enrique usually refused to pay, as he had done with the city inspector who complained about the two-faced sign. Often the angry extortionist issued Enrique a citation. Enrique usually fought it, losing hours of what little free time he had. One bribe he was unable to avoid was the one required to get his "free" license to practice medicine. The license is issued to verify that a person really is a doctor. It has no revenue-collecting purpose. But in 1987, it had cost Enrique fifteen thousand pesos, about a day-and-a-half's pay. At that, it was sort of a bargain. The Health Ministry official who had demanded it had initially asked for forty thousand pesos.

"It seems I'm working just to enrich these crooks," Enrique said.

Why did he put up with all this, I asked him. Why not go to a small town, where people were begging for doctors, where the air was clean and traffic light? Enrique said he had tried that for a while. He did his one year of compulsory national service in a small town near the Arizona-Mexico border. But that town had too many doctors for him to stay there. Besides, residents, when it came to something important, went across to Douglas or Bisbee to have American doctors do the work. For a few weeks Enrique also practiced in a small village in the state of Guerrero. But his contract was not renewed. He was not one of them. He was not accepted.

Nezahualcóyotl was where he belonged, he said. This vast, destitute metropolis was his mistress, his lover. It was not always pleasing. He'd been robbed at gunpoint twice at the clinic in the last five years. But it was ever fascinating and needful of him. Well, then, I asked, was there at least some way the government might improve the horrific health conditions in Neza, as some called the sprawling city of three million? That wouldn't be easy, said Enrique. Neza was caught in a vicious circle. For things to improve, the government would have to solve the problems of the economy, housing, education, malnutrition, and crime. As an interim measure, it could spend more on health care, he said. But health had never been a high government priority.

Enrique was right about that. Mexico spends less per person on health than most countries in Latin America. Hospital beds are scarce. Little is spent on preventive dental care. About one in five Mexicans gets no medical treatment at all. While about 80 percent of Mexicans are eligible for insurance-paid medical care in some type of clinic or hospital, many, including all Enrique's patients, use private doctors. They do it because they aren't treated like charity patients, and the service is faster. Mexico's rich go one better. For annual checkups or anything serious, they fly to Houston or some other nearby U.S. city to be treated by American doctors. For many, it's so regular a thing that they have Blue Cross–Blue Shield coverage.

If the government wanted to increase health spending, Enrique noted, it would have to rearrange its budget priorities. That wouldn't be as easy as it once was. About 60 percent of Mexico's income from exports goes to pay interest on the immense foreign debt. Oils exports, a major source of export income, dried up substantially in the 1980s when oil prices dropped. Billions of pesos more are needed to finance the staggering domestic debt. That debt reflects a whopping government budget deficit caused by profligate spending. Poor agricultural policies force the government to spend billions more on imported foodstuffs such as milk and even corn, the most common staple in Mexico's tortilla-intensive cuisine.

Health priorities were all screwed up too, in Enrique's view.

The Pan-American Health Organization has said the same thing. In 1986, it criticized Mexico for focusing too much on curing disease and not enough on preventing it. It said that different health agencies had conflicting health plans, that medical services were inadequately distributed, that there was insufficient health coverage for the public. Such points were right on target. Mexico actually has too many, not too few, doctors. They are all bunched up in cities, with hardly any in rural areas. Unemployment among doctors is openly mentioned in speeches by the health minister. Inexplicably, the government, which runs the medical schools, seems transfixed with the idea of churning out more doctors, especially specialists. Focus on specialization has produced breakthroughs that have brought Mexico worldwide recognition, such as its pioneering treatment of Parkinson's disease. But, as Enrique pointed out, "We don't need any more specialists. We are dying of diarrhea."

"Your readers are going to need a handkerchief after reading all this," Enrique joked after we wound up our informal critique of Mexican medicine. With all the misery he saw, I asked, had he ever needed a handkerchief? Of course, he responded. Some cases, just a few weeks before, had brought him close to tears, he said. After hearing about them, I could see why.

The case of the three-year-old girl was the saddest. It was so maddeningly typical of what could happen in the conditions of poverty and ignorance that plague Neza and other slums that ring the capital. The little girl's mother, a single parent, had to work each day. She earned the minimum wage and could not afford to pay someone to stay with her little girl. There were no public preschools or day care centers where she lived. Unable to think of anything else, the woman locked the little girl in their house when she went to work each day. When she returned home one night, she found the little girl a bloody mess, an emotional wreck. During the day a man had climbed in the house's window and raped the little girl. She had been unable to escape through the padlocked door.

"What kind of animal does that?" asked Enrique. "An animal— that's all he was."

Depressed by his own stories, Enrique said he wondered sometimes why he went on. The emotional cost of his practice was draining. He was making little as a doctor. Sometimes people didn't pay at all. Enrique showed me the list of clients who owed him money. Others took the prescriptions Enrique gave them. But he knew they would never get them filled, because they couldn't afford to.

"That man has herpes," said Enrique after one patient left. "He needs a medicine from the United States that costs more than fifteen dollars. There is no way he can buy it."

Enrique had had no vacations since he began his clinic five years before.

"If I don't work, I don't eat," he said.

He had six years to go on the ten-year mortgage on his house. The house was nothing special—two bedrooms, a dining room, kitchen, bathroom, and yard.

"My family wants the finer things in life—a nice home, good clothes," he said, "the type of things they see watching reruns of *Ben Casey, M.D.* or *Dr. Kildare*. They don't understand the way things are."

Enrique fell silent for a while. Then he asked me if I knew what *masoquismo* meant. "Masochism," I replied. "Yes, that's it," he said. "Maybe I am a masochist."

I knew that, deep down, Enrique was just joking, although it was a black joke. He knows why he stays in Neza. He had said it himself. People rely on him. On the days I visited him, many of his patients came just to talk. Some came to tell him that the pressures of everyday life were getting to them. They were looking for a calming voice. Enrique was their father confessor. A sixty-two-year-old man wanted to know if a new fiber cereal would be good for him. He paid nothing. He made a point of staying in the waiting room. As many do, the man had said, "I have a question, doctor. This is not a consultation." Consultations cost money; questions do not.

"My friends ask me why I don't leave Neza, why I don't move my clinic closer to my house," he said. "The answer is simple. How could I leave these people? They trust me. Who would help them?"

· 6 ·

The *Chavo*

I first realized that it wasn't going to be a run-of-the-mill rock concert when the flying body hit me in the back. I guess nothing about the concert should have come as a surprise. After all, my hosts for the evening were El Morsa ("The Walrus") and El Chino ("The Chinaman"), two members of Los Sex Pistols, a street gang that rules a joyless little patch of Mexico City called Barrio Norte.

The flying body belonged to a member of the audience. I never did get his name. He was just one of several overwrought fans who would stand up periodically and hurl themselves down the auditorium's sloped concrete bench seats toward the stage below. The fact that there might not be a body such as mine to cushion the headlong dive from the waiting concrete seemed of little import to these kids. El Morsa said they really weren't considering the risk of what they did. They just got a little carried away by the music.

Mexico's version of punk rock was what I had come to hear, so I listened more closely to see what might cause such insanity. I heard the lead singer of Masacre 68, the group on stage, scream "Hunger! Misery! Repression!" over and over to a heavy-metal tune that had as much feedback as melody. The young crowd hollered along, belting out every word of the song. Except for the strident, atonal nature of the music, they might have been die-hard fans at a Bruce Springsteen concert, singing along with the Boss. The words they sang, however, were not exactly lyrics from "Born in the U.S.A." or "Tunnel of Love." One went: "I demand death for the president!" Another began: "Let's toast to death." I heard the angry, alienated message. It didn't do to me what it obviously was doing to the frenzied Mexican crowd. But then I didn't live in Barrio Norte.

The body hurlers were joined in their insanity by fifty or so leather-clad fans who jumped up on stage to dance in front of the band. Dancing isn't really the right word for what they did, al-though punk-rock aficionados call it slam dancing. What they did was really more like a choreographed gang fight. It was a males-only event. Slam dancing is considered too dangerous for girls, El Morsa explained, as he eyed a punk lovely with purple hair and a T-shirt that read: "I came. Did you?" As far as I could tell, slam dancing consists of running, hopping, or skipping as fast as you can in a counterclockwise oval pattern. While in motion, you try to hit as many other dancers as possible with your elbows or knees. A few crazed fools dance clockwise, something akin to doing the limbo under a John Deere combine. One poor soul who chose the clockwise pattern got knocked off the stage and landed at my feet. His head hit the edge of a concrete step, opening a bloody, four-inch gash above his right eyebrow. One of the Sex Pistols got up from his seat and casually rubbed a little concrete dust and some cigarette ashes into the dazed youth's wound to stop the bleeding. The young man, dressed in a black leather vest that said ¡Peligro! ("Danger!") on the back, bounded back up on stage and rejoined the other dervishes.

I never did find out if El Morsa, a tough guy in anyone's book, was a Norman Mailer fan. But he did not dance. He was at the concert for the music. Like the others, he knew all the words. "Corrupt police! Crooks! Murderers! You want the right to kill a thousand people," he and his pals sang along, rocking in unison right and left to the beat. El Morsa was obviously enjoying him-self, getting into the music. But then El Morsa liked anything that reviled the Mexican government.

El Morsa was dressed in a black leather motorcycle jacket and green pants with horizontal slits purposely cut in a ladder pattern all up and down the front of the legs. His pants were neatly bloused into a pair of calf-high, black military boots. Here and there on this punk uniform he wore safety pins, the jewelry of his set, and a large silver crucifix, which hung defiantly from one of the zippers of his jacket. On the back of his jacket he had written *Goberino de mierda* ("Government of shit").

El Morsa was a new breed among Mexico's alienated youth. Like others, he had once looked outside Mexico for his antiheroes and his music. Mariachi, salsa, and the safe, sweet rock music of Mexico had always been too bland for kids like him. In search of a social message and an outlet for their frustrations, El Morsa and others had turned to the United States or Europe for rock's leading edge. When El Morsa had joined his gang some ten years before, that edge had been punk rockers like the Sex Pistols, the English group whose name El Morsa and his buddies had copied. Sid Vicious and Johnny Rotten were their icons. The gang liked the fact that the Sex Pistols' songs reviled almost anything. Now gang members have trouble even recalling who plays with the Sex Pistols. Only the group's shocking name remains of use. These days, the gang and other Mexican youths have turned their attention to a new, hard-edge Mexican music of aboveground groups such as El Tri and Botellita de Jerez, and underground favorites such as Masacre 68 and Xenofobia. The music talks of life in Mexico's streets—of hunger, misery, repression, as Masacre 68 would put it.

I had come to hear this new message. I'm familiar with and like a lot of different types of rock. But when Masacre 68 began to play, I felt like Benny Goodman at an early Elvis concert. One might say that Masacre 68, which took its name from the murderous government response to student protests in Mexico City in 1968, was ahead of the avant-garde. Their music wasn't commercial enough for them to have a recording contract or record albums, as El Tri and some other new groups did. Masacre 68 fans had to make crude, bootleg cassettes of their concerts, using cheap, hand-held tape recorders. El Morsa had all their songs on tape. If I would just listen to what Masacre 68's songs said, El Morsa had told me when I met him earlier that day, I might get a better idea what made the Sex Pistols tick, what made them so angry.

I must admit that when I first heard that some of Mexico City's 700,000 gang members were punk rockers, I found it such a delicious image—so un-Mexican—that I knew I had to talk to these guys. It was a good story. Besides, there was the serious side. Mexico's economic crisis and the government's inadequate, corrupt response to it had been increasing social alienation among the Mexican public since I arrived in the country. This was especially true among Mexico's youth, who were coming into the work force a million strong each year at a time when there weren't a million new jobs for them. Street-gang members were the most alienated of Mexico's youth. Anarchic punk rockers, I figured, must be the most alienated of all. I wanted to find out what was happening as all that anger built up.

The Sex Pistols' turf, Barrio Norte, is not a place you find on the Gray Line tour. You wouldn't want to wind up alone there at night—or even in broad daylight, for that matter, some of my Mexican friends had warned me. But one rainy Saturday, I drove out anyway to where the paved streets of the city end and the stony lanes of Barrio Norte begin. I parked my car, flipped on an antitheft ignition switch, locked the doors, and turned on an alarm connected to a couple of air horns. Thinking back, maybe I was just a little worried about the neighborhood.

I saw a couple of young toughs leaning against a building. I asked them where I might find the Sex Pistols. One was sniffing glue, the drug of preference among the poor in this section of town. The other one—the one who still knew what day it was—told me how to get there. As I walked away, he yelled out, "Are you sure you want to go down there, man?"

I had been told that I would know I was in Sex Pistol territory by the graffiti. When all the available outside walls of houses and factories were covered with Sex Pistol messages, that's where the Sex Pistols would be. Down a rutted hill, around some abandoned buildings, I found the Sex Pistols—or, rather, they found me. As I walked along a wall covered with British flags, skulls, and a slogan that read "Jesus is dead. Punk is not," I was braced by two members of the gang. Sardonically addressing me as *jefe* ("boss"), they wanted to know what I was doing in Barrio Norte. I explained who I was and that I wanted to talk to the leader of the Sex Pistols. After a few tense moments, it was agreed that I could talk with El Morsa, who is the closest thing to a gang chief in a gang that rejects all leaders.

The Sex Pistols' turf is a cramped, six square blocks of bad drainage and worse houses. It's located in an area where the city used to mine sand. The thirty or so members of the gang can usually be found not far from the old mines, sitting on the curb of Norteños Street, which serves as an informal clubhouse. The gang members, who range in age from seven years old to twenty-three, were at first leery about talking with me. They said they had to be careful. I might be working for the police, their arch-enemy, or maybe even the CIA. In my best bluffing voice, I told them that if they didn't want to talk, I'd find some other street gang to write about. Publicity for a rival gang was apparently too much for them to bear, so they put bravado and menace aside. And we got down to business.

We established the basics pretty fast. The name, of course, had come from the English punk group. The original Sex Pistols were *anti-sistema,* and so was the gang that took their name. It was a perfect fit. Trust no one but your *cuates* ("pals")—and never the government. All for one and one for all. That was the creed the gang lived by.

There were no qualifications to join. Unlike street gangs in the United States, you didn't have to kill anyone or commit a crime to prove your worthiness. If you lived in the neighborhood, you joined. If you didn't, the gang might wonder why.

There were no special gang colors or uniforms or bandanas, although anything with leather was cool. Nobody had the money to shave the sides of his head regularly or to buy hair mousse to build his hairdo up in the pointy Mohawk style of punk rockers. Most of the gang just affected a bushy butch cut that was the closest thing that gang members could afford.

Members did drugs, although nothing hard. Cocaine and heroin were too expensive and hadn't really caught on with Mexico's poorer classes the way they have elsewhere. El Morsa and his pals smoked marijuana when they could afford it and sniffed glue when they could not, they said. But when I saw them, they were mostly into tequila.

A few of the gang had spent time in the city jail, although no one had done a stretch in the penitentiary. José Antonio Gonzá-lez, the gang's court jester, had done the most time, including a four-month stint in jail for destroying property in the course of a fight with another gang. But I really didn't get the sense that he or any of the gang were really bad people. They laughed easily. They had a sense of outrage about injustice. These were not the vicious, murderous, cruel youths one found among the Bloods or Crips of Los Angeles or the El Rukns or Vice Lords of Chicago. But you couldn't tell that by the image the police had painted of them.

A few months before, the Mexico City chief of police had said in off-the-cuff remarks that he'd like to give a 100,000-peso reward (about three weeks' pay at the time) to any cop who shot a gang member. Gangs, he said, were a pollution that could spread across the city if not controlled. The city attorney general said the answer to the gang problem was to reduce the age of majority from eighteen to sixteen so police could throw more kids in Mexico's already overcrowded jails.

I'm no sociologist. The closest thing to expertise that I brought to my analysis of the Sex Pistols was my memory of the Jets and the Sharks in *West Side Story*. But a commonsensical assessment of why Mexico had produced the Sex Pistols or the thousands of other city street gangs was that they were, as one of the Jets might say, the product of "a social disease."

Spanish director Luis Buñuel captured the essence of these boys' lives a few decades ago in his classic film *Los Olvidados* (The Forgotten Ones). In 1988, things were about the same as Buñuel had found them in his day. Maybe they were a little worse. Most of the boys had completed no more than six years of grammar school. Even the married ones, such as El Morsa and José Antonio, lived in the close quarters of their parents' homes with five or more brothers and sisters. Their neighborhood, Barrio Norte, didn't have enough facilities for the thousands who lived there. There were two grammar schools for 1,500 children. There weren't enough recreation facilities. Most important, there weren't enough jobs. Without jobs, gang members turned to petty crime to survive. Strong-arm robbery was the preferred method to get a little something from a passerby when money couldn't be found in other ways to put food on the table. In desperate times, admitted José Antonio, you sometimes had to use guns, machetes, knives, or rocks, the armaments the gang used in warfare with other gangs in the area.

"The [prices of] basic products go up all the time," explained José Antonio. "The salaries don't go far enough. There is no work. That's why we have to steal."

The city was making some attempt to reach gangs such as the

Sex Pistols. The hope seemed to be to stem the crime wave that had swept over Mexico since its economic crisis began in earnest in mid-1982. A few months before, José Antonio had signed up in a Ministry of Education program to teach gang members how to become carpenters. There was no guarantee, however, that there would be any carpentry work when he finished. The concert I attended was one of a series of *tocadas de rock* that the government had organized so that the gangs might blow off a little steam. In a much-publicized effort, the police had also organized soccer matches between on-the-beat cops and the gangs to develop better relations. But the Sex Pistols complained that it was just a publicity stunt. Once the reporters went home, the cops came back into the barrio to round up gang members in nighttime sweeps. They beat them senseless in a search for suspects in crimes they could not solve. They arrested some. Others they let go if the bribe was big enough.

To me, it made no sense not to make a sincere effort to turn these gangs around. Deprivation and poverty had killed any hope of a better future that these *chavos bandas* ("boys' gangs") might once have had. With a regular diet of gang rumbles and snatch-and-grab robberies, these *chavos* were criminals-in-training. If someone did not stop them today, tomorrow they would join the growing hordes of drug traffickers, car thieves, bank robbers, burglars, and kidnappers who had brought crime to plague proportions in Mexico's big cities.

Thinking about the fate of gangs was not an idle intellectual exercise for me. I had been a crime victim several times in Mexico. Frankly I was getting a little sick of it. In the four years I lived in Mexico City, I had three car radios stolen. My car trunk was broken into and hundreds of dollars of gifts were ripped off. My office was burgled twice. My secretary was mugged once. My maid was mugged twice on the way to work and had her pocket picked once in church. Her husband, who sometimes tended our garden, was robbed and beaten to a pulp on his way home. And the woman who looked after our son was molested on the bus just a few blocks from our house.

Mexico City, with a population about the same as New York City, regularly registered about 3,500 intentional homicides each year that I lived there. That was about twice the New York number. Bank robberies had become so common that the government had had to station special police, equipped with body armor and automatic weapons, outside city banks. Robberies, especially auto theft, had become pandemic. According to the police, 70 percent of these and other crimes were being committed by youngsters between the ages of fifteen and eighteen, the majority of whom belonged to gangs.

The reported crime rise was bad enough in Mexico City and other major urban areas. But underreporting masked an even more serious problem. Homicide rates were regarded as fairly accurate, because it's hard to hide a body. But many daily robberies went unreported because people felt the police weren't capable of solving them—or would demand money to investigate. Some people feared investigating police might take anything robbers had left behind. In my own case, I never bothered to report any of the thefts of my car radios. Maybe I got discouraged after I learned from insurance-company sources that a police ring was a key element in city auto thefts.

Crime, in its own way, had become many people's response to Mexico's economic crisis, and to the ineptness and corruption of the government. Anyone who beat the system was, at least among the disadvantaged, a hero. Rafael Caro Quintero was a hero of sorts to the Sex Pistols. He was Mexico's best-known drug dealer. Even though he had been caught and charged with the sensational 1985 torture-murder of U.S. Drug Enforcement Agency undercover agent Enrique Camarena, he was still a Robin Hood figure to many Mexicans, including El Morsa and his pals.

"Free Caro Quintero!" they shouted when I brought up his name.

They liked the fact that Caro had spent a lot of his drug loot on his hometown and other poor communities. He had built schools and roads that the government had not. But most of all, they liked the fact that he had thumbed his nose at the system. That's what the Sex Pistols did. They thumbed noses. They lived to shock, through their clothes, their music, their graffiti, and their lifestyle of studied anomie. If anyone held an antigovernment demonstration, they joined it. The cause did not matter. If it was *anti-sistema*, that was enough. They ignored legal niceties. José Antonio and El Morsa were married, as far as they were concerned. But they had gone through no formal ceremony, had no marriage licenses. They lived in what Mexicans call *unión libre* ("free union").

"I don't care what people think," El Morsa said about not having a marriage license. "It's just a piece of paper. It means nothing. I will not be controlled by the majority."

When I talked with the gang, Mexico was in the middle of its 1988 presidential campaign. El Morsa and the Sex Pistols had no real interest in the outcome. They were intrigued a bit by the populist, maverick candidacy of Cuauhtémoc Cárdenas, whose father, Lázaro, is regarded by many poor Mexicans as the last true president of the people. But they assumed the candidate of the ruling party, Carlos Salinas de Gortari, would beat Cárdenas one way or another, just as Salinas's predecessors had beaten all comers for the last sixty years. When I asked if there were any figures in Mexican history—presidents, poets, writers, anyone— whom the gang regarded as admirable, I just got a collective laugh.

"History is the past," said José Antonio. "The future is in the future. We live for right now. The government is just going to screw us, so why should we think about the future? We know what it will be."

The gang didn't think too highly of Mexican industrialists, either. Business people were social leeches, they said. Gang members talked in a left-wing cant about exploitation of the classes by transnational companies. But the Sex Pistols were no fodder for communism or Marxism. They blasted the United States as an imperialist power that imposed its will on the region. But they had no love for the Soviet Union, which they branded as equally imperialist. They espoused no ism but anarchism.

I kept coming back to the word "anger." Sociologists talk of alienation to explain gang formation. But anger is what I saw. After talking with the Sex Pistols, anger is what I felt, too. I guess "wasted potential" was what I thought of most. These were kids who could be reached before it was too late. I was sure of that. Here was El Morsa, whose real name, he admitted, with embarrassment, was Humberto Camarillo. El Morsa had obvious leadership talent and a savvy street sense that sprang from a ready but unpolished intelligence. And yet, at twenty-three, here he was scraping by as a street sweeper, earning, when he could, the minimum wage of three dollars a day to support his family of three children and a wife. As the man in the movie says, he could have been a contender. But unless something changed, he was going to turn out a bum or worse.

This would-be bum, though, had had enough inner substance

and spirit to try to write a play. He hadn't finished it. But he and José Antonio, a few years before, had felt moved enough by police brutality and government insensitivity to the poor to start a play about gangs and Mexican society. The effort was nothing unusual. Other gangs had produced poets and song writers. One song I ran across while in Mexico was penned by members of another punk rock gang, Los Mierdas Punk ("The Punk Shits"), which ran around Nezahualcóyotl, a big slum northeast of Mexico City. It went:

> Putrefaction has arrived.
> We are already here, the Punk Shits,
> To dance, to make things sour, to boil.
>
> We are the generation of horror.
> It's as if the whole world were seeing me.
> I hate the world.
> I'm like a fucked person.
> The world is putrid and me too.
> They see me, and they are left
> with the temptation to be like me:
> extremely putrid.
> The whole world is putrid.
> They don't know what they want.
> They don't know what they are.
> They don't have feelings.
> It's as if I were seeing myself
>   in a mirror.
> For that, I love the mirror.
>
> We are the future of Mexico.
> There is no future.
> There is none. There is no love.
> There is none. There is no glue [to sniff].
> I am shit. I don't want more love.
> Autoputrefaction . . . autoputrefaction.
>
> You know what will happen to me?
> I shall rot. I shall rot.

There is a lot of desperation, alienation, and anger in that song. But there is a lot of thought as well for someone with less than a grammar-school education. A mind that composed that outcry of anguish is a creative mind. But the way things are in Mexico— and likely to be for some time—it's not a very positive force of creation.

These kids, the future of Mexico, are products of a shocking grammar-school dropout rate. They come from broken homes. Some are orphans. Some are kicked out into the street when their fathers or mothers remarry. They have been beaten. They have been pressured to go into the streets to earn money in any way they can so their families or they can survive. Is it so surprising that some of them—an astounding number, really—will turn against a society that shows them no love and little care? It works that way in the South Bronx, Watts, and the South Side of Chicago. Why should it be any different in Mexico?

.   .   .

When there was a break in the music at the concert, I took the opportunity to ask El Morsa if he thought he might be coming back to such events ten years from now, or even later. "Do you think you'll be in the gang when you're forty?" I asked. He said he hoped he'd continue his interest in punk rock forever, although he was always searching for something new in case punk did not last. He didn't imagine that he would ever leave Barrio Norte, and he had no real ambition to do so. Barrio Norte was where his friends were. He felt comfortable there. He liked the people. He had no dream to have a lot of money or a big job. He had no hope of having a flashy car or an expensive home. When you reject the society in which you live, you don't espouse its dreams, he said. There was only one thing he wanted, he said. And it sounded like the real El Morsa, the real Humberto Camarillo, crying out.

"I'd like something that permits me to use my head," he said. "I'd like to write. I told you about the play José Antonio and I started. I'd like to do something like that. But I never seem to be able to finish anything."

· II ·
Politics

· 7 ·

The *Priista*

At exactly 1:48 P.M. on Palm Sunday, 1988, Cuauhtémoc Cárdenas's seven-car motorcade crossed the state line dividing Guerrero from Michoacán. He was home again.

Between 1980 and 1986, Cárdenas had been governor of Michoacán, where his famous father, Lázaro, had been born and gained fame, first as a revolutionary general and then as the most popular president in modern Mexican history. Through myth and lore and actual fact, Cuauhtémoc Cárdenas had become a very popular politician himself, sometimes siding with the people when his unpopular but powerful party would have preferred otherwise.

He had always sided with the people. He was, after all, his father's son. In the minds of many, his father, who was president between 1934 and 1940, had been the last real politician of the people. With the blood of Tarascan Indians in his veins, he was a *mestizo* (a mixed-race Mexican), like 90 percent of Mexicans. Every president since Cárdenas had come from more patrician stock. Each had had skin a little lighter. Each had acted a bit more aloof. None had the dirt of everyday life under his fingernails. The people wanted to believe that Cárdenas, the son, would bring back those populist times, when oil fields were expropriated, when land was seized from the rich and given to the poor, when the president walked among the people and listened to them. Cuauhtémoc Cárdenas wanted them to believe it too. Like his father before him, he was now running for president.

In some ways, it was natural that he should run. How could one not run for president with a name like Cuauhtémoc Cárdenas? Cuauhtémoc was the last Aztec emperor, whose dark skin and chiseled profile one could see in the visage of the fifty-three-year-old candidate. Cárdenas was a Mexican name with the dynastic magic of a Kennedy or a Roosevelt in the United States. As if his name were not enough, he had been born on May Day in the year his father had become president—May Day, the day most of the world celebrates as Labor Day. A birthday for a man of the people.

Like the warrior prince Cuauhtémoc, young Cárdenas prepared himself early for power. He passed through youth with little of the callowness of his contemporaries. He learned the history and politics of Mexico at his father's knee. He attended school in the Pacific port town that now bears his father's illustrious name. He attended the national university in the capital and became a civil engineer. He studied in France and Germany and polished his world view. His father's party, the Institutional Revolutionary Party (PRI), which has ruled Mexico since 1929, was happy to have such a fine young man as a potential political candidate. He seemed the epitome of a *Priista,* as party members are called. But the party, which most Mexicans simply call the PRI, would soon learn that young Cárdenas's plans for the political future were not always the same as its own.

The party quickly found work for young Cárdenas, who in his spare time traveled his state getting to know its people in small towns and mountain villages. In successive government posts, he moved from project developer to subdirector to undersecretary. But his response was not the usual one of cloying gratitude. To others, young Cárdenas seemed to expect such work, almost as a birthright.

About halfway through the administration of President Luis Echeverría Alvarez (1970–76), party elders began to get the idea that there was something radically different about this son of Lázaro Cárdenas. He began to show worrisome independence. Even worse, it appeared he was a man with a mission. In speeches, he sounded almost messianic. For a party that venerated public unity and obedience above all, there could be nothing worse.

What caught the attention of party leaders during Echeverría's time was Cárdenas's call for greater party democracy. PRI leaders always talk a lot about how democratic the party is. But the reality was something very different. The party was run by an elite. The elite was run by the president, who was treated more like an emperor than a chief executive. The country worked the same way. There was a national legislature and a judiciary. But the senators and deputies and judges were just rubber stamps for the president and the party elite, most of whom held powerful government posts. Among his imperial rights, a Mexican president has always been able to pick the PRI's gubernatorial candidates personally, like a king naming a new duke or count. The party then ratifies the president's choice at its conventions. The PRI, which controls more than 95 percent of all Mexico's federal, state, and local offices, has never lost a presidential or gubernatorial election since it was formed, so a president's selection of a gubernatorial candidate is tantamount to election. But young Cárdenas had a revolutionary suggestion. He said the selection should be the choice of local party leaders, if not the rank and file. He said the age-old tradition of *dedazo*—the president's act of pointing his royal *dedo* ("finger") at the candidate he wanted—should be scrapped. Cárdenas went further. He said he should be the candidate.

President Echeverría, who had chosen the senior Cárdenas as his political role model, did not pick Cuauhtémoc Cárdenas to be the governor of Michoacán. But Cárdenas was not snubbed completely. How could the party punish him? There was that name! Cárdenas was ignored for a few years. But at the end of Echeverría's term, perhaps in hopes that Cárdenas had learned his lesson, he was redeemed and made a senator of the republic. Later the same year, he was named undersecretary of forest and fauna resources, a vital post for his agriculture-intensive home state. Four years later, Echeverría's successor, José López Portillo, made Cárdenas governor of Michoacán, a post Cárdenas's father had held half a century before.

By most accounts, Cárdenas was a good governor. He adopted the strict, frugal style of his father. He insisted that laws be obeyed, even laws no one had paid much attention to for decades. His father had not drunk liquor or smoked. In that spirit, Governor

Cárdenas enforced long-ignored blue laws banning the sale of liquor on Sundays. What corruption he could find, he did not tolerate. That left more money in the state treasury for the public projects that the money had been intended for in the first place. He urged those interested in succeeding him as governor to step forward and declare. Don't wait for a decision by the president, he said. He brought a new pride to his state. When police from a neighboring state came into Michoacán in hot pursuit of drug traffickers, the tall, dour, Lincolnesque Cárdenas ostentatiously had the officers apprehended and threw them out. He publicly chastised them for violating his state's sovereignty. Call me the next time and ask my permission, he told them. People began to take notice. They talked of dignity. They talked of respect. In private, they talked of revolution, of the Mexican Revolution.

Revolution was something on Cárdenas's mind too. Not a new revolution. He was happy with the principles of Mexico's 1910 Revolution. In the face of dictatorship, blatant vote fraud, massive income disparity, and excessive foreign entanglements, the revolution had promised effective suffrage, no reelection of presidents, land reform, and a strong sense of national sovereignty. What Cárdenas was not happy with was the implementation of these principles. His father, he felt, had been true to the revolution. In his most notable act, he had nationalized Mexico's oil fields in 1938, throwing U.S. and European oil companies out of the country. Support for the expropriation was so fervid that rich and poor Mexicans alike contributed family heirlooms, jewelry, life savings, and even chickens to help Mexico compensate foreign oil companies for their lost mineral rights. He was the first president to expropriate widespread tracts of land—about forty-five million acres—for the landless. He helped *campesinos* ("peasants") organize politically and give them a real place in the party. He campaigned to integrate the millions of illiterate, malnourished, pure-blooded Indians into the general population.

The way Cárdenas saw it, sometime after his father left office, the PRI, which calls itself the party of the revolution, got sidetracked. The "land and liberty" battle cry of revolutionary leader Emiliano Zapata had been forgotten. Corruption, arrogance, bureaucratic inefficiency, and stupidity had squandered the oil, gold, and silver wealth that God had bestowed on Mexico. Education, housing, and health conditions had improved since the disastrous, murderous days of the revolution. But conditions remained embarrassingly bad. People were hurting. The rich stayed rich, while the poor got poorer. The country was being run by a party elite of counterrevolutionaries. That's what Cuauhtémoc Cárdenas was thinking when his term ended in 1986.

This was not what President de la Madrid was thinking, however. His six-year term was winding down. It was time to do what all his predecessors, including Cárdenas's father, had done before him. It was time to pick his successor. PRI officials vehemently assert that Mexico is a modern democracy. Indeed, it has a rule of one man, one vote in presidential elections. But that one man is the sitting president, and only his vote counts. For a while, at the beginning of Mexico's post-revolutionary history, the president consulted what the party called the revolutionary family in picking his successor. The family consisted of the top party elders: former presidents, powerful revolutionary generals, and the like. They had some say in the choice. But in the 1980s, the revolutionary generals were all gone. Mexico hadn't had a general as president since Manuel Avila Camacho had succeeded Cárdenas. The only living former presidents, Luis Echeverría and José López Portillo, were in disgrace because of charges of corruption and repression. And so the choice was de la Madrid's alone.

In the fall of 1986, de la Madrid leaked to the press a list of people he might consider as his successor. It was not a list with his fingerprints or name on it. It was made public by a powerful party leader, who privately let PRI officials know that it was the president's list. Party officials let others know. In its own limited way, the list was a nod toward greater democracy in Mexico. It was really only a nod toward greater democracy for the PRI. But in Mexico the PRI, whose red, white, and green colors are the same as those of Mexico's flag, has really been the only party with a chance of winning the presidency, so one could make the argument that more democracy for the PRI meant more democracy for Mexico. At least that's the argument that *Priistas* made.

By making his list of *presidenciables* (those of presidential timber) public, de la Madrid gave party leaders and the public a chance to complain about a potential candidate's lack of ability, or to dig up some secret that might disqualify him. It also gave the president a chance to observe his candidates to see who acted presidential and who did not. None of the candidates would say anything publicly about himself or the others, of course. That is not the way of Mexican politics. The first rule of Mexican presidential campaigns had always been that a candidate could never say he wanted to be president. One had to be worthy but not eager.

Almost immediately, it became clear that some on the initial list had been put there merely to honor them for past performance or favors. By late fall, the talk in the corridors of party power, where rumor is king, centered on three men as de la Madrid's possible choice: Alfredo del Mazo González, whom de la Madrid had plucked from the governor's seat in the state of México to make his energy minister; Manuel Bartlett Díaz, the interior (security) minister, who had run de la Madrid's presidential campaign; and Carlos Salinas de Gortari, a young bureaucratic infighter who was the minister of planning and budget, the post de la Madrid had held when he was handpicked to be president by his predecessor, López Portillo.

If logic were the controlling factor, many party insiders said, the president was going to pick del Mazo, whom de la Madrid had once described as the brother he wished he had had. Del Mazo had an excellent party pedigree. Like Bartlett and Salinas, he was a political "junior," a man whose rise in the party started because of his father's influence and power. Del Mazo's father had been governor of the state of México, the most populous of Mexico's thirty-one states. Young del Mazo was also a friend of labor. He had worked in a labor-union bank on his way up the political ladder. There were stories that his godfather was Fidel Velázquez, the octogenarian leader of Mexico's most influential labor group, the Confederation of Mexican Workers (CTM). Whatever the truth, Don Fidel made it known privately that del Mazo was his choice. Don Fidel detested the bald, wiry Salinas, an economist whom he considered the architect of de la Madrid's policies of economic austerity. As far as Velázquez could see, all those policies had done was to cut the earning power of the Mexican worker. He tolerated Bartlett, whose Interior Ministry had shown the sort of heavy hand in elections that veterans such as Velázquez though was necessary. But he was backing del Mazo because he was the only one of the three who had been elected to anything. Don Fidel and many others of the party's old guard were in a struggle for the future of the party. As they saw it, the party was increasingly being run by government bureaucrats who had never been elected to anything. They wanted a politician to lead the way.

De la Madrid had not been a politician. He was a lawyer who had been brought into government by his onetime law professor, López Portillo, a nonpolitician who had been brought into government by his predecessor, Echeverría, a nonpolitician. All three were what party veterans derisively called *técnicos* ("technicians"). They were men who had not come up through the party ranks the hard way. They were of a generation that had grown up in Mexico City. They had spent little time in the countryside. They could call few *campesinos* or workers their friends. They went to the same grammar and high schools. They all studied abroad. With their fathers' help, they moved ahead politically. They joined *camarillas* (political cliques) in hopes that the head of their clique would be picked for a powerful political post and bring them into his department or ministry. In their wildest dreams, the head of their clique would be picked as the party's candidate for president, as happened when de la Madrid was chosen president and made ministers of Bartlett and Salinas, who belonged to de la Madrid's clique. As ministers, they became clique leaders themselves. If all went well, one of them would become the next president. This was what the party had become. But in the view of Velázquez and many old-timers, this was not what the party was supposed to be. It had been created as the party of peasants and workers who had gone to the barricades to end dictatorship. But now faceless technicians with calculators for hearts were running things. Like Cuauhtémoc Cárdenas, Velázquez thought something had gone awry.

What the party had become in the 1980s was probably not what President Plutarco Elías Calles had envisioned when he decreed the PRI into existence in late 1928 amid considerable political chaos. In the years following the beginning of Mexico's 1910 Revolution, the first great social revolution of the twentieth century, things had gotten out of control. Revolutionary hero had turned on revolutionary hero. No one wanted to follow anyone else. Francisco Madero, who had had the backing of nearly everyone when he toppled the dictator Porfirio Díaz, was seized and shot by those who thought that they could do better. After that, all the great names of Mexico's revolution were murdered seriatim. Zapata, Venustiano Carranza, Pancho Villa, and Alvaro Obregón all died violent deaths. In the mayhem after the 1928 assassination of president-elect Obregón, Calles, then called El Jefe Máximo ("The Supreme Leader"), created a party he called the Party of National Revolution (PNR). *Campesinos,* workers, bureaucrats, intellectuals, and the army were all given a fair say. All would share the political spoils. Over the years, these groups, all suspicious of each other, came to realize that this unlikely coalition of rivals was the only way for Mexico to have a workable government. This stable but ruthless political organization would become the envy of coup-prone Latin America. Every president elected under the new party's regime had finished his term. From year to year, one group's share of seats in the senate or the chamber of deputies, or of governors' seats, would go up or down. But the four warring groups stayed together. In 1946, with most of the great revolutionary generals dead, things were so regularized that party leaders were able to tell the once-boisterous military that it would no longer be an official sector of the party. The military would be well taken care of, its officers were told. Occasionally there would still be a governor's post for a general or two. But the once-powerful army would become a tame pussycat, the only armed forces of no real threat to a Latin American government. With the army out of the political fray, three sectors of the party—bureaucrats, workers, and *campesinos*—would battle it out for political power under the rubric of a new party name, the Institutional Revolutionary Party, or the PRI. The revolution had been institutionalized. It had grown up. Or so people were told.

With the coming to power of Miguel Alemán Valdés (1946–52), the revolution took on a buttoned-down look. University-trained politicians elbowed aside the wild adventurers who had fought in the revolution. Occasionally there would be a flare-up of discontent. But the party put down whatever dissent it found. Though it did not shrink from threats, its main tactic was co-optation. If someone got too noisy in his complaints or if his power base outside the party was growing a bit too fast, he was offered things: money, an office, women, cars, a government or party post. Those who said no were often sorry they had.

Over the years, the party has become an improbable collection of people of every political stripe from Communists to Fascists. Those on the right are kept happy by being given a say in domestic and economic policy. Police and security forces keep a tight watch on leftist or guerrilla elements that might threaten the government. Economically, Mexico has become more or less capitalist, despite significant government ownership of industry. After bitter objection from the left, Mexico joined the General Agreement on Tariffs and Trade (GATT) in 1986, a move designed to make it a real-market economy. As an offset, those on the left get foreign-policy concessions. Still fuming over the loss of half Mexico's territory in the 1847 Mexican-American War, the leftist Foreign Ministry often sets Mexico against the United States, the principal ideological enemy of Mexico's government. Mexico opposes U.S. efforts in the United Nations and Central America. It maintains warm relations with Cuba, even during times when the rest of Latin America follows the U.S. lead in ostracizing the island Communist nation. It trades with Comecon, the Communist common market. Though it has not joined the Organization of Petroleum Exporting Countries (OPEC), it sometimes follows OPEC's anti-U.S. lead.

Mexico's anti-U.S. feeling is similar to its attitude toward any foreign military power. Some think this feeling stems from the fact that every foreign power that has invaded Mexico has beaten it on the battlefield—the Spanish, the French, the Americans. With nothing much to crow about in its military history (even its famous Cinco de Mayo holiday honors a battle won in a war lost), Mexicans have fashioned a foreign policy grounded in principles of national sovereignty, nonintervention, and peaceful resolution of disputes. A strange little museum in Mexico City, the Museum of National Interventions, epitomizes this attitude. On long lists on the museum's walls, the government has recorded every violation of its sovereignty—every war, every skirmish, every time two gringos stepped over the Rio Grande. It is sort of a museum of ignominy. But it says volumes about how Mexicans feel about outsiders. The United States, by the way, is the biggest bad guy of all in this museum. The United States was, after all, the last country to invade Mexico, where the U.S. Marines reached "the halls of Montezuma" (really Moctezuma). In Mexico's military colleges, the United States is the country that Mexico's army officers war-game against, not unlike U.S. officers war-gaming against the Soviet Union.

Those who cannot be accommodated within the party are often farmed out to some of its satellite parties, such as the Popular

Socialist Party (PPS) and the Authentic Party of the Mexican Revolution (PARM). These two parties have typically endorsed the PRI's presidential candidates. In return, their candidates have been given seats in the national legislature, even when the votes that their parties received did not justify it. The PRI-controlled government has also financed their activities.

With the coming to office of technocrats Echeverría, López Portillo, and de la Madrid, the party's "popular" sector, which represents the bureaucracy and some small-business interests, began to grow in influence at the expense of the *campesino* and worker sectors. At least, that's the way the *campesino* and worker sectors perceived it. The *técnicos* and their offspring began to take on the characteristics of the *nomenklatura* ("privileged class") of the Soviet Union and other Eastern Bloc countries. They were self-perpetuating, living only to continue in power, handing it down from father to son. In their own minds, they were the *vanguardia* ("vanguard") of the party, those who knew best where the revolution should go.

Velázquez and other party veterans did not hide their dissatisfaction with the conservative economic policies that de la Madrid and Salinas had proposed to solve Mexico's problems of high unemployment, hyperinflation, and massive foreign debt. Velázquez and his labor colleagues were Socialists at heart, wanting more income distributed to the poorer classes and more government control of the economy.

The debate between the *técnicos* and the other sectors of the party would have been enough to make 1987 an interesting run-up to the 1988 presidential elections. But into this fray stepped the man from Michoacán. He had a solution to the complaint that the party had moved too much to the right. The party should make him its standard-bearer. The son of Lázaro Cárdenas would return Mexico to the road of revolutionary rectitude.

In saying that he wanted to be president, Cárdenas broke the rules. Those who want to be president are known as *tapados,* or "veiled ones." They are veiled because their campaign to be president is not supposed to be obvious. While these veiled candidates remain apparently inactive, their supporters, led by the members of their clique, fan out quietly across Mexico to enlist the support of clique members whose leaders are not secretly running for president. Those who hop on the bandwagon early are rewarded most heavily. Those who don't join until it is too late come to regret it. Private dinners are held to introduce the *tapados* to important business leaders. Questions are asked about views on this subject and that. No *tapado* every says, "I will do this if I become president." But everyone gets the idea. Eventually these leaders of business, labor, and the party are called in by the president to give their impressions. No one ever says, "Mr. President, I like Señor So-and-so." The president may be told that Mexico needs a man who understands the sacrifices that the workers or the peasants have made to help Mexico through its times of austerity. Others may stress that the next president must understand the need to continue Mexico's transition from a government-dominated, protected economy to more of a modern, market economy, no matter hard it might be on the poor. No names are mentioned. But everyone knows who is being talked about. In the unwritten rules of the game, no one who gives his views to the president tells any one else what he said. In the end, the president pretends that he made his pick based on a consensus of opinion. But because no one knows what that consensus is except the president, he is free to pick anyone he wants. As history has shown, he often has, much to the consternation of party elders who have to pretend that some obscure cabinet member was their preferred choice all along rather than the onetime front-runner.

When the president makes known his choice, who is known as the *verdadero tapado* ("the real veiled one"), or *el bueno* ("the good one"), the party holds a national convention and goes through the motions of nominating him. The nominee tours the country, getting to know its people and problems, in what is more a triumphal victory tour than a political campaign. An election is held some months later in which the pitifully weak opposition parties of the right and left oppose the PRI nominee. He wins, usually gaining more than 70 percent of the vote cast.

That, at least, is the way things worked until Cuauhtémoc Cárdenas stepped into the picture. In the fall of 1986, while Mexico's attention was focused on the three principal *tapados*—del Mazo, Bartlett, and Salinas—Cárdenas let it be known that he too wanted to be considered as the party's presidential candidate. The response of party officialdom was underwhelming. This was not the way things were done, some grumbled. But Cárdenas did not slink away into the darkness. Spurred by what seemed an inner sense that he was right, he created a reform wing of the party with the unlikeliest of partners. He called it the Corriente Democrática

("Democratic Current"). In public pronouncements, the Current's leaders charged that Mexico's political system was undemocratic and condemned the majority of Mexicans to poverty. They attacked the government's economic policies as capitalistic, which was a lot closer to the truth than the government's characterization of the policies as revolutionary nationalism. They complained that Mexican values were being subordinated to foreign interests, despite leftist rhetoric of the government. The Democratic Current said it stood for many new things. But what caught the public's attention was its call for more democracy in the way the PRI selected its presidential candidate. There was talk of adopting a caucus method of selection, or even a primary, methods many other countries used. What was strange about this was that Cárdenas's partner in reform was Porfirio Muñoz Ledo, who had once been the president of the PRI and had shown little previous signs of being a reformer. Quite the opposite, he had run the party during times when the PRI-controlled government used blatant vote fraud to steal local elections from opposition parties.

On that Palm Sunday that Cárdenas returned to Michoacán, I asked him how he had linked up with Muñoz Ledo. During a campaign stop in the tiny village of Arteaga, up in the southeastern mountain ranges of his beloved state, he explained a political marriage that many found bizarre.

"I found him to be a man of intelligence, of political skill and experience," he said of Muñoz Ledo, as he munched on a plate of barbecued meat that local admirers had put before him. "I believed and still believe that he truly wants reform."

Skeptics had an unkinder explanation. Muñoz Ledo was dead politically within the PRI. He was looking for a new horse to ride. Once a *tapado* himself, Muñoz Ledo had been passed over. Later he was named Mexico's ambassador to the United Nations and became president of the U.N. Security Council. He was a controversial envoy. He got involved in some incidents that embarrassed his country. When his tour of duty finished, he returned home in semi-disgrace. The party had nothing to offer him. That was its mistake. One did not send into oblivion a man who once thought he would be president of Mexico. One did not spurn a political tactician as brilliant as Muñoz Ledo. As the party would learn, if Muñoz Ledo could not get its attention in traditional ways, he would break tradition.

Muñoz Ledo knew about the discontent within the party regarding its rightward drift. He had observed the impatience of Cárdenas with the party's new ways. He knew he could do little in his own name to forge a new political career. But with a man named Cuauhtémoc Cárdenas heading a movement, anything might be possible. If Cárdenas forced the PRI to make him its presidential candidate, Muñoz Ledo would be back on top again, or at least headed there. If Cárdenas lost the nomination battle, Muñoz Ledo would be no worse off than he already was.

Conspiracy theorists in Mexico—and there are many—will try to tell you that the creation of the Democratic Current was just a ploy by the PRI to make it appear that there was a struggle for democratic reform within the party, to steal the issue of democratic reform from an unusually interesting field of opposition presidential candidates. Some said the Democratic Current was designed to become the new PRI, so the old PRI could trick people into thinking Mexico had undergone reform. Diehards even stuck to such theories when Cárdenas was thrown out of the PRI and agreed to be a presidential candidate for another party. When that happened, the conspiracy theorists argued that the PRI intended to kite the vote totals of Cárdenas's new party to reduce the influence of Mexico's leading opposition group, the right-wing National Action Party (PAN). My own theory—and it is only a theory, because I think such things are unprovable in Mexico—is that the PRI did not plan the Democratic Current. But it found it useful once it appeared on the scene. The Current's demands lent an air of democratic struggle and excitement to the party at a time when the PRI was very worried about having the July 1988 presidential vote marred by a high rate of abstention.

The key indication that the party welcomed the Current was the number of stories in Mexico's censored press about Cárdenas and Muñoz Ledo. If PRI leaders had wanted to make Cárdenas and Muñoz Ledo political nonentities, they could have done so. But they did not. The Democratic Current attracted a lot of attention and intra-party support. But in August 1987, PRI leaders said the fun was over. The PRI's president, Jorge de la Vega Domínguez, announced that the party would consider six fine men as its nominee—and only six. The veiled ones were unveiled. Cárdenas's name was not on the list.

On the surface, this appeared to be something of a democratic reform. The candidates, who had never before been allowed to state political views publicly before being nominated by the party, were asked to make presentations at party headquarters. The six, who included the front runners del Mazo, Bartlett, and Salinas, as well as de la Madrid's education minister and attorney general and the mayor of Mexico City, all gave long speeches. No one made waves. Everyone said what a wonderful president de la Madrid was. Then the candidates all went into virtual seclusion. Behind the scenes, however, they and their aides worked feverishly to destroy their rivals. The following month, President de la Madrid announced that he would meet with each of the six. When each came out of the president's office, reporters searched for clues—facial gestures, body language, anything—that might indicate how the interview had gone. Del Mazo was down. Bartlett looked good. Salinas was moving up. That's what the press said, anyway. The first weekend in October, top party leaders met in secret, ostensibly to consider all that they and the president had learned about the candidates. De la Vega went to talk to the president after the Saturday meeting. Early the next morning, it was announced that Salinas, hardly a consensus choice of the rank and file, had been chosen. The official story was that a sort of caucus had picked him. But no vote was ever released. Everyone knew what had really happened. As had always been the case, the president had picked his successor, and everyone in the party had to pretend the party had done it and wasn't it a grand idea.

Everyone did not include Cárdenas, who chose to accept the presidential nomination of the normally pro-PRI Authentic Party of the Mexican Revolution (PARM). In a new sign of independence, it had been the first of several opposition parties to make a pact endorsing the reform ideas of the Democratic Current. The PPS also wanted Cárdenas to be their candidate. He accepted their nomination as well, as he did that of the Mexican Social Workers Party (PST), which renamed itself the Cárdenist Front for National Reconciliation. With the Democratic Current, he put them all under an umbrella group, which he named the National Democratic Front. The real left-wing opposition parties of Mexico— the ones that had not been the running dogs of the PRI for decades—also wanted Cárdenas for their standard-bearer. Most of them had unified under the banner of a new party called the Mexican Socialist Party (PMS). The candidate they had in mind,

Heberto Castillo, said he'd step aside if Cárdenas beat him in an all-left, winner-take-all primary. But Cárdenas rejected the idea. Then, just a month before the July elections, Castillo resigned as the PMS candidate after he got Cárdenas to agree to a twelve-point political program acceptable to the PMS.

Cárdenas's new coalition was an amazing array of ideologies. The PMS included the old Communist party of Mexico as well as several Socialist groups. But Cárdenas told me his acceptance of the PMS nomination did not change his political views. "I am a nationalist and a revolutionary," he said. That's why he felt most comfortable with the PARM of all the groups that backed him, he said. As its name implied, revolutionary nationalism is what the PARM is all about, he noted. In Cárdenas's frame of mind, that was very apt. The PARM's past blind support of the PRI was of no import, he said. The future was the key. For him, the future meant getting back to revolutionary principles. Cárdenas had the strange idea that the Mexican constitution should mean what it says. It guarantees decent housing for all Mexicans and the right to assemble politically without government interference. It talks of adequate education and minimum levels of health. Cárdenas wanted a new, easier payment schedule for Mexico's one-hundred-billion-dollar foreign debt. With the money spared from debt payments, he wanted more spent on education, health, social security, and credit for *campesino* farmers. He criticized the PRI's selling off of strategic state-owned industries in its efforts to modernize Mexico's economy. He said Mexico was selling too much oil, that it should save petroleum for the future when it would be worth more. The PRI had let too many foreign companies come into the country to exploit Mexicans through low wages, he said. Mexico should join OPEC and the Non-Aligned Movement. He attacked the PRI's Economic Solidarity Pact (PSE), which had frozen wages more than prices. He called it a "pact of aggression" against the average Mexican. He said President de la Madrid had "lost the moral authority to lead the Mexican people."

This was the populist message Cárdenas took on the road. Whether it was the message or the man, many loved what they saw and heard. Wherever he went, he was greeted enthusiastically. While I interviewed him in Arteaga, a poor town of eighteen thousand people, men and women repeatedly came up to his chair to touch his sleeve or his shoulder. They said nothing. They just wanted to touch him, the son of the great Lázaro Cárdenas.

Cárdenas ran a frugal campaign. He had to. The PRI-controlled government doled out campaign finance funds to each opposition party. Some said the PRI's candidate spent in a day what Cárdenas spent during the whole race. This may have been an exaggeration. But there was a tremendous imbalance. In any town one could see slick Salinas posters and colorful banners strung from building to building across busy streets. Salinas had funds for campaign buses, airplanes, television commercials, flyers, banners, flags, rallies, bribes to reporters, lavish campaign meals, and walking-around money. Cárdenas rode around in a Chevy station wagon and got his meals from peasants who barely had enough to eat themselves.

Despite such advantages, the PRI scheduled party or government events to coincide with Cárdenas rallies. The party seemed bent on drawing attention away from Cárdenas at any cost. It seemed afraid of him. PRI-controlled government workers took down monuments to Cárdenas's father and removed street signs with his revered name. No sense in giving Cárdenas any free publicity, the thinking seemed to be. On March 18, 1988, when Mexico celebrated the national holiday that commemorates Cárdenas's nationalization of the Mexican oil fields, the ceremony led by President de la Madrid was perfunctory, noticeably short, even though it was the fiftieth anniversary of the event. It was as if Stalin had been asked to give homage to the founders of the Russian Revolution and discovered he had to mention Trotsky. Likewise, anniversary stamps, flags, banners, and buttons all avoided use of Lázaro Cárdenas's name.

The PRI also used the leverage it had over millions of Mexicans who depend on it for government jobs or the continued provision of basic services. It was not surprising, then, that on election day in July 1988, Cárdenas did not win—at least not officially. Salinas was declared the victor, amid charges of vote fraud and claims of a Cárdenas victory. Cárdenas told me in Arteaga that he expected vote fraud. As a lifelong *Priista,* he knew how the party worked. In speeches such as the one he gave in Arteaga, he told voters openly that he needed a victory of landslide proportions so that it would be politically impossible for the PRI to deny his win through fraud.

"Do you really think the PRI will let you win, no matter how many votes you get?" I asked him.

"Not if they have a choice," he responded.

I asked him the question that politicians hate to answer in the middle of a campaign.

"But what if you don't win?" I said. "What will you do?"

Like a good politician, he responded that he expected to win. But when pressed, he said: "I am in this struggle for the long term. I shall not quit. I shall not retire."

Many of my colleagues viewed Cárdenas as a Mexican Don Quixote, a man with no chance of victory, who tilted at political windmills and lost. I must admit that I too regarded Cárdenas as quixotic when he first burst onto the political scene. He seemed the unwitting captive of the mad political genius Muñoz Ledo, Othello to Muñoz Ledo's Iago. But close up, I saw a sincere man, perhaps a man who knew the overwhelming odds he faced in confronting the leviathan PRI. I saw a man who knew when a fight was worth waging, when it was time to put reason aside and face the juggernaut. As it turned out, he did pretty well against stiff odds. Even the PRI's official tally admitted that he got a third of the votes cast, an astounding showing for an opposition candidate. Some pundits said the vote marked the beginning of a new chapter in Mexican political history. They said it signaled the end of the PRI's six decades of one-party rule and perhaps the end of the PRI itself. Others, more conservative, said the vote would at least force the PRI to become more democratic, both within the party and in the national chamber of deputies where it had won only a slim majority that was insufficient to approve constitutional changes without some opposition support. That remains to be seen.

Somewhere down the road of Mexico's history, Cuauhtémoc Cárdenas may win his battle to get the revolution, as he sees it, back on track. In the meantime, he will be a gadfly who nettles the PRI when it makes a wrong turn. He will be a noisy conscience for the party and the country. Even without a revolution, that's not a bad epitaph.

· 8 ·

The *Panista*

Sonora is an improbable hotbed of Mexican politics. No one disputes that it's hot. It's the political part that's implausible. Going outside for any reason in Sonora's breathtaking, sauna-like heat seems daffy. But to go out just to press the flesh seems downright masochistic. Much of the year, the afternoon air heats to about 115 degrees Fahrenheit. Sometimes it's hotter. Maybe that's why people call Sonora "Hell's Waiting Room." Even the lizards sweat.

If this were a logical world, Sonora, a large, inverted triangle of land tucked into the northwest corner of Mexico, would be populated with only dust-covered scorpions and a few wiry descendants of the Yaqui, a mean, savage Indian tribe that once roamed this sizzling skillet of a state. But a hardy brand of pioneers was drawn to Sonora, first as miners, in the last century, later as farmers and cattle ranchers, in this one. Almost two million of their independent, ornery, bragging, prickly offspring now make the state their home and have made this patch of desert bloom. Cacti and tumbleweed were once the main crops of Sonora, many of whose people affect straw cowboy hats and pointy-toed leather boots. Now the landscape, which comprises about 10 percent of Mexico's territory, is flush with alfalfa, winter wheat, safflowers, soybeans, corn, chick-peas, grapes, peaches, strawberries, broccoli, asparagus, cotton, white potatoes, and, hidden here and there, a little marijuana. Fish from the Gulf of California are plentiful. And Sonora's grain-fed cattle produce the tastiest steaks in Mexico.

Sonorans, who have carved out their own destiny with little help or interference from the government, have always felt they know better than anyone else how to do things. Some of Mexico's best-known revolutionaries, such as Adolfo de la Huerta, Alvaro Obregón, and Plutarco Elías Calles, have come from Sonora, as have Fernando Valenzuela, the ace pitching star of the Los Angeles Dodgers, and Arturo Durazo, the infamous former police chief of Mexico City (1976–82) who was indicted on corruption charges during the administration of President Miguel de la Madrid (1982–88). De la Huerta, Obregón, and Calles all became presidents of Mexico in the murderous days that followed the 1910 Mexican Revolution. They backed up their desire for power with bullets as well as ballots. That contrariness continues. In modern times, Sonora has produced some of the most outspoken opponents of the Institutional Revolutionary Party, known generally as the PRI, which has ruled Mexico since 1929. One of these nay-sayers is Adalberto Rosas López.

For most of Rosas's life, he has farmed corn, potatoes, and winter wheat in the New Yaqui Valley, just outside Ciudad Obregón. His father, Ignacio, started in Sonora as a field hand. In 1945, Ignacio bought twelve meager acres of wooded land in the Old Yaqui Valley with borrowed money. Many thought him crazy to work the land because there was no apparent source of water nearby. But Ignacio cleared the land by hand and dug irrigation ditches with shovels and mules. By 1983, when he died at the age of seventy-five, the Rosas family had about a thousand acres, which Adalberto Rosas now farms with his six brothers.

In normal times, Rosas might have remained a quiet farmer all his life. But a few unexpected events set things in motion to make him the well-known, maverick politician he is today. The first happened in 1953, when Rosas was only eleven years old. His maternal uncle, Maximiliano, was murdered in his home by some members of the ruling political party. The nighttime shooting occurred just hours before Maximiliano was scheduled to make public some fraudulent activities of the management of the *ejido* ("communal farm") on which he and the party men worked. The triggerman was caught and sent to prison for a few years. But the party leaders who were the brains behind the killing were not punished.

"What impressed me was how the government repressed those who fought the system," said Rosas, a tall, beefy man whose above-average height and weight make him a typical Sonoran.

Thirteen years later, though still not drawn to politics, Rosas would be shocked by the PRI's conduct in the 1966–67 gubernatorial campaign in Sonora. In that race, some reform-minded members of the PRI demanded that the rank and file be allowed to pick the gubernatorial candidate instead of party leaders, as was the custom. Party leaders refused and picked a very unpopular candidate. To deal with expected dissent, the governor formed a goon squad, which Sonorans dubbed the Ola Verde (the "Green Wave") after the green hats they wore. Squad members kidnapped and sodomized prominent male supporters of the reformers. They circulated photographs of the denigrated men to humiliate them.

"I was just a spectator in politics at the time," said Rosas, "but it made a big impression."

In the anti-PRI atmosphere that developed after the Green Wave excesses, Don Jorge Valdéz, a leader of the opposition National Action Party (PAN), was elected mayor of Hermosillo, Sonora's capital. Six other PAN candidates won mayoral seats in Sonora too. A young Rosas, just graduated from the University of Sonora as an agricultural engineer, listened to the speeches of Valdéz and other Panistas, as members of the PAN are called. Their message of free enterprise, religious freedom, and real democracy made sense. It began to take hold in Rosas's consciousness. But work on the family farm came first. Rosas and his fiancée, Bettina, were planning to get married, so political activism was put on hold for a while.

It would be a decade more before Rosas would become a member of the conservative PAN, Mexico's leading opposition party. In the meantime, he did what many PAN members do. He joined business groups. He became vice president of the local farmers' credit union. A gifted athlete with an outgoing style, the gregarious Rosas impressed his colleagues. In 1979, PAN leaders asked him to run for mayor of Ciudad Obregón, where he had an in-town home not far from his farm operations.

"I liked the idea," said Rosas, whom his friends call El Pelón

("Baldy"), a nickname he got stuck with when he had extremely short hair during his stint in the Mexican army. "I was thirty-seven years old at the time."

Though he had no previous political experience, Rosas threw himself into the campaign with energy and creativity. He used gimmicks. He broke the rules. Rosas had thousands of business cards made up in blue and white, the colors of the PAN. He passed out seventy-five thousand of them personally in Ciudad Obregón, using a door-to-door style that had never been seen in Sonora. His early nomination, his name recognition, and his unorthodox style prompted the PRI to name Francisco Obregón, son of the former Mexican president, as Rosas's opponent.

Only about 3 percent of the electorate had bothered to vote in prior mayoral elections, according to private PAN counts. People had had no real incentive to vote because no real opposition had ever confronted the PRI in these races. Rosas decided it was time to wake people up. He engaged in stunts to whip up interest. If the PRI candidate was to meet with local teachers, Rosas got there early and met with them as well. If the PRI was to hold an event at a fair or rodeo, Rosas would parachute in to attract attention. Other times he arranged to appear as a performer, driving a motorcycle up a ramp and through a fire-ringed circle between acts. He also insisted on calling Ciudad Obregón by its original, Indian name, Cajeme. He said that to use its official name would be free publicity for his opponent since the city had been named for his famous father.

Notwithstanding all these publicity stunts, Rosas didn't really expect to win. The PRI was so well organized that they rarely lost. When they did, election officials, who were PRI members, often issued vote totals at odds with unofficial counts by opposition poll watchers. But, again, unexpected events moved Rosas's political career forward. The sitting governor had a spat with Rosas's opponent. Sticking it to his own candidate apparently became more important to the governor than stopping a PAN candidate from winning. President López Portillo was in the midst of a political reform campaign. He had promised clean elections as yet another means of trying to get Mexico's feeble political opposition to continue running against the PRI. He wanted to keep up the pretense that Mexico is a real democracy. Finally, Rosas's share of the vote was so overwhelming—about twenty-two thousand votes to eight-thousand—that it would have been difficult to deny his win.

The PRI had some explaining to do when the official count was issued. In prior elections, when there had been little voter interest, the PRI had insisted that about forty-five thousand people had voted in Ciudad Obregón. In Rosas's hotly contested race, the final figures showed that less than thirty thousand votes were cast.

"There was a real scandal about the numbers," said Rosas.

Just as Rosas had been a different kind of candidate, he became a different kind of mayor. Most PRI mayors had had an imperious style, sending for people peremptorily when they needed to talk to them or just ordering them to do something without benefit of consultation. Rosas, who loves to be outdoors, would drive from his office to the countryside to talk with the lowliest farm worker. He let it be known that he would deal fiercely with corruption. As mayor, he was able to name a new police chief. But he was stuck with the city's street cops, who had a reputation for demanding bribes of the citizenry. Nonetheless, people began to come to him with complaints of police harassment and even of torture in jail.

Though popular with the people, Rosas was snubbed by the PRI-dominated officialdom of the state. When the governor would come to town for parades or a speech, Rosas would not be introduced or even invited to sit on the dais. When López Portillo came to town, Rosas went to the airport to welcome him, as was the mayor's duty. But he was told he was not welcome to join the president's motorcade. The PRI governor cut the budget for the city, so there was less to go around. But Rosas kept a tight watch on graft, so what money he got went further.

By law, Rosas could not succeed himself. But he helped his party's new mayoral candidate to campaign. The new candidate looked like a winner too. But Rosas and party leaders were worried that the PRI would never allow two PAN victories in a row in Ciudad Obregón out of fear that the PAN would establish an unshakable foothold there. On election night, Rosas, ever the nonconformist, decided to keep all the ballots, ballot boxes, and official tallies in Ciudad Obregón for a public vote tally. The state legislature ordered him to hand over the voting material. He refused. He cited state law to show that the legislature only had the power to declare an election void or valid—not to tally votes.

Rosas made his count, which showed the PAN candidate had won. But the state legislature overruled him and declared the PRI candidate the winner. (Later they changed the law so that the legislature could count the ballots if, mysteriously, official tallies disappeared—as they often did.) Rosas was later sentenced to three years and three months in jail for disobeying the legislature. But he got an injunction to suspend the sentence. The threat of jail hung over his head, however, until March 1985, when the courts threw the sentence out.

By then, Rosas had become the gubernatorial candidate for the PAN for the July 1985 elections. Actually, his candidacy had begun in March 1983, when he decided to run 750 miles from the southern tip of Sonora up to the state's northern border with Arizona in what he called a March for Democracy. As he had done before, he handed out his blue-and-white business cards to thousands of potential voters as he ran along the way. Many Mexicans ran part of the way with him during his thirty-seven-day marathon. In addition to shedding quite a few pounds under the blazing Sonora sun, he got mountains of free publicity. He wrote a book, *Edict of Shame*, about the 1982 mayoralty and his fight through the courts to avoid jail. By the time the PAN nominating convention took place, he had no real rivals.

In late 1984, the atmosphere looked propitious for another Rosas win. A new Mexican president, Miguel de la Madrid, had taken office in December of 1982. He had promised to do something about the rampant government corruption that had so characterized the López Portillo administration. He promised cleaner elections too—as López Portillo had. In 1983, de la Madrid's first real year in office, his party recognized several opposition mayoral victories, especially in northern border states, where antagonism against the PRI was the strongest. But PRI veterans began to grumble privately that if the party was going to recognize all opposition victories, they'd soon be out of power. As 1984 began, the mood turned blacker. PAN candidates claimed mayoral victories in Piedras Negras and Monclova, in the northern border state of Coahuila, and in Chemax, in the Yucatán. Angry *Panistas*, faced with official proclamations of PRI victories in those cities, seized the city halls. Violence broke out and captured headlines. The PRI made some concessions to quell unrest. In Piedras Negras, for example, they substituted a more suitable PRI member as mayor and gave the PAN half the seats on the city council. But the questionable PRI victories stood. Privately, PAN officials were concerned that the reforms de la Madrid had talked so much about were over. But publicly they began to say that Rosas had the best chance in modern Mexican history to become the first non-PRI candidate to be elected a state governor.

Since Sonoran Plutarco Elías Calles formed the PRI in late 1928, the party had never lost an election for president or governor. Rosas was bucking a strong trend. The PRI, in fact, controlled about 95 percent of all federal, state, and local offices. Undaunted, Rosas conducted an enthusiastic campaign in the oppressive heat of Sonora. Both his ebullient style and the possibility that Mexico was about to turn an historic political corner attracted about two hundred foreign journalists to the state for the elections. I was one of them.

I interviewed Rosas in November of 1984. I found him an engaging man who genuinely believed that he might win. To me, however, his chances depended not so much on his political experience or personal appeal as on the official attitude of President de la Madrid and his party toward the elections. De la Madrid seemed to take Rosas's challenge seriously. As is the president's privilege, he picked Rosas's challenger: Rodolfo Félix Valdés, his minister of communications and transportation. He also said publicly that he wanted clean elections in 1985. After all, the whole world was watching. State party officials didn't seem to pay much attention, however. Their view seemed to be that they were going to be around long after de la Madrid's six-year term was over. They wanted to stay in power.

Whatever the thinking of local party officials, the vote fraud that I and my colleagues saw on election day was astoundingly brazen. When I was growing up in Chicago, where people know a thing or two about kiting vote totals, there was a famous local character called Lead Pencil Louie. He used to put a piece of pencil lead under his fingernails. When the paper ballots were being counted, he would slyly make an extra "X" on the ballots of those who had voted for opponents of the Democratic machine. That would make the ballots invalid. But Louie was a paradigm of finesse compared with the ham-handed stalwarts of the PRI in Sonora. Rough-looking men in cars with no license plates pulled up to polling places and stole ballot boxes. Some ballot boxes were so stuffed with votes before the polls opened that the first voters in line could not get their ballots into the boxes' slots. At some polling sites, mysterious men showed up claiming to be official PAN poll-watchers, only to be confronted by real PAN watchers later on. Thousands of phony voter-registration cards were printed up and handed out to PRI loyalists so they could vote more than once. Voting lists were inflated with ghost voters. Polling places in PAN strongholds were moved at the last minute to make it difficult for PAN voters to cast their ballots.

PRI efforts to deceive foreign reporters were equally clumsy. Just minutes after the polls were scheduled to close, PRI officials appeared in the lobby of the Holiday Inn in Hermosillo, where most of the foreign reporters were staying. They handed out a sheet of initial results, purporting to show that the PRI had swept a number of precincts. The results seemed bogus for a number of reasons. Most precincts couldn't have made such quick tallies, because closely watched official counting went on into the early morning. Moreover, most results had been rounded off to the nearest hundred. The PRI would have had us believe that Rosas had lost 800–0, 700–10, 800–10, 600–0, depending on the precinct. It may be that party officials just weren't capable of sophisticated fraud. After all, they had never had so many outside observers monitor a local election. But I tend to think they were just sending the world a defiant message that they were in charge of Mexico and would run it as they pleased.

The official count showed that Rosas carried precincts only in Ciudad Obregón and Hermosillo. The PRI said he got 116,000 votes, even though, in the previous election, the PAN senate candidate had gotten 127,000 votes after a lackluster campaign. By Rosas's count, ninety tally sheets for precincts in the capital were "lost." When the state legislature used its new power to count the ballots in those precincts, they said Rosas hadn't won any of them. The official count showed that Rosas carried no precincts in Agua Prieta, a PAN bastion. Rosas supposedly got no votes in Pueblo Yaqui, where he was born and had 500 relatives.

PAN officials had promised demonstrations in the streets if their election victories were denied them. People did appear for a while to make known their discontent. But the hubbub quickly died down. When the foreign press left town after a few weeks, the controlled Mexican press dropped the story too. The following year, PAN officials again tried to persuade reporters that their candidate in neighboring Chihuahua was going to be the first opposition governor in modern times. They said the PRI was running scared. As proof, they noted that the PRI had replaced its usual candidate selection by party leaders with a more democratic caucus selection in mayoral races in a bid to blunt the PAN's criticism of the PRI's antidemocratic ways. The PRI had promised to do the same in the next state legislative contests. But few foreign correspondents bought the idea this time. We had learned our lesson in Sonora. Our cynicism proved a justifiable attitude. The fraud in Chihuahua was brazen too. The PRI won. The PAN launched a short campaign of civil disobedience, getting its followers not to pay their light and phone bills for a while. But the state-owned light and phone companies weren't crippled financially as PAN leaders had hoped. They just shut off service. After a few months, the campaign was forgotten.

In the 1988 presidential election, civil disobedience was the PAN watchword again. Before the election, party members wrote protest slogans on Mexican peso notes as a means of spreading their message of discontent. The government announced that such bills would not be considered legal tender. The protest petered out. Manuel Clouthier, the tubby, gruff, bearded presidential candidate of the PAN, promised violence if he won and was denied victory. By the official account in July, he did not win. And post-election protests fizzled after a burst of hot rhetoric about fraud.

In the same elections, Rosas, bitter but unbowed, ran for the Mexican senate. Not surprisingly, he didn't become the first PAN senator in modern Mexican history. The outcome of Rosas's race did little to help or hurt the PAN's long-term fight to govern Mexico one day. In a talk we had just before the 1988 elections, Rosas acknowledged that the PAN couldn't really think about achieving that goal until it became a national party in the real sense. It wasn't even organized in all of Mexico's thirty-one states. It was still head and shoulders above the opposition parties of the left. Despite a good showing by Cuauhtémoc Cárdenas, the left's presidential candidate in 1988, the left remained a bickering, disorganized force nationally. The PAN didn't seem to have the fire in the belly that Rosas did when he conducted his campaigns. Rosas seemed willing to scorch a little earth in the effort to oust the PRI from power. He lamented that his colleagues didn't have the same eagerness to go the extra mile.

"A PAN victory," he told me, as we sat in a potato field owned by his neighbor Don Miguel, "would take a real hunger on the part of the Mexican people." Panistas, he said, hadn't been hungry enough in their fizzled civil-disobedience campaigns in Sonora and Chihuahua.

"People didn't stick with it," he said. "To fight, I think you first have to do without. If people realize that not paying a light bill would mean doing without air conditioning in the summer or without refrigeration for their food, they are less likely to fight. It would be easier not to pay the bills, if you can't pay."

People soon wouldn't be able to pay, he said, if Mexico's economic crisis continued. Given what Rosas called the bankrupt ideas of the PRI, he had little doubt that there would be more crisis. He almost seemed to warm to the prospect, to welcome the economic purgative that might, at last, bring real democracy to Mexico.

"When we suffer," he said, "then we will become citizens."

· 9 ·

The *Fayuquero*

Most big cities have a rough section where gangsters, smugglers, drug dealers, and muggers can put their feet up and let their hair down. In Mexico City it is called Tepito, a sprawling, center-city neighborhood of slum housing and chockablock open-air stalls of the famous Thieves' Market.

In the glory days, old-timers will tell you, one could regularly find a body in a roadside ditch almost every morning in Tepito. Sometimes the corpse was someone who had ventured into Tepito a bit too naively in search of thrills or some of the contraband goods for which the neighborhood is famous. Sometimes it was the victim of an all-too-frequent rape. Tepito was loaded with hard characters. One did not go there without good reason.

In more recent times, Tepito hasn't exactly gone uptown. But it has become more respectable. Middle-class people visit it to browse through its colorful market, though it is hardly what one would call safe. Gangs of young toughs still roam Tepito's streets, such as Avenida de Trabajo ("Work Avenue") and Avenida de Carpintería ("Carpentry Street"), whose names are vestiges of the days when Tepito was mainly a neighborhood of tradesmen. One can still be robbed by some fourteen-year-old who has become frighteningly handy with a knife or pistol. The chance of having one's pocket picked is more than average. But more and more of Tepito's merchants, who for years have been smugglers or sellers of contraband, have gone legit. Among them is Luis Hernández, whose transformation into an honest businessman is the story of a recent, drastic change in Mexico. It's a change that is dragging the country into the economic twentieth century just as much of the world prepares to enter the twenty-first.

Oscar Lewis told the early story of Luis's life, for Luis is one of the *Children of Sánchez,* whom Lewis made famous in that classic 1961 study of poverty in a Mexican slum. To protect Luis from any government retaliation for his candid comments, Lewis changed Luis's name to Manuel Sánchez, the gregarious, Runyonesque, story-telling, womanizing eldest son of the family. Lewis subtitled his book *Autobiography of a Mexican Family.* But it was much more than that. The searing look at Luis's family, at its problems of child beating, alcoholism, army desertion, poverty, and infidelity, was the stuff of Dickens or Dreiser.

Luis's early years were an agonizing search for satisfying work and true love. He had bad luck with both initially. But by the time I met Luis in late 1986, he had become a happy man, though certainly not a rich one.

As a young man, he had drifted from one employer to another, switching jobs as casually as he changed socks. He gambled. He drank. He fought. With his pals Donkey, Three Daily, Rat, and Dirty Face, Luis generally gave delinquency a bad name. He became an early initiate of the sexual world. At eight years of age, he tried unsuccessfully to have his first sexual intercourse. He visited his first whorehouse at thirteen. A sexual fever got hold of him. He tried to have sex with the impoverished women whom his father hired to clean the Sanchez's tiny house. But, as Luis will tell you, his randy father, a leathery-skinned peasant from Veracruz, always seemed to beat him to it. At the age of fifteen, the sexually precocious Luis took María as his common-law wife. She was nineteen. Luis was in love. But like all of his contemporaries, he saw nothing wrong with infidelity. It was a Mexican man's right, he had been told all his short life. He exercised that right frequently. He had a particularly torrid affair with one woman. But he discovered that he really loved his wife more than anything. When she died suddenly while he was off philandering, Luis, guilt-ridden and grief-stricken, went into a depression. He fled the harsh reality of Tepito and wound up in the United States. There he worked as a *bracero* ("laborer"). He learned a little English. He became acquainted with the American way of life. He learned about the myriad products that the booming U.S. economy provided people, products one could not find in Mexico. An idea came to him for a new line of work. He would become a smuggler.

It was hardly a surprising choice of jobs, given the illicit traditions of Tepito. Since the days of the Spanish Conquest, Mexicans, chafing at the import restrictions of whatever government was in charge, have gravitated toward those who offer the forbidden fruit of foreign-made items. The term for such contraband items, *fayuca*, is said to derive from the archaic Spanish term *bayuca*, which meant "tavern." On Mexico's Caribbean coast, in a tavern called simply La Bayuca, pirates and other brigands first brought smuggled items to Mexico. Ever since, anything that smacks of contraband has been called *fayuca*, a corruption of *bayuca*. *Fayuca* sellers have been called *fayuqueros*. When one says *fayuqueros* in Mexico, the name that comes to mind is Tepito.

Over the years, Luis—and later his son Victor, a second-generation *fayuqueros*—has sold a variety of items that have not always been imported in total observance of Mexico's restrictive, Byzantine customs laws. Using someone else's truck, they have traveled to U.S. border towns, such as Laredo, Texas, to buy televisions, watches, clothes, cutlery, tape recorders, and other items that Mexicans could not find in Mexico, or could find only at ridiculously high prices. Like the good capitalists one finds all over Tepito, Luis and Victor saw a need and filled it.

Tepito is the epitome of an efficient, capitalist market. Luis, an uneducated man with the street savviness of a New York wholesale merchant, calls it a *cuna*, or nursery for capitalists. For a price comparable to that found in the United States—plus expenses for transportation to and from the border, lodging there, and bribes to the police along the way—one can find items in Tepito that cost two or three times as much elsewhere in Mexico. Tepito's merchants are proud of their competitive tradition. They belittle the price-gouging of other Mexican merchants. But they will admit to you that there would be no Tepito or markets like it in Monterrey, Puebla, and other Mexican cities if Mexico didn't have such a strange economic system.

That system is often described as mixed. It is a mixture of capitalism and state ownership of the economy. The easiest way to understand what that means is to take a look at a little history. Under the dictator Porfirio Díaz (1876–1911), Mexico promoted foreign investment in oil, gold, silver, agriculture, textiles, and railroads in hopes of quickly opening up world markets to Mexico's then-fledgling economy. Díaz thought the road to prosperity was faster through superior foreign technology, capital, and know-how than through purely Mexican means. His methods produced good results. Earnings from exports, including coffee, henequen, sugar, vanilla, chicle, cattle, copper, zinc, lead, graphite, and antimony, increased about 6 percent annually during his politically repressive reign. He did encourage some domestic manufacturing through easy import rules on items that Mexican businesses needed, and through high protective tariffs on those they did not. He also encouraged exports, reduced taxes, and kept transportation costs low. When revolutionaries threw Díaz out in 1911, they were primarily interested in ending political repression. But they rejected everything he stood for. They renounced his reliance on foreign investment and technology. They promised to redistribute agricultural lands that he had allowed to be concentrated in the hands of a few in the name of production efficiency. Post-revolutionary chaos prevented much of this planned reform until the formation of the Institutional Revolutionary Party (PRI), which, under one name or another, has ruled Mexico since 1929. The party's first elected president, Lázaro Cárdenas, expropriated vast tracts of agricultural lands and turned them over to peasants. In 1938, he nationalized Mexico's oil fields, which had been run mostly by U.S. and European companies before then. He adopted a nationalistic, somewhat socialistic, approach to economics. He raised customs duties to discourage imports. He inaugurated a policy of "import substitution," which involves making at home what one has been purchasing from abroad—and then banning the previously imported goods.

Post-revolutionary Mexico turned inward economically for about a decade. But World War II forced it to look outward. Though still bitter about the disastrous outcome of the 1847 Mexican-American War, Mexico's government provided vital items to its archenemy, the United States. Key commodities and morphine made from Mexican-grown poppy plants went across the border.

With the United States focusing all its production on the war, Mexico had to stimulate its industries even more to produce the consumer goods it had been importing. With this new blend of trade, Mexico experienced unexpected growth. Politicians found they liked the prosperity that came with it. The composition of Mexico's economy began to change. During the time of Miguel Alemán (1946–52), the importance of manufacturing rose. So did corruption linked to unprecedented profits. With manufacturing's rise, agriculture, which had enabled Mexico to become a net exporter of food, began to decline. Foreign companies were encouraged to invest in developing Mexican industry, though they were not given the green light to come in willy-nilly. In the 1950s, big U.S. firms were allowed to concentrate in the automobile, food-processing, rubber-tire, chemical, drug, and electrical-appliance industries. General Motors, Ford, Chrysler, Goodyear, Firestone, General Electric, Kellogg, Campbell, Heinz, Proctor & Gamble, Colgate Palmolive, and Coca-Cola became familiar brand names in Mexico. In the 1960s, European and Japanese companies came in. Well-known foreign products made it seem to tourists that Mexico was just another capitalist economy, albeit a poor one. But this was not the case.

As this part-manufacturing, part-agricultural, part state-controlled economy developed, so did a social pact. The warring factions of the ruling Institutional Revolutionary Party (PRI)—workers, peasants, bureaucrats, and the army—were kept happy by what seemed an ever-expanding economic pie to share. Economic growth rates, often in the 5-to-8 percent range annually, meant more jobs were being created. Real salaries were going up. A middle class was being created where once there had been none. But the middle class developed middle-class tastes. Mexican industry had to produce even more consumer goods and make better housing available. A still large poor class had to be kept happy, too. The government began to subsidize the basics of life—tortillas, milk, beans, rice, beef, chicken, fish, cooking oil, telephone calls, buses, trains, movies, electricity, gasoline, and natural gas. In 1961, it created the National Company for Popular Sustenance, known as Conasupo, whose subsidized retail outlets serve as supermarkets for the poor. It controlled the prices of unsubsidized, basic goods. That made voters happy but created havoc within industry. Businesses often found that rising costs forced them to sell goods at a loss if they stuck to the official price. In quiet protest, they withheld goods at the factory, awaiting a new price increase. The normal laws of supply and demand went out the window. Common shortages began to occur.

I often could tell when the Ministry of Commerce was about to raise prices on controlled items. Milk or apple juice or canned dog food or flour or yeast or several other things I regularly bought would suddenly disappear from the shelves. When public protests about such shortages reached fever pitch, the ministry would cave in and authorize a price hike. Usually officials said they didn't want to raise prices, but an increase was necessary to end the crisis. The public, aware of what the game was, often stocked up on such items, as I came to do. One could see wealthy matrons or their maids in the supermarket check-out line with twenty or thirty quarts of milk in their baskets. Hoarding only exacerbated the shortages.

By 1970, this hodgepodge of economic policies was, strangely, producing high annual economic growth rates. Astoundingly, these rates even kept pace with (and sometimes exceeded) Mexico's dangerously high population-growth rates. Mexico had become self-sufficient in food, steel, and most consumer items. It imported a lot. But mostly it bought foreign capital goods for domestic industry rather than luxury consumer items. Foreign investment was creeping up. Debt and budget deficits were not really a problem, as they would become later. It seemed as if Mexico's unorthodox economic formula might just work. But it didn't seem so for very long.

One could argue that the roots of the economic crisis that Mexico finds itself in today go back to the straitjacketing politics of the 1910 Revolution. But the crisis did not begin in earnest until the presidency of Luis Echeverría, who took office December 1, 1970. His leftist policies of increased subsidies, greater state participation in the economy, foreign borrowing to finance social improvements, and initial neglect of runaway population growth were the seeds of today's troubles: triple-digit inflation, double-digit unemployment, a foreign debt of more than a hundred billion dollars, and an underdeveloped domestic industry. Mexico's overreliance on oil, huge reserves of which were discovered the year Echeverría left office, was the capping folly to an economic philosophy that would haunt Mexico for the rest of the century.

It is easy in hindsight to take potshots at what now appear to be misguided, if not stupid, decisions. To outsiders, it seems silly for an underdeveloped country that lives right next door to the world's largest market not to stress exports as a key element of its economic policy. It is often said that South Korea or Taiwan would kill to get a hundred yards of Mexico's two-thousand-mile border with the United States. Why then has Mexico largely ignored this potentially lucrative opportunity? Why does it limit sales of oil to the United States to 50 percent of its export total? Why does it not encourage foreign investment from the United States and other industrial leaders as the cheapest, fastest way of developing Mexican industry, as Canada did? To ask such questions, however, is to ignore Mexico's history, which, right or wrong, is very anti-American. Japan chose to put aside the memory of two atomic bombs and a humiliating defeat in World War II in order to become one of the United States' best trading partners. This has not been the case with Mexico, where official anger about hundred-year-old military losses and decade-old diplomatic insults smolders as if such offenses occurred last week. You can argue about the logic of such an attitude. But you can't deny it exists.

Mexicans, led by the left wing of the PRI, have argued since the 1910 Revolution that to hitch Mexico's economic destiny to the United States would mean being economically and culturally swamped by its giant neighbor. It was not just that they wanted Mexico to be its own man politically and economically. They hated the United States. It had, after all, stolen half of Mexico after the Mexican-American War and had generally done what it could to thwart the 1910 Revolution. It was hardly the country that Mexican politicians wanted to emulate. Perhaps that explains why modern Mexico chose instead the path of revolutionary nationalism. Under that philosophy, the state is the leading player in the economy. President Miguel de la Madrid called the state the rector of the economy, a term his successor and onetime chief economic adviser, Carlos Salinas de Gortari, embraced in his 1988 presidential campaign. *Paraestatales,* or state-owned industries, dominate many industries, including steel, cement, domestic airlines, coffee, railroads, newsprint, electric power, the telephone system, fertilizers, and, of course, oil. It makes sense for the government to own some of these industries. But others are clearly the stuff of private enterprise. With bureaucrats in charge, many have become cash-sucking, unprofitable businesses.

Oil is one business that could have been private. But history and politics have made oil, and any natural resource, part of Mexicans' "national patrimony." To let foreigners or even private Mexican businesses exploit such resources is unpatriotic, any politician can tell you, even if it makes good economic sense. Before it became apparent that Mexico had some of the largest oil reserves in the world, this attitude didn't make too much difference. Oil played a key, though not a dominant, role in the Mexican economy. But when the massive size of Mexico's oil reserves became apparent in the late 1970s, it suddenly became very important how well oil was handled as a resource. Mexico's government vowed not to make the mistake that Iran and Indonesia had with their petroleum riches. Their economies had become addicted to oil revenues. They went boom or bust with the mercurial rise or fall of world oil prices. Corruption reigned. But Mexico did fall prey to the easy money of oil exports. It soon distorted its economy into an oil-reliant one permeated by corruption. At one point, three quarters of all Mexico's export revenues came from oil. Some politicians made billions from it.

Revolutionary nationalism likewise called for some imports to be banned, officially or de facto, as happened with foreign cars. Others, particularly luxury consumer items, were subject to high tariffs that discouraged most purchases. Such restrictions were designed to protect Mexican industry, which, on the surface, is an unlikely beneficiary of the policies of Mexico's ruling party. Party rhetoric regularly brands business as a counterrevolutionary enemy of the state. The explanation of this strange protection is that the PRI, ever nervous about losing power, uses protectionism to blunt the appeal of the leading opposition group, the conservative, pro-business National Action Party (PAN).

This approach has had good political results, denying the PAN full business support. Economically it has been a disaster, though. Mexican businesses have never developed an entrepreneurial tradition. They have gotten used to little risk, even less competition, and quick, sometimes breathtaking, profits. With little outside competition, manufacturers feel little pressure to make quality goods. The poorest of Mexicans have no choice but to buy appliances that fall apart in months instead of years, or ready-to-wear pants that do not fit and have little style. When I first arrived in Mexico I remember seeing a headline that said: "40 Percent of Light Bulbs Defective." I thought this a bit farfetched for an item that other nations make in quality-controlled assembly lines. But I soon discovered that quality control was not a standard part of Mexican manufacturing. Recognizing this, every Mexican hardware store and supermarket has installed a testing device so buyers can determine if the light bulbs being sold actually work. Everyone uses them.

Car parts were another item of shoddy production. About a year after I bought a new, made-in-Mexico Volkswagen, I found one morning that my horn did not work. I had it checked and was told it had burned out. "Burned out?" I asked incredulously. "I've never heard of a horn burning out." "It happens all the time," the repairman told me. "Your mistake was buying a Mexican horn. They only last a year. I have an imported horn here if you don't want any more problems." Poorer but wiser, I bought it.

Many Mexicans have responded to shoddy goods by voting with their feet. Those who can afford it go to the United States or Europe to buy clothes, electronic goods, perfume, or other items regarded as inferior if made in Mexico. Those who can't come up with the price of an airplane ticket go to places such as Tepito. Even government officials succumb. I often saw contraband televisions and videocassette recorders in government offices. In fact, one of Mexico City's leading black markets, Correo Mayor, thrived right under the windows of the national palace, where Finance Ministry officials in charge of cracking down on contraband had their offices.

With the 1970 election of Luis Echeverría, things began to change in a way that would spell the end of black markets such as Correo Mayor and Tepito, at least as Luis Hernández had known such markets all his life. Echeverría thought himself a populist, the first real leftist since President Cárdenas. It was an apropos time for a populist politician. Mexico's population growth had taken off, creating severe problems of poverty, unemployment, and strained social services. Echeverría went on a spree of public-works building for Mexico's growing public. He increased subsidies for basic goods and services dramatically. He launched massive state projects such as Mexico's Cancún and Ixtapa resorts, and the white-elephant Sicartsa steel plant in Michoacán. Rather than raise taxes to cover such spending, Echeverría borrowed money. Rather than focus on the limitations of his own economic policies, he blamed unfair world commodity prices for Mexico's financial woes. He kept the peso overvalued, which made luxury imports and foreign vacations cheap. An overvalued peso also made it cheap for Mexican industry to import needed capital goods. All those imports, combined with a feeble emphasis on exports, soon produced a whopping trade deficit. Overvaluation of the peso also encouraged Mexicans to bet against their currency by converting their savings into dollars to wait for an inevitable devaluation. That devaluation came just before Echeverría left office in December 1976. The peso, which had once been worth more than the U.S. dollar and had circulated as legal tender in the United States, was cut in value from 12.5 pesos to the dollar to 29.

In 1973, Echeverría had fired his finance minister, Hugo Margaín, when Margaín announced publicly that the Mexican treasury had run out of money, largely due to Echeverría's spending. Echeverría said he'd find a finance minister who could find the money Mexico needed to finance social and state-industry projects. He found José López Portillo, who three years later became his successor. López Portillo found the money by borrowing it. It was the beginning of an extraordinary borrowing binge in which foreign banks, flush with petrodollars after the 1973 Arab oil embargo, were willing accomplices. By the end of López Portillo's regime (1976–82), the Mexican government and Mexican businesses owed foreign banks about $85 billion, the most of any nation in the world. With the equivalent of seventy billion barrels of oil and natural gas in the ground, the banks assumed that Mexico was a good credit risk. But toward the end of López Portillo's administration, world oil prices began to fall. And while it was clear Mexico had enough petroleum collateral in the ground to assure that it could pay back all those loans some day, foreign bankers got a little worried about whether Mexico could make its payments month to month.

With oil revenues down and government spending still up, orthodox economic rules called for López Portillo to cut spending or devalue the peso or both. Devaluation would make Mexican goods cheaper, boosting export revenues. But Mexico was in the midst of a presidential campaign. López Portillo did not want to hurt the image of his party's candidate, Miguel de la Madrid. More important, López Portillo, a proud, arrogant man, did not want to hurt his image in history. He did not want to be remembered as a president who left Mexico in a financial shambles. He continued to think that he could use Mexico's oil wealth to mask the fundamental structural problems of the economy. Like Echeverría, he kept the value of the peso artificially high. The U.S. dollar became the cheapest thing in Mexico. Everyone began to buy it, even maids and shoe-shine boys. Mexicans became common visitors to Las Vegas, Vail, Houston, Los Angeles, and New York. They bought real estate, clothes, electronic goods, and everything in sight. Those poor foreigners living in Mexico found it irrationally expensive. But madness has its limits. By February 1982, López Portillo found he could wait no more to do something about the economy. After promising to defend the peso "like a dog," he surprised everyone and devalued it to forty-six to the dollar. Devaluation was only one thing Mexico's economy needed. But López Portillo, the victim of presidential election–year politics, refused to do anything else until the July presidential election was over. When it was, he moved quickly, ordering price increases at state-owned enterprises. That boosted government revenues and help cut the budget deficit. Later, he imposed partial foreign-exchange controls. On August 12, he closed all foreign-exchange markets and froze all dollar accounts in Mexico, including those of hundreds of thousands of resident Americans. He converted the dollar accounts to peso ones at an official rate considerably below that available on a suddenly flourishing black market. In the crisis atmosphere, Mexican officials began to talk openly about not being able to make payments on the immense foreign debt, much of which was owed to U.S. commercial banks. A. U.S.-led rescue package was arranged that infused billions of dollars into the Mexican economy. Notwithstanding this intervention, the peso fell to 120 to the dollar. But the worst appeared over.

Business and foreign confidence had slipped so much in López Portillo's final months that he appointed two men slated for de la Madrid's cabinet, Jesús Silva Herzog and Miguel Mancera, as his new finance minister and president of the central bank respectively. That helped a bit. But López Portillo's preoccupation with his place in history led him in September 1982 to nationalize Mexico's banks, the most sweeping expropriation since Cárdenas's seizure of the Mexican oil fields. Confidence in the government slumped to an historic low. When de la Madrid came into office on December 1, 1982, he found he had inherited the world's largest foreign debt, a battered peso, a recession, nearly triple-digit inflation, high unemployment, and a huge government budget deficit. The time for foreign scapegoats and the populist claptrap rhetoric of Echeverría and López Portillo was over, de la Madrid decided. He told the Mexican people they would have to tighten belts and endure an economic policy of austerity. He talked of a "national process of renovation." For the rest of the world, this was an orthodox approach. But for Mexico it was downright— well, counterrevolutionary. De la Madrid's policies would tilt things in favor of the middle class and, to some extent, toward business at the expense of workers and peasants, who considered themselves the true heirs of the 1910 revolution. During his six years in office, de la Madrid called his economic policy many things. Known principally by their initials, his economic plans were variously called the PIRE, the PAC, and, finally, the PSE. Few will remember what the initials stood for. But the plans were all fundamentally the same. They headed Mexico in the same rightward direction economically. The government pledged to cut public spending in order to reduce the budget deficit (and the amount of internal borrowing required to finance that deficit). Cutting government spending meant that subsidies for the basics of life would be cut back. The price of bus and subway tickets soared far beyond inflation. Gasoline prices went up extraordinarily, too. Ridiculously cheap intra-Mexico air fares were replaced with more realistic ones. Air service to out-of-the-way cities was ended. The government began to unload many state-owned industries, whose mindlessly managed, red-ink operations were a key drag on the budget. De la Madrid undid some of the damage of López Portillo's bank nationalization by selling off bank-owned stock in non-bank companies. He even sold minority shares in the banks themselves. But all his tightening up had its price. By the end of his administration, economists estimated that the average Mexican had lost about a third of his or her earning power because once-subsidized or controlled prices had gone up so much faster than wages. Some said they had lost more.

De la Madrid's progress in solving Mexico's economic problems was mixed. Unemployment went up as the government and the economy were unable to keep pace with the million new persons entering the work force each year. To make a living, out-of-work Mexicans took to the streets, selling a dizzying variety of goods from makeshift stalls and at street corners. They created an underground, market-oriented economy of impressive proportions. Economic growth, in negative figures when de la Madrid took over, went up, then down, then up. The size of the economy shrank in dollar terms, as did Mexicans' wealth, measured by their individual shares of the economy. High double-digit inflation went down, then became triple-digit inflation. Public spending was cut back. The budget deficit (as a percentage of the gross domestic product) went down, then up again. The domestic debt (the amount Mexicans owe themselves) soared. Through debt swaps and payment stretch-outs, de la Madrid brought Mexico's draining foreign-debt interest payments down, though Mexico's debt total remained high. Partly because of new loan money, the level of international hard-currency reserves, the money Mexico uses to pay foreign debts and buy imports, rose to impressive levels. Foreign investment, always extremely low compared with other countries, was opened up a bit to get Mexico moving in key areas, such as high technology. The longtime 49 percent ceiling on foreign ownership of companies operating in Mexico was changed to 100 percent in certain fields, under certain conditions, one of which was an emphasis on exports. The dollar volume of non-oil exports rose, as did their percentage of total imports, moving Mexico away from an oil-dependent economy.

When historians look back, they may or may not decide that de la Madrid's economic tactics were the ones that finally got Mexico's problems of inflation, debt, budget deficits, and unemployment under control. But I think they will find that the most significant step he took to get Mexico on the road to permanent fiscal health was his decision to sign the General Agreement on Tariffs and Trade (GATT) in August 1986. The GATT agreement changed the whole structure of the Mexican economy. It bound Mexico to end protectionist measures, such as high tariffs and impossible-to-obtain import permits. That meant Mexico had to open its long-protected market to foreign competition. Mexican leftists had long attacked membership in GATT as a counter-revolutionary move that would make Mexico a satellite of the dreaded United States. They warned that U.S. products would surely dominate the Mexican market under free-trade conditions.

De la Madrid counterargued that GATT allowed a ten-to-fifteen-year period of adjustment during which Mexico could do some things to protect and develop its fragile, underdeveloped domestic industry. But he also made it clear that Mexico had taken the plunge into the market system of economies. Privately, his advisers talked about emulating the economic models of South Korea and Taiwan. To assuage the left, de la Madrid promised that the state would still hold on to certain strategic industries, such as oil and steel. But it would privatize much of the rest, perhaps even the telephone, electric, and airline industries. Those industries that remained under state control would have to show a profit, he said. Private businesses would have to get their acts together, too. Those that did not get lean and mean and produce high-quality, competitively priced goods would go bankrupt. Those that survived would prosper. If all went well, Mexico would be able to create jobs for the million youngsters coming into the market each year. Mexicans as individuals would get richer, more educated. On the downside, party old-timers warned, better-off Mexicans would want more democracy, a development that could threaten the PRI's sixty-year reign of power. In a simple stroke of the pen, de la Madrid had loosed an irresistible force in Mexico. No one knew exactly what impact it would have.

In the short run, the government said, it hoped the expected influx of foreign goods would keep inflation down. It expected that imported goods, produced by efficient foreign factories, would underprice Mexican goods. In 1987 and 1988, high-quality goods did begin to trickle into Mexico, but not quite as the government had imagined. Large Mexican enterprises tended to dominate much of the importation of such goods. In Mexico's long tradition of easy, quick profits, these conglomerates offered such goods at two and three and four times the U.S. retail price. Price-gouging was a hard habit to break, apparently. Comparable Mexican goods remained less expensive and overpriced. Many Mexicans, enthralled with being able to buy imported goods for the first time legally, bought them even though they were obviously quite dear.

Strangely, some foreign goods did not appear at all. Maybe Mexican businesses hadn't yet awakened to the profit possibilities of imports. Maybe foreign companies thought Mexico was too poor a market to warrant the effort. Whatever the cause, you just couldn't buy some things in Mexico, even though they were widely available elsewhere. I remember checking prices in late 1987 on portable computers, one of the hottest business and consumer items in the United States at the time. I found that only IBM was offering such a computer in Mexico. It had just appeared. It was a made-in-Mexico version of its clunky "convertible" model, not an import. In the United States, IBM had encountered keen competition from Toshiba, Zenith, and other portable-computer manufacturers. It had had to drop its U.S. price on the portable to about $1,500. Occasionally it offered it at $895 on sale. But in Mexico, its portable cost $2,750 and was offered in a less capable version than the one available in the United States. By the time I left Mexico in mid-1988, no other portables had appeared to drive this price down or to force introduction of an up-to-date model.

I found the same pattern with other products. Italian wines, generally never before available in Mexico, appeared in 1987. But they sold at three and four times what they could be purchased for at retail outlets in the United States. Legally imported Snickers bars appeared in early 1988. But they sold for 1,900 pesos ($.85) at a time when U.S. supermarkets sold them at three for $.99. I saw similar high prices charged for U.S. plastic baby bottles, compact discs, Fisher-Price toys, and hundreds of other desirable items. Such prices were hard to explain, since the maximum tariff on most imported items had been reduced from 100 percent to about 20 percent. Some merchants insisted they had to charge high prices because imported goods were being bought in small quantities and took a long time to sell. It is true that the market for such items was small in Mexico, where half the workers make only the minimum wage. That did not explain, however, how merchants in Tepito were able to sell such items for one third or one fourth the price found in major department stores and small shops.

The government noticed this price difference too. It openly encouraged Tepito merchants to end their criminal ways and become Mexico's leading, legal discount merchants. Obviously, the government wanted Tepito sellers to create price pressure on other Mexican businesses. Merchants, such as Luis Hernández, jumped into the fray. At first, the *fayuqueros* were more organized than the government. Luis and his son Victor took a 1987 trip to the U.S. border to buy some watches and other things. They had heard that the new post-GATT tariff on such watches was quite low—certainly a lot lower than the bribes they had always had to pay to customs agents, highway police, and city cops to get contraband goods from the Texas border back to Tepito. They tried to do things legally when they presented the watches to customs officials at Nuevo Laredo. But no one there had the new tariff books yet. They were forced to pay bribes just as in the old days.

By early 1988, Luis and Victor were able to pay the new tariffs at Nuevo Laredo. But the valid customs receipts they got did them little good when they were stopped by other Mexican officials as they drove back to Mexico City. Some who stopped them were police who refused to recognize the validity of legally imported goods. These officials had always received a bribe for letting *fayuca* through—sometimes railroad cars of *fayuca*. They did not want to lose their traditional source of income. Others were traffic cops who stopped them for not having the right truck transport license for a federal highway or for Mexico City streets. In either case the result was the same. Luis and Victor had to pay a bribe to get the goods back to Tepito, a bribe they tacked on to the price they charged customers for the imported goods.

When I talked with Luis in April 1988, he said he didn't think he'd ever be able to afford the special permits and license plates required to drive a truckload of imported goods from the border to Mexico City. But he was happy that at least local police wouldn't be able to harass him any more for selling *fayuca* in Tepito once he got the goods home. He was happy too that he'd have no more hassle with customs agents in Nuevo Laredo. Crossing the border wasn't going to be a problem either. In February 1988, Luis, based on his fame as one of the Children of Sánchez, had persuaded the U.S. embassy to issue him a permanent visa that allows him to travel to the U.S. border area to buy consumer goods. As long as Mexico City's department stores and small shops show no signs of developing a discount tradition—and in the spring of 1988 there were no immediate signs of that—he and other merchants in Tepito would be able to make a living, he told me, maybe even a very good living. Mexicans have not traditionally been educated, demanding shoppers, Luis noted. But a growing number were realizing that Tepito, despite the danger of being mugged, was a place where they could find bargains, legal bargains.

When I first met Luis in late 1986, his future was not so bright.

His U.S. visa had expired. He hadn't been able to renew it. Without it, he hadn't been able to cross the U.S. border legally, so he'd been forced to scrounge around Mexico for things to sell on commission. Furniture, real estate, antique jewelry—he sold whatever he could get his hands on. It was a time of personal turmoil, too. Luis's house, the house Oscar Lewis had made famous in his book, had been damaged in the twin earthquakes that had hit Mexico City in September 1985. It had taken City Hall nearly a year to get around to tearing Luis's damaged house down so it could build him a new one. I met him the week the bulldozer arrived.

While he waited for his new house, Luis, like all his neighbors, had nowhere to live. He moved in with Victor, at whose kitchen table I met and interviewed all the Children of Sánchez, except his sister Cristina, whom the family had lost track of. The government was supposed to deliver a new house to Luis by early 1987. Luis got his new house, though later than originally promised and at a substantially higher mortgage payment. The old house had carried a monthly payment of only 500 pesos, a ridiculously low sum that had been set when the peso was still a stable currency. These were times of austerity, however, City Hall officials said. Mortgage payments would have to rise with inflation. But payments would be kept to the equivalent of one third of the minimum wage, the wage most Mexicans earn. That, at least, is what the officials said. In the fall of 1987, not long after Luis and his family moved into his new house, his payment was 28,000 pesos a month ($17.00). By April 1988, it had jumped to 71,000 pesos a month ($31.50), or 150 percent more, while the minimum wage had increased only 43 percent.

Luis complained that the increase was just another indication of the impact of de la Madrid's austerity policies. Despite government efforts, inflation remained out of control, sapping what little wealth the poor had. In advance of the July 1988 presidential elections, the de la Madrid government had announced a new economic plan called the Pact of Economic Solidarity (PSE). It was supposed to freeze wages and prices and squeeze triple-digit inflation out of the economy. Later, wages would be indexed monthly to the inflation rate of a special market basket of items. What was in that basket was never made quite clear to Luis, he said. The peso-U.S. dollar exchange rate was frozen artificially too, at about 2,300 pesos to the dollar, even though, under normal economic rules, the difference between U.S. and Mexican inflation rates warranted a continued devaluation of the peso. There is little doubt that wages were kept down under the new plan. Inflation went down, too, at least the inflation of things in that mysterious market basket. But the prices Luis and other Mexicans paid didn't seem to be holding quite as well, he complained.

"Look," said Luis, "the plan is a trick. When the elections are over, prices are going to go up. Everyone knows that. My housing payment will probably be five hundred thousand pesos by then. The PSE is just election-year politics. It does nothing to deal with inflation—except to make it worse."

Luis was no trained economist. But as a street merchant for nearly thirty years, he had an innate sense about the economy.

"We all know what has to be done to control inflation," he said. "You have to cut [government] spending. That means the price of gasoline will go up. It's still subsidized, you know. The price of many things must go up. Prices have to get realistic, even though that's going to be very, very painful.

"It would help if the government would stop corruption. That causes inflation too. But we don't expect miracles. They have made a valiant effort to moralize the police. You can see some of it around here. The police don't bother us as much as they used to. But the police have to eat. They have families. They don't earn very much. What are you going to do when you have to choose between hunger and morality? The answer is obvious."

Luis was skeptical whether de la Madrid's PSE plan would ever solve Mexico's problems of inflation, unemployment, and the foreign debt. But he did think Mexico's economic future would be quite different because of de la Madrid. It would be different because of GATT. Foreign trade was something Luis knew about. As a *fayuquero,* Luis had been in foreign trade all his adult life, you might say. With all the new imports coming in, he said, either Mexican companies would have to produce comparable items and sell them at competitive prices, or Mexicans would wind up buying mostly foreign goods. If Mexican goods got competitive, Mexican businesses would prosper, maybe even become modern. If foreign goods won out, though, many Mexican companies would go bankrupt. Whatever happened, the face of Mexico was going to change. De la Madrid had rolled the dice. Everyone was waiting to see if they came up snake eyes or seven. It was still too early to tell which way it would go, Luis said. But based on what he had seen so far, he worried that foreign goods might dominate Mexican ones.

"We Mexicans have a prejudice against Mexican goods," he said. "Something that says 'imported' has a certain *categoría* ["class"] to it. People want the foreign product, especially if it is for a gift." Besides, he said, Mexican businesses were spoiled, resistant to change, and more than a little inexperienced in the ways of the world. Maybe they'd wake up; maybe they wouldn't.

Did he think, I asked, that Mexicans could ever do what the Japanese had done? The Japanese, I reminded him, had changed the meaning of "made in Japan" from cheapness and shoddy quality to a symbol of high-priced, quality merchandise.

"I don't know," he said. "They [Mexican companies] have quite a challenge. They've never had to work hard before. I don't know if they can do it. Some probably think they can get the next government to quit GATT and go back to the old ways. You see their complaints about GATT every day in the newspapers. Whatever happens, it's going to be very interesting to watch."

· 10 ·

The *Pepenador*

The Santa Fe garbage dump is no more, and therein lies a story. For me, the story begins on a personal note. Santa Fe was where my garbage went after the rumbling behemoths of the city garbage service picked it up. But I did not discover the story of Santa Fe by following the trucks. I followed my nose.

What little wind there is in the Valley of Mexico, where Mexico City and its suburbs are located, prevails from the northwest. That meant that the wind generally blew away from my house toward the thousands of tons of crud suspended in the valley's polluted air each day. But every once in a while, the wind would turn around and blow toward me. The first time it did, I noticed not only noxious auto-exhaust fumes but a terrible stench. I asked someone what that horrible smell was. "That," I was told, "is Santa Fe."

The smell alone was enough to draw even the mildly curious out to Santa Fe. But my first visit to the dump to end all dumps was made for professional, not personal, reasons. In September 1985, while I was reporting on the aftermath of the two killer earthquakes that had hit Mexico City that month, I discovered that much of the rubble was being trucked out to Santa Fe. I had heard that scavengers who worked the dump often made a good living recycling odd bits of garbage. I thought it might be a good story if someone was benefiting from a disaster that had inflicted so much misery.

I drove out to Santa Fe one weekend, although some friends had warned me that the local denizens of the dump had just beaten up a Mexican reporter. They hadn't liked what his newspaper had written about them. I had a hostile reception, too. My car was surrounded by a knot of scavengers who apparently did not want me to see what was going on inside the dump. I managed to persuade them to let me talk to their leader so he could decide if I would be allowed to stay. The leader, Pablo Téllez Falcón, was drunk as a skunk, so I talked to one of his lieutenants, Felipe Castillo. He said I could come back in a few days when "Don Pablo" might be feeling better.

Santa Fe sat atop the same ridge of valley foothills as my house. But it was higher up and afforded a more spectacular view of the valley and the mountains and volcanoes that ring it. At least it was a great view on that handful of days each year when one could see the valley and peaks through the smoke, ozone, and suspended particulates that made it the most polluted urban landscape in the world. Santa Fe itself presented a view of a different sort. It was a vast tableau of garbage. Sprawled across 150 acres of land was garbage as far as the eye could see. In man-made landfill pits, noisy bulldozers pushed mountains of garbage from here to there. What garbage was not in these manufactured canyons had been tossed down the sides of every available hill and slope, as if garbage-truck drivers had had to dump their loads in a hurry, like drug traffickers spotlighted by the authorities. Garbage was strewn along the dusty access roads that led to the heart of Santa Fe. In fact, the road into Santa Fe had been built on garbage. My car, I was told, was sitting on about 230 feet of garbage, the accumulated detritus of nearly five decades of dumping at Santa Fe.

The shocker was that some 2,500 people were living on all that garbage. By day, they scurried over mounds of newly arrived refuse like hungry ants at a picnic. By night, they slept on compacted garbage that had provided a steady income for three generations of scavengers. At first, it was hard to imagine that anything of value could be found amid this gargantuan collection of trash. I looked and saw rotted fruit, cracked eggshells, fetid meat, crushed milk cartons, crumpled aluminum foil, broken soft-drink bottles, discarded clothes, half-eaten tortillas, split banana peels, dried chicken bones, and soiled paper diapers. The trained eye of the scavengers looked and saw money. Lots of money.

In Mexico, scavengers are called *pepenadores*. In Mexico's version of Spanish, *'pepenar'* means to scavenge or pick up things that are scattered about. That's what the *pepenadores* did. Their name derives from the nahuatl (Aztec) word *pepena*. Thus, *pepenador* is a term used almost exclusively in Mexico. The brand of garbage picking in Mexico is pretty singular too.

In the 1940s, a few families, desperate to earn a living, surreptitiously moved into Santa Fe and a few other city dumps and claimed them as their own. They were the lowest of the low. They were hoping to find a little something of value that had been tossed out by the more fortunate. No one rushed in to dispute their claim. Garbage-dump squatters don't have many rivals. Eventually, people got used to them. City officials, who did virtually nothing to treat the capital's solid wastes, came to realize that the *pepenadores* performed a service. They sorted out trash that could be recycled: glass, aluminum foil, paper, cardboard, copper, bent steel rods, and the like. What could not be used the *pepenadores* would burn to make room for the next day's waste. A modus vivendi developed. In a crude way, the *pepenadores* became part of the establishment. They even joined the ruling political party and became stalwarts.

Over the years, the *pepenadores* developed an intricate system for deciding who had the right to sort out the various types of garbage and who would get to sell it. Mexicans say a "mafia" came to control the garbage business in the valley. Certainly the garbage men who came to my door had all the characteristics of mobsters. If I wanted my garbage picked up, I had to give them a "tip." No tip, no garbage pickup. But I found the *pepenadores'* system more feudal than criminal. The *pepenadores* are like a medieval clan. Their rights to scavenge are based on heredity. With few exceptions, one has to be born into a *pepenador* family to become a *pepenador*. Like the Middle Ages, those who hold power within this tight-knit clan are the meanest, most ruthless, most cunning of the lot. The baddest of them all was Rafael Gutiérrez Moreno, who in his time ruled with varying power over some fifteen thousand scavengers at seven open-air garbage dumps in the city. His subjects and the Mexican press called him the King of the Garbage Pickers. He used the political clout of his clan—and the group's absolute loyalty to the ruling Institutional Revolutionary Party (PRI)—to become a member of the national legislature. In the process, he became a very rich man. He took in an estimated sixty million pesos (fifty-five thousand dollars) a month, according to court records at the time of his murder in March 1987.

Gutiérrez, who was born and died in a city garbage dump, acted like the king he was. He left a legend that is the stuff of soap operas and Balzac novels. He died in spectacular fashion too. He was murdered in his sleep at about 2:00 A.M. on March 19, 1987. At the time of his death, he had ruled the *pepenadores* for about twenty-five years. The courts found that his onetime common-law wife, Martha García González, had hired Juan Carlos Roque Sáenz to kill Gutiérrez after he had informed García that he was going to take another common-law wife. García promised Roque Sáenz six million pesos ($5,500) for the job, giving him 300,000 pesos as a down payment. After the murder, there was a mad scramble for the fortune that Gutiérrez had left. A strongbox was found in a sauna at his lavish home at the Santa Catarina dump. Accounts differs as to its contents. But it contained as much as 3.5 billion pesos' ($3.2 million) worth of loot, according to another of the king's wives, Guillermina de la Torre Malváez. She made an attempt to become the queen of the garbage pickers after Gu-itiérrez's death created a power vacuum. She cited the twenty-two years she had lived with the king—and the eight children she had borne him—as basis for her claim. Gutiérrez was also thought to have had bank accounts in the United States and Europe with other money he collected as king of the garbage pickers. It's hard to say how much Gutiérrez was really worth at his death. But the squabble over his riches set off a probate fight that kept the Mexican press buzzing for months. Scores of children came forward to claim they were Gutiérrez's sons or daughters. The courts recognized twenty-seven children as legitimate heirs. Residents of the Santa Catarina dump, where Gutiérrez had reigned, insisted that he and his many wives had fathered more than a hundred children on his way to achieving a personal goal of 180 offspring. If local lore can be believed, Gutiérrez also exercised *droit du seigneur,* sometimes demanding that the wives and daughters of Santa Catarina's *pepenadores* be sent to him to spend the night in his bed.

If Gutiérrez was the king of the *pepenadores*, one of his dukes was Don Pablo Téllez Falcón, whose realm was Santa Fe, just as it had been his father's before him. When I came back to Santa Fe after my first, unsuccessful visit, Don Pablo, a short, heavyset man with eyes like coin slots, was indeed sober. Once I was announced, Don Pablo, just up from a post-lunch nap, came out to greet me. He was still wiping the sleep out of his eyes as he emerged from the darkness of his shack into the brilliant sunshine of late afternoon. Don Pablo took a seat on a tree stump under a canvas awning that jutted out from the side of his ramshackle house. As I explained what I wanted, he stroked the enormous head of one of his dogs, an aggressive female mutant malamute. Don Pablo got very testy at my questions. I had it all wrong, he said. All the *pepenadores* were getting from the earthquake sites were huge clumps of concrete and twisted steel that had once been the floors or walls of now-destroyed buildings.

"You can't sell those things to anyone," said Don Pablo, who said the rubble was being used as a base for a new soccer field that the *pepenadores* were building on top of sifted garbage. Don Pablo said he wasn't surprised that I thought the way I did. *Pepenadores* are very misunderstood characters in Mexican society. They are the butt of exploitational newspaper stories that depict them as some kind of garbage-eating savages. Just because *pepenadores* lived on garbage amid blankets of flies, hundreds of junkyard dogs, scores of bloated pigs, and the odd defecating horse or cow, did not mean they were without dignity. *Pepenadores* had built their homes with their own hands. They had a grammar school, sports facilities, electricity, and community water facilities. They voted regularly. They made an above-average wage, although no one got rich, Don Pablo was quick to point out.

I looked around. I certainly did not see wealth, but I didn't see much dignity either. I saw dirt-floored homes with walls made of flattened oil drums and roofs of corrugated metal and sheets of turquoise garbage bags. On my previous visit I had seen a little smudged-faced urchin, who had offered me a choice of fruit or vegetables from a sack of dirt-encrusted bananas, oranges, apples, and carrots that someone down in the valley had thrown out a few days before. I saw people coughing and wheezing, the effects of breathing in the contaminants that so much garbage generated. I saw desperation.

Don Pablo saw something different. He saw decades of survival and a way of life. At the time, the members of his group, which he described as a social organization, were making between 1,300 and 1,500 pesos a day. That was slightly more than the 1,260-peso-a-day ($2.65) minimum wage that the majority of workers in the valley were making at the time.

"Sometimes it's more, of course," chirped Castillo, "like when you find a gold medal or something valuable in the garbage."

Finds of treasure weren't occurring much anymore. Since mid-1982, Mexico had been gripped by an economic crisis. Even the quality of the garbage had gone downhill. People, particularly the maids of the city, were picking over the garbage before it got to Santa Fe. The garbage from the valley's rich areas was the worst, said Castillo.

"It seems all we get from them is grass clippings," he complained.

To compound the *pepenadores'* problems, Mexico was at last coming out of the Dark Ages in its attitude toward the environment. A small band of *ecologistas,* or environmental activists, was demanding that the federal and city governments do something about the pollution that was choking the Mexico City area. At the top of their list was shutting down Santa Fe, or at least modernizing its operations through sanitary procedures or closed-oven burning. Bacteria and parasites were proliferating in the rank putrefaction that could be found all across the mammoth dump. Germs or viruses were carried into the valley by millions of fleshy black flies that fed on the garbage. Other poisons were carried into the atmosphere by the winds that blew across the site. Spontaneous fires spewed infectious material and acrid smoke into the air, creating an acute health danger for many of the valley's eighteen million residents. The health of the *pepenadores* was a scandal, too.

"These people don't understand us," Don Pablo told me. "If we had to burn the garbage or do what they say, we couldn't make a living. We need all the garbage we can get. Garbage is our life."

Don Pablo and the *pepenadores* did not win that fight. With orders from President Miguel de la Madrid and Mexico City mayor Ramón Aguirre, it was announced in December 1986 that Santa Fe would be closed. Santa Fe was the last of the city's open-air dumps to be shut. But shut it was.

In March of 1987, Don Pablo's *pepenadores* began working a new landfill site, just up the foothills from their old home. It is called Los Prados de la Montaña, or "the Meadows of the Mountain," which sounds a lot nicer than it looks. Los Prados is a gaping seventy-foot-deep hole, excavated out of the side of a mountain and spread out over about fifty-five acres. It is expected that it will be filled up in about five years, if the current delivery of 2,500 tons of garbage a day continues. Then the *pepenadores* will have to move even farther outside the valley to the Barranca de Tlapizahuaya, a deep gorge whose holding capacity is supposed to suffice for what city officials call the medium term.

At Los Prados, which can't be seen from the valley, many of the old *pepenadores'* rules are the same. Certain families have the right to sort out aluminum foil or cardboard containers or glass bottles. Certain families have the right to buy bags of such items and to sell them in bulk to recyclers. But other rules are different. Open fires, for example, are banned. The garbage is not allowed to sit and rot as a festering point for flies and disease. Each night, bulldozers level out what is left of the day's trash after the *pepenadores* have picked over it. The refuse is covered with a special type of dirt that packs well and is supposed to provide an impermeable seal between one day's garbage and that of the next. If the garbage graders do their job well, the contaminants of Los Prados's stored solid wastes will never again seep into the valley's underground aquifer as pollutants did for some fifty years at Santa Fe.

The *pepenadores* have to leave when the bulldozers arrive. They have from 7:00 A.M. until 7:00 P.M. to collect what they can. No longer can they live on the garbage. Across the road, in an area called Tlayapaca, the city has built modular homes for them, much like the temporary housing that thousands of victims got after the 1985 earthquakes. The new scavengers' village is to have regular electric, water and sewage service, its own market, a grammar school, a children's garden, a medical dispensary, and recreation areas.

•   •   •

In March of 1988, the government instituted a new get-tough environmental law aimed at curbing polluting businesses and cars. The government, in the midst of a presidential campaign, was doing a lot of crowing about how much they had accomplished to clean up the environment. Their critics were expressing a lot of doubts. I had not been back to Santa Fe since my talk with Don Pablo after the 1985 earthquakes. I thought the reported crackdown on Santa Fe might be a good indication of how serious the government had really gotten about the environment.

When I arrived at Santa Fe, I found that most of the pitiful shacks in which the *pepenadores* had lived for generations were still standing. However, the open-air landfill sites that had so alarmed environmentalists were gone, covered over with the special dirt that city officials said would protect people from the leagues of garbage below. The city was building a park on top of the new dirt. Apolonia Martínez de Correa's two-room shanty was still standing, but not for long, she said. The government had told her she and her family of ten children would have to move out in about two months. She didn't know where she'd be going. Her husband had hereditary rights to buy used milk cartons and other cardboard items from *pepenadores* who extracted such things from garbage at Los Prados. But the family didn't make enough money to buy one of the 510 new modular homes that the government was building at the Tlayapaca site. Mrs. Martínez de Correa had been told that a new house there would cost between two and three million pesos ($833 to $1,325). Her husband paid her and each of their children a weekly salary of 50,000 pesos. That was a little more than the 8,000-pesos-a-day mandatory minimum wage that the majority of workers in the valley made for a six-day week in 1988. But 50,000 pesos a week did not make one rich. The dirt-floor Correa house had only a little kitchen and one room where all twelve Correas slept, ate, and socialized. There was electric service, but no bathroom. Water had to be hauled by plastic bucket from a community tap toward the center of the *pepenadores'* village.

Two million pesos for a new house was the equivalent of forty weeks' pay for any of the Correa clan. If they could save all the money the entire family earned in a week, they could come up with that sum in about three and a half weeks. But that, of course, was impossible. The family needed what it earned just to survive. The Correa family was better off than most in that respect. Everyone was working. The national unemployment rate was about 18 percent of the work force, so there was that to be grateful for. But not everyone was in good health. Mrs. Martínez de Correa said she was having trouble breathing. Maybe it was all those years of inhaling garbage fumes, she said. One of her little boys had a heart problem, too. Even with the family's above-average finances, there wasn't much she could do for him.

By birth, everyone in the family had the right to work at Los Prados and at any landfill site the government might open later. But where was the family going to live, asked Mrs. Martínez de Correa, a plump woman with graying streaks in her jet-black hair. "My family has been here for a very long time—fifty years," she said. "Where will we go?"

By her count, some 208 *pepenador* families had already moved out of Santa Fe. Some had moved away from Mexico City. They were looking for new jobs elsewhere in the country. They would be *pepenadores* no more. Others had moved to a poor neighborhood called San Antonio. It was farther from Los Prados than the model village at Tlayapaca. But people could afford the housing. As they had so many years before, they could build their own homes on cheap land. Maybe she would go to San Antonio, too. But right now, she said, all she was thinking about was sorting out milk cartons. She and her brood had bought bags of such cartons from fellow *pepenadores* earlier in the day at eighty pesos a kilo, less than two cents a pound. By day's end they had to flatten the cartons out so they were ready for the recycler who would come and pay them eighty pesos a kilo plus a tidy profit that financed the family's wages.

"We have no plans," she said of the inevitable move from Santa Fe. "We will have to go somewhere. I don't know where. Right now we are working day to day."

It had been an act of political courage for the government to bring the curtain down on the long saga of Santa Fe. There had, of course, been political pressure to do so from do-gooder groups such as the Mexican Ecological Movement and the Group of 100, a collection of poets, artists, writers, musicians, and other Mexicans who had grown tired of breathing poisoned air. But the ruling PRI party, which has been synonymous with the government since 1929, doesn't have much of a record of responding to public complaints. It had shown even less inclination to turn on a loyal political ally such as the *pepenadores,* who had always voted for PRI candidates as the price for informal government recognition of their squatter status.

The action against Santa Fe was a little surprising. The government had been slow, even resistant, about doing anything about Mexico's undeniable environmental problems. Even when it could deny the problems no longer, it argued that environmentalists had exaggerated them. Then something unexpected happened. In the winter of 1985–86, Mexico City suffered the worst thermal inversions in its history. Since the 1970s, these aberrational layers of upper-level warm air had kept a lid on all the contaminants that the capital's cars and factories had put into the cool, low-level air of valley mornings. But the government had always been able to rely on a rising morning temperature to lift the inversion before noon. That winter, however, the inversions stayed in place, putting an airtight lid on the bowl-shaped valley and creating a pressure cooker of pollution. People with enough money took their children to the countryside. Marchers took to the streets. The government realized it had not just an environmental problem on its hands but a political one. Slowly and begrudgingly it began to act. The federal environment ministry, known as SEDUE, began to issue daily reports on the level of the leading pollutant in each quadrant of the city, as well as for the downtown area. A rating of 0 to 50 for each pollutant was considered "Good"; 51 to 100 was "Fair"; 101 to 200 was "Poor" (100 was the internationally recognized tolerable maximum); 201 to 300 was "Very Poor"; and 301 to 500 was "Dangerous." From the beginning of the program, a rating of 50 or under was very rare anywhere in the city, and 100 to 200 was a typical reading during the May–October rainy season. The level would have been higher, but daily deluges in the rainy season washed much of the pollution out of the air, leaving its corrosive residue on people, houses, and cars. In winter, when particularly cold morning air sometimes kept thermal inversions in place later than normal, one could regularly see readings of 200 to 300. At that level, environmentalists warned that people should not exercise outdoors. They said people with respiratory problems—and there were hundreds of thousands of them in the valley—should stay indoors. That was fine for some, but many had to go outside to work in order to eat.

The government told the public that the valley's 2.5 million cars, most of them badly in need of a tune-up and few equipped with emission-control equipment, were the main culprits in creating the most polluted environment in the world. It announced that Pemex, the state-owned oil company, would offer a new low-lead gasoline to replace the leaded regular gasoline that Mexico had used for years, notwithstanding the widespread switch elsewhere to unleaded regular. A new gas, "Nova Plus," did replace the old regular gas. But a strange thing happened. The pollution got worse. Ozone levels soared. Environmentalists had the explanation. After independent studies of samples of the new gasoline, it was discovered that it still contained a lot more lead than U.S. unleaded gasoline—and a lot more hydrocarbons. Hydrocarbons were added so Mexican cars could still run smoothly without the high-performance lead additive. But the hydrocarbons also produced ozone. If the hydrocarbons had been processed through a catalytic converter, ozone levels would have been lower, environmentalists said. The government insisted there was no real proof of this. It refused to provide environmentalists with details about the new gasoline's formula. It also refused to require catalytic converters on cars until 1988—and then only on new-model cars. One reason why the government dragged its feet on emission controls may have been that catalytic converters would send car prices up, a politically unpopular act. But the government may also have been concerned about whether Pemex could supply enough truly unleaded gasoline for Mexican cars. "Nova Extra," an unleaded gasoline made available for tourists who drove cars with catalytic converters in Mexico, was often in short supply. At times, it had to be imported from abroad, an embarrassment for a country that celebrates the 1938 nationalization of Mexican oil fields as a national holiday.

The government seemed to be more concerned about the reaction of Mexicans as car owners than Mexicans as beings who breathe. There may have been some political sense to this. Although pollution levels are published daily in Mexico City newspapers, more city residents read comic books than newspapers. Most people get their news from the radio, which reports little about the environment and does not give pollution readings. With such limited dissemination of information about pollution, it's not surprising that Mexicans have not developed much of an environmental consciousness. The sad part is that if they knew what pollutants such as lead were doing to the mental and physical development of their children, they would be enraged. Maybe that explains why the government-influenced press doesn't tell them.

Mexicans do know about cars, however. A car is a symbol of

social status and, in some cases, the difference in whether one gets to work or not. Just as their U.S. counterparts had, Mexican environmentalists ran up against this love affair with cars in efforts to clean up Mexico City's air. One campaign in particular was a fiasco. Under the slogan *Un día sin auto* ("One day without a car"), environmentalists set up stands all over town to get capital residents to give up use of their cars one day a week in hopes of reducing pollution levels. The campaign goal was to sign up half a million of the valley's 2.5 million car owners. About 400,000 *Un día sin auto* bumper stickers were handed out. But program officials estimated that only about 75,000 persons put them on their cars. And no one knew how many drivers had actually reduced the use of their cars. The program also got negative feedback from testy Mexican car owners, including an outburst of bumper stickers that read: "I drive every day, I pollute every day, and I don't give a damn."

Notwithstanding a generally listless public concern about the environment, what criticism there was did rise notably as the 1985–86 thermal inversion crisis became apparent to everyone. President Miguel de la Madrid apparently sensed trouble and moved to head it off. In addition to ordering the low-lead gasoline, de la Madrid, who had created Mexico's first Environment Ministry, fired his environment minister. The minister was already under a cloud because of charges of corruption. De la Madrid issued a twenty-one-point statement of plans for improving the environment. City buses were to be outfitted with less-polluting engines. Car owners were to be asked to submit to voluntary emission testing. In mid-1988, testing became mandatory for some used cars, after complaints from environmentalists about the ineffectiveness of voluntary testing. The government said it would close open-air dumps, such as Santa Fe. As part of a plan of decentralization, some government agencies and some of the worst-polluting factories would be moved out of town. Some polluting cement factories were closed. Others factories, including a Pemex refinery north of Mexico City, were forced to switch to less-polluting natural gas as their chief operating fuel. Government workers planted twelve million new trees in the valley to create more "green lung" areas. Most of the trees died.

Despite all these efforts, the following winter the pollution seemed worse. Undaunted, de la Madrid's new environment minister, Manuel Camacho Solís, said in January 1987 that the government would take one hundred more steps to improve the environment. But when the rainy season began that May, pollution had gotten so bad that even the daily deluges did not help. The steely gray that Mexico City children had come to think of as the natural color of the sky had become a permanent fixture.

The government had clearly awakened to environmental problems. But in many cases it talked a much better game than it played. Camacho promised to institute an emergency drill to close down Mexico City factories or force them to reduce operations if pollutions levels got too bad. In 1987, as far as he was concerned, that was never necessary. Not until February of 1988, when some pollutant levels hit 298, did the government shut some factories—and then only for a few days. Not surprisingly, when the government's self-described, get-tough environmental law went into effect in March 1988, many critics didn't have much faith in it. Its requirement of mandatory emissions testing for passenger cars would be undercut by Mexico's tradition of bribing police to avoid laws that cost too much to obey, they said. The law's required fining or shutdown of polluting factories would be effective only when the government got tough with the employer most responsible for pollution: itself.

Many of the worst polluters among the valley's thirty thousand factories belonged to state-owned industries. That was a key part of the problem. The government could, of course, shut down its own factories without the legal fight it might encounter from private enterprises. But to do so would put thousands of people on the streets at a time when the crippled Mexican economy already wasn't able to create enough jobs for those who wanted them. One third of all the jobs in Mexico were in the valley. Alfonso Ciprés Villareal, president of the Mexican Ecological Movement, said it best when he told me: "The truth is, there is more interest in Mexico in the economy than in the environment. A man would rather have a job in a polluted city than have no job at all."

That was the crux of it. Cleaning up the environment would cost money. Americans had discovered that distasteful fact in 1970 when the U.S. environmental movement got off the ground. U.S. businesses had dragged their feet when cleanups were demanded. U.S. firms had argued that cleaning up the environment was a luxury that would cost jobs and add little to production.

Mexico was going through the same process in the late 1980s. The difference was that Mexico had a lot less money to spend on cleanup and a lot more people out of work.

The magnitude of Mexico's environmental problems was greater, too. Mexico City, which some local wags called "Make-Sicko City," was the worst of all. No one had to tell you about how bad the air pollution was. All you had to do was breathe. Water was wasted at an alarming rate. The city, which drew much of its water from underground aquifers, was sinking a few inches each year. Uneven sidewalks and sunken building floors could be found all over the capital. And yet home owners or their maids continued their mindless ritual of watering down their sidewalks each morning, even in the rainy season. Noise pollution from unmuffled cars and buses was beyond belief in some neighborhoods. It was a key contributor to a widespread, environmentally caused depression that people jokingly called "chilango neurosis," after the nickname used for residents of the capital. Acid rain was killing what few trees were left. Land use had become so saturated that the city had run out of places to bury people.

While the enormity of problems was greater in the capital, the immature, uninformed, self-destructive environmental attitude that one found there was hardly the exception. In Tijuana, one found slow-moving progress in dealing with acute water pollution. It plagued not only the one million residents of that huge, growing border town but San Diego as well. The attitude could be seen in the state of Veracruz, where the white-elephant Laguna Verde nuclear power plant was being foisted on the people, even though environmentalists warned the plant was unsafe and could become the next Chernobyl. One saw it in the apocalyptic skies above the Pemex refineries of Minatitlán, on the Gulf of Mexico. It could be seen in the disappearing rain forests of Chiapas and in the deforestation of thousands of acres of Mexican trees by poor people who needed wood to heat or cook, or by unscrupulous land developers. Wondrous species of fish and fowl were becoming extinct with barely a whimper. In Mexico's farm fields, *campesinos* were using DDT, Paraquat, and other pesticides banned throughout the world. In factories across the country, workers were being maimed or killed because no one cared about industrial safety or the proper disposal of toxic wastes.

With this type of attitude, it wasn't surprising that Mexican environmentalists had few positive things to say about the government's environmental performance. But they did praise the program to wipe out Santa Fe. Some doubted whether the dirt used to cover the garbage was really impermeable. Others lamented the health hazards that *pepenadores* still faced by working in garbage all day without the benefit of even a simple paper face-mask. They pointed out that thousands of tons of garbage were never making it to sanitized landfills such as Los Prados, that thousands of small, clandestine, open-air dumps still existed in the valley, that enormous amounts of garbage just sat rotting at the curb. But what had been done at Santa Fe, the most notorious and obnoxious of the city's dumps, they said, was impressive. Maybe, just maybe, some optimists began to say, Mexico was growing up environmentally.

I wondered what Don Pablo might have to say about all this. I went to see him the same week I talked to Mrs. Martínez de Correa. He was running a little late, the guard at the gate of the Los Prados landfill told me. I waited, and around 10 A.M. a garbage truck pulled up with Don Pablo in the passenger's seat. Dressed in dirty tan pants, an army fatigue jacket, and a baseball cap, he slid out of the truck and landed with an unsteady plop on the ground. He was drunk again. I introduced myself and reminded him of our interview in 1985. I told him I wanted to talk with him about what had happened to his *pepenadores* since our chat.

"I'm not talking to anyone, you *pinche cabrón* ["fucking cuckold"]," said Don Pablo, weaving a tipsy path toward the landfill's new office complex. Don Pablo never made it to the office. He was just too drunk. Two officials of the city's solid-waste office, who had taken the place of Felipe Castillo and Don Pablo's other lieutenants, put Don Pablo's slack arms around their shoulders and carried him back to the truck. Hector Samano, a city engineer who had become one of the new bosses of the area's garbage operations, told the driver to take Don Pablo home.

Samano was clearly nervous that I had come to Los Prados. He didn't want to talk much about what had happened to Santa Fe. I came back a couple of times, but he kept coming up with new excuses as to why he couldn't give me an interview. Los Prados was clearly an improvement over Santa Fe. Mrs. Martínez de Correa had summed up the difference nicely: "There are a lot less flies." But Samano didn't want to tout the government's achievement. I thought I knew why. To do so, he would have to talk about the fact that, slowly but surely, the government was putting an end to the embarrassing existence of the *pepenadores*.

A year before, the death of the king of the *pepenadores* had given the government the opening it needed to move against the ever-loyal *pepenador* clan. Through his political clout, the king had blocked the government's plan to close Santa Fe and other polluting dumps. His death ended the political protection he had so long given the *pepenadores*. It also cleared the way for environmentalists to push for a program of supermarket-based collection centers where people can sell the cardboard, glass, plastic, and other items that had so long been the lifeblood of the *pepenadores*. To me, all this spelled the end of an era. But no one seemed to want to talk about it.

· 11 ·

The *Campesino*

A few pieces of the puzzle are still missing. But most of the facts are known. Late in 1987, Francisco Arias, the mayor of Independencia, gave his mandatory state-of-the-city report. And all hell broke loose.

The cause of the commotion was money and, more basically, land. As became evident from the mayor's report, a lot of money was missing from the treasury of the *ejido,* the communal farm organization that manages hundreds of acres of land around Independencia, a tiny hamlet in southern Mexico. How much money was missing is in dispute. Some of the *campesinos* (peasant farmers) say it was about 200 million pesos ($115,000). Others say it was less. Everyone said the mayor took it. Some *campesinos* said they had proof. Others relied on rumor. In rural areas, that's often enough to convict. Persuaded by one or the other, about a thousand *campesinos* marched en masse on December 4, 1987, down Independencia's dusty streets to Mayor Arias's office. They demanded a meeting and an accounting. Conveniently, the mayor was out of town. Infuriated, the *campesinos* seized the city hall and vowed not to leave until the mayor appeared. The mayor's spokesman said he would call for a negotiator to come from the state capital to resolve the matter. A negotiator was not acceptable, the protesters yelled back. They wanted the mayor.

The mayor did come the next day. But he brought with him about seventy armed members of the state attorney general's police. They arrived in large vehicles. According to testimony of many of the *campesinos,* the police came out of the vehicles shooting. The official version was different. The attorney general said the first shot was fired by the *campesinos,* although no gun was ever produced. State authorities said the police were just responding to unwarranted civilian violence. They had to restore social peace, they said. What is not disputed is that during forty-five minutes of chaos, raw fear, and bullets in the air, four peasant farmers fell dead. One policeman died, too. Some said he was the victim of cross fire from his colleagues. The death toll eventually rose to eight, but that count took a few more weeks to become official. For those weeks, the additional four were listed merely as "disappeared."

In Mexico, "disappear" can be a transitive verb, a deadly part of speech. Police can "disappear" someone. They make him disappear. That is what happened to Abelardo Velasco, who was in his forty-ninth year when police shoved him and three other demonstrators into a truck and drove off after the shooting had stopped and the gunsmoke had cleared. In the days that followed the bloody encounter in Independencia, there was no immediate word about the fate of the four men. Independencia is a remote farming outpost in the south of Chiapas, the most southern and backward of Mexico's states. People die or are tortured in such places with little notice from the rest of the country. Maybe that's why the mayor made no apologies for the extreme force that had been used that scorching afternoon. In fact, no one in authority said anything. Nothing at all.

A few days later, three more *campesinos* were killed in another Chiapas town in another dispute over land and the money it produces. In the edgy atmosphere that followed, other long-festering complaints boiled over. *Campesinos* seized ten other city halls. The local bishop finally mobilized reaction against state authorities. Some members of left-wing opposition parties made public demands for the resignation of the governor and the attorney general. Finally, three weeks after the Independencia incident, a member of the federal chamber of deputies came to visit the families of the dead and the missing. He said everything humanly possible was being done to find Abelardo Velasco and the three others. If, God forbid, they should turn up dead, he said, the government would, of course, provide "humanitarian aid" to their survivors as it was to the families of those already dead. He mentioned a figure: one million pesos ($571).

Maybe it was coincidence, but a few days later, after a somber Christmas, scratching dogs broke the surface of shallow graves not far away from Independencia near the El Progreso communal farm and found four bodies. Authorities at first refused to admit that the remains were those of the missing men, despite positive identifications by their families. Later, the attorney general's office—the office whose police had come to Independencia—began referring to the wives of the four missing men as "the widows." Eventually a man from the office delivered not one million but two million pesos to each of them.

"A *campesino's* life is worth more than that," said Abelardo Velasco's widow, Romelia.

"Two million is what you get if you kill a dog," said Abel Espinosa López, who sat in Romelia's modest home one cloudless May day, talking bitterly about the needless death of his father, Adolfo, another of those "disappeared."

By that May, just five months after her husband had died, Romelia had already spent some of the money the government had given her. It was hush money as far as she was concerned. But she took it. She needed it to farm the three hectares (7.5 acres) of land that she and Abelardo had once tilled side by side. Under the rules of the *ejido*, Romelia did not own the land. The *ejido* did. But she did have the right to cultivate those three hectares as long as her energy kept up. She could keep what profits she made. She wasn't sure how well she could farm the land without the strong back of Abelardo to help her. But farming was all she knew, so she took the government's money and spent it on fertilizer and seed for the spring planting. The money was enough, but just enough. There would be no extra for clothes or a better education for the four children she now had to rear alone.

Farming is an expensive proposition in Mexico, especially for the many peasant farmers such as Romelia who only have small plots of land. As government farm aid dwindles in times of economic crisis, farming is getting more expensive all the time. It was not supposed to be this way. That's what the 1910 Revolution was all about, was it not, asked Romelia as we talked in her two-room adobe hut under the baking, late-spring sun. Had not *campesinos* shed the majority of the blood in that violent upheaval? "Land and liberty" was the rallying cry of peasant leaders. Middle- and upper-class revolutionary leaders halfheartedly mouthed it too to keep *campesinos* in the fight against the dictatorship of Porfirio Díaz. They knew land was an emotional issue for *campesinos*, most of whom were Indians with a visceral attachment to land because of custom and history. They knew that most of that land had been taken from the peasants unjustly during the long decades of Díaz's rule. Three-and-a-half million poor Mexicans were landless when the revolution began. One percent of the population owned 97 percent of the land, thanks to Díaz's preferential policies. Half the land was owned by 835 families.

The revolution would change all that, the *campesinos* were told. A decree in 1915 promised to redistribute land to the peasants who had once owned it. The distribution went slowly, however. By 1930, only 6 percent of the land had been handed out. With the 1934 election of Lázaro Cárdenas, a president of the people, the parceling out finally began in earnest. Some forty-five million acres were given to the poor during his six-year term alone. Somewhere along the way, however, the idea of land reform went awry. The rhetoric continued. The *campesinos* and their progeny were still told they were the heirs of the revolution. But, more and more, they began to feel like its orphans.

Economics was partly the culprit. So was geography. In the 1940s and 1950s, Mexico was in the process of industrialization. It needed income. Mexico was still largely an agricultural nation. The most logical source of funds for new factories and infrastructure was revenue from agricultural exports. The small plots of land that *campesinos* typically got under revolutionary land reform were hardly suited to high production, however. Few such plots were farmed with tractors or other modern techniques. Hand planting and plows pulled by oxen were more common, and still are. Therefore, the government curbed its expropriation of large farms. With no drop in the fervor of its revolutionary rhetoric, it began offering arid, remote tracts to peasants with promises of future irrigation projects. It channeled scarce farm credit into big, existing agricultural enterprises as the quick fix it needed for sizable agricultural export revenues. The large farms flourished and showed production gains far in excess of the *ejido* lands of the peasants.

Peasants got non-arid land as well, but typically it was the worst available. And there wasn't enough of it to go around for the burgeoning *campesino* population. The size of *campesino* plots decreased. The average U.S. farm is about 430 acres. But two thirds of all Mexican farms are less than five hectares (12.5 acres), just like the farm that Abelardo Velasco's widow now tends. Though the plots became smaller, peasants' share of farm land grew from about 10 percent in 1930 to 50 percent in 1970, roughly their share today.

With such limits on land to be handed out, the number of landless peasants went up, not down. Out-of-control birth rates in the 1960s and 1970s created excess demand for land by poor Mexicans who believed the political rhetoric that told them that such land was their revolutionary right. By 1970, the number of peasants who did not have land had grown to 4.5 million—50 percent more than before the revolution. By the time President José López Portillo (1976–82) came to power, the government had to announce that it had run out of land to expropriate. In the future, said López Portillo's successor, Miguel de la Madrid, the government would only be able to hand out land that was not used properly by existing owners.

There wasn't much good land to begin with. The United States grabbed about half of Mexico, including much of its best agricultural land, after the 1847 Mexican-American War. Mexico was left with 192.3 million hectares (475 million acres), about one third of which is totally unusable for farming because of lack of water. Mexico has a six-month rainy season, but the rain often falls in the wrong places. Some of the rivers in Mexico flow through territory unsuited to cultivation. Only about a quarter of the cultivable land in Mexico gets enough water. In any given year, Mexican farmers plant only about seventeen million hectares of crop land, about a third of which has to be irrigated. Four out of ten years, Mexico is affected by drought, as it was in the early and late 1980s.

Campesinos, the majority of the Mexican population during the revolution, also found themselves a shrinking minority. Two thirds of Mexicans now live in cities, only a third in the *campo*, or "countryside." But those rural third, out of fear or loyalty, produce half the votes for the Institutional Revolutionary Party (PRI), which has ruled Mexico since revolutionary fighting ended in 1929. As much as anything, that political fact explains why Mexican agriculture is in such a mess these days. Politics, not economics or common sense, governs the way the government treats farming, especially peasant farming.

Politically motivated pricing and credit policies explain why Abelardo Velasco was clearing only three thousand pesos ($1.33) a day in a good year and eight hundred pesos ($.35) a day in a bad one before his death. The year he died was a bad farming year, said Abelardo's brother, Agustín, who netted eight hundred pesos a day in 1987.

"Eight hundred pesos buys a kilo [2.2 pounds] of beans," said Agustín, who noted that Abelardo could have made ten times that amount in Mexico City, and a hundred times as much as an undocumented worker in the United States if he had forsaken farming. But Abelardo did not forsake farming and had no plans to do so, said his wife, Romelia, even though the future hadn't looked any better than the past. In fact, it had looked worse.

Credit was getting tighter. When you could get loans, said Agustín, the interest ran high, as it did in 1987 when government banks charged 73.75 percent. Though that rate seems high, it was less than half the level of inflation that year. The banks, all owned by the government since nationalization in 1982, were making the loans at a loss. But it was not as much of a loss as it once had been. For political reasons, the government had been subsidizing farm operations for some time. For many years that made sense. By keeping *campesinos* happy—or at least by keeping their anger under control—the government kept millions down on the farm at a time when big cities could not accommodate them. It was also easier for the ruling party to get out the vote in high numbers in the isolated countryside where heavy-handed tactics weren't so noticeable. As its popularity waned, the party needed more and more of the peasant vote each year. Subsidies spent on this political-pacification program reached an insane level of $3.5 billion during President López Portillo's administration. But when an economic crisis hit Mexico in López Portillo's last year, the free lunch ended. The next president, Miguel de la Madrid, threw out López Portillo's high-spending program of agricultural incentives and guaranteed prices and substituted a more modest one of his own.

Guaranteed prices that the government promised to pay farmers for crops were deteriorating. Such prices had fallen about a third in real terms during de la Madrid's administration. What money the *campesinos* were paid didn't go as far because the government was also raising the subsidized prices of basic food items. It had kept such prices artificially low for decades as another means of keeping the poor quiet while ignoring economic reality. Milk was a good example. After the economic crisis began, it became so expensive that many poor people had to stop buying it. But it remains illogically cheap. Dairy farmers often get so little for their product that they chose to slaughter their herds rather than produce milk for customers. Others skim off all the fat solids they can to use in other products. Some even water the thin fluid that remains. Some refuse to deliver milk to stores until price ceilings are raised. When milk is available, it often goes sour within a day of purchase.

The bizarre thing about this is that Mexico's vast regions of high-mountain altitudes are perfect for dairy farming. Mexico could be one of the best dairy-farming countries in the world. But cockamamie government policies have made Mexico the world's no. 1 importer of dry milk to compensate for the shortages such policies have created.

Few dispute that Mexican agricultural policies are nonsensical. But everyone agrees that there are limits to what any Mexican president can do about them. Politically, it is impossible to say that the *ejido* system must go because it no longer makes sense, even though that is the case. It would be easier for a U.S. president to end U.S. farm subsidies or to cut Social Security payments. For eight decades, Mexico's poor people have listened to speeches that have told them that land reform was the very essence of their revolution. To take their tiny farms from them now would appear counterrevolutionary. In fact, it would be to do exactly what the leading opposition group, the conservative National Action Party (PAN), has recommended: move toward big, private farms that allow economies of scale. Already the government has nibbled at the *ejido* system as best it can. But it has not been without political cost. Credit still goes mostly to big, productive farms that produce the exports that Mexico's cash-strapped economy needs. But those large-scale operations are changing the face of Mexican agriculture. Every year, especially in the more conservative northern states, such farms produce more fruits and vegetables for export to the lucrative U.S. market. Such crops are labor-intensive. They create a lot of jobs. But as landless *campesinos* or subsistence peasant farmers move north to take such jobs, they come under the influence of the north's antigovernment leaders.

Likewise, more strawberries, broccoli, and asparagus means less land for Mexico's traditional crops, such as corn and beans. The situation has become so ludicrous that Mexico, once a net exporter of such foodstuffs, has become a net importer. Worse, it has had to borrow money to import food that is the very essence of Mexican life. Most of the tortillas sold in Mexico City are now made with U.S. corn.

In the late 1980s, this subtle change in Mexican agriculture still looked like a good political gamble. The prosperous north was more politically demanding. But through better candidates, small democratic reforms, and a bit of vote fraud, the PRI held on to the most important state and local offices. Likewise, enough *campesinos* were staying on their small plots of land, despite widespread illiteracy and malnutrition. Winter fruits and vegetables were making enough money to finance the importation of corn and other basic grains that a growing Mexican population needed. But the gamble was likely to become more of a long shot in the 1990s, the experts warned. Many predicted the crunch would come when consumer demand for basic grains would rise as Mexico came out of its economic slump in the century's last decade. Mexicans, the experts said, would want to resume eating chicken and beef in amounts similar to pre-crisis times. Livestock producers would need more U.S. grain to fatten poultry and cattle. Mexico would have to find the hard cash for such imports. That increased demand for grain would likely increase inflation, which, in turn, would devalue the peso and make those imports more expensive.

This worrisome prospect is hardly of small interest to Americans. In the late 1980s, U.S. farmers, reacting to the bad news of Mexican agriculture, sold Mexico more than a billion dollars a year in agricultural products. If the experts were right, they would sell Mexico even more in the 1990s. Such a boom in U.S. agricultural exports, however, would have its downside. If Mexico can't pay for all the food imports its people will need, more undocumented workers are likely to cross the U.S. border in search of work and survival. Those who remain behind could become violent as they protest worsening living conditions. Violence could mean more Independencias or worse.

As grim as this future looks, it was hard to see how things could get much worse for the family of Abelardo Velasco. His wife, Romelia, a diminutive, dignified woman with skin hardened and tanned by years of working the fields, is now the nominal head of an enormous brood of children, grandchildren, and various in-laws, all of whom live in her dirt-floor, two-room house or in the one-room lean-to that sits next to it. Her house has electricity, something that less than half the homes in Chiapas have. But there is no indoor plumbing. Potable water must be hauled in pails from a well about a mile away.

It's not certain that the violence is over for her or other *campesinos*, either. The killing and clubbing last December in Independencia was rare for its intensity and magnitude. But violence has become a way of life for Mexico's twenty-five million *campesinos*, especially those of Chiapas. Human-rights groups regularly report the deaths of a dozen or so peasants each year in Mexico due to "political" causes. More than a hundred are killed each year for unknown reasons. Often the violence starts with the *campesinos* themselves. Spurred by the revolutionary rhetoric of politicians, groups of peasants, helped by all-too-willing left-wing opposition parties, seize plots of unused land or land they claim is illegally owned by some rich person. They cite their right to it under the Mexican constitution. Authorities, who otherwise speak of such rights with reverence and passion, often ignore them in the face of mob action. They take harsh measures against *campesinos*, citing peasants' lawlessness and unwarranted violence as justifications.

If things do get more violent, they are likely to be their most savage in Chiapas, whose two million residents are still living in a nineteenth-century world of serfs and landlords. Chiapas has always been a little different. When Mexico gained its independence from Spain in the early 1800s, Chiapas was part of Guatemala. It joined Mexico later, when it became disenchanted with its own government. The Guatemalans have never quite accepted this loss of territory. The bellicose ways of the Guatemalans partly explain why Mexico's central government regards Chiapas as a security risk.

Many Chiapans are more Guatemalan than Mexican in cultural outlook. The presence of thousands of Guatemalans in Chiapas in recent years—mostly refugees from the long civil war in their own country—has made the Mexican government even more anxious. Large numbers of Mexican army troops are permanently stationed in Chiapas. In January 1983, an army general, Absalón Castellanos Domínguez, was made governor of the state. Castellanos Domínguez's reputation as a firm hand was not his only qualification for office. His family had long owned thousands of acres of farm land in Chiapas. His brother Ernesto, in fact, owns large tracts around Independencia—thousands more acres than appear legal under the revolutionary land-reform laws of Mexico.

Violence in Chiapas and elsewhere is often the tool of *caciques,* or local land bosses. They use gangs of cheap gunsels called *pistoleros* to impose their will on local peasants. In many ways, *caciques* rule the same way as harsh hacienda owners did during the era of the Díaz dictatorship, when *campesinos* lived in peonage. *Caciques* often own the stores that *campesinos* must buy from. Sometimes they have a stranglehold on local credit. They frequently monopolize the transportation needed to get crops from field to market. Around Independencia, one could argue that the mayor, who has strong ties of friendship to the governor, is the local *cacique.* But the real *cacique* is the governor, who during his term used locally stationed forces of the army and the attorney general's police as his *pistoleros* to keep Independencia's peasants and Chiapas's other *campesinos* in line. His police regularly rounded up peasant leaders as well as student and teacher activists who were demanding more *campesino* rights. Torture was the main investigative tool used to get information that police wanted, according to several human-rights groups. Particularly hard hit were independent *campesino* organizations like the Emiliano Zapata Campesino Organization (OCEZ) and the Independent Center of Agricultural Workers and Campesinos (CIOAC), neither of which follows the compliant path of pro-government peasant organizations. Perhaps it was just coincidence, but Abelardo Velasco belonged to one of these rebel organizations, as did most of those killed in Independencia.

Violence can also come at the hands of drug traffickers who exploit the impoverished nature of *ejido* farming by persuading or forcing peasants to plant marijuana or opium poppies in place of corn or beans. Those not put under the thumb of drug criminals often become the victims of land grabbers. Cattle raisers, with the help of government bankers, entice illiterate *ejido* members to sell off lush timberlands for what seems like big money. That's what happened near Las Margaritas, one town over from Independencia. Wooded lands are cleared, and the new owners sell the resulting lumber at eye-popping profits. The cleared acreage is turned into grazing ranges for cattle. Cattle are an excellent source of export income, given the rising demand in the United States for livestock. But unlike corn, beans, or rice, cattle don't require many *campesinos* to tend. When the money from land sales runs out, *campesinos,* landless and jobless, face starvation or an unplanned move to the big city or the United States.

President Reagan thought he had the answer to such acute agricultural problems. He proposed a North American accord whereby Mexico, the United States, and Canada would each do what it did best toward the most efficient production of agricultural and manufactured goods in the region. High technology would be one of the United States' contributions. Cheap labor would be one of Mexico's. Famous economists and conservative politicians said the same thing. With the right technology and planning, they predicted, Mexico could become the U.S. breadbasket. But to do so, Mexico would have to scrap the *ejido.*

For Romelia, the widow of Abelardo Velasco, that would be unthinkable. As hard as her life is now, as hard as she expects it to be, eliminating the *ejido* is not an option, she said. If the experts had asked her, Romelia would have told them that land gives meaning to the *campesino's* life, just as it did to Mexico's Indians before the Spanish Conquest more than four centuries ago. In thought and soul, millions of Mexico's *campesinos* are still Indians. Land is their anchor, said Romelia, whose arms and legs were unashamedly smeared with the soil of her meager fields the day I came to visit. Land is the *campesino's* future, even though that future now seems uncertain. Land is all they know. Without land, *campesinos* would be adrift, like so many tufts of corn silk in the sultry Chiapas wind.

· 12 ·

The *Policía*

Mexicans have strong feelings about their police. A newcomer doesn't even have to ask. In casual conversations, viewpoints pour out. To say that Mexicans hate their police doesn't quite capture the feeling. Abhor? Loathe? Revile? Well, yes, those are all closer, but still not quite it. Abominate! Yes, that's the feeling I encountered when talking with Mexicans about the police. Mexicans abominate their police.

Behind this unbridled antipathy is the perfectly justifiable fear that any encounter with Mexican police could involve extortion, robbery, torture, or even murder. That's what happens *after* the police arrive. Maybe that's why people joke that Mexico is a country where a kid can play cops and robbers by himself.

The most common fear is police extortion. That's the legal term for it. But what's involved is bribery or, as Mexicans call it, *la mordida*. *Mordida* means "bitten." It's an apt slang word, because what the police do is put the bite on you, often fabricating offenses to do it. In Mexico City, the official motto of the city police department is *Protección y Vialidad* ("Protection and Highway Service"). But bribe demands are so common there that many say that the motto should be *Collección y Venalidad* ("Collection and Venality").

The bribes can be crushing. Some Mexicans go to extremes to evade them. While doing a story on how Mexicans drive, I met a man who had crawled away from the scene of an accident, even though badly injured, rather than undergo police questioning. He had been the victim in this accident. His car had been hit by another whose driver had run a red light. But he had a lot of money on him, the payroll for his small company. He feared most of it would be gone by the time he got out of police hands.

Bribes to traffic cops are so established a fact of Mexican life that many people pay them as if they were highway tolls. I knew one man who paid the corner cop a weekly tribute so he could make an illegal left turn each morning to save time on the way to work. I saw others hand cops money from their car windows without even bothering to make a full stop, after they'd been waved to the curb for supposed offenses.

With all these stories in mind, I thought I had misunderstood Tonio, my office assistant, when he said, "I know a policeman who doesn't take bribes." At the time, I was working on a story on Police Day, a December 22 holiday designated to honor the police. After all the complaints I had heard about the police, I found the holiday a bizarre idea. I wondered if local cops found it a little funny, too. I asked Tonio if he knew any policemen who would be willing to talk about bribery in Mexico. Tonio said he knew one. But Agustín González might not be exactly what I had in mind. Agustín not only refused bribes, he was against them.

Tonio was a good source on Mexican cops. During his off-hours, he drove his father's cab. As a veteran Mexico City driver, he had been stopped many times by the police. That's logical. Most Mexican police aren't paid enough to live on, let alone enough for the bribes they have to pay to superiors for good assignments, promotions, and maintenance of vehicles. They always seemed pressed to find extra cash. What more handy source of cash is there than cabbies, who take in fares all day long?

Until the day Tonio met Agustín, his experience had always been the same when he was curbed by the police. Whether he was at fault or had merely been stopped on a pretext, he was asked for a bribe to be let go. He always paid it. With Agustín, it was different. Agustín was a Mexican oxymoron, an honest cop.

Like any self-respecting Mexican driver who has run a red light and been caught, Tonio offered Agustín a *propina,* a tip, to forgive the offense. Much to Tonio's surprise, Agustín said no. Tonio was dumbfounded. No policeman had ever refused a bribe before. It wasn't natural. Tonio was visibly confused. He didn't even know what to do next. Would he be arrested? Would his car, God forbid, be impounded? Where did one pay a traffic ticket? In all his years of driving, Tonio had never been issued one. Everything had always been arranged at the curb. What would happen now? Agustín seemed to understand Tonio's confusion. He told Tonio not to worry. He would let him go this time. But he warned Tonio to be careful in the future. He also told him not to be so eager to offer a bribe. The ticket for running a red light carried a fine that was less than the bribe Tonio had offered.

This was the closest thing to a man-bites-dog story that I had heard in Mexico, so I asked Tonio to set up a meeting with Agustín that weekend. He did, and that Saturday we drove out to the northwestern reaches of the city for a rendezvous with a moral oddity.

Agustín's corner was the intersection of Las Armas and San Isidro streets in the Azcapotzalco neighborhood. It's right on the city line, in an industrial neighborhood of cheap apartments and smoke-belching factories. It was coffee-break time when we arrived, so we waited in my car for Agustín to return. When he did, I decided to watch him unobserved for a while to see if he acted any differently from the way he had treated Tonio.

It was clear Agustín took pride in his work. His blue serge uniform was immaculately pressed. His black lace-up shoes were buffed to a high gloss. His plastic police whistle hung neatly at his neck. He wore white gloves, which he used to accentuate his arm-signaling, like a batonless maestro at the podium, a Toscanini of traffic. Now and then Agustín would interrupt his "conducting" when some driver committed a traffic violation. He'd signal the person to pull over. He'd lean down to talk, resting his elbows and forearms easily on the car's windowsill. In friendly fashion, he'd lecture for a while. Sometimes he'd let the person go. Other times, he'd write out a ticket. But as far as I could tell, he never took any money.

After about half an hour of watching, we got out of the car. I had Tonio introduce me. I told Agustín that he seemed to be having fun at what he did, conducting and all. He laughed and said his job was *bonito trabajo,* "beautiful work." He had been doing

it for twenty-six years and had no plans to quit. It was a dangerous job, though. Many Mexicans drive recklessly, he said. In the
early-morning dimness, poor drivers kept their headlamps switched
off to save wear and tear on the lights. Often they didn't see Agustín
until the last minute. He had never been hit, but it wasn't for
want of opportunities, he joked.

Corner traffic cop was hardly a cushy post. Agustín's day began
early. He had to be at his station by 6:00 A.M. He had an hour-
and-a-half commute by bus from his modest one-story concrete
home in the Ajusco neighborhood, so he was up before dawn.
Much of the year, the penetrating chill of the capital's high-altitude mornings hung in the air. Cold mornings could be followed
by sun-baking afternoons. Other times, Agustín was as likely to
be drenched by the daily deluge that typified the rainy season.

At fifty-two years of age and in good health, Agustín said he
could remain a policeman for at least another decade. But in four
years he'd be eligible for retirement at full pay. Many might jump
at the chance to receive the same pay for not working as for
working. But Agustín said he wouldn't retire if his superiors felt
they needed him. He was a man not only of honesty and pride,
but of duty. What was strange about all this, of course, was that
Agustín felt it an honor to be a policeman in an era of police
dishonor. He said he'd become a policeman again in a minute,
notwithstanding all the embarrassing revelations that had come
to light about his colleagues' criminality.

The brunt of the morning rush hour had passed. I asked Agustín if we could move into the park that abuts his intersection to
talk about bribery. I asked him how extensive he thought corruption was among the police. He admitted that such things, regret-
tably, did exist, but he was reluctant to estimate how widely. I
asked him what he thought about notorious cops in other Mexican police forces. I brought up the case of First Commander Jorge
Armando Pavón Reyes, a high official of the federal judicial police. Pavón Reyes's relationship with Rafael Caro Quintero, Mexico's best-known drug dealer, was so established that he was willing
to take a check for sixty million pesos (then $270,000) to let Caro
flee Mexico right under the noses of pursuing U.S. Drug Enforcement Administration officials. It was a particularly bold act
because the DEA wanted Caro in connection with the highly
publicized 1985 murder of Enrique Camarena, a DEA under-

cover agent. Agustín chuckled at the audacity of Pavón Reyes, but he declined to make any generalizations about how many other federal police were as venal.

We talked a bit about torture, which many Mexican police use as their prime investigative technique in solving a criminal case. Mexican police receive very little training on how to amass clues or handle evidence. They're more Inspector Clouseau than Lieutenant Columbo. Some speculate that this is why they feel compelled to turn to torture to solve a case quickly. But to torture someone, you first need to arrest a suspect. Mexican police often have trouble doing that. Even the most publicized, politically embarrassing crimes, such as the Christmas 1985 robbery of Aztec and Maya treasures from the National Museum of Anthropology, or the May 1984 machine-gun murder of journalist Manuel Buendía, typically went unsolved while I lived in Mexico.

Sometimes police didn't try to solve a case because they didn't have enough money to do it. Norman Carlson, an American I interviewed in 1985 while he was trying to find the murderers of his son and three others, got no cooperation from the police in the state of Guadalajara until he agreed to pay for gas for squad cars to be used in the investigation.

Even when crimes involved Americans, whose tourist patronage Mexico relies on for about two billion dollars in revenues each year, Mexican police seemed unable or unwilling to catch and prosecute those responsible. After Jewel Strain and her husband were robbed in 1985, Mexican officials at first appeared to be falling all over each other to show interest in catching the guilty parties. But when the Strains, of Granbury, Texas, were brought to a prison in the state of Querétaro, supposedly to identify some suspects, the Strains found the men had been released just before they had arrived. A sympathetic prison official pulled them aside and told them that the men had been released because they were active-duty policemen.

Bobby Stone and his wife, Freda, of Brownsville, Texas, were robbed and she was raped, also in 1985. Stone, a former U.S. Border Patrol officer, provided Mexican authorities with police-artist sketches of the assailants. But when the Stones were asked to come to identify some men who had supposedly confessed to the crime, they found the men, all of whom had been roughed up, looked nothing like the sketches. Stone said the police obviously wanted to get someone, anyone, to confess to the crime to clear it from the books.

A study by the U.S. embassy in Mexico City found that few serious crimes against Americans were ever resolved. But Americans were not being singled out, U.S. officials pointed out. Few serious crimes against anyone in Mexico are truly resolved.

When police did get a suspect, they often got an amazingly quick confession out of even the hardest cases, including Caro Quintero. One technique that seems particularly effective involves mineral water and chile peppers. Peppers or fiery chile powder are put into a bottle of Tehuacán, Mexico's best-selling mineral water. The carbonated mixture is shaken. The resulting geyser of water is forced up a suspect's nostrils. The pain caused by this suffocating procedure has been described as excruciating by those who have testified to international human-rights groups about it. Americans got a close-up glimpse of this practice in August 1986. A scandal erupted after some Mexican state police used it to interrogate undercover DEA agent Victor Cortéz, whom they had arrested as a supposed drug dealer. It is so widely known a technique of police torture that Mexicans have dubbed it *tehuacanazo*. Cortéz said he had also been tortured with electrical shocks to his body. The eleven police officers, all from the state of Jalisco, were suspended during an investigation. Cortéz provided Mexican authorities with a deposition about the torture. But when he declined to return to Mexico to testify personally, nothing was ever done to punish the men.

Torture is forbidden by the Mexican constitution. But after a particularly well-publicized spate of police-torture revelations in the mid-1980s, Sergio García Ramírez, President Miguel de la Madrid's attorney general, admitted that torture was widespread among Mexican police, though not "institutionalized." One indication of how ingrained the torture tradition runs among the police occurred in 1985, when some Mexico City area officers were charged with torturing some accused car thieves. One policeman protested the charges vigorously. He told Mexico City reporters that he and his colleagues couldn't have been the ones responsible. "We are not that stupid," he said. "When we want to torture someone, we give him shocks on the tongue and testicles. No way do we leave visible marks on the body."

Likewise, after the September 1985 earthquakes in Mexico City, bodies of several Colombian drug dealers were found covered with cigarette burns amid the rubble of the detention cells of the city attorney general's office. According to reports in the government-influenced press, the attorney general, Victoria Adato de Ibarra, admitted that the men had been arrested without due process, but she denied they had been tortured. She told an investigative committee of the federal chamber of deputies that her police sometimes used torture. But there had been no need to do so in this case, she testified, because her office already had the information it needed from the suspects. Amid protests, she later resigned and was made a judge of the Mexican supreme court.

In the spring of 1988, those same police tortured a state police commander to death. Sub-commander Pablo Estanislao Aguilar of the state of Mexico was bound, beaten, and suffocated while in police hands, because the attorney general's police suspected he was behind the murder of the son of one of their commanders. The torture-murder created such a stink that the Mexico City attorney general fired his chief of police and most of his subdirectors and commanders.

Agustín nodded knowingly as I ticked off incidents of police abuse. He knew torture existed, of course, he said. But he insisted he had no personal knowledge of it. I could see Agustín was reluctant, maybe even worried, about discussing this point, so I returned to familiar ground. I told Agustín about some of my own experiences with traffic cops. I wanted to see if my encounters had been typical.

It hadn't taken long for me to meet the police. Just a few weeks after I had arrived in Mexico, I was stopped by two officers in a patrol car. The officer driving told me in stern tones that my car did not have the required decal in the back window to show I had paid my annual car tax, the *tenencia*. It was a serious violation, he added. Without that sticker, I could not drive my car farther. It would have to be impounded. Though new in the country, I had already been regaled by many Mexicans with horror stories about cars that had been stripped of everything valuable while parked in police impoundment lots. My car was brand-new. I did not want this to happen, so I appealed to the officers' reason. I pointed out that I had paid the tax. I had a receipt to prove it. The problem, I explained, was that the local *delegación* ("ward") office had lost thousands of paid applications for the stickers, including mine. It might be months before I got a decal, a clerk had told me. The officers were not sympathetic. The driver did say, however, that I might avoid all the bother of impoundment if I paid a fine directly to him. He would pay it for me as a "courtesy" to a foreigner in Mexico. I had just come from shopping. I had very little in cash on me. I told him I didn't have that much. In desperation, I said I couldn't afford to be without my car because I was a journalist. I needed it in my work, I told him. I pulled out my press credentials from Los Pinos (the Mexican White House) and the Interior Ministry, which controls internal security. Veteran journalists had told me to use my credentials in a pinch, with the police or anyone else. Even more than money, they said, the police understood power, the political power of a credential issued by the president or the interior minister. The officers conferred as they examined my IDs. After a while, I got a "Why-didn't-you-show-us-these-in-the-first-place?" look from the two, who suddenly realized that they had wasted their time trying to get a bribe. Credentials returned, I got a snappy salute as the driver said, *"Que le vaya bien,"* wishing me a safe journey. The driver turned to get back into his car. But, as an afterthought, he pivoted and asked me if he and his partner might have a little money for *refrescos* ("soft drinks"), since all our talking in the afternoon sun had caused quite a thirst. I was so relieved to be out from under the threat of impoundment that I gave them the few pesos I had. Later, as I thought about it, I became angry at myself for paying anything. After all, I had done nothing wrong. But I had a better appreciation for the fear and anger most Mexicans must feel when they are stopped by the police.

"It looks bad," admitted Agustín at the end of my story. "There's no doubt about it. It looks bad."

It doesn't have to be this way, however, he added. What was necessary, he said, was leadership. All the president or the chief of police had to do was tell citizens not to pay the bribes anymore. People should demand their tickets if they've actually committed an infraction, he argued. As in Tonio's case, the fine would probably be less than the bribe. If they hadn't done anything, then they should challenge the charges. Most policemen wouldn't want to be bothered with all the delay and red tape a challenge would involve, he said.

Agustín admitted that drivers such as Tonio, who often drove as they pleased, had become used to the "convenience" of paying fines on the spot. Others liked the ease of paying the cop on the beat a "tip" so they could double-park rather than hunt for scarce parking spaces. It would be hard to break them of this attitude, he agreed. More important, when I pressed him, he admitted that if past performance was an indication, government leadership against corruption was unlikely.

Every modern Mexican president, it seems, has launched an anticorruption program in the face of the embarrassing graft of his predecessor's administration. But not much happens after the policy is announced. Certainly that was the case with President Miguel de la Madrid. His administration (1982–88) followed that of José López Portillo (1976–82), whose reported grabs for public funds were excessive even by Mexican standards.

Unfortunately for de la Madrid, López Portillo was indiscreet about how he used the inexplicable wealth he amassed. In the final year of his term, he built a multimillion-dollar housing complex for himself and his family on a hill overlooking one of the busiest commuter routes in Mexico City. It was so visible a flaunting of his booty that people dubbed the complex "Dog Hill," a mocking reference to López Portillo's promise to defend the peso "like a dog"—a remark he made shortly before he devalued the peso drastically in 1982.

López Portillo's spokesman tried to downplay the lavishness of the ex-president's house in the Dog Hill complex. He told me it was a *pinche casa* ("fucking little house") that had just one bedroom, a living room, a dining room, a kitchen, a bathroom—and a five-story library containing forty-thousand books and a spiral staircase. Mexican newspapers also reported that López Portillo had digs in France, Spain, and the Valle de Bravo, a weekend vacation area west of Mexico City. López Portillo also built a two-million-dollar villa in Acapulco for his mistress, Rosa Luz Alegría, whom he made his minister of tourism. However, his wife, who spent millions on shopping sprees abroad, occupied the villa before his mistress could move in. López Portillo had to build his paramour another house.

In López Portillo's last year as president, public hatred for him was so palpable that candidate de la Madrid had to make criticism of corrupt government officials a key part of his platform. In the Mexican style, however, de la Madrid never mentioned López

Portillo or anyone else by name in his complaints.

De la Madrid began his anticorruption campaign with a flourish. He created Mexico's first controller general's office, whose sole function was to discourage and root out corruption. He disbanded Mexico City's dreaded secret police. He fired hundreds of federal police suspected of corruption. He required all top government officials, including himself, to file income statements. His administration said it would go after big fish and quickly instituted a fraud prosecution against one of López Portillo's cabinet members, Jorge Díaz Serrano, who had headed Pemex, the state-owned oil company—and been a rival of de la Madrid's for the presidency.

On closer examination, the program proved to be a lot less than met the eye. Several officials got star treatment once arrested. Díaz Serrano, who was charged with a thirty-four-million-dollar fraud involving the sale of two tankers to Pemex, wasn't exactly doing hard time when I visited him in jail in 1987. He was in the midst of throwing a birthday party for his wife, complete with a mariachi band. He had some of the best-pressed jail uniforms of anyone I saw there. And he had a personal computer in his cell to keep track of his case and his continuing business affairs. He was later convicted and sentenced to ten years in prison and fined more than fifty million dollars. His sentence was quickly cut to five years in prison, the amount of time he had already served while awaiting conviction.

After Díaz Serrano was picked up, few other high-level arrests were made. It became clear that what de la Madrid had in mind was not wiping out official corruption but merely returning it to historic levels. The housecleaning of crooked federal cops also began to backfire. Hundreds of out-of-work cops, who had only known a life of crime while on the force, became modern-day highwaymen. Thousands of public officials failed to file their income statements on time. None of the reports on file was available to the public. In its 1987 annual report, the controller general's office stated that the most important results of de la Madrid's anticorruption campaign (known in Spanish as renovación moral) "are not easily quantifiable." Officials of that office told me that the biggest achievement of the anticorruption campaign had been to deter officials from committing crimes, although it was impossible to say how many they had deterred.

No charges were ever brought against López Portillo, even though a simple net-worth analysis of his wealth compared with his known income would have given many prosecutors plenty of ammunition. I asked the controller general's office why no action had been taken against the former president. The official response was that no evidence had been found. Mention was also made of the political crisis that might ensue if a former Mexican president were prosecuted, something that had never happened. Unofficially, as one of the controller general's aides walked me back to my car after the interview, I was told that presidents often become rich because people give them things. "It's not against the law, my friend," the smiling aide said.

The de la Madrid administration would also prosecute Agustín's onetime boss, Arturo Durazo, the chief of police in Mexico City during López Portillo's administration. It was a halfhearted, comic-opera prosecution. Durazo, who had openly lived the life of a multimillionaire on a modest salary, fled Mexico at the end of López Portillo's administration. He had been accused by many, including former aides, of drug trafficking, murder, and extortion. Despite such serious allegations, the Mexican police really didn't look for him very hard. It was the U.S. Federal Bureau of Investigation that ultimately captured Durazo, finding him on the lam in Puerto Rico in June 1984.

Durazo's apprehension created a dilemma for the de la Madrid government. If they failed to prosecute so notorious a fugitive, de la Madrid's anticorruption program would be exposed as a sham. But bringing Durazo back had its hazards. He knew enough to put a lot of officials in the administration—his former colleagues—in jail if he talked. The government decided in favor of an extradition petition. But they just barely made the U.S. court deadline. And the crimes they listed in the petition were the least serious ones Durazo had been accused of.

The petition said nothing about Durazo's alleged drug-trafficking activities, even though Durazo had been implicated in drug trafficking in a 1976 indictment by a Dade County, Florida, grand jury. Likewise, there was no mention of Durazo's supposed involvement in the mass murder of a group of Colombian drug dealers. According to Durazo's own colleagues, at least twelve Colombians and a Mexican were tortured and dumped into the Tula River sewer system so Durazo could get his hands on the estimated five million dollars in cash the Colombian gang had when they were arrested. Some said more had been murdered. That was the testimony of José González González, Durazo's former security chief, who wrote a best-seller about the Durazo era.

De la Madrid's government did say it wanted to prosecute Durazo for extortion, illegal possession of weapons, and possession of contraband. After a lengthy series of hearings, a U.S. judge allowed Durazo to be extradited in April 1986. But he threw out the contraband charge (involving possession of items that had not been legally imported to Mexico) because it was not a crime in the United States.

The government's lawyers made fools of themselves pursuing the arms charge. Some of the weapons, it turned out, were antiques. Many weren't operational. Some blew up in investigators' faces when test-fired. Others, all automatic types, could only be possessed by army personnel under Mexican law. But Durazo pointed out that he had been given a four-star army general's rank by his boyhood friend, López Portillo.

That really left only the extortion charge, which allegedly involved payments that thousands of Mexico City police were forced to make to Durazo and his henchmen as the price for getting a job, a particular assignment, or a promotion. When the proceedings against Durazo finally began, it seemed the government was also bent on purposely blowing prosecution of this charge. Scores of witnesses had signed statements confirming the system of extorted fees. Mexican prosecutors charged that Durazo alone had taken in $2.5 million in such fees in his six years as police chief. But when witnesses against Durazo were called to affirm their statements in court, many could not be found because they had fled the country. All the rest, save two, recanted, claiming that they had been tortured into testifying against the rotund former police chief. Prosecutors explained that the witnesses had been intimidated or paid off by Durazo or his friends. While Durazo tied prosecutors in knots, he lived well in jail. He had his cell fitted with a color television, a videocassette recorder, a Jacuzzi, and wall-to-wall carpeting.

Durazo said González González, one of the two who did not recant, had made up stories about him in order to sell books. He said he knew nothing of the Tula River murders. He claimed that the money he had received from underlings had been mostly

Christmas gifts. Durazo denied all financial wrongdoing. In a 1983 statement, Durazo admitted to a net worth of $640,000, which was still a lot of money for someone who never earned a salary of more than ten thousand dollars a year. U.S. prosecutors who handled Durazo's extradition proceeding estimated he was worth a minimum of $7 million. Mexican prosecutors thought his fortune might be more like $200 million.

Despite his denials, Durazo, on a police official's modest salary, managed to acquire a $2.5-million hilltop mansion in Mexico City, a Pacific beach hideaway modeled after the Greek Parthenon, a dog track, a horse track, nineteen thoroughbred horses, a bull ring, a personal disco modeled after the defunct Studio 54, a fleet of antique cars, a collection of expensive jewelry, and bank accounts with millions of dollars on deposit. When the U.S. judge considering Durazo's extradition asked how this was possible, Durazo's lawyers responded: "Shrewd investments."

The other witness who stuck to his guns was Ramón Mota Sánchez, who succeeded Durazo as police chief. He resigned and disappeared shortly before he was to be called to ratify his limited statement against Durazo. After months of awkward searching, prosecutors finally got Mota to make a brief appearance. Not having been one of Durazo's colleagues, the former army general merely confirmed he had found incriminating documents in Durazo's office when he took over as police chief.

Near the end of de la Madrid's administration, the courts still hadn't been able to convict Durazo. But even if he were to be convicted, it's unlikely the government would ever prosecute him for drug trafficking, murder, or the other serious charges people have made against him. Under the U.S.-Mexican extradition treaty that governed his return to Mexico, Mexico would need to obtain special permission from the U.S. State Department to go beyond the crimes listed in the extradition petition. Typically, this permission is not granted.

Agustín had met Durazo once. It was a ceremonial visit on one of Agustín's anniversaries on the force. Durazo had received Agustín in his lavish downtown office, dressed in his trademark powder-blue police uniform. I asked Agustín what impression he had gained of Durazo.

"He didn't ask me for a bribe," Agustín said, flashing a little smirk.

I reeled off some of the other famous bribe cases that had come to light during my stay in Mexico. In 1986, Alfredo Rios Galeana, a former cop who had become Mexico's most notorious bank robber, paid off a Mexico City jail warden to let him escape. He robbed a bank on the way out of town and was never recaptured. In 1985, after he was arrested in Costa Rica and returned to Mexico, Rafael Caro Quintero, the drug kingpin who bribed Commander Pavón Reyes with a check, availed himself of jail guards' openness to bribes. In January 1986, it came to light that Caro had in his cell gold Rolex watches, expensive cowboy boots, stereo systems, non-prison-issue clothing, and $630,000 in cash. According to his lawyer, all these items were stolen by prison guards, who apparently felt Caro wasn't giving them enough. An investigation was launched into why Caro had such luxuries in his cell. But no results were ever made public. A few months later, DEA officials who visited Caro's cell said he had been permitted to knock down the bars between his cell and those of his co-defendants to create a "suite" for his gang. It had a marble-floored sauna, Oriental carpets, a private, fenced exercise area just outside, and a live-in cook to prepare Caro's favorite meals. On days when prisoners were allowed to bring in their wives for conjugal visits, DEA officials told me, Caro was allowed to entertain a bevy of hookers in his suite.

Bribes also kept Mexico's most wanted drug dealer at large for years, according to the DEA. One of Caro Quintero's partners, Miguel Félix Gallardo, was sighted several times in Culiacán, the capital of Sinaloa, a major drug-trafficking state, after Caro was arrested. Gallardo was wanted for questioning in the murder investigation of Enrique Camarena, the DEA agent whose February 1985 murder was allegedly masterminded by Caro. When I visited Culiacán in 1986, several people told me that Gallardo had just thrown a big party for his goddaughter in the capital. He had sent out fancy invitations to state bigwigs, indicating the date and place of the fiesta and his sponsorship of it as the girl's godfather. Federal anti-drug police insisted they were unable to locate him because most of the state anti-drug police were on his payroll. Local police supposedly warned Gallardo of federal moves to capture him and refrained from passing on information about his whereabouts to federal officials.

Agustín didn't deny that corruption was rampant within police or prison ranks in Mexico. But it was obvious that he didn't really feel comfortable talking about whether this cop or that warden might be crooked. He did feel strongly, however, that it wasn't necessary to be corrupt to get by as a cop.

"We're not here to charge for infractions," he said. "My job is to keep traffic moving. We [the police] are here for the citizens. We are here for Mexico."

Agustín lamented that bribery was the first response of the majority of Mexicans when they encountered the police.

"I don't allow it," he said firmly. "I try to educate them about what to do. I tell them they can pay the fine in a bank or the *delegación* office."

That was a laudable goal, but hardly an easy one to achieve in a city where most drivers never take driving lessons, where thousands don't have a driver's license, and where millions don't bother to get accident insurance. Making honest drivers out of Mexicans would also be tough because of the country's easy atmosphere of corruption. From the days of the Aztecs and the Spanish conquistadors, there have been corrupt Mexican officials whose rampant greed has infected many aspects of Mexican life. Even the 1910 Revolution, which threw out the corrupt dictatorship of Porfirio Díaz, did not end corruption. A fine portrait of turn-of-the-century corruption in Mexico is found in B. Traven's novel *Government,* the story of Don Gabriel, whose uses a low-paying civil-service job in his village to enrich himself. In the opening paragraph of the book, the author states the philosophy of Don Gabriel's fellow civil servant, Don Casimiro: "He served his country not for his country's good, but in order to profit at its expense. If a man can earn no more as a servant of the State than he can by running a snack bar, there is no reason whatever why he should aspire to devote his energies to his country's service."

I had grown up in Chicago, where, at one time, a good policeman always had change for a twenty-dollar bill. Vote early and often, was the slogan of local Democrats—and, some would argue, still is. But despite all the crooked city hall pols, grifting state legislators, and bent White House aides I encountered in the United States, nothing prepared me for the breadth of corruption I found in Mexico. Crooked union officials skimmed millions from revenues of state-owned companies. Government officials stole millions more from public treasuries. Bureaucrats wanted bribes to perform routine services. Customs officers took bribes. Immigration officers took bribes. Many police, of course, took bribes.

All these bad examples of officialdom have had an impact on the citizenry. Many adopt a larcenous approach in business, watering down or short-weighting products or turning out dangerous or shoddy goods. Their attitude seems to be that any trouble can be resolved with money to the right person. Businessmen keep double sets of books to evade income taxes. Others routinely deal in cash to hide income and attract customers by promising not to charge Mexico's oppressive 15-percent national sales tax. Thousands of Mexicans staff a thriving black market where millions of Mexicans, including government officials, shop for contraband goods that have been smuggled into Mexico to avoid customs duties. This is not to say that Mexico is the most corrupt country in the world. It is not. During my time in Mexico, Latin American countries such as Noriega's Panama and Stroessner's Paraguay overshadowed Mexico when it came to crookedness. They were veritable kleptocracies. Unlike those two, Mexico drew the line at selling citizenship or shelter to ex-Nazis, on-the-lam drug dealers, or famous assassins. But sometimes the magnitude of corruption in Mexico was breathtaking. In 1985, the governor of the state of Morelos fired the entire state police force after looking into how widespread police corruption was. When drug dealer Caro Quintero was arrested in the same year, he confessed that he had just about every state policemen in his home base of Jalisco on the take as well as many high police officials elsewhere. In the same year, it was discovered that drug dealers had thousands of acres under cultivation for marijuana in the state of Chihuahua. Hordes of peasants were used to harvest the drug. They kept the project a secret for years because they were paid two and three times their normal wages. Army troops were on the drug dealers' payroll, too. Soldiers kept curious outsiders away from the marijuana fields and bought takeout lunches each day for the workers.

Bribery, to be frank, is what many Mexicans (and resident foreigners) think of first when they wanted to get something done. It's an insidious attitude of epidemic proportions. It is probably the most serious obstacle to Mexico's becoming a modern, developed nation. General Mota Sánchez, while he was Mexico City's police chief, once captured the scope of this unstated assumption about Mexicans' venality. In response to complaints about police corruption, Mota said it would be unrealistic to hope that he or the de la Madrid government could eliminate it entirely. "The police cannot be an island of purity in a society like ours," he said, "but we will try to reduce corruption to the level of the rest of the country."

More than a few Mexicans were astounded when I told them that I was going through all the time-consuming legal steps required to adopt my son, Alex, in Mexico. The normal method of adoption is to pay a woman for her baby and then register the child as one's own, never telling the authorities or the child what really happened. If a clerk at the birth-certificate registry office raises an eyebrow, one can always offer a "tip" to move things along.

Even the Mexican courts are up to their gavels in bribery. Leaders of local bar associations openly complain that many judges are on the take, handing out justice to the highest bidder. Trial lawyers regularly bitch that they have to pay "tips" to court clerks and judges just to get routine papers filed. Defense attorney Hector Montoya Fernández got so riled up about the need to pay people off in the Mexico City court system that he held a press conference in 1985 to charge that the courts were "teeming with rats, filth and corruption, with only a few honorable exceptions." He said court officials "were nothing but booty hunters who keep lawyers on both sides of a case running around uselessly until they [the lawyers] decide to accept the corrupt system and pay. This is the only way to see action on a case."

In this sea of corruption, Agustín was as improbable as a salmon swimming upriver. When I met him, he was making about eight thousand pesos a day ($4.75). That was about a third more than the typical Mexican. But he clearly wasn't getting rich on it. He rented his house from his in-laws. He'd probably never be able to save enough to buy his own home, he said. But Agustín had become rich in other ways. His parents had only finished grammar school. He hadn't gotten beyond high school. But his oldest son was in a national university, studying architecture. Two others of his six children were in college preparatory schools. The other three, with prodding from their parents, were likely to follow suit, he said.

It wasn't easy getting his kids that far, he admitted. Tuition was nominal in the public schools. But sacrifices had to be made to pay for books, supplies, and clothes. To economize, his kids used books from libraries when they could. They were encouraged to study hard and discouraged from too much time in front of the television or in the street. Agustín and his wife often went without so his kids would have what they needed.

"You can get by," he said. "Obviously you can because here I am. The salary is sufficient."

•   •   •

In early 1988, I drove back to Azcapotzalco. I guess I just wanted to deal with that doubt that had been at the back of my mind ever since I had met Agustín. "Was this guy for real?" I had asked myself more than once. I had told some of my Mexican friends about Agustín. Without exception, I was informed that I had been taken in. Cynicism about the police ran deep. I decided I would watch Agustín one more time, again unobserved, to see if this was the man Diogenes had so long searched for.

I chose the morning rush hour again, because it was easy to park nearby and remain unnoticed. I brought some binoculars. I wanted a close-up look at Agustín's conversations with drivers he stopped. I felt a little funny using binoculars. But I wanted to see if money was passing, however so slyly. I watched Agustín for a better part of two hours. He did not disappoint. He did nothing untoward.

I thought about talking with Agustín again. But what would I say? I couldn't very well congratulate him for passing the honesty test after my two hours of spying. I left Agustín as I had found him, a happy man in a job he loved, a rara avis for my life list.

· 13 ·

The *Periodista*

In many countries, 1968 was an extraordinary year, a year of violence, a year of change. Mexico was no different. There were riots in the streets of Mexico City, just as there were in Chicago, Paris, and Prague. The precise reasons for the demonstrations were never quite clear. Students led the protests, as they did elsewhere. But they weren't united in their complaints. When police bashed in heads during a clash between rival student groups, however, a disorganized mob became a movement. Other Mexicans, perhaps looking to vent anger about the authoritarian ways of President Gustavo Díaz Ordaz, took to the streets, too. One famous silent protest drew 400,000 people.

This visible unrest came at an embarrassing time for Díaz Ordaz. The 1968 Summer Olympics were set to begin in October. Mexico was the first Third World nation to be given the honor of the games. The government had chosen peace as its Olympic theme to show that the poor nations of the world had a better way than the bellicose superpowers. But when increasingly violent disturbances showed no sign of easing as the games approached, Díaz Ordaz decided he had had enough. When a noisy crowd gathered on October 2 at the Plaza Tlatelolco, concealed soldiers opened fire without warning and killed hundreds.

Many of those who survived were jailed. Others fled the country. Those in exile were exposed to then-radical ideas of feminism, gay liberation, and grass-roots democracy. Many in Mexico look upon the massacre at Tlatelolco as a pivotal event in Mexico's history, one that still reverberates in the country's political development. Some say its impact is roughly equivalent to that of the riots outside the 1968 Democratic National Convention in Chicago, or the 1970 killings at Kent State University. But another, less-noticed event of 1968 had just as profound an effect on Mexico. A few months before the 1968 massacre, Julio Scherer García became editor of Mexico's leading newspaper, *Excélsior*. Scherer, an incorruptible journalist, was in the right job at the right time to make a difference. And he did.

Excélsior's coverage of the events of 1968 was unsparing. Díaz Ordaz, surprised by the magnitude of negative public reaction to his savage crackdown on the protesters, wound up a recluse for the short remainder of his term. When he anointed Luis Echeverría as his successor, the stage seemed set for six more years of unrest. Echeverría had been Díaz Ordaz's interior minister. It was he who had carried out Díaz Ordaz's brutal plans for the Tlatelolco dissidents. Echeverría had called Scherer regularly in 1968 to demand that *Excélsior* tone down its coverage of the protests and the post-massacre crisis. Scherer had refused. A tense relationship developed. But when Echeverría became president, he seemed to change. Not long after he assumed office in December 1970, he freed a number of the dissidents who had been arrested in 1968. He said Mexico needed a "democratic opening" to restore the political balance after the harsh years of Díaz Ordaz's regime. He encouraged the press to be critical of the government.

His leftist rhetoric was taken a bit too literally by some. Armed guerrillas began appearing in rural areas, especially in the state of Guerrero. Small bands of rebels, such as the Party of the Poor, gained a reputation as folk heroes. Urban guerrillas, such as the Revolutionary Action Movement (MAR), sprang up too, with the clandestine help of the Soviet Union and North Korea. By early 1971 it must have appeared to Echeverría that his democratic opening was getting a bit out of hand. When an MAR plot to make Mexico another Vietnam was uncovered in March 1971, his government's atmosphere of tolerance for dissidence got decidedly chilly. In June 1971, Echeverría's real feelings about protest emerged. In that month, students staged the first mass protest in Mexico City since the 1968 Tlatelolco massacre. A few thousand gathered to support a strike in Monterrey. Out of nowhere, a band of paramilitary goons known as Los Halcones ("The Falcons") appeared and killed about two dozen demonstrators. Echeverría blamed the killings on right-wingers. He said the right was trying to undermine his democratic opening. Some leftists bought this. But shortly thereafter, political dissidents, the first of about four hundred began to "disappear."

All the while, Scherer kept a spotlight on unfolding political events. *Excélsior* also kept Mexicans informed about how Echeverría's populist, big-spending economic policies were going sour. The government's budget deficit was soaring. So was the amount of foreign debt Echeverría was incurring to finance it. *Excélsior* wrote about the growing corruption of the administration. It criticized Echeverría for failing to end widespread social injustice. In the process, it broke the tradition of Mexico's historically tame, self-censored press. It became, in the words of one Mexican historian, the real legislative power in the country. It checked and balanced Echeverría's emperor-like presidency. It filled the vacuum left by the rubber-stamp national legislature.

Clearly, Echeverría would have liked to put out this new flame of press freedom. But moving against such an established institution as *Excélsior* would have been like a U.S. president trying to muzzle or shut down the *New York Times*. *Excélsior* had been founded in 1917, in the midst of the Mexican Revolution. It was twelve years older than Echeverría's party, which had ruled Mexico since 1929.

Echeverría bided his time on direct action against *Excélsior*. But he began to move against it in subtle ways. With no complaint from his supposedly left-wing government, conservative business leaders, many the private political allies of Echeverría, initiated an advertising boycott in 1972 against *Excélsior*. They said they were protesting the paper's leftist editorial line. *Excélsior* dropped from first to fourth among newspapers in advertising lineage. After four months, however, *Excélsior* had not buckled under to business demands for a new editorial line. The boycott was ended when Echeverría, who could have stopped the protest the first day, ostensibly came to the paper's rescue by ordering state enterprises to cover the deficit created by the private sector's actions. *Excélsior* had some breathing room for a while after that. Some other publications were not so lucky. In 1974, police raided the offices of a tiny weekly magazine called ¿*Por Qué?* It had reported on guerrilla activities. The reports hadn't been supportive of the guerrillas. But Echeverría seemed to equate coverage with sympathy. The police wrecked ¿*Por Qué?*'s facilities, closed the magazine down, and held the staff prisoners at an army torture center for two weeks, according to several reports. The magazine's reporters were beaten and threatened with death if they resumed publication.

Things turned particularly sour between the president and the paper after *Excélsior* criticized a 1975 vote by Mexico in the United Nations. In that shocking vote, Mexico sided with about seventy other countries, many of them in the Communist bloc, on a resolution that branded Zionism as a form of racism. At the time, Echeverría was campaigning to become U.N. Secretary-General after he left office in December 1976. He was also lobbying to win the Nobel Peace Prize. Widely publicized criticism by his country's leading newspaper certainly did not help either cause. Echeverría probably wanted to crush Scherer and his paper right after the vote. But 1975 was the wrong time to attack *Excélsior*. The process for picking a new Mexican president had begun. Echeverría, as was a Mexican president's prerogative, had picked his finance minister, José López Portillo, to be his successor. His choice would be legally ratified at suspenseless presidential elections in July 1976. Getting the public to accept a Mexican president's undemocratic selection of his successor has always been a delicate matter. It was not the sort of thing that would have been helped by cracking down on Mexico's most respected newspaper. Echeverría decided to wait until after the elections for his frontal assault on *Excélsior*. But he intensified his subtle campaign against it.

Channel 13, the principal government television station, withdrew its substantial advertising from *Excélsior*. *El Nacional*, the government newspaper, began attacking *Excélsior* by name. Other newspapers, under pressure from the government, chimed in. In February 1976, the Mexican Editorial Organization, a group in which Echeverría was financially involved, bought *Excélsior*'s principal competitor, *El Universal*, as well as the papers of the *El Sol* chain. Both would benefit from Echeverría's behind-the-scenes campaign against *Excélsior*. In June, when a group of peasants seized a few hundred acres of land that *Excélsior* owned, Televisa, Mexico's largest television network, slanted its already pro-government coverage against *Excélsior*. *Excélsior* had been depending on development of that land to produce needed operating revenues. Such seizures were common in Mexico. Revolutionary promises of land reform were often invoked by poor Mexicans who wanted land but did not have the money to pay for it. In cases where title was shaky, a common situation in Mexico, the squatters sometimes got the land. The government would support them in a public show of revolutionary fervor. In this case, there was no question that *Excélsior* was the rightful owner. But the government did nothing to evict the squatters. One explanation may have been that the group was headed by Humberto Serrano, a member of the national chamber of deputies and a political ally of Echeverría's. The mute response of government to violations of *Excélsior*'s rights was a pattern that would grow.

When the July 4 presidential elections were over, *Excélsior* spoke out on the subject of the land seizure. Scherer, a man of dignity and propriety, had thought public complaint during the campaign would have been unseemly. He told readers that *Excélsior* was getting no help from the government, a situation he found "alarming." Readers did not learn, however, of an even more distressing development. Conservative members of *Excélsior*'s staff had demanded an extraordinary session of the cooperative that owned *Excélsior*. The right-wing rebels, secretly backed by Echeverría, made no bones about their intent to use the assembly to oust Scherer as editor. Echeverría's direct attack had begun.

When the meeting took place, on July 8, the rebels were joined by outside agitators, some of whom came armed. Pleas to the police for help went unanswered. Scherer sensed that there was a real danger of loss of life in the explosive atmosphere of the meeting. He and his two hundred followers walked out. The rebels took over *Excélsior*. The paper that had become the best Spanish-language newspaper in the world under Scherer became safe and tame again. It remains so today.

Scherer, however, did not become safe and tame. By November he had started *Proceso*, a muckraking weekly magazine that has been a thorn in every president's side since its first issue. With a circulation of only 75,000, *Proceso* does not have the impact of

Excélsior, which claims a daily circulation of 200,000. But *Proceso* is the most fearless, most respected publication in Mexico. It is the best single source of what is really going on in the country. It has regularly exposed corruption in Mexico's vital oil industry. It has written about atrocities by the normally sacrosanct Mexican army. It published the first articles on the allegations of murder, drug trafficking, and extortion against former Mexico City police chief Arturo Durazo, once one of the most feared men in Mexico. It broke the story about the White Brigade, a secret government military unit that used illegal methods to crush armed guerrillas between 1977 and 1980.

Proceso's beginning as a muckraking magazine was a difficult one. The government controls all the newsprint in the country. An angry Echeverría didn't want to sell Scherer's new operation any paper. Buying imported newsprint would have been extremely costly, so Scherer cajoled a couple of his competitors into selling *Proceso* some of their surplus newsprint. *Proceso*'s first edition was published. Some 100,000 copies were sold. Three weeks later, Echeverría's term ended. Scherer and *Proceso* got a new lease on life. The new president, José López Portillo, was Scherer's cousin. He promised full press freedom, just as Echeverría had. Things did get better for a while. But government tolerance did not last, despite blood ties. Family feelings did not stop Scherer from publishing the embarrassing truth about what was wrong with Mexico and why his cousin was to blame.

Proceso has survived more than a decade. But it has not been a financially enriching experience for Scherer personally. He remains a man of modest means. It could have been otherwise. Many reporters and editors become quite rich, thanks to monthly bribes and subsidies that the government provides to journalists to keep them in line. Taking money from the government must have been an especially strong temptation for Scherer. His family had been wealthy once. He had had the taste of riches. But hard times had hit his family. His once-wealthy banker father went bankrupt. The three Scherer children were told they would have to look for work. The Scherers were formal types, with more than a few professionals in their ranks. In upper-middle-class style, they discussed history and culture at the dinner table. In mealtime homilies, Scherer's father and mother had stressed the need to be socially useful, productive, honest. "Responsibility" and "dignity" were words commonly heard between soup and dessert. When financial fortunes went bad for his father, Scherer decided to try his hand at journalism. No one had ever been a journalist in the Scherer family. Such a career was not exactly what his parents had had in mind. But they did not try to stop him. Scherer is glad they did not. He found he loved reporting and writing. He has never regretted his choice.

From the beginning, Scherer rejected all sinecures from the government, an attitude that made many of his more pliant colleagues suspicious of him. He demands the same of his reporters at *Proceso*. His magazine does buy its newsprint from Pipsa, the state-owned newsprint monopoly, which significantly subsidizes the price of paper. *Proceso* also accepts a few ads from state-owned industries and government agencies. Revenues from government advertising don't add up to much. But they might have been a considerable source of income given the large portion of the economy that the government controls. At some newspapers, such publicity amounts to 75 percent of total advertising revenues.

Scherer also forbids *Proceso*'s reporters from accepting the government's monthly cash bribes, known as *embutes*. Mexican reporters make very little, typically sixty to seventy dollars a week. Those *embutes* (also called *sobres* or *igualas*) can amount to two or three times their regular salaries. Reporters who cover the president, the finance minister, or Pemex, the state-owned oil company, can make even more. If they work for a major newspaper, especially if they write a column, they can become rich.

Scherer likewise bans acceptance of money that is handed out on presidential or ministerial trips, or during coverage of political campaigns. In the oil-boom days of President López Portillo, reporters typically got their airfare, hotel, and meals paid for by the government during such trips. On foreign presidential visits, they also got $1,000 a country as "walking-around" money. During President Miguel de la Madrid's administration, in keeping with the atmosphere of economic crisis, the *embute* practice was temporarily ended. After coverage got a bit critical, however, it reappeared. Walking-around money for foreign trips also continued, although at less spectacular levels than in López Portillo's day.

Proceso does not accept *gacetillas* either. They are articles written by the government or private citizens and published in a newspaper or magazine for a fee. Only a few newspapers, such as the English-language *Mexico City News,* mark such copy as advertising. Some newspapers are so accommodating that they run such stories under the byline of the reporter who normally covers the agency or company paying for the story. In hotly contested elections, the ruling Institutional Revolutionary Party (PRI) will typically buy a *gacetilla* for the space normally reserved for a newspaper's lead story. The headline over the *gacetilla* might say something like "PRI Wins in Landslide!" The story would not be likely to say anything about vote fraud or opposition protests. The same story, with exactly the same wording, might appear in several other papers.

Just to make sure that a reporter doesn't mind being pushed aside for a story written by the people he covers, the reporter gets a commission on each *gacetilla.* Some reporters are so comfortable with this arrangement that they suggest *gacetilla* topics, serving as both reporter and ad salesman in the process.

Proceso's course of financial independence has cost it not only money but access to top government officials. Scherer, who has interviewed Fidel Castro, Konrad Adenauer, Salvador Allende, John F. Kennedy, Willy Brandt, Augusto Pinochet, and other heads of state, was never granted an interview with President de la Madrid, who talked with other Mexican reporters. De la Madrid did not, however, try to punish *Proceso* for any of its many articles that were critical of his administration. The same was not true for López Portillo, who saw cousin Julio publish photographs of López Portillo's lavish five-mansion complex along with stories about his inexplicable accumulation of wealth during the height of Mexico's oil-boom years. In 1982, López Portillo ordered all government entities to withdraw advertising from *Proceso,* creating a temporary financial crisis.

Normally, no other Mexican publications publish stories about a president's personal or financial life. Stories about the Mexican army are also extremely rare unless they are flattering or superficial. A Mexican *periodista* ("reporter") doesn't have to be told what to write and what not to. The self-censorship that is the norm in the sold-out world of Mexican journalism has unwritten rules that everyone understands. If reporters do break the rules or misinterpret them, they will invariably get a call from a top government official who will question their patriotism if not threaten them. During de la Madrid's time, this function was performed by Fernando Pérez Correa, the undersecretary of the Interior Ministry, and by Manuel Alonso, de la Madrid's spokesman. If the reporter or editor won't heel under, sometimes he or she will get pressure from the boss. The boss may get a call from the government, or he may just be worried enough about government reaction that he will act on his own. This is what happened when Pete Hamill was editor of the *Mexico City News* in 1986. Hamill, a noted U.S. journalist, had called for hard-hitting coverage of a university strike that the government did not like. The government, probably sensing that a call from Pérez Correa or Alonso would be futile with a journalist of Hamill's stature and integrity, said nothing to him directly. But after several weeks of straightforward student-strike stories, Hamill was called in by the *News*'s owner, Romulo O'Farrill, Jr. O'Farrill said he wanted the paper to take a more antistudent line. Hamill refused and quit. The new editorial team did what O'Farrill wanted.

Government restraints on television news are similar. Few calls have to be made to complain about Mexican television programs. The government controls a good portion of the channels in Mexico. The pro-government Televisa network controls most of the rest. Just in case, though, the government regularly inspects scripts of television shows, which stations must provide in advance. There isn't much trouble with radio news, either. It is the single most important source of news for Mexicans. But its short news programs, rarely accompanied by commentary or analysis, tell Mexicans little that would disturb the government. One exception was the live radio call-in show of Francisco Huerta. His program, *Public Opinion,* presented a particularly nettlesome problem for the government, because officials had no chance to screen and censor the callers' usually antigovernment comments. To eliminate the problem, the government just eliminated the show. There was less of this during de la Madrid's time. But in early 1988, the antigovernment economic commentaries of Nilda Morell were dropped after the government put pressure on the network that featured her program on its stations.

Foreign television programs are also watched closely. About 350,000 homes in Mexico get cable service that provides shows from the three major U.S. networks, PBS, and ESPN. Officials from Pérez Correa's office often tell Televisa, the principal cable operator, when not to broadcast programs that are negative about

Mexico. Most news programs are delayed in transmission so that they can be viewed ahead of time. This has given government officials a chance to black out critical reports on Mexico by the *MacNeil/Lehrer Newshour* and the *CBS Evening News,* among others. All local U.S. news programs from border cities such as San Diego and El Paso have been permanently blacked out because they regularly report on U.S.-Mexican border problems. The *MacNeil/Lehrer Newshour* was dropped from cable service for about a year after one critical report on Mexico during de la Madrid's term. In early 1985, Cable News Network's *Headline News* service was also canceled following the network's concentrated coverage of violent opposition demonstrations in the border town of Piedras Negras.

If a call from the government is not enough, a reporter may find himself or herself the subject of personal attacks by columnists on the payroll of the government. This even happened to reporters of the *New York Times* and the *Wall Street Journal* during my four years in Mexico. Reporters who hit particularly sensitive subjects may experience worse. Adolfo Aguilar Zinser, a reporter for *Unomásuno,* a left-wing Mexico City daily, was kidnapped in 1984 in a paramilitary-style operation. His unidentified abductors told him he was being punished for some articles he had written on Mexico's handling of Guatemalan refugees. Released unharmed, he considers himself lucky. An alarming number of crusading Mexican journalists have just been killed. According to Freedom House, which monitors human rights worldwide, more Mexican journalists were murdered in 1987 than those of any other country. The most famous assassination of a journalist occurred in May 1984, when Mexico's best-known columnist, Manuel Buendía, was gunned down in broad daylight in Mexico City. He had many enemies. He had written frequently about corruption by former Mexico City police chief Arturo Durazo, graft in the oil-workers' union, spying by the U.S. Central Intelligence Agency, and clandestine activities of the Mexican ultra right. The government officially condemns such murders. But it rarely brings the murderers to justice. So far, there is no proof of any government involvement in such atrocities. Some political observers speculate that some of these murders, especially those outside Mexico City, may be a reaction to the inadequacy of Mexico's libel laws. Rich business executives, large land-holders, or powerful local officials—the typical targets of hard-hitting, some-times libelous, news coverage—have little legal recourse against reporters whom they feel have libeled them. They may just de-cide, this theory goes, that execution is the only real remedy they have.

With all these restraints—fear of loss of subsidies, intimidating calls, shutdown of one's publication or show, kidnapping, disap-pearances, and murder—it is not surprising that there is not a full airing of ideas in Mexico's press. But this is not to say that Mexico has a fully censored press. Even Scherer will tell you that. The continued publication of *Proceso* attests to it. There are cer-tainly worse examples of censored media in Paraguay, Guate-mala, Honduras, Chile, and other countries in Latin America and elsewhere. In Mexico, one can regularly see articles critical of the ruling party and of government policies in many newspapers such as *Unomásuno, El Financiero, La Jornada, El Diario de Yucatán,* and *El Norte (de Monterrey).* The *Mexico Journal,* an English-language publication that first appeared in the fall of 1987, also provides unvarnished reporting. During the 1988 presidential campaign, there was also regular coverage of all the antigovern-ment complaints of opposition candidates, although the volume of coverage of the ruling party's candidate, Carlos Salinas de Gor-tari, dwarfed all opposition coverage combined. Some Mexican cartoonists, especially those of *Proceso,* can be vicious. Some even lampoon the president, once an unheard-of affront. But to focus on the existence of critical newspaper coverage is to miss the point. Most Mexicans don't read newspapers or magazines. Even less read critical intellectual journals. More read comic books than read a newspaper. Most get their news from radio and television, which are not critical at all. The most popular television news program, Televisa's *24 Hours,* rarely says anything against the government. Its largely discredited host, Jacobo Zabludovsky, is openly anti-left and pro-government in his frequent snide asides during the program. Occasionally, as happened during a natural-gas disaster in Mexico City in 1984 and during Mexico City's 1985 earthquakes, Zabludovsky let the unsparing eye of the camera show Mexicans what was really happening in the streets. But these were the exceptions, not the rule.

The real issue in Mexico is not freedom of the press but free-dom of information. There is none. Even under the rules of self-censorship, Mexican reporters could write quite a bit about Mexican life if they could get information about it. But Mexican bureaucrats regard information as power, something they give out only for something in return. Sometimes even the president doesn't get the facts he needs to make informed decisions because his underlings are playing power games over the required data. Rumor, hearsay, and gossip are highly valued, for sometimes they are all there is. Frequently they appear in the press reported as fact.

High Mexican officials often talk in elliptical sentences that do not respond to reporters' questions. Out of inordinate respect or fear, reporters rarely point out that a question was not answered. Interviews with the president never get beyond the softball-question phase. Frequently, officials in the news spotlight just refuse to grant interviews. There is no tradition of the public's right to know.

This dampening effect on the circulation of ideas and information spills over into other media. The least affected medium is books, probably because books have the least impact. Mexicans don't have enough money to buy books, or not enough education to want them or understand them. Only 6 percent of Mexicans buy and read books, according to the 1980 census. Through the government-financed *Fondo de Cultura Económico* (the Economic Culture Fund), the government also determines, to a large extent, which books will be published. The *Fondo*'s endorsement can be very important in total sales because *Fondo* paperback editions are often chosen as Mexican classroom texts. Films are censored, but usually of sexual rather than political material. Few Mexican films deal with Mexican reality, and virtually none with politics. Self-censorship is the rule in such areas, rather than the government's direct hand. Mexico once enjoyed a golden age of films in the 1930s and 1940s. But much of what is found in theaters these days comes from the United States or Europe. Those films that are Mexican are mostly mindless comedies or violent shoot-'em-ups.

Even pure intellectual thought gets co-opted through government financing of think tanks, scholarships, prizes, and grants. The National Research System, set up in 1984, awards grants of up to $450 a month to about two thousand intellectuals. Likewise, intellectuals who write columns for newspapers that accept *embutes, gacetillas,* or other government subsidies are often restricted by the newspaper's own idea of what the government will and will not tolerate. Some intellectuals have shown a tendency since the current economic crisis began in 1982 to be more independent. On issues of vote fraud, environmental reform, and the economy, a small number are speaking out, choosing penurious independence over government bribes. Gabriel Zaid, in his book *The Presidential Economy,* has challenged the wisdom of the government's traditional domination of the economy. The Group of 100, a collection of Mexican writers, artists, and other intellectuals, has complained about Mexico's abominable environmental conditions and gotten the government to make some limited reforms. But many Mexican intellectuals remain like the characters in Arturo Azuela's novel *Shadows of Silence.* They write spare articles in obscure publications, pretending they have struck a vital blow for freedom. They argue among themselves about who has done the most to advance Mexican intellectual thought. Privately, they indulge in self-pity about how little they have done. Their fecklessness is tragic for Mexico. With no real opposition from political parties, the Catholic Church, the army, or other traditional centers of power in Latin America, intellectuals could make a difference if they had the courage to do so.

Strangely, the government has largely left alone one of the most popular media, comics. Just as Mexicans are gaga over *telenovelas* ("soap operas"), they are nuts about *fotonovelas,* the name for most comics in Mexico. About seventy-five million Mexicans read a comic book a week. One can find Superman and Spider Man comics at the corner newsstand. But the most common comics are adult stories about cowboys, cops-and-robbers, or true romance. Maybe the values touted in such stories explain the government's indifference to what comics say. Typically one finds themes of male domination, female obedience, respect for government authority, honor in poverty, and acceptance of one's grim lot in life as God's will. For example, in *Trampa por un Maldito* (Trap for a Bad Guy), a Western, Waneka, an Indian from the state of Sonora, spends most of the story discovering that her bandit father is a drunken, murdering louse. In the end, he dies, as does Waneka and her brother. Mexican comics don't go in much for Hollywood endings.

Women fare particularly badly in comics. The government does nothing to stop this despite official pronouncements about the equality of women under the law and the need to show them more respect. In many comics, one can see women in the midst of a striptease, women mud wrestling, or women in a variety of skimpy clothes that bare breasts and buttocks. Garter belts and G-strings seem the favorite costumes of comic artists who try to outdo each other in coming up with new angles to look down a woman's blouse or up her skirt.

Comic publishers argue that this low-level literature is about all the average Mexican's sixth-grade education can handle. They insist they provide an educational service by teaching readers, in some comics, about world history. Some comics may give Mexicans a rough outline of Roman or Greek history. But the average comic writer needs a little brushing up on current events. One of my favorite out-of-whack modern comics told a story about Mayim, a voluptuous Egyptian. The plot had Mayim trick an American, Alex Copek, into planting a bomb aboard a U.S. airliner. Mayim wanted to get revenge for the U.S. bombing of her village. Why the United States would have bombed its ally Egypt, which gets about two billion dollars in U.S. foreign aid annually, was never explained.

· · ·

Faced with such manipulation of ideas and expression, it's a wonder that anyone in Mexico bothers to try to get the truth out. It's particularly improbable that Julio Scherer is one of those trying. Now a grandfatherly sexagenarian with wispy gray hair, he hardly looks the part of a to-the-barricades rebel. An affable man in relaxed settings, he is painfully shy when asked to state his views on anything.

Scherer hardly ever grants an interview, a bizarre posture for a professional journalist. He can get violent in his zeal to avoid them. Once, when a Mexican television crew set up an ambush-style interview, he grabbed the crew's camera cable, pulled the camera forcefully to the ground, and stalked off. In my own case, after numerous unsuccessful requests by phone for an interview, Scherer finally agreed to let me talk to his associate Froylán López Narváez to see if Froylán could answer my questions. I got quite a bit about Scherer's personal and professional life from Froylán, whom I had known before. But some questions required personal responses. I narrowed them down to one typed page.

Reluctantly, Scherer agreed to see me a few days later and answer my questions. When I arrived, he came out of his office, in shirtsleeves and casual pants. We chatted briefly. I asked if we could begin the interview. At the last minute he begged off. "I'm too embarrassed," he said. "I don't like interviews."

As a compromise, we agreed that I would leave my list of questions and my tape recorder. Froylán would later turn the recorder on and ask the questions for me. Later, I could pick my recorder up. After a few days, Scherer said even a tape recorder was too intimidating. He preferred to write out his responses. I knew he had written two books, one on his experiences with the last four presidents of Mexico, the other a biography of the Mexican painter David Alfaro Siqueiros. Maybe, I thought, he only feels comfortable giving his views in print. I humored him. But after two weeks of excuses as to why he couldn't find the right words to write down, I went back to talk to him personally. I caught him in the hallway on his way to lunch.

He was terribly apologetic. "I know I've been a *pendejo* ("asshole") about this. But I wanted to get the answers right. It's hard for me. I'm searching inside me for the proper way to say it. I'm not finding what I need."

My questions had really boiled down to two. I wanted to know why he had passed up government bribes to journalists when all his contemporaries had not. After reading his writings, talking to his friends, and meeting him in person, I thought I had the answer to that one. He was just a decent man, the victim of a good upbringing by parents of integrity. The second question was more important, for I wanted to know if he thought there would be more freedom of the press in Mexico in the future. Would Mexicans finally get the data they needed to make informed decisions? Would they be allowed to speak out more? I knew I had time for just one question, and this was the one I asked him. With no tape recorder in front of him, with no intimidating blank piece of paper in his typewriter, he answered immediately. It was just one journalist talking to another.

"There are so many factors we don't know about yet," he said. "Things, of course, are better now than under Echeverría and López Portillo. That wouldn't be hard. Whether they will get better, though, I couldn't say for sure. I hope they will. But then I always hope for the best."

· 14 ·

The *Evangelista*

There are those in San Juan Jaltepec who say that their village's luck changed when they got a new patron saint. All villages in Mexico adopt a special saint who is supposed to watch over them. For centuries, the patron saint of San Juanito, as most call the tiny settlement, had been San Juan Bautista, or St. John the Baptist. But some time early in this century—no one seems to remember exactly when—there was a change. Things were going very badly for San Juanito. The village priest suggested a new patron saint might bring better luck. He proposed a switch to the Virgin of Candelaria.

The Virgin was known to bring good luck to children if they were brought before an image of her shortly after their birth. Sometimes she even performed miracles, it was said. Another village already had the Virgin as a patroness. But that was all right, the priest had said. Her goodness was big enough for San Juanito, too.

To make the switch, the villagers bought a three-foot-high plaster statue of the Virgin. Her white countenance now looks down from the altar upon a sea of brown faces that worships her from the cold marble floor of the village church.

While the Virgin's miraculous abilities seem to focus on infants, the story goes that if you ask her for something else—better crops, good health, a son—you might get that too. But if you do, you have to offer some sacrifice in thanks on her feast day, February 2. Typically, people bring flowers, such as the red gladioli and yellow mums that festooned the altar that February night that I visited San Juanito's church. But gifts of candles and homemade clothes for her statue are common, too.

I was in San Juanito, a Zapotec Indian hamlet in the state of Oaxaca, because of my maid Adelaida. She was born there. As a devout Catholic, she grew up believing in the Virgin's miraculous powers. Something had happened to make Adelaida believe the Virgin had performed a miracle for her. It was time to pay the Virgin back.

Adelaida's husband, Félix, had been robbed in late 1987. He didn't have much money on him at the time. The muggers, angry that they had wasted their time, beat him senseless. For weeks, Félix could not use his arms or hands. He had to quit his job as a construction worker. The prognosis for his recovery wasn't good. One doctor said it would be necessary to amputate one of Félix's arms because of the swelling. Adelaida did not accept the diagnoses. She prayed to the Virgin. Félix, for whatever reason, began to regain the use of his arms. His stiff hands began to flex again.

Adelaida did not listen to doubters who argued that Félix had just made a normal recovery. She knew it was the Virgin. That meant she had to go back to San Juanito to make an offering. Adelaida did not have the money to make the thirteen-hour bus trip from Mexico City to San Juanito. She pleaded with me for a loan. She told me that she and Félix had to place a crown on the altar of the Virgin on her feast day, which was fast approaching. For Adelaida, it was an enormous amount of money, about a hundred dollars. It took her weeks to pay it back. It left her with hardly anything to live on in the meantime.

To a stranger, this might seem a senseless squandering of a hundred dollars. But such financial excesses for fiestas or feast days are as Mexican as tortillas or sombreros. Mexicans are a ritual people. They have been making sacrificial offerings to the gods since long before the Spanish brought their crushing brand of Catholicism to the country in the 1500s. Some speculate that peasants, such as those who live in San Juanito, first made such offerings to placate the gods. Perhaps they did it out of fear, perhaps to prevent the gods from becoming envious of the good fortune of their earthly charges. Others think people just hoped that money would beget money, that strength would come through waste, just as some think an orgy regenerates one sexually. For Adelaida, the need to spend the money seemed purely a matter of fervor and of faith.

Adelaida had spent big money once before on a religious feast day. That time it was for celebrating the Day of the Dead, Mexico's combination of All Saints' Day, All Souls' Day, and Halloween. Many Mexicans believe that on the night between November 1 and 2, lost loved ones can communicate with the living if the right rituals are followed. Adelaida had lost a daughter to childhood illness, and her father was dead. She felt a need to communicate with them, so she borrowed money to buy ingredients for her daughter's and father's favorite meals. According to pre-Hispanic legend, one is supposed to lay out the meal on the graves of the deceased. The graves serve as picnic sites for the loved ones of those who have died. Waiting relatives often gorge themselves and get a little drunk while waiting to hear from those in the beyond. The favorite meals, supplemented with skull-shaped sugar candies and *pan de muerto* ("bread of the dead"), are supposed to entice the departed back to the world of the living—at least for the night. Adelaida told me she had been visited by her daughter and her father during past days of the dead. "How do you know?" I had asked. The wind had blown out a candle once, she said. Another time, a glass had tipped over. Those were the signs one looked for.

This sort of religious fervor was something I had run into all over Mexico, where an Indian tradition of religious fanaticism and violence has given the *mestizo* (mixed-race) nation a sort of folk Catholicism that the Church of Rome tolerantly accepts under the umbrella of ecumenism. I had seen poor Mexicans crawl for miles on their knees, inflicting bloody wounds, as they made pilgrimages each December 12 from their villages to the Basilica of the Virgin of Guadalupe, the patron saint of Mexico. They were paying her back for prayers answered. Each year, I had followed with fascination the stories of young men who played the role of Jesus in Easter pageants. They got so immersed in their parts that they allowed themselves to be crucified. Other actors pounded stainless-steel spikes into their flesh, leaving them with the stigmata for the rest of their lives. I decided to go to San Juanito with Adelaida for a few days to see if I could learn a little more about this extraordinary fervor.

If the Virgin of Candelaria had brought San Juanito good luck, I just couldn't imagine what the little *pueblo* must have been like when times were bad. Old-timers told me the post-Virgin transformation of San Juanito had been a "miracle." But they were hard pressed to point to specifics, such as bumper crops, when I asked how things had changed. San Juanito, as far as I could tell, had little of anything. It was a sorry collection of thatched-roofed mud huts and not much else, save the thirty-foot-high blue-and-white Catholic church whose twin domed bell towers stood glistening in the sun on high ground in the village's center. Pigs, chickens, and malnourished dogs roamed the unpaved streets at will, dumping their wastes where they would. There were no sewers or piped-in water. No home had a sink or bathroom. People bathed themselves outside, relieved themselves outside, as the animals did. There was no electricity, so only the moon and a few camp lanterns illuminated the village at night. No power meant there were no refrigerators to preserve food or chilled drinks to slake a hot afternoon's thirst. No one had a phone. There was no public transportation to the nearest paved highway, a hard hour's drive away. Almost no one had a car or truck, so the highway was really several hours' walk away along the crude back road that had recently been scratched into the ocher soil and rocky foothills that lay between the remote village and the highway.

San Juanito had a public grammar school, but the nearest high school was in Maria Lombardo de Caso, a small town more than an hour's taxi ride away. The taxi ride cost five thousand pesos (about two dollars), which was a day-and-a-half's pay for the agricultural work that the majority of San Juanito's residents did. Adelaida's husband, Félix, summed up San Juanito's situation best as he took me on a tour. "*Somos jodidos aquí,*" he said. "We're fucked here."

San Juanito was so poor and remote that it didn't even have its own priest. About every six weeks Father Octavio Vilches came from Mexico City to say Mass and hear confessions. But the rest of the time, people in San Juanito were on their own. Father Octavio, of course, had come for the Virgin's feast day. It was, after all, the most important holy day in the village. The massive secular fiesta made it a memorable social event as well.

There were five or six horn-and-drum bands that blared and thumped out music throughout the fiesta, which began on the eve of the Virgin's day. They played with more effort than talent, but they created an amusing atmosphere. There was dancing in the streets at night, fireworks, a somewhat comical bullfight with one of the local farmer's white Brahman bulls, a basketball tournament, and a series of Masses to honor the Virgin.

I knew that Father Octavio would be busy with Masses and other work, so I left myself plenty of time to talk with him about the importance of the Virgin to the village and about the fervor of religion in Mexico. I proposed an interview for any hour that was convenient. He said he'd think about it. A few hours later, I received a note saying an interview was impossible.

I wasn't really that surprised at his refusal. Religion isn't just a complicated affair in Mexico, it's a sensitive one. Even though 90 percent of Mexicans say they are Catholic, the Catholic Church is on shaky ground in Mexico. Throughout Mexico's revolutionary history, the church has always backed the status quo, earning an enduring enmity from the rebels who overthrew the establishment and their descendants who now rule Mexico. Anti-Catholic legislation first started appearing in the 1830s, two decades after the 1810 revolution. Laws against the church hit a high point under the reforms of President Benito Juárez in the middle of the last century. They were codified in the 1917 revolutionary constitution under which Mexico is governed today. That charter contains a dizzying number of antichurch provisions, which apply to all religions but which principally affect the Catholic Church. It denies legal status to any religion. Marriage in the church is not recognized. All citizens must be married civilly before any church ceremony. It proclaims that church buildings and lands are state property. Catholics and others may use the churches, but they need government approval to make alterations or additions to them. Churches can't run religious schools. Priests and ministers are denied the right to vote and may not wear clerical robes in public. Church leaders are banned from making public political comments. All parish priests must be native-born Mexicans, and their numbers are limited.

While that's what the law says, enforcement of these prohibitions isn't as harsh as it was in the late 1920s, when priests were rounded up and forced to marry in order to break their vows of celibacy. Those who refused were executed, like the famous "whiskey priest" in Graham Greene's novel *The Power and the Glory*. In 1926, the Catholic Church's opposition to the 1917 constitution led to the Cristero rebellion, a state-versus-church civil war that lasted until 1929. Many died, including President-elect Alvaro Obregón, who was assassinated in 1928 by a religious fanatic. Things remained tense but generally nonviolent through the 1930s. It was not until President Manuel Avila Camacho (1940–46) proclaimed that he was a Roman Catholic believer that religious peace was truly restored.

Many Mexican officials have had a schizophrenic attitude toward anticlerical laws ever since. As the ruling party's popularity has declined, political leaders have been reluctant to enforce the prohibitions literally, given the overwhelming Catholic nature of the voting public. Many officials, in fact, are devout Catholics themselves, who quietly send their children to schools that are titularly run by Catholic laity but, in reality, are church schools. The constitution bans any public celebration of Masses or other religious ceremonies. But when Pope John Paul II visited Mexico in the 1980s and held several open-air Masses, no government official tried to stop him. Many foreign priests operate in Mexico, despite a legal ban, because the Catholic Church has trouble getting enough Mexicans to become priests. Likewise, outspoken church leaders, such as Mexico City's Archbishop Ernesto Corripio Ahumada, are allowed to make veiled antigovernment remarks in the press. But most priests keep a pretty low profile, obviously hoping that keeping out of trouble may eventually help the church regain some of its former influence.

This was certainly the case with Father Octavio, whose polo-shirt-and-slacks outfit gave no hint of his real profession to an outsider. After he declined an interview, I found out he had a special reason for not wanting to anger the government with comments to the press. A small band of *campesino* leaders, affiliated with the ruling party, was trying to organize San Juanito's peasants who worked the coffee, corn, and bean fields of the region. That was a threat to Father Octavio's church. For generations San Juanito's people had always turned to the church for guidance in times of trouble. If party officials outside San Juanito helped the local organizers, the church might lose influence.

Many of San Juanito's 2,600 residents already voted for the PRI. That was mostly pragmatism. They wanted to make sure San Juanito would continue to receive what little it got from the government. But if residents, many of whom regarded the church as their guiding force in life, became more dependent on the PRI, San Juanito might eventually become what most of Mexico had: nominally Catholic, but secular in its heart.

Father Octavio also had Melitón Contreras Hernández to worry about. Melitón had been born in San Juanito thirty-seven years before. Like Adelaida, he had moved to the Mexico City area a few years back in search of work. He became a metal worker, doing specialty jobs on big construction projects. One of those was a church for a Switzerland-based Protestant group, known as the Word of God Church. Such Protestant groups had been making significant inroads in Mexico. The government had made the Catholic Church an official enemy of Mexico because of its anti-revolutionary role. But Protestant churches carried no such political baggage. Quietly but firmly they preached their message, even though public proselytizing was banned by Mexican law.

While Melitón was still doing metal work on the Word of God building, he observed church members "testifying" at prayer meetings in the still-unfinished structure. Melitón, a drinker and marijuana smoker who had regularly pilfered materials from the projects he worked on, was impressed. "I saw lawyers, doctors, even a drug trafficker testify to the Lord. I thought that if they could be saved, maybe this church was something for me, too."

Melitón had been a Catholic up to this point. But, by his own admission, he hadn't been a very good one. With little support in Mexican society for religious values, and with active government hostility toward Catholicism, he had not found what he wanted in his church. He had been born into Catholicism but had not chosen it himself. There was a fervor inside Melitón for things religious. And the people of the Word of God Church set it off.

Melitón joined the church, bringing along his wife and six children, all of whom had been baptized Catholics. Mexican women are particularly zealous about religion. I told Melitón I was surprised that his wife had converted as well.

"She saw I was becoming a better person in the church," he said. "She was impressed too."

Melitón had moved up the ranks in his new church. He had been made a "worker." His job was to return every few weeks to San Juanito, whose people he preached to in the Zapotec tongue he had used most of his life. He was intent on converting them to a literal belief in the Bible, a key tenet of the church. He had started his work just three months before I met him. Already he had converted about thirty villagers.

Melitón wasn't in San Juanito by chance. He had come specifically to counteract the religious impact of the Virgin's holiday. His stark prayer meetings provided a marked contrast to Father Octavio's lavish liturgy. At the Mass celebrated on the eve of the Virgin's feast day, Father Octavio, dressed in a white alb, began by hearing confessions. He gave people time to place candles and flowers on the altar in front of the Virgin's statue. Then, donning a red-and-white silk chasuble over his alb, he began the Mass proper. Once begun, he would now and then stop to swing the chain-held incense-holder through the air, filling the small church with wispy gray smoke. He went through a series of prayers, each different. Some one hundred parishioners made a standard response that began: "*Santa María, Madre de Dios . . .*" ("Holy Mary, Mother of God . . .").

On the fringe of the village, Melitón, dressed in navy slacks and matching sleeveless sweater, led about twenty of his flock through a candlelit reading of Corinthians on the importance of faith. His faithful sat on rough-hewn wooden benches, transfixed at his words.

"Do not let them hurt us; do not let them hide anything from us," began Melitón's oration.

"The Bible says all idols are an abomination," Melitón told his group. It was a not-so-veiled message: worshiping the Virgin of Candelaria was morally wrong. More subtly, he was making an attack on Mexicans' widespread adoration of the Virgin of Guadalupe, the patron saint of Mexico. This was dangerous ground. Although the government's revolutionary tradition requires it to be antichurch, no official is so politically stupid as to attack the Virgin, the most unifying force among Mexico's people. The government doesn't even allow the Mexican press to question the miracle involving the Virgin, who supposedly appeared to a dark-skinned Indian peasant, Juan Diego, in 1531 on the site of the former temple of Tonantzín, an Aztec earth goddess. Melitón and others in the Word of God's flock, however, dared to ask the questions many wondered about in private. Wasn't it convenient for the Catholic Church that the Virgin appeared in the guise of a dark-skinned Indian woman, in a place where an Indian goddess had once reigned? Wasn't the Virgin's "miracle"—leaving an imprint of roses on Juan Diego's cloak—a convenient sign for non-Catholic Indians to make an easy transition from their pagan beliefs to Catholicism? Wasn't the Virgin's request that a church be built on the site of Tonantzín's temple a convenient way to replace an Indian place of worship with a Catholic one?

"Idolatry, it's all idolatry," said one of Melitón's converts, Francisco Alvarez, in whose house I stayed during the celebration of the Virgin's feast day. "They mean nothing. The Virgin of Guadalupe is an idol, too. She means nothing at all."

This sort of remark, Francisco said, had caused Father Octavio to speak out against Melitón's tiny cell of *evangelistas*, the name Mexicans use for all Protestants.

"It's difficult to be an *evangelista* in a small village," said Francisco. "In other villages, they have killed us."

Despite such sniping, Melitón was not discouraged in his work. People who had known him before as a poor peasant now saw him dressed in tasteful blue suits and nice sweaters. He was a success, a man at peace with himself, a happy man, and, above all, a confident man.

"As the Bible says, the righteous are bold like a lion," said Melitón.

Boldness was behind Melitón's plan to build a Word of God church in San Juanito. Funds had been being collected. A site had been chosen. With a few more converts, Melitón would be able to ask for a pastor.

Melitón had been able to attract the curious to his prayer meetings, even though he offered a life of moral vigor and probity. The church had some activity almost every night of the week, be it prayer meeting, Bible reading, or song singing. It allows no drinking, no adultery, no lying, no criticizing of one's neighbor. It's a tough row to hoe, Melitón admitted. But it's a life many Mexicans want, he insisted, once they find the leadership to show it to them. It hasn't been easy to show everyone, Melitón noted. As in many villages with indigenous populations, San Juanito is plagued by men who fall down drunk from bouts with mezcal, the local cactus-based moonshine. Witchcraft, important in the Zapotec tradition, is still practiced too.

"We have *curanderos*, ["herb healers"], *brujas* ["witches"], and *hechiceros* ["sorcerers"]," Melitón said. "We are in a struggle for the souls of Mexicans."

• • •

At 6:00 A.M. on the Virgin of Candelaria's feast day, the bell of the church of San Juan Bautista awoke me in Francisco's house. The din of one of the brass-and-drum bands was rousing residents for early-morning Mass and other festivities. I dressed quickly and went outside to join the band-led procession that would ramble through town. In the parade was a young man from the next village, Santiago Yaveo. He had come to San Juanito to celebrate the feast day.

"Are you one of them?" he asked me.

"One of whom?" I said, wondering if he meant an American, since I was the first gringo ever to visit the village.

"The *evangelistas*," he said. "I saw you talking with them."

"No," I replied. "I am not an *evangelista*."

"Are you a Catholic?" he continued.

"I was baptized a Catholic," I said. "Now, as one says in Mexico, I am *jubliado*—retired."

"You are a Catholic forever," said the serious young man, seeing no humor in my remark. "We need Catholics to help us. These *evangelistas* are in my village, too. They are stealing souls. They must be stopped."

I had had Jehovah's Witnesses and Pentecostalists knock many times on my door in Mexico City. I had listened politely and told them I wasn't interested in conversion. They always went away, I told the young man. "All you have to do is say no."

That was not enough, he said. They must be stopped.

"We have killed some," he said. "We will kill some more."

Since both Melitón and Francisco had said that some of their church's workers had been murdered, I didn't take these words lightly.

"Is it a Catholic thing to do—to kill someone?" I asked.

I got no answer.

"Have you killed someone?" I pressed on.

Still no answer.

"Would you kill one of them?" I finally asked.

"If they provoke us," the young man said, "it is justified. We are talking about souls."

The young man left and headed for Mass. I stayed in San Juanito for a little while after that. But by mid-morning I felt there wasn't much point in staying longer. I had come looking for the meaning of religious fervor. In an unexpected way, I had found it.

· III ·
Values

· 15 ·

The *Cómico*

¿Qué Nos Pasa? is a weekly comedy show, one of the most popular on Mexican television. Each Tuesday, for half an hour it offers a biting, satirical message on the foibles and frailties of the Mexican character. Tardiness, elaborate lies, obfuscating speech—all are fair game for the show's band of players. Some find its content unpatriotic, if not downright subversive. Maybe that's why its host, comedian Hector Suárez, gets calls from the government telling him to shut up, and anonymous threats from others warning him what will happen if he doesn't. The government's airlines regularly lose his luggage, too, Suárez notes. But maybe that's nothing personal, he jokes. In Mexico, that happens to everyone.

I met most of the characters in this book by chance or in the course of my work as a reporter. In the case of Hector Suárez, I sought him out. I was looking for someone who could take me through the complicated, convoluted elements of the Mexican character. I wanted to get behind the stereotypes. I wanted the mysteries explained. I had thought about talking to Mexican poet Octavio Paz. He wrote *The Labyrinth of Solitude*, the classic study of the Mexican personality. I had also thought about Carlos Monsiváis, a Mexican intellectual who has become the leading analyst of the Mexicans of the 1980s. But I decided that an even better choice would be a Mexican *cómico,* a "comic." Who better than a comic examines the strengths and faults of his own people? I started looking for Mexico's version of Robin Williams or David Letterman. Most people I asked told me to look for Hector Suárez.

Suárez, now at the peak of his career, has seen it all in Mexico. Born some fifty years ago in a rough barrio of Mexico City, he enjoys enough wealth to have a Mercedes-Benz, a comfortable colonial-style home in a fashionable area of the capital, and a weekend house in the country. He has become the highest-paid movie star in Mexican film history. In his thirty-year career, he has been in some three dozen films. Some, like *El Milusos* (The Handyman), have won international praise. But his pride and joy is his weekly show, *¿Qué Nos Pasa?* Each Tuesday night, its title asks Mexicans: "What's Happening to Us?" More specifically, a brief message at the beginning of the show asks viewers if they see themselves in the parodied characters about to appear. What Suárez has done is provide a weekly vehicle for examining who Mexicans are.

Suárez, the private man, is not what one would expect. On television, his characters run from zany to dumb. In person, he is intelligent, thoughtful, and, to the chagrin of the government, polemic. Brought up by his grandmother, who once fought with the revolutionary forces of Emiliano Zapata, he has become a social guerrilla with a dangerous weapon: a sense of humor.

His most famous persona is the mustachioed Ciriaco, an idiotic-looking man in overalls and a New York Yankees baseball cap with the bill turned up. Ciriaco runs around saying *"¡No hay!"* That means "There aren't any." It draws a laugh every time. If you are Mexican, you know why. Given Mexico's economic crisis, the government's heavy, inefficient hand in running much of the economy, and private enterprise's indifferent attitude toward customers, *"¡No hay!"* is a phrase heard often in Mexico. There are always shortages of something—inexplicable, maddening shortages. Ciriaco started out helping Mexicans laugh at this misfortune. But his *"¡No hay!"* punch line has become a symbol of so much more since *¿Qué Nos Pasa?* began in 1986. *"¡No hay!"* is a battle cry for anyone who wants to complain about the shortcomings of life in Mexico. Grammar and high schools now hold *"¡No hay!"* contests in attempts to wipe out shortcomings in grades or schoolroom cleanliness. Suárez regularly goes to schools to hand out prizes to winners. His *"¡No hay!"* character hit such a nerve among Mexicans that one can find Ciriaco posters and bumper stickers all over Mexico, especially in the homes, shops, and rattletrap cars of the poor.

Suárez's *"¡No hay!"* routine has also forced many Mexican merchants to stop saying *"¡No hay!"* The shortages continue, maybe a little less severe than before. But now the person behind the counter feels a bit ridiculous saying *"¡No hay!"* when something isn't in stock.

"They try to think of some other way to say it," laughed Suárez, who hopes the merchants' next step will be to do something about the shortages themselves.

Suárez enjoys putting the heat on those who exhibit tendencies that he considers harmful to his beloved Mexico. He is pleased that his mordant show is having an impact by making Mexicans think about how they act. Even the powerful have cleaned up their acts. Fidel Velázquez, long the best-known labor leader in Mexico, was parodied by Suárez for his tendency to talk forever without saying anything. During Mexico's times of economic crisis, Velázquez, a leader in the pocket of the government, had little good news to tell workers, so he chose to obfuscate when asked about wages or the economy. When Suárez put the spotlight on Velázquez's little game, Velázquez became more direct in his public pronouncements. Sometimes he even stopped wearing his trademark horn-rimmed glasses, duplicates of which Suárez used in his act to let everyone know whom he was ridiculing.

Suárez also got the government to make Mexican cigarette manufacturers change the required health warning on packs of cigarettes. The warning had said: This product can be harmful to your health. Suárez asked his audience, *"Can* be harmful? Are Mexican cigarettes or tobacco different? Everywhere else in the world, cigarettes *are* harmful. Are Mexican cigarettes superior?" Warnings now say: This product is harmful to your health.

Mexican airline pilots are infamous for never telling passengers why the plane has been delayed or what is wrong. Suárez skewered this arrogant attitude, too. Now, when he experiences flight delays, pilots frequently come back to apologize and tell him what is happening. But they still don't tell anyone else.

"At least it's a beginning," shrugged Suárez.

Getting the merchants, Fidel Velázquez, the cigarette manufacturers, and the pilots to change their errant ways were small victories in Suárez's efforts to make Mexicans better human beings. But he knows that final victory is far away. He is trying to get Mexicans to change a lifetime of bad habits and attitudes. He is trying to change a culture. Others who have examined the Mexican character have blamed a number of negative Mexican characteristics on the Spanish conquistadores. Hernán Cortés and his ruthless band beat an indigenous people into a feeling of inferiority. In many cases—too many cases, according to Suárez—this downtrodden feeling has stuck, long past when there was any justification for it.

"Mexico is a first-class country," said Suárez. "The problem is we have a lot of fifth-class people."

Suárez said it would be easy to blame the government, whose repressive policies keep people in fear and sap their confidence. But the real ones to blame, he argued, are Mexicans themselves.

"Mexicans don't have the courage to be themselves," he said. "[Their shortcomings] are problems they should solve themselves."

Just in case inertia might hold them back a bit, Suárez concocts skits every week to give his fellow Mexicans a cultural kick in the pants. He zeros in on those habits or characteristics he finds the most damaging to Mexico's future. For example, in one ¿Qué Nos Pasa? skit, a man has had a car accident on a busy expressway in Mexico City. At risk of his life, he stays with his car on the shoulderless road as he waits for an insurance agent he has called. Many hours later, the agent finally arrives, showing no remorse for his tardiness. When the man complains about the delay, the agent replies incredulously that he had no idea the man was a stickler for punctuality. After examining the wreck, the agent tells his client that his car, now shaped like an accordion, might prove to be quite an asset—easy to park, more economical on gas, easy to maneuver through Mexico City's overly narrow streets. That's a good thing, the agent adds, because his company won't be reimbursing the car owner for the damage. His company, he explains in his most illogical manner, does not pay for accidents caused by the irresponsibility of third parties.

"Kafka would go crazy here," laughed Suárez, whose heroes in theater are, appropriately, Kafka, Ionesco, and Strindberg.

The skit's intended themes were the Mexican concept of time, lying, and the lack of logic in daily life. They are all key to under-standing who Mexicans are, Suárez said. Other skits focus on cruelty, the Mexican attitude toward death, vanity, officiousness, black humor, alcoholism, the common use of double entendre, and the tendency to screw someone before he or she screws you. All these harmful characteristics sprang from the same roots, said Suárez. All could be eradicated if Mexicans would just realize that those roots have been dead a long time.

In the beginning—that is to say, around 1519, when Cortés arrived—there was some need to keep your head down and avoid eye contact with authority, Suárez acknowledged as we began a series of talks about Mexicans at his home in the San Jerónimo neighborhood. The sixteenth century, especially the Spanish ver-sion of that century, was not one dominated by notions of human rights and democracy. It was dominated by domination. The res-idents of what Cortés called New Spain had to do what they were told. For some, this was easy. The Indian kings and priests who had ruled before Cortés had had a dictatorial approach to govern-ing too. But the Spanish injected a new element: a feeling of cultural inferiority for the subjugated. The new rulers of Mexico told their subjects that they were worthless. They treated many of them like slaves. These indigenous people—Aztecs, Mayans, and the like—felt shame that they had been vanquished by a smaller Spanish force. Their shame was passed down to their progeny, including those *meztizos* who were the fruit of cou-plings between the Spanish invaders and Indian women. The Spanish brought priests to instruct the conquered and their de-scendants in the "one true faith"—Catholicism. They taught the mysteries of that religion and some rudimentary Spanish—but lit-tle else. Those whom they taught developed a feeling of igno-rance. They lost confidence. In 1810, the year Father Miguel Hidalgo shouted "¡Viva Mexico!" one warm September night, Mexico began its erratic move toward independence. It experi-enced emperors and tyrants in the century that followed, enjoy-ing only a brief period of democratic reform under Benito Juárez, the only pure-blooded Indian president Mexico has ever had. In the early twentieth century came another revolution, this one against a Mexican dictator instead of a Spanish one. Mexico had been free of Spain for more than a hundred years by this time. But even the catharsis of a century of rebellion and revolution had not cast out the demons let loose by Cortés and his men. Many Mexicans were still acting as if they had to cower in the face of power—not just government power but any kind of power. Nearly eighty years later they were doing the same thing, complained Suárez.

This "tremendous feeling of inferiority," as Suárez calls it, is exhibited in many ways. On one side, it may involve timidity or even servility in speech or action. On the other, one sees a cruel, reckless bravado, which some call machismo.

There are many servile sayings in Mexico. Most of the Spanish-speaking world says "*¿Cómo?*" when it wants to say "What did you say?" or "Huh?" In Mexico, one says "*¿Mande, usted?*" Literally, this means "Order me," as in, "I didn't hear you. Order me again." Rich and poor, educated and illiterate use it. If a Mexican wants to say "May help you?" he or she says: "*A sus ordenes*" ("At your orders"), or "*Su servidor*" ("Your servant"). When they are finished waiting on you, they say: "*Para servirle*" ("I did it to serve you").

Much of this is false servility. A waiter, when asked for the check, may reply: "*¡Con muchísimo gusto!*" ("With the utmost pleasure!") and then ignore you for half an hour. When President Miguel de la Madrid's tourism minister first met my wife, he said to her: "*A sus pies*" ("I am at your feet"). Obviously he did not intend to prostrate himself before her. Educated people, like the minister, explain that they are only trying to be courteous—in the extreme Mexican way. But other Hispanics roll their eyes when they hear such fawning.

Likewise, Mexicans, more than most Hispanics, speak in a roundabout way when they want to tell you something. They rarely say directly what it is they really want or mean. One of Suárez's heroes, Cantinflas, the famous Mexican comedian, has parodied this tendency of circumlocution so much that this style of speaking has become known as *cantinflismo*. Suárez mocked one common example of this tendency in a *¿Qué Nos Pasa?* skit that involved a wealthy woman who comes to a government office to complain about her real-estate assessment being too high. She tells the bored tax clerk, "*Venía* [One was coming] to this office to complain about my assessment." The clerk, played by Suárez, replies: " '*Venía*'! What do you mean, '*Venía*'? Don't you mean '*Vengo*'? Why don't you just say 'I came' to complain?"

"People hide behind such fuzziness because they don't want to take responsibility for anything, they don't want to make any promises," Suárez said.

Speaking indirectly to avoid confrontation or commitments has led to a remarkable creativity in use of language, Suárez thinks. Nowhere else in Latin America does he find use of Spanish so rich, so layered in meaning. Double entendre has become the plaything of Mexicans, especially in a sexual sense. Mexicans speak in multiple meanings without effort. Even the simplest Spanish words can be traps for the uninitiated, as I found out when I first arrived in Mexico. For example, the first time I went to a market, I asked the man behind the counter, "¿Tiene huevos?" I thought I was asking, "Do you have any eggs?" In Mexico, however, huevos ("eggs") can also mean testicles as the laughing customer alongside me explained. A helpful friend recommended that, in the future, I ask the more indirect question "¿Hay huevos?" ("Are there any eggs?") Likewise leche ("milk") can mean sperm, chile ("chile pepper") can mean penis, and chi-chi ("chic") can mean tits.

Mexicans have also become creative about lying, which Suárez calls the Mexican cancer.

"Lying is our daily bread," he said. "The first thing a Mexican learns to do is lie. Life is a continuous lie. A Mexican lies to protect himself. He does it because he is vain. He does it to give himself value. Mexicans don't feel as they have a real place in the world, so they invent one."

People will inflate their wealth or accomplishments or the degree of their friendships with powerful people, Suárez noted. Unlike Spain, few people except older Mexicans are called Don as a title of dignity. Instead, Mexicans like to use Licenciado, which shows that they have a college degree. Few have a degree, however. But this doesn't stop many vain Mexicans from printing up business cards with Licenciado before their names. Others will hang up pictures of themselves with famous politicians, even those they curse in private as crooks and thugs. They want their friends to think they are important.

Faced with the possibility of recriminations or punishment for their actions, Mexicans will deny responsibility at all costs. They will lie, of course, said Suárez, but indirect speech is important too. I had noticed this right away, I mentioned. Shortly after I hired a maid, I came home one night and was told: "Se cayó el florero" ("The vase fell down.") "Did it fall by itself?" I asked.

"Was there an earthquake? Did someone knock it over?" The only answer one will get to such interrogations is: "*¿Quién sabe, Señor?*" ("Who knows?").

A key reason why people lie, Suárez said, is that they often don't know the answer to a question. They lie because they don't want people to think they are ignorant. They are ashamed of their ignorance, even though no one could be expected to know the answer to every question. In a country where the average person has finished only six years of grammar school, this aching feeling of ignorance is widespread. Any stranger who asks directions in Mexico, Suárez warned, may become the victim of this Mexican tendency. To maintain *dignidad* ("dignity"), many Mexicans will avoid ever saying: "I don't know." A lost foreigner is likely to hear: "Go straight ahead for a while and ask the next person." The site the stranger is seeking might be just a few feet to the left or right—or behind—but invariably the advice will be to proceed straight ahead. Likewise, Mexicans who are lost are loath to ask someone how to get where they want to go. Suárez said he frequently has to yell at his obstinate chauffeur to ask someone where an address is.

Mexicans also create masks to shield themselves from those who might hurt them. Most Mexicans have *apodos*, or nicknames, that give them an image that may be nothing like they really are. Such names are generally bestowed by one's closest friends, who usually pick out some distinctive physical characteristic or habit of a person. El Pelón is someone who is bald or has thin hair. El Gato is someone regarded as having a swift cleverness. A friend of mine, Luis Hernández, was called Golden Beak because of his facile way with words. One of his best friends was Three Daily, because that was the number of times a day he tried to have sex. Cruel friends can stick a buddy with an unfortunate nickname, such as El Moco ("Mucus") or El Rata ("The Rat").

Negative names are part of a widespread cruelty that many Mexicans exhibit as a means of self-defense. Many feel that their fate in life is to be screwed by someone, just as the Spanish screwed the Indians of Mexico, just as many leaders of Mexico have screwed their fellow citizens. Some Mexicans react by trying to screw someone else first. They *chinga* someone. *Chingar* means to do violence to someone, to rape someone figuratively or literally. A *chingón* is someone who succeeds in screwing someone else. It is a term of admiration. People say "*¡Qué chingón!*" when they mean "What a guy!" Many foreigners mistakenly think *chingar* just means to have intercourse. It can, although, more directly, this distinction goes to *joder*. *Chingar* means so much more. A *chingadazo* is a heavy blow. A *chingadera* is a dirty trick. A *chingaquedito* is an irritating person. "*Vete a la chingada*" means "Go to hell!" And Mexicans blackly refer to themselves as *hijos de la chingada* ("children of the raped"). Having been raped in one way or another through the centuries, Mexicans have decided it is better, said Suárez, "*que chingo que me chingues*" ("that I hurt you before you hurt me").

Bureaucrats exhibit this tendency of trying to screw someone. They typically ignore people's requests for simple services. Often they demand a bribe to perform them. Mexicans call this *el pequeno poder* ("the little power"). There are so few occasions when people feel they have power over their own or others' lives that they seize every precious opportunity they get. Mexicans' concept of time reflects this. Many foreigners mistakenly think that all Mexicans have a *mañana* attitude about doing everything. Everything is done slowly, perhaps out of a native laziness, outsiders think. Obviously such people have never driven in the frenzied atmosphere of Mexico City traffic or had Mexicans shamelessly butt in line at the bank or the supermarket. Time is power, Suárez explained. When it is a Mexican's own time that is involved, things can't be done fast enough. But when it is someone else's time, then what does it matter if one shows up two or three hours late for a dinner party? Being late is a Mexican's way of showing others that they don't have power over him. It is a little protest—one of the few that can be made—about how little control a Mexican has over time or anything else.

This sort of attitude hardly leads to great national camaraderie. Suárez tells the familiar Mexican joke about a grandmother who tells her grandson to separate the lobsters they have caught into dark ones and light ones. The dark ones (representing Mexicans) should go in the basket without the lid, she says. The light ones (representing Americans) have to be put in the basket with the lid. "Why, *abuelita* ["grandma"]?" asks the boy. Because the light ones are smart, says the grandma. When one figures how to get out of the basket, it will help the others until all have escaped. "But what about the dark ones?" asks the boy. With them, there will be no problem, the grandma says. As soon as the first dark one tries to get out, all the others will try to pull him down.

This self-denigrating humor is also illustrated in another oft-told Mexican joke about God and one of his archangels, Suárez said. God is creating the world, and the archangel asks if it is fair to give Mexico so much—gold, silver, oil, beautiful mountains and lakes, thousands of miles of sandy beaches, wonderful fruits and vegetables, and millions of acres of lush trees. "Oh, don't worry," God replies. "I'm also going to give it Mexicans."

This sort of black humor pervades Mexican culture, Suárez noted. It is yet another example of how Mexicans try to protect themselves by hurting others. My most vivid memory of this tendency came after a 1984 natural-gas explosion in San Juanico, a slum north of Mexico City. I reported on this tragedy, Mexico's worst industrial accident. Hundreds of lives were lost as an exploding gas plant leveled an adjacent neighborhood. Despite the humorless nature of this tragedy, dozens of San Juanico jokes sprang up within days. One could hear them on the streets and even on the radio. One went: Q. How do you fit ninety kids from San Juanico in a Volkswagen? A. Put them in the ash tray! Another was: From now on, San Juanico's feast day will be Ash Wednesday. Writer Carlos Monsiváis has suggested that one reason why Mexicans engage in such humor is to make themselves feel superior to those who have suffered. Suárez suggested that it might also be an attempt to deny the reality of the disaster by belittling it. In this respect, he said, such jokes weren't much different from Mexicans' attitude toward death. Many foreigners hear that Mexicans laugh at death. They celebrate the Day of the Dead in early November by eating sugar skulls and having picnics on the graves of their loved ones. Laughing at death, however, said Suárez, does not mean that Mexicans are not afraid of it.

"Mexicans fear death," he said, "so they want to be death's friend. They think that if they are his friend, he won't do anything to them. This is why a Mexican plays with death. Sometimes he even shouts at death to show his courage. He calls death a whore. But he is really terrified by death. He just lies about it."

• • •

"Look," said Suárez, after we had been talking for about three hours, "I don't want people to get the idea that there are only negative things to say about Mexicans. I talk about the vices because I love Mexico and because they bother me." Mexicans are hard-working and courageous, Suárez thinks. Above all, he likes their ingenuity. But isn't it a shame, he asks, that all their creativity has to be channeled into unproductive activities such as obfuscating speech, double entendre, and lying.

"Mexicans have great potential, but we don't use our ingenuity in productive ways," he said. "If we could channel this ingenuity in the right way, we could become a world power. I'm a bit of a chauvinist in saying that we have a brilliant minority, people like Octavio Paz. But we are only a few. I love Mexico. I adore it. It is a magic place. But I hurt because of its faults. That's why I point them out. I want us to change."

Suárez said that shows like his are not enough to make Mexicans act more responsible and become more productive. The government must lead, too, although he admitted this was unlikely. If the government encouraged people to be more independent and confident, they would demand more democracy. And the government might lose some of the frightening power it has.

If the government were inclined to reform people's characters, it had a once-in-a-lifetime chance to do so when two earthquakes struck Mexico City in September 1985, Suárez argued. During the aftermath of the earthquakes, many Mexicans took their lives into their own hands for the first time. They acted bravely. They showed confidence and independence. Gone was the normal attitude of leaving things up to the government. Gone was the fatalistic view that nothing can be done because that's the way life is. Few uttered that ubiquitous phrase "¿Ni modo?" ("What else can one do?"). Mexicans pitched in block by block to dig out victims buried under tons of rubble. Courageous tunnelers, who became known as "the moles," burrowed through cement and twisted steel to snatch fading lives from death's door. Mexicans felt good about themselves, Suárez said. They seemed to be waiting for someone to tell them that things had changed, that they were worth something. But no one did. Instead, the authorities told people that the earthquakes had not been a punishment from God. It was not their fault, the officials said, as if everyone assumed that it was.

Suárez blames not only the government for failing to lead. He reproaches Mexican mothers and fathers for continuing to instill feelings of dependency and inferiority in their children. He faults them for telling their kids that social plagues, such as Mexico's widespread corruption, are inevitable, unconquerable.

The picture is not all grim, however, he said as we finished up our colloquium. Changes are afoot, he insisted. Since the government of President Díaz Ordaz massacred student protesters just before the 1968 Mexico City Summer Olympics, Mexico has been a different country, in Suárez's view. The differences have been slow to surface. But they are there. The government is letting the press print more critical things. Opposition politicians have emerged and are increasingly vocal. But political leaders will not be the ones to change Mexico, Suárez believes.

"We must begin in the home," said Suárez, who has done just that. Ten years ago he got his alcoholism under control and now tours prisons and schools warning others about this and other socially destructive behavior. In a land of machos, he has become what he calls "a hundred percent feminist." He considers his Spanish wife his best friend. He gives his two teenage kids regular lectures about how to be good citizens and sensitive human beings.

"My son and daughter know what the truth is," he said. "They know that things aren't perfect. But they also know that things can get better. They know that we can go forward as a nation."

· 16 ·

The *Maricón*

From what little he remembers of it, Juan Jacobo Hernández's childhood was quite normal. Until the age of six, he lived in León, in the state of Guanajuato. His memories are mostly gauzy images of playing with his brothers, sisters, and friends—except for one bizarre incident. At age four, he was sitting one day in a playpen with a number of his friends. As young boys will do, they began to examine and play with each other's genitals. Some adults discovered them and became very upset. The adults told the boys that such things were not nice and certainly nothing to be done in public. At the time, Juan Jacobo didn't understand what he had done wrong. Eleven years later, he would discover why the adults had been so upset.

In 1948, Juan Jacobo's family moved to Mexico City. He began school and studied a lot, encouraged by his mother and father, who had above-average educations. He made friends easily and quickly became one of the gang. When he turned fifteen, however, his world changed completely. He doesn't remember what triggered the realization. But in that sixteenth year of life it dawned on him that all of his friends were boys. He had no girlfriends, and no desire to have any. He realized he was a homosexual.

Juan Jacobo's parents probably suspected something. But, like most Mexican parents, they said nothing. Juan Jacobo didn't say much either. Mexico is the land of machismo. Being gay not only rejects the most important cultural value pounded into little boys, it can also be downright dangerous.

In 1964, at age twenty-two, Juan Jacobo finally did tell his parents and his seven brothers and sisters that he was gay. His father, now a retired electronics technician, said nothing. He still refuses to talk with Juan Jacobo about anything. His mother, a retired secretary, talks with him but has never really understood, as she might put it, what went wrong. His brothers and sisters are split. Some ask him about gay life, though only sparingly. The others, mortified at what their friends think about Juan Jacobo, can barely keep up the small talk when he enters the room.

Since his admission to his family, Juan Jacobo has come to grips with his sexual preference. He gives every sign of enjoying life immensely, despite the hostility one can find toward gays in Mexico. In the mid-1960s, he went bisexual for a while. He had a torrid affair with a woman who seemed intent on saving him from himself. But Juan Jacobo has no inner doubts about what he is now. He is gay, pure and simple. He regards his past liaisons with women as fanciful flings, departures from real life.

Juan Jacobo might have remained a closet gay whose secret life was known only to his immediate families and his lovers. But Mexico, like many nations, went through radical times beginning in 1968, the year Mexico City hosted the Summer Olympics. Student protests and deaths in the streets started a lot of people thinking about their rights. Mexican gays were no exception. Many of them, bitter with the taste of government repression, fled Mexico for a while. Others bolted in 1971, when more were killed in Mexico City's streets during antigovernment protests. In the United States and Europe, young men such as Juan Jacobo picked up ideas of gay liberation. They picked up audacity, too.

Imbued with this new courage, Juan Jacobo came out of the closet in 1972. He surprised quite a few of his friends, not to mention his superiors at the Catholic boys' school where he was teaching. There had never been any real trouble at school because of Juan Jacobo's sexual preference. Nonetheless, after he went public with his gayness, he moved on. He speaks French and English in addition to Spanish. He used his language skills to earn money as a translator for a while. But the theater was his real passion. He acted in a lot of experimental plays. Eventually, he wound up teaching theater analysis and English at the National Autonomous University of Mexico (UNAM), a bastion of left-wing thought where he had received a bachelor's degree in French letters some years earlier.

When I met Juan Jacobo in June of 1987, he was on sabbatical from UNAM to work as an editor of *Macho Tips*, Mexico's only regularly published gay magazine. The Acquired Immune Deficiency Syndrome (AIDS) scare had reached Mexico. Gays and left-wing parties were marching in the streets to demand that the government do something about the plague of the twentieth century. Juan Jacobo, whose magazine was publishing graphic, how-to articles on safe sex, was among the march leaders. I sought him out.

At the time, the United States had 40,000 confirmed cases of AIDS. Mexico had only 500. There was some finger-pointing in Mexico, as there had been in the United States. But the target was not the Mexican gay community. Not burdened by puritanical tradition, no Mexicans declared that God was punishing Mexican gays for their perversions. The farthest some government officials would go was to argue that Mexican cases of AIDS were mostly the fault of gay Americans or Europeans who had transmitted the disease to unsuspecting Mexicans. More than wrath, there was fear. Health treatment and basic hygiene are substandard in Mexico. Government officials were scared they might have an AIDS epidemic on their hands. They were so frightened that they began dealing with the gay community as they would with any other important sector of Mexican society—with respect. They seemed to realize that more gays had AIDS than any other population group. More were going to die of it. Therefore the cooperation of gays was vital to blunting the spread of the disease. What was fascinating about this was that under normal conditions, the government, like most of the Mexican people, would never have admitted that homosexuality even existed in Mexico. Gays had always been nonpersons. But AIDS had forced the government not only to let homosexuals march in the streets. The controlled Mexican press was told it was all right to write about it. Mexicans were not being allowed anymore to pretend that gays did not exist.

The policy was a two-edged sword. Gays did pitch in to help

the Mexican Health Ministry get its anti-AIDS campaign under way. There was no sniggering or displays of discomfort as health officials met with leaders of the gay community to plot strategy. An AIDS information center was opened in the summer of 1987. The government ran ads in most newspapers to let people know that AIDS could not be transmitted casually. In no-nonsense terms, the ads explained what AIDS was and was not, and how to avoid it. The government provided free testing for AIDS under conditions of strict confidentiality. The unexpected kicker in all this was that many Mexican gays found they liked the new openness about their existence. In what seemed a pivotal social event, they began talking about gay rights with a fervor not seen in more than a decade.

Socially, the new gay overtness was only a toe in the water. One did not see thousands of gays coming out of the closet that year. But the long-felt fear about being exposed as gay began to wither ever so slightly. Gay leaders began to talk, however hesitantly, about a new era of homosexuality in Mexico. They had no illusions that Mexico City would soon become the San Francisco of Mexico, with its own Castro district, political candidates, and gay-pride parades. Mexicans' attitudes against gays were too ingrained for that, they knew. But—ironically, thanks to AIDS—it might be just a little easier to be gay in Mexico. People might be a little more tolerant, some gays began to say. I found that an intriguing prospect for a society that worshiped at the altar of machismo.

One night I announced to my wife that I would be home late because I was going to cruise the gay bars of Mexico City's Zona Rosa. My wife looked a little nonplussed at first. But I quickly told her that I wasn't proclaiming any new sexual preference. I had just arranged with Juan Jacobo to show me around the night spots that he and his friends frequented. If I was going to understand this profound transformation of Mexican society, I needed to spend some time with Mexican gays.

My classroom was El Taller, a basement-level gay disco on Florencia Street in the Zona Rosa, the capital's center of good restaurants and fine shopping. My teachers were Juan Jacobo and several of his friends, including an American visitor, Dr. Clark Taylor. From the street, it's easy to walk past El Taller. Its nondescript entrance makes no attempt to invite clients in. People come to El Taller because they've been told about it. Juan Jacobo described El Taller's decor as "a little butch." Its walls and ceilings were a montage of gears and cogs, industrial pipes, and electrical coils. Most everything was painted red or black. We arrived around seven. The crowd was pretty thin, about fifty young and middle-aged men, casually dressed. It was a weekday. But even if it had been Saturday night, it would have been early for Mexico City, which parties very late. Juan Jacobo had picked this night because Mario Rivas was performing. Mario was Juan Jacobo's lover and had been since 1980.

Mario wasn't going to be on for a while, so Juan Jacobo, Dr. Taylor, another of Juan Jacobo's friends, named Andre del Valle, and I began to talk about how gay life in Mexico was different from elsewhere. Dr. Taylor, who has written extensively on homosexual life in Mexico, said there were some things that foreigners would notice right away. For example, stylish clothes aren't as important, nor are fantasy costumes. Some American gays are fond of playing roles when they go out at night to meet other gays, Taylor noted. They dress in motorcycle leathers. Those who are hustlers play the Midnight Cowboy. Mexicans don't dress this way at all, Taylor said. There are *padrotes,* or hustlers. But most can't afford cowboy gear. Even if Mexican gays could afford a costume, he said, they wouldn't get all rigged out in leather. In Mexico there is no leather cult, an idea spawned in Northern Europe.

"Here it's more common to be yourself," said Juan Jacobo. "You wear the clothes you have."

American gays' preoccupation with looking tan, muscled, and youthful also doesn't exist among Mexico's homosexuals. Most Mexicans are *mestizos,* of mixed Spanish-Indian origin. They already have dark complexions. Tanning just isn't as important. A well-developed body is appreciated, but again, Taylor said, few people have the money to go to health clubs to work out.

Picking people up is different, too. "The life," as gays call homosexual living, is mostly in the streets. There are no gay community centers and few places other than some secluded bars where gays can meet. Juan Jacobo has met most of his lovers while going from one place to another in Mexico City. Others he has linked up with in public bathhouses, which many straight Mexicans use because so many homes are without bathrooms.

Crowded subway cars are another favorite haunt. Juan Jacobo's technique is to give men "the look." It's hard to describe it, he said. He just knows how to give it and what it looks like in return. Mostly it's in the eyes, he said. If he gets a look back, he starts up a conversation to see if there is interest in a cup of coffee and perhaps something more.

The difficulty in meeting people may explain why Mexican gays aren't as particular as American or European homosexuals about looks. They are happy to find anyone. Age, so psychologically important to many gays in the United States, just isn't a very key value in a gay Mexican relationship. Fat gays date handsome gays. Short gays date tall gays. In fact, said Taylor, many middle-aged and older gays come down to Mexico from the United States, knowing they will be better treated than at home.

"What's important here is whether you have money," interjected Juan Jacobo. "If you have money, you can have any lover you want."

Sexual equality of partners is not as widespread in Mexico, either. Influenced by ideas of sexual liberation and equality, American gays have increasingly adopted sexual roles that allow each partner to be the dominant or submissive lover, depending on one's mood. But the old-fashioned gay relationship, derived from male-female roles of the '50s and '60s, prevails in Mexico. One partner is typically the *activo,* or what Dr. Taylor called the inserter in the anal sex that is the purest form of homosexual activity. The other is the *pasivo,* or insertee. The *pasivo,* in some cases, adopts the role of a woman so thoroughly that he may wear dresses and makeup and affect extremely effeminate behavior.

Rather bizarrely, persons who act as an inserter in male-male sex acts are not always considered homosexuals in Mexico. "Masculine homosexuality is regarded with a certain indulgence insofar as the active agent is concerned," writes Mexican poet Octavio Paz. "The passive agent is an abject, degraded being. This ambiguous conception is made very clear in the word games or battles—full of obscene allusions and double meanings—that are so popular in Mexico City. Each of the speakers tries to humiliate his adversary with verbal traps and ingenious linguistic combinations, and the loser is the person who cannot think of a comeback, who has to swallow his opponent's jibes. These jibes are full of aggressive sexual allusions; the loser is possessed, is violated, by the winner, and the spectators laugh and sneer at him. Masculine homosexuality is tolerated, then, on condition that it consists in violating a passive agent. As with heterosexual relationships, the important thing is not to open oneself up and at the same time to break open one's opponent."

Many male prostitutes who consider themselves heterosexual or at most bisexual offer their services to homosexuals as inserters but never as *pasivos*. They refuse to hug or kiss those homosexuals who hire them. All of this, I was told, stems from the rather complex idea of machismo in Mexico, an attitude that pervades so much human activity in the country.

Foreigners have the mistaken impression that machismo in Mexico has to do with aggressive behavior that is blind to danger. This is not the case. In some Hispanic countries, machismo means doing whatever is necessary to defend one's honor. In Mexico, it has more to do with the fear of betrayal and the ability to suffer pain. Some Mexicans argue that the fear of betrayal and the fragile masculinity that makes Mexicans act so macho stems from the time of the Spanish Conquest of Mexico. Conquistadors violated Indian women, some of whom remained with the Spanish soldiers, spurning their own men. The most famous of these was La Malinche, an Indian woman who served as Hernán Cortés's concubine and translator. Her name is synonymous with betrayal of what is Mexican.

Of machismo, Paz also says: "For other people the manly ideal consists in an open and aggressive fondness for combat, where we emphasize defensiveness, the readiness to repel any attack. The Mexican 'macho'—the male—is a hermetic being, closed up in himself, capable of guarding both himself and whatever has been confided to him. Manliness is judged according to one's invulnerability to enemy arms or the impact of the outside world. Stoicism is the most exalted of our military and political attitudes. Our history is full of expressions and incidents that demonstrate the indifference of our heroes toward suffering or danger. We are taught from childhood to accept defeat with dignity, a conception that is certainly not ignoble. And if we are not all good stoics . . . at least we can be resigned and patient and long-suffering. Resignation is one of our most popular virtues. We admire fortitude in the face of adversity more than the most brilliant triumph."

Machismo is no different with homosexuals. In fact, given the stoicism required to be homosexual in Mexico, Mexican gays, one could argue, are the most macho of all Mexicans. For some gays, the pressure to be macho is so great that they pretend they are really bisexual. They make forays into the gay world, telling friends they are so oversexed that women alone will not satisfy them. Sometimes they get drunk to explain away their behavior. When they are done, they return to their wives and children. For most gays, however, machismo means being able to endure the rejection of their families, who feel ashamed, or their fellow workers, who shun them. The luckiest gays are those who only have to humor parents who persist in the pretense that their son is not a homosexual. Humberto Hermosillo, a gay Mexican director, captured this pretense of parents in his droll film *Doña Erlinda y Sus Hijos*. In it, a mother persists in trying to marry her son off to a nice woman, ignoring all the while the existence of his obviously gay lover, whom she writes off as no more than a close pal.

Threats or violence can require stoicism too. Homophobic Mexican men are prone to shout "*maricon*," "*joto*," "*puto*," or other epithets that are the equivalent of "queer" when they see men they think are gay. Some gay-bashers go beyond that, beating up homosexuals indiscriminately or, sometimes, killing them.

"I've had three researchers who have been murdered," said Dr. Taylor, who is affiliated with the Institute for Advanced Human Sexuality in San Francisco and has taught classes at Stanford University's medical school and at San Francisco State.

Police are also a threat. Typically, they stake out known gay bars, picking out potential blackmail victims. They check out people's clothes and cars. They are looking for rich gays, government officials or business executives who don't want their colleagues to know they are gay.

"If you're rich and get caught," said Dr. Taylor, "you pay and pay and pay."

Notwithstanding all this menacing, in some ways it is easier to be gay in Mexico than in many countries. Mexico is what Dr. Taylor called a "homo-social" country. Men go out socially with men. They spend hours together on the street. They think nothing of putting their arms around each other's shoulders in public. They give each other hugs—*abrazos*—which are an important Hispanic form of greeting and a desired sign of respect. Some hold hands while walking. They touch their own genitals in front of others with none of the self-consciousness of American men, who have a much more prudish body language.

With all of this camouflage, Mexican gays can transform a cantina into a gay bar without most of the clients realizing it. Dr. Taylor explained how this might happen. Mexican gays might pick a bar with a mariachi band or a bullfight motif. They would sit together, hidden amongst tables of Mexican women or of families celebrating a birthday or wedding. Maybe only the shoe-shine boy would know what is really going on. He would keep track of who is gay and where the police are. For tips, he would pass a message that So-and-So wants to buy So-and-So a drink. The man offering the drink might be waved over to join the table, or a meeting could be arranged later on. As the hours grow late, the heterosexuals would leave, and more and more gays would arrive. Those few heteros who remain would ignore what is happening. But the later it gets, the gayer it gets.

The key to enjoying all this cultural protection, said Dr. Taylor, is not getting caught flagrante delicto. "You can be gay as a goose," he said, "but if you get caught, you may be ruined for life." As long as straight Mexicans can have some fig leaf to cling to in refusing to acknowledge that a boy or man is homosexual, they will use it. They provide what Dr. Taylor called counterfeit secrecy. Andre put it best: "Here in Mexico, appearances are more important than reality." If one gives straight Mexicans no choice but to accept one's homosexuality, however, one can expect vilification, violence, or even worse.

My ABC lesson finished just as Mario came on stage and began to tune his guitar. Mario, dressed in leather pants, a sailor shirt, and a rhinestone belt, had not yet begun when a rumpus occurred behind us. A reporter-cameraman-soundman team from one of the government television stations had arrived. They had come to El Taller to film the gay community *in situ* as part of their coverage of the AIDS crisis. The owner of El Taller announced to the hundred or so clients assembled what was about to occur. He advised those who wanted to remain incognito to move to the side of Mario's stage, out of camera range. I must admit I was hoping Juan Jacobo, Dr. Taylor, and Andre would want a little anonymity. But no such luck. When I returned home in the early hours of the morning, I told my half-awake wife that

I had good news and bad news. The good news was that I was going to be on television. The bad news was that some of our friends might start to whisper if they saw me.

The cameraman panned the dimly lit bar. His blazing spotlight illuminated the faces of the crowd, including those of our group. Most of his videotape recorded Mario, whose songs such as "Ángel, My Sweet" and "Put Your Hand Here" seemed to make the crew even more uncomfortable than they had been when they came in. Mario sang of love in the night in out-of-the-way places. From time to time, he blew kisses to fans or friends in the audience, who applauded rabidly after each number. After about an hour, Mario took a break. The talk turned to AIDS.

Dr. Taylor said he was in town to give some "safe sex" lectures designed to help Mexicans avoid AIDS. His writings had earned him the nickname "Dr. Safe Sex," he told me. He had copies of his *Guide to Safe Sex* with him. One publicity blurb on the cover caught my eye. The reviewer had said of the book: "It should be next to the KY Jelly on everyone's bed stand."

Juan Jacobo was a safe-sex promoter, too. He told me he always carried condoms, and even handed out freebies to friends. The condoms were not always well received. Mexican men—gay or straight—have traditionally disliked condoms, which are thought to reduce sensitivity and are not considered macho. Some caveman gays even reject condoms as an unmanly way of dealing with AIDS. Dr. Taylor acknowledged that it would take some doing to get the sexually febrile Mexicans to accept the protection of condoms and dental dams as erotic accompaniments to foreplay. To arouse interest, he had drafted some suggested come-on lines in his book, which was intended not only for gays but for the many Mexican women whose husbands or lovers were bisexual. One proposed foreplay remark was: "I can't wait to get my mouth around your condom-clad rod." I told him this didn't do too much for me. But maybe I just wasn't in the mood.

The government, which often pretends sex does not exist, had even gotten into the safe-sex act. Each week, it gave away thousands of matchbooks with vibrantly colored condoms inside. It ran safe-sex ads. It deferred to gay leaders for the best advice on how to avoid the spread of the disease. But Juan Jacobo was not as sanguine as some others that all this government-gay cooperation might one day lead to at least a quasi-respectable status for homosexuals in Mexican society. As we had seen in the United States, he remarked, the numbers of AIDS cases can grow geometrically. With only a few hundred cases to worry about in mid-1987, the Mexican public hadn't really reacted yet to the danger of a possible AIDS epidemic. Mexican dentists weren't wearing surgical gloves. Hospital workers weren't demanding extraordinary protection. Parents of schoolchildren were not up in arms about infected students. If the number of confirmed cases did grow dramatically, however, as some health officials thought it might, then things might turn very nasty. Mexicans did not have a very positive attitude toward homosexuality in the first place, Juan Jacobo reminded me. If the numbers went up, it was unlikely the public would look beyond the gay community to fix the blame.

"Right now," said Juan Jacobo, "people are saying AIDS is a public disease, not a gay disease. That's good. But I fear there could be a backlash."

. . .

Almost a year after that night at El Taller, I decided I should see what had happened to all those hopes and promises that Juan Jacobo and the others had talked about. Was macho Mexico at last accepting gayness, as so many other nations had? I phoned Juan Jacobo. He wasn't there, but Mario answered. Mario said Juan Jacobo was in Europe. He was giving some seminars on gay life in Mexico and presenting a play he had written. I asked Mario if he could stop by sometime to talk about what had been happening in the time since we had met. He agreed. One rainy Tuesday afternoon he arrived at my door.

In the months that followed the beginning of the government's anti-AIDS campaign, there had been no backlash, he said. In fact, there had not been much of anything. The presidential campaign of 1988 began in earnest in October 1987, when the ruling party had named a candidate, Carlos Salinas de Gortari. The amount of publicity about him and the opposition candidates had pushed AIDS off the pages of Mexico's newspapers. Daily reports about the government's latest economic plan to save Mexico made the AIDS crisis seem even more invisible. What did not disappear was the problem. The number of AIDS victims continued to grow.

Juan Jacobo quit *Macho Tips* around the time Salinas was

nominated, Mario told me. Juan Jacobo hadn't liked what the magazine represented. It was careful, conservative, and safe. Its photographs of men were not very provocative. They were certainly less pornographic than those in the heterosexual skin magazines. Juan Jacobo thought Mexican gays needed more. With Mario and some other leaders of the Mexican gay movement, Juan Jacobo had spent the beginning of 1988 trying to launch a biweekly gay newspaper. The newspaper, to be called *Mexico Gay*, was supposed to be all the things *Macho Tips* was not. It would provide serious debate about gay issues. It would present gays as more than the stereotype of limp-wristed sissies. It would demand gay rights.

This editorial line mirrored the plot of Juan Jacobo's play. Called *The Dark Side of the Moon*, it was a work about a transsexual named Brenda who gets arrested and beaten up by the police on her way to a fiesta. Brenda, whose character is based on a real person who was savagely beaten by the police, represents the most embarrassing personification of gay life. She is a man-woman who has developed women's breasts through injections and has had her sexual organs changed. This outrageous human species is what the police like to hold up to the public as a typical homosexual, even though transsexuals strain the definition. Juan Jacobo used Brenda to show that even this vain demimonde creature on the fringe of gay life could have dignity, inner beauty, and a desire for respect and human rights.

Mario, whose delicate features, soft speaking voice, and wispy black hair belie a personal ferocity, said he wasn't sure the government would allow a newspaper to publish a serious message of gay normalcy. Nor did he know if hands-off treatment of the newspaper would be a harbinger of official reaction to a host of other gay projects for the late 1980s: community centers, gay records, gay music festivals, and many other things that had become commonplace in other countries.

"I think there have been sufficient advances in public opinion for [the newspaper] to succeed," said Mario. "I worry about how the right [wing] will react, of course. I hope things will go well. But if they do not, we will survive. We have for a very long time."

· 17 ·

The *Mentalista*

During my first weeks in Mexico, a number of people told me there was something different—something, well, *magic* about the place that I should be aware of. I thought little about such remarks at first, writing them off as quaint chauvinism. But months later, an incident in the tiny village of Tepoztlán made me think that there might be something to this.

Tepoztlán, which some call "the city of magic," has a curious history. Tucked into a stunning mountain setting just off the Mexico City–Cuernavaca highway, it was once a fiercely Indian town. Now its indigenous residents have to rub elbows with the capital's elite, who use it for a weekend hideaway. But Tepoztlán's indigenous residents still proudly recount how it was one of the few towns the Spanish never really conquered.

When the conquistadors first arrived in the village, they tried to do what they had done in many other Indian towns in their zealous pursuit of Catholic converts. They set out to destroy all vestiges of local Indian gods. Tepoztécatl was the village deity. His stony statue stood in a pyramid chamber atop one of the several mountains that ring the village. Armor-clad Spanish soldiers climbed the mountain, a hike many tourists now make, and hurled Tepoztécatl's image down the steep, rocky incline. But a strange thing happened. After its long roll downward, Tepoztécatl's statue came to rest unscathed. As far as the Indians were concerned, it was a miracle, Tepoztécatl's message that neither he nor his people were to be dominated. As one might imagine, the Spanish priests didn't make many converts after that.

As I was researching this history for a story on the town, I met Alejandro and Pamela Sánchez. They ran a pottery shop, just down the block from El Encanto, Tepoztlán's magic bookstore. Both had attended the University of California at Berkeley. I found them highly intelligent and well-read. But as we began to talk about Tepoztlán's reputation for magic, some strange stories began to creep into their conversation. Alejandro, who is Mexican, let it drop casually that he knew a *nagual* named Don Félix who lived nearby. *Naguales,* some believe, are witches who can change into animal form as night falls. They and assorted generic *brujas* ("witches") live in the verdant hill country around Tepoztlán, locals say.

Pamela, an American, said nothing about whether she believed in witches. But she told me a bizarre tale about their son Ian and a local *curandero*. A *curandero* is an herb healer, but some believe that most witches call themselves *curanderos* to hide their real profession. A few years before, Ian had gone on an unexplained crying jag at the home of a friend. Alejandro and Pamela tried everything to get him to stop. But they couldn't. Finally a Mexican friend told them that it was likely that someone had put a *malo ojo,* an "evil eye," on Ian. Only a *limpia,* a ritual cleansing by a *curandero*, would stop the crying, the friend said. Desperate, Alejandro and Pamela took Ian to a *curandero,* who passed an egg from a black chicken over the boy to draw out any evil forces from his body. The yolk of the special egg would absorb the evil, the *curandero* told them. For whatever reason, Ian stopped crying. Strangely, Pamela added, every time Ian now passes the house of the friend where the crying began, he bursts out crying.

My response to this story was sort of a mental "Hmmm." My short stay in Tepoztlán and the few weird stories I had heard there about magic and witches had certainly not made me a convert to the occult. But I wasn't writing such things off either as so much nonsense. I left Tepoztlán sensing that something was in the wind.

Perhaps it was this open-mindedness about the subject that led me some months later to visit a fortune-teller. I consider myself a logical, pragmatic person. I'm from Illinois, not Missouri, but in most cases, you've got to show me. I don't have much patience with charlatans, quacks, or phonies. Even chiropractors are a bit suspect in my book. So what was I doing that fall day heading to the center of Mexico City—with some eagerness, if I'm honest about it—to see a fortune-teller? After all, I'm a college graduate. I have a law degree from an Ivy League university. Fortune-telling is just so much bunkum, isn't it? That's what I heard myself mumbling without too much conviction.

If I had still been living in the United States, I probably would never have dreamed of such a visit. I had passed many a store-front office of tarot-card readers and palmists with nary a thought of going in. As far as I was concerned, they were fakers who took money from suckers. But after a couple of years in Mexico, somehow it was different, more acceptable. Mexico was a magical place, wasn't it? That's what people were always telling me. Maybe that explains why, when one of my best friends gushed about this fortune-teller she regularly used, I heard myself say, "I'd like to see her."

On a tiny side street not far from Mexico City's national palace, I was to look for the apartment of Doña Mari. The grim, decrepit edifice was hardly what I had expected. A tiny green wooden door opened onto a long, dark corridor with a stairway at the end. The building was a tenement with chain-link fences and concrete floors in the public areas, South-Bronx style. There were no names in the mailbox slots. It was very anonymous. I had expected to see some sort of sign outside, something with symbols of the zodiac, advertising Doña Mari's fortune-telling business. But there was none. As I was to find out, Doña Mari did not want to publicize her powers, nor did she charge for her services.

"I only do it for friends," explained the diminutive woman who opened the creaky wooden door of the second-story apartment. I was a friend of a friend. That was good enough to gain me entrance to her dining room, where she did her sessions. Doña Mari knew nothing about me and asked nothing before we began. Friend of a friend. That and my physical appearance were the only clues she had about my past and my future.

I sat down at her square wooden dining table as she prepared to begin the session. She fixed herself a glass of a foul-looking green herbal drink. She got a pack of cards out of a nearby drawer. She took a magnifying glass from a cabinet. She applied some ointment to her temples. The session began.

At age eighty-three, Doña Mari's eyes were not too good. Even with her owlish-looking, thick glasses, she still had to use the magnifier to read the lines in my palm, which is what she did first. Some of what she told me was pretty much what one might expect. I had a long lifeline and would live until I was ninety. But I was stunned when she said I was about to quit my job and embark on a new project, a project "involving a lot of papers." At the time, I was just finishing up my reporting tour of duty and about to begin this book. But she had no way of knowing that. She also said I had some concerns about having enough money for the project. But I shouldn't worry, because money was coming soon. How could she have known I was worried at the time about whether I would get a book contract with an advance? How did she know that a few weeks later my agent would call and say I had one?

Doña Mari also said that I'd be moving to another country the following year. It would be a country where people spoke a language something like Spanish. Again, she was on target. My wife had just been told that she would be transferred to Brussels in June of the following year. I was going too. The language of Belgium is French, which, like Spanish, is one of the family of Romance languages.

Palm reading done, Doña Mari asked me my birth date and turned to the cards, a well-worn deck with Egyptian characters. Using the cards to focus her vision, she went through some of my past. She knew that I had changed careers at some time in the past. She used the word "career," not job. Some fifteen years before, I had given up the practice of law for journalism. She ticked off some aspects of my personality that were on target: pragmatic, in a hurry, even-tempered. With only one minor exception—she said my wife talked too much—she was dead bang on with every comment.

After the forty-five-minute session was over, she showed me around her apartment, leading me by the hand like a small child as she padded from room to room in her dog-eared bedroom slippers. There were indications of a strong religious belief. I saw several pictures and statues of Jesus Christ and the Virgin Mary.

Above her bed, there was a photograph of her grandfather. He had had "second sight" too, she said. He was a Spanish count, born in the sherry country that surrounds Jerez. But she had never known him. He taught her nothing. He had died before she was born.

On another wall was a photo of Doña Mari dressed like a gypsy, complete with a crystal-ball prop. She giggled irrepressibly when I asked about it. Back in the 1940s, some friends had persuaded her to tell fortunes in the lobby of a Mexico City movie theater as sort of a lark. But her career as a gypsy lasted only a few days. As word got out about her abilities, would-be patrons began jamming the lobby, ignoring the movies inside. Eventually the crowds spilled out onto the street. The police shut the operation down.

Though she was billed back then as a fortune-teller, Doña Mari refers to herself as a *mentalista,* or "mentalist." Sometimes she prefers *clarividente* ("clairvoyant"). But she stresses that she has never made a living telling fortunes. A widow, and retired when I met her, she had spent most of her life in humdrum jobs, such as clerking at her father's hardware store while growing up in the state of Querétaro. She learned early about her powers of vision. At the age of three she began telling others about their lives. She thought there was nothing special about it. It just came out naturally. Her playmates thought it a game. When it became clear, however, that her predictions were coming true, others didn't think it was a game at all.

When Doña Mari moved from Querétaro, she left behind her reputation as a fortune-teller. She made no attempt to kindle interest in her abilities among her new friends in Mexico City. But one day, they just sort of slipped out. She was visiting the home of a family friend. The owner of the house remarked that he had lost something and was bedeviled by the fact that he could not find it. Without missing a beat, Doña Mari, who had never been in the house, told him where it was. After that, word spread about her gift, and friends of the house owner began calling on her for similar advice.

"I have some families who have been coming to me for three generations," said Doña Mari, whose oversized cardigan, thinning hair, and gnarled skin give her the look of a benevolent, woolly gnome.

After the house tour, we moved into her small parlor, a tidy room of ancient furniture and old linoleum. I asked how visions of the future came to her. Was it possible that she was only reading people's thoughts and hopes, something that students of parapsychology think is a more probable human power than fortune-telling? No, she didn't think she was a mind reader. In fact, as she had with me, she normally asked people to clear their minds of thought at various stages of her sessions.

From where did she think she got her abilities? It wasn't magic. She knew that. Most probably it was something hereditary. Her grandfather, she reminded me, had the power. Her daughter, who lives in the state of Sonora, has it too.

"But she doesn't like it," Doña Mari said. "Thoughts come into her head. She doesn't want them."

Doña Mari accepts her power. But over the years she's adopted some rules about using it. She would never abuse it, she said. For example, she has never used her visions of the future for personal gain. Even though she might have become rich by looking at the future of the stock market or the price of gold, she never has, she assured me. The poverty of her apartment seemed evidence of that.

"I don't invent things," she added. "If the news is bad, I have to tell it."

I joked that it must have been interesting to have been able to tell so much about her husband. In a country where men often are philanderers, she must have known if her husband was cheating on her. Doña Mari said she forgets what she says almost as quickly as she says it. Her mind seems to be more a medium than a receptacle for such thoughts.

"Is that right?" she often asked after she told me something.

Doña Mari's real name is María. The Doña is just an honorific Mexicans give older people of stature. She told me her last name. But she asked me not to use it.

"When people hear what I do," she said, "they might think I'm a witch."

Was that so bad? I asked. What difference did it make what people thought? In Mexico, she said, it made a difference. In Mexico, people hate witches.

Many Mexicans I met were truly spooked by the idea of a witch. These included educated Mexicans who professed no belief in them—and tried to persuade me that no one in Mexico really put much stock in such primitive ideas. When I first arrived in Mexico City, I hired Emma Hernández, a temporary secretary who was from a wealthy family. She was one of those who pooh-poohed the idea of superstition and witchcraft. But after we got to know each other, she would occasionally start a conversation with, "I don't believe in witches, but. . . ." She'd then proceed to tell me a story about how this friend or that had hired a witch/*curandera* to put a hex on a lover, or to get rid of a cold or cough that the doctor wasn't able to handle. Emma even admitted once that she'd hired a *curandero* to put a hex on an ex-lover.

"It was kind of a joke," she said, somewhat embarrassed at the revelation. "But I hoped it would work. And it did, I think."

Putting a hex on lovers or ex-lovers—to bring them back or make them miserable—is one of the most common uses Mexicans make of *curanderos*. *Limpias* to counteract the evil eye is another. But many *curanderos* are legitimate herbal healers. They use plants to cure disease, just as doctors use pills based on the pharmacological properties of those plants. For example, *curanderos* use *epazote,* or "wormseed." Doctors have found it's a powerful preventative and cure for intestinal parasites. Other *curanderos* use *cabeza de negro,* which, it turns out, contains progesterone. It helped lead to the discovery of the birth-control pill, which was achieved in Mexico.

Even after my session with Doña Mari, I still had a healthy skepticism about magic and witches. Psychic phenomenon was one thing. The occult was something else. But with my interest in magic, the occult, and parapsychology piqued, I made a trip out to a market I had heard some bizarre things about. Officially, it is called the Sonora Market. But Mexico City residents refer to it as the Witches' Market, even though one can also buy pots, pans, produce, straw baskets, wooden spoons, and hundreds of other items there. No one at the market actually admits to being a witch. But in a little corner, under a sign that says simply *Herbolaría,* ("Herb Shop"), one can find a *curandero* or two.

In one of the shop's stalls I found María de la Luz Rivas. Others had told me she was a *curandera,* as a female herb healer is called in Spanish. But at first she refused to say if she did *limpias* or other *curandera* works. She was highly suspicious, perhaps because gringos aren't the normal clientele for her services. I started to walk away, but her grandson grabbed me by the arm to ask how much I might be willing to pay for a *limpia*, the service I had inquired about. Rivas was charging a dollar plus the cost of the herbs she used. But a better price might be arranged, the grandson said.

I asked what Señora Rivas used to cure *la gripe*, the generic name Mexicans use for any cold-type ailment. A turkey egg, he replied, using an Indian word for turkey rather than the Spanish one. Rivas also used branches of the pirul tree and, not to be unmodern, magic aerosol sprays.

Still giving me the fish-eye, Rivas admitted that she was indeed a *curandera* and that she'd be willing to do a *limpia*. But, the octogenarian herb healer added, for it to work, "you must have faith."

What else might a *limpia* be useful for? I asked. With the right herb or ingredient, almost anything, she replied. Pieces of the nogal cactus or the roots of the *sangre de grado* plant reversed baldness. Begonia leaves were good for diabetes. Dried viper skins, of the type which sat in a basket near her feet, would get rid of cancer if you ground them up and took the powder with water three times a day. But if someone has put the "evil eye" on you, then a *limpia* is what you need. Turkey eggs were important, of course, because of the yolk's special power to absorb evil. But Rivas also used a special body soap that contained the ingredients of "seven magic plants," according to the box it came in.

Magic soaps come in a variety of forms. There were soaps that would allow you to dominate your lover, soaps to let you win at gambling, soaps that brought good health. Aerosol sprays promised to do the same but in a more convenient form. My favorite soap was the one that promised domination over your lover. Its box had a drawing of a man kissing the bottom of a woman's foot. I bought a bar. But, to my disappointment, my wife remained as independent as ever after I showered with it.

I must admit that I didn't have too much faith in the bar. And, as Señora Rivas said, you've got to have faith. I found that especially difficult, however, after having read the label of a can of magic spray I also bought. It was a can of all-purpose magic spray. With one easy-to-use application, I could guarantee myself luck in gambling, domination of my wife—all the good stuff, Rivas said. But when I examined the label later, I noticed the can and contents had been manufactured not in Mexico but in the very nonmagical United States. Perhaps stringent U.S. truth-in-advertising laws explained why the can carried the disclaimer (in English only): "Contains no magic properties whatsoever."

Mexicans also buy a lot of amulets for good luck from the Witches' Market and others like it throughout Mexico. Amulets, which are sometimes called *piedras imán*, are often made from the base of a plant that is decorated in baroque fashion with crosses, horseshoes, tassels, beads, body parts from religious statues, and pictures of Jesus and Mary. For the less religious, the market offers skins of dead skunks. A stall owner told me they are good for curing anemia and sixty other diseases if one drinks the liquid produced from soaking the skins in water overnight. I knew I didn't have enough faith to try that!

Maybe it's to be expected that Mexico, a nation of *mestizos* (those of Indian-Spanish blood), would have so much interest in magic, the occult, superstition, and herb healing. Magic was very important to the Aztecs, Mayas, Zapotecs, and other indigenous peoples of Mexico. Just a few blocks from where Doña Mari lives, Aztec witches tried to hex Hernán Cortés to prevent him from conquering Mexico. But their magic was insufficient. Historians attribute Cortés's success to the horses, steel swords, and guns his small band had—weapons unknown in the New World. But the natives had another explanation: Cortés had brought his own, more powerful witches from Europe.

A lot of Indian superstition and beliefs persist in the twentieth century, especially in small towns where people are uneducated and retain Indian ways. In the Yucatán, where descendants of the Mayas live, some people still believe that a blue bird that flies over a child's crib at night will make the child sick. Others think that if you see a snake with red eyes or a tarantula taking care of its newborn, it's bad luck. This attitude, which one can find sporadically in big cities, makes it easier for *curanderos*, would-be witches, and others to make a good living. Mexico, of course, has its lighthearted superstitions. A black cat crossing in front of you is bad luck, just as it is elsewhere. And if you spill salt, you're supposed to gather up the grains and dissolve them in water to avoid the worst. A fork dropped at a Mexican dinner table means a guest is coming. But there are more sinister superstitions as well, particularly those used to explain medical ailments. These beliefs persist even though medical science has shown they have no basis in fact. Many Mexicans, for example, believe that *vientos* ("winds") or *aires malos* ("bad airs") cause respiratory ailments, cramps, toothaches, and even paralysis. One might argue that the wind and air in pollution-plagued Mexico City are things to be avoided, superstitions or not. But the belief that Mexicans have in bad winds and airs exists in unpolluted villages and dates back before the days of serious pollution in the capital. Even on the hottest of days in high-altitude cities in mountainous Mexico, one can see bus and car passengers who refuse to roll down a window, preferring to sweat inside their vehicles rather than let "bad airs" inside. Those who walk to work in the often chilly but never cold mountain mornings will be swathed in scarves or towels as their protection, as if prepared for an arctic snowstorm.

Some peasants believe that bad airs from whores or a loose woman can harm newborn children or fetuses. A loose woman, who is said to have an *aire de basura* ("garbage air"), is supposed to cause a fetus to be born blind if she enters the house where a pregnant woman lives. A newborn babe will develop eye pus if such a woman walks into his room. Sicknesses caused by "garbage air" can be cured, the belief goes, by washing the baby's eyes with water boiled in the umbilical cord of a firstborn child.

Other Mexicans believe that persistent anger can lead to a generic bad feeling, which Mexicans call *bilis,* or an overflowing bile. As far as I could tell, most of this feeling was psychosomatic. It probably could have been cured by taking a few Tums. But Mexicans have their own myriad ways for curing *bilis,* which some regard as the national illness.

When an illness is persistent, many Mexicans think it has been caused by someone who has cast an evil eye on them. In turn, say Mexicans, one can usually find some justification why someone put the evil eye on you. To avoid such spells, peasants will tell you, you should not display wealth ostentatiously or be obviously envious of others' good fortune. Many Mexicans also believe that if they are suddenly frightened or shocked they may die. Others fear they will lose consciousness or have persistent body chills. A lot of people consult doctors to cure this fright-caused condition, which is called *espanto.*

Mixing hot and cold things is to be avoided, too. For example, many Mexicans would never stand in front of a hot fire or space heater to warm themselves after taking a bath. Water, even if it is hot bath water, is a "cold" substance (except when it is in the form of ice, when it's considered "hot"). Fire is "hot." To mix hot and cold this way, I was once told, might cause leprosy. Similarly, many Mexicans would never think of having a cold drink after working up a sweat on a long run. Again, that would be mixing hot and cold. If you gave a sweaty Mexican a cold drink, he or she would probably wait for it to warm up to room temperature before drinking it.

After four years of hearing such stuff from our maid, the nurse who looked after our baby, the man who mowed our lawn, the mailman, and assorted others I thought a bit loony on the subject, I never did buy any of it. But the session with Doña Mari remained pretty vivid in my mind. I found it unsettling, hard to explain in my logical universe. Perhaps to allow me to understand it better, I began to send friends to see her. As much as anything, I wanted to see if her predictions for them and her knowledge about their past were as uncannily accurate as they had been with me. First, I sent my wife, Sally. Without being told who Sally was, other than a friend, Doña Mari again predicted an imminent change of residence to a place where people speak a language somewhat like Spanish. She said Sally would live into her eighties. She got details about my wife's past correct.

Her remarks were somewhat similar to what she had told me, so one might suspect she was telling everyone the same fortune. But another friend, who accompanied Sally, got a completely different reading. At the time, he was desperately trying for a new job. Eerily, Doña Mari, without having been told anything about the friend's background, told him, first thing, that he would be getting a new job shortly. Within six months he had one.

Before we left Mexico for Belgium, I also took another friend to see Doña Mari. My friend Millie had just found out that her live-in boyfriend of more than ten years had been fooling around with another woman. Millie, who didn't want to break up the relationship, had come to Mexico while her boyfriend decided if he would stay or move out. When her session began, the first thing Doña Mari told Millie was that she had had a bad emotional experience with her boyfriend. Doña Mari went on to describe what she saw ahead for the relationship. Second thoughts for him. Second thoughts for her. The rest of the session was the "usual." Doña Mari told Millie things about her life, about her former marriage, about things Doña Mari simply shouldn't have known. She said Millie would live a long time. When the session ended, Doña Mari gave Millie a hug and said good-bye. We made our way down the stairs and through the corridor and walked outside into the crisp air of twilight. Millie hadn't said much inside, even though she had been eager to see what Doña Mari would say about her future with her wayward boyfriend. She was unusually quiet.

"What did you think?" I finally asked, able to hold back no longer. My friend, an educated woman who makes a six-figure salary, replied: "It was pretty remarkable. Spooky really. Pretty spooky."

· 18 ·

The *Güera*

When Felicia Mercado was growing up in Tijuana, she was considered a pretty child. But no one, except maybe her parents, made very much of her looks. Though Felicia is Mexican, her parents were able to send her to grammar and high school in San Diego because they had been born in the United States. With her blond hair and light skin, she looked much like the other Southern California sunshine girls who were her classmates.

She was nice-looking. But, as she will tell you, she was hardly considered the class queen or anything. Adolescence often makes young girls see bodily imperfections magnified far beyond what they really are. Blemishes and baby fat take on nightmarish proportions. Felicia was as susceptible as the next girl to such insecurities. She worried about her looks. She has pictures of herself in those bothersome times. But only very, very close friends get to see them these days.

Her teenage years finally passed, although there were times when Felicia thought they never would. The beauty of her childhood returned. Felicia became a lovely woman. She was thankful for beauty. But she didn't dwell on it. Certainly she was not thinking about her chances in beauty contests when a friend suggested she enter one. But she did. And that was the beginning of everything.

She became Miss Tijuana and was crowned queen of Maza-tlán's Carnival, a competition many Americans enter. She won whatever local or regional contest she entered. Then someone suggested she go for the big one. She should compete to become Señorita México—Miss Mexico.

When Felicia entered the Señorita México beauty pageant in 1977, she was told by the judges that she had a very good chance of winning. Between the lines, the nervous officials seemed to be saying that she would win. But there was one small obstacle. It was the way she looked. Felicia has stunning good looks. A flowing mane of natural blond hair frames a face of luminous skin and radiant, seductive blue eyes. She is tall, with an appealing figure. In these feminist times, those not wanting to offend might call her statuesque. Caveman types would say she's built.

"So what's the problem?" someone might have asked the judges. The answer is that, in Mexico, beauty can be a tricky thing, especially when politics are involved. Which woman represents Mexico as Señorita México is a very political thing indeed. Winners, of course, must be beautiful. There is no talent competition. Judges don't care how well you can play "Lady of Spain" on the accordion or whether you can do a Mozart concerto on your thighs with wooden spoons. They just want you to be a looker. Felicia is surely that. When she strolls through a restaurant, she can cause an outbreak of male whiplash, as I found out when she showed up to meet me at a Mexico City watering hole. Insufficient beauty was not her problem with the judges. What she lacked was the right kind of beauty, a political beauty. She was in a Mexican beauty contest. But she did not look Mexican. In fact, she looked sort of gringo.

In real life in Mexico, it's great for Mexican women to look like an American. People who do look that way consider themselves lucky. Women who are light-skinned and have blond hair and blue eyes are the stuff of many Mexican men's dreams. But Felicia was not dealing with reality. She was dealing with politics, Mexican politics. The official government policy is that Mexico is proud of its racial origins. Government pamphlets, books, films, and museums glorify the historic accomplishments of the Aztecs, the Mayas, the Zapotecs, the Toltecs, the Olmecs, and other Mexican indigenous groups. The government tells people that the Mayans were the first to come up with the mathematical concept of zero, that they created a calendar more accurate than the one most of the world uses today. They point out that the Aztecs were organizational geniuses whose talent for conquest was rivaled only by that of the Incas. Mexican Indians were no slouches when it came to cultural achievements either, as the heroic murals of Mexican masters Diego Rivera, David Siqueiros, and José Clemente Orozco make clear. Indians are beautiful. Indians are intelligent. Indians are dignified. Mexicans are better off because of Indians' contributions to history. This official message is not only commendable. It makes political sense. Ninety percent of Mexicans are pure or part Indian. Long ago, the government realized that Mexicans could not be proud of themselves if they could not be proud of their Indian past. But most Mexicans have not bought the message. Pure-blooded Indians—as many as ten million Mexicans—are treated as social inferiors. They are generally among the poorest and least educated of the Mexican population. When a Mexican feels that someone has done something particularly stupid or ignorant, he or she is likely to exclaim: "Indian!" Classified newspaper ads frequently ask for *apariencia agradable* ("agreeable appearance"). Translation: "No Indians." The prevalence of poverty and illiteracy among Mexican Indians, their humiliating conquest by the Spanish, and the history of human sacrifice and cannibalism among some of Mexico's indigenous peoples all make many Mexicans feel embarrassed about their country's Indian heritage. Even Indians themselves often feel ashamed.

In shunning their Indian past, Mexicans have established a standard of beauty that is passing strange. The majority of Mexicans are *mestizos,* a racial blend that stems from the mixture of members of the Indian tribes that once roamed Mexico with the Spanish invaders who conquered them. Most Mexicans have dusky to dark skin, with black or brown hair and, most commonly, brown eyes. As with any racial group, one can find beautiful Mexicans and ugly Mexicans within this *mestizo* group. But if you were to poll Mexico's *mestizos,* most would tell you that anyone with hair, skin, or eyes in color tones lighter than they have is considered more beautiful, maybe even smarter. This cultural self-hate runs so deep that many Mexicans feel the ideal of beauty is the physical opposite of an Indian: a blue-eyed blond. If he or she looks American or Northern European, so much the better. Anything but Mexican. When a daughter or son is born with blond hair or blue eyes, there is rejoicing within the family. The family knows that the little boy or girl will have an easier time in life. Companies that advertise dish-washing liquid, toilet paper, wine, bathroom cleaners, and a host of other products use blond models exclusively, as if the viewing public were all Scandinavians. My favorite is the ad campaign by Superior Beer, a blond-colored lager. It uses a blond woman who is known simply as La Rubia Superior ("The Superior Blond"). Not taking any chances with imagery, the company uses an American model to portray what has become one of the most recognizable symbols of Mexican beauty.

To get some hint of how strange and twisted the notion of race and beauty has become in Mexico, it might help to recreate the population of the United States hypothetically. Imagine what it would be like if 90 percent of Americans were black or partly black in origin. Imagine that the U.S. government put out a steady drumbeat of publicity lauding the accomplishments of black writers, sculptors, scientists, and other blacks of achievement. Imagine that, despite all this, the 10 percent of the population that was not black felt they were the superior ones and treated the majority like dirt. Imagine, finally, that the majority agreed with the minority and tried to emulate them. This is roughly what has happened in Mexico.

When I came to Mexico, I was surprised to discover the extent to which this feeling of racial inferiority made people sensitive about the color of skin. The only parallel I can think of is Americans' onetime fixation with how much "Negro" blood a person had. In the last century and for a part of this one, one could hear now-antiquated terms such as quadroon and octaroon when people were trying to determine who could legally pass for white and who could not. In a similar way, modern Mexicans refer to themselves as *negro* (very dark-skinned), a term that can have the epithet weight of "nigger!" if shouted in the right way; *moreno* (medium dark); *medio-moreno* (light-to-medium dark); or *blanco* or *güero* (white). When my wife and I adopted a Mexican baby, many Mexicans remarked how lucky we had been to get a child who was such a *blanquito,* a "little white one."

Despite all the importance given skin color, Mexicans bristle if you suggest that racism exists in their country. Denials come forth even in the face of irrefutable evidence. One of the most popular comic books in Mexico is *Memín Pingüín*, the name of a little boy who looks like Little Black Sambo and whose mother is the spitting image of Aunt Jemima. The title character is the butt of unending jokes about his stupidity. When I once asked the publisher of *Memín Pingüín* if he had ever tried to sell the comic to Mexican-Americans in the United States, he replied that it wasn't feasible. "People would say it was racist," he said. "But we have no racism in Mexico, so we can do it here."

Notwithstanding such denials, many Mexicans do all they can to look whiter and blonder. Even Indian women peroxide their dark hair, looking as improbable as they do pathetic in their attempts to pass as blondes. *Rubia* is Spanish for "blond." But *güero* (*güera* for women) is the most common term one hears in Mexico for someone with blond hair—or for anyone with lighter-than-average skin or hair. I was often called *güero*, even though my hair is predominantly gray with some dark brown underneath. Felicia, too, is a *güera*. But as a *güera* she could not win the Señorita México contest, she was told. It just wouldn't look right, the judges said. It would offend government policy. Even though ninety-nine out of a hundred Mexican men might pick her as the most beautiful entrant in the contest, she could not win as things were. To win, reality had to be suspended. And it was. The judges asked Felicia to dye her hair brown. It would make her look more Mexican, they said. Felicia did, and became Miss Mexico.

Felicia is back to being a blond these days. She works in the "real" world of television soap operas and films. Television casting officials and movie directors know what the Mexican public wants. They want a blond. Felicia knows that, to some extent, her success has been the result of her blondness. Blondness got her a start. She did some television commercials. That led to a film. Then came the *telenovelas*. *Telenovelas* are Mexican soap operas. Mexicans are every bit as avid about their soaps as Americans are about theirs. When the best of the soaps are on—say, at nine-thirty at night—it's just a waste of time to call most Mexicans at home. Either there will be no answer or the maid will tell you the Señor or the Señora will call you back. Felicia has been in a couple of *telenovelas*. When I met her, she had just finished *Rosa Salvaje* (The Savage Rose), which, like all Mexican soaps, runs for a limited time rather than for decades as some U.S. soaps do. Felicia has made a career playing "bad girls," vampy women with the integrity of a tramp. Her character Leonela in *The Savage Rose* was no exception. The plot of *The Savage Rose* gives you some idea of how the public has come to see her. It was as implausible as a Wagnerian opera. The lead character, Rosa, is a poor Mexican of *morena* complexion. Felicia played Leonela, a *güera* bombshell. Rosa grew up in a poor neighborhood. She falls in love with Ricardo, a rich Mexican with the tenderness of Alan Alda and the virility of James Garner. They get married, which infuriates Ricardo's greedy family. They think Rosa is not only beneath Ricardo in breeding but a threat to their claims on the family fortune. Ricardo's mother, Dulcina, has a scheme to lure Ricardo away from Rosa. She invites Leonela to live in the family mansion, where Rosa, Ricardo, Dulcina, and a lot of other people too numerous to mention seem to hang out. Leonela seduces Ricardo. Rosa finds them in bed. Rosa leaves Ricardo but discovers later that she is pregnant by him. She survives a kidnapping-murder attempt masterminded by Ricardo's mother, who gets her comeuppance when her family loses all its money in a legal complication. In the meantime, Rosa learns that she is really the daughter of a filthy-rich woman, her long-lost mother. Ricardo discovers that, in his heart of hearts, he has never really stopped loving Rosa. At Rosa's hospital bedside he admits that he did stray a bit with Leonela. But, after all, she had looked pretty irresistible in lingerie. Everything is set for a reconciliation between Rosa and Ricardo, except that Leonela stands in the way. The scriptwriter manages a train crash in which Leonela dies in spectacular fashion. Rosa and Ricardo are remarried in the Basilica of the Virgin of Guadalupe, the equivalent of having your ceremony in St. Patrick's Cathedral in New York.

OK, so it's not Shakespeare. Maybe it's not even Jackie Collins. But such roles have made Felicia very popular in Mexico.

"They love to hate me," she said, laughing about the evil characters she has played.

Felicia had gained particular fame as Leonela because *The Savage Rose* had become such a tremendous ratings success. She thought it had been popular because good (Rosa) had won out over evil (Leonela et al.), an always popular ending with stories. I had a different theory. I thought it had become such a hit for the same reason that Felicia had become Señorita México. The writers and producers had suspended reality. In the soap opera, the poor *morena*, Rosa, vanquishes the rich *güera*, Leonela. It doesn't happen that way in real life very often. It was nice for the majority of viewers—dusky and dark-skinned viewers—to be able to root for one of their own for a change, and see her win.

I found it very sad that many Mexicans only seemed to feel this way in the world of make-believe. The problem of deciding what is Mexicanness and how Mexicans should feel about themselves has been haunting Mexico since the days of the Spanish Conquest. The Spanish, with superior weapons and tactics, beat the native Mexicans squarely in battle, and then drilled into the vanquished notion that Spain was superior not only in military matters but in every way. Those who were conquered were inferior, they were told. Those who intermarried with the conquered were not as inferior as purebloods. But certainly they were not the equals of Spaniards or *criollos*, the name for those born in Mexico of Spanish mothers and fathers. This conqueror's idea stuck even though many Indian groups fled to the mountains or other remote areas to try to preserve their customs and traditions. Millions of Indians were not integrated into what became Mexican society. They did not learn to speak Spanish, the lingua franca of the new country. Those who did "progress" in this new, mixed-race society looked down on those who retained Indian ways, even though many Indians felt their traditions were something to be proud of.

As Mexico moved through nineteenth-century independence and its era of legal reform into twentieth-century revolution, a debate arose about what to do about those millions of Indians who persisted in living outside what the majority regarded as the Mexican mainstream. Revolutionary leaders, many the descendants of *criollos*, talked about whether to integrate these millions into Mexican society—and how. To leave them as they were seemed unthinkable, leaders decided. Plans were formulated and implemented. Over the decades, those plans have been about as successful as those of the Great White Father in the United States.

One strain of revolutionary thought—that of intellectual José Vasconcelos—was to foster the concept of *La Raza*. In this notion, Mexico was populated with a unique, proud race that had sprung from the Spanish conquest of Mexico's indigenous peoples. Hernán Cortés and his band were hated figures for all the cruelty they and Spanish Catholic priests had inflicted on the native people and their land. Cortés and his repressive progeny could hardly serve as models in the post-revolutionary era, even though *criollos* made up much of Mexico's political leadership. Better to focus on Mexico's indigenous past, Vasconcelos thought. But many Indians ignored his idea. They just wanted to be left alone to farm in primitive fashion as they had for centuries. They displayed an indifferent, even submissive approach to life, accepting fatalistically whatever befell them.

Some Mexican writers argued that Indians were a burden on Mexico, that they should be snatched out of their primitive existences for their and the nation's good. D. H. Lawrence put this negative view of Mexican Indians into his novel *The Plumed Serpent*. His heroine, Kate, expresses hopelessness about the state of Indians.

"Aztec things oppress me," she [Kate] said.

"Perhaps the Aztecs never asked for hope," the General said.

"Surely it is hope that keeps one going?" she said.

"You, maybe. But not the Aztec, nor the Indian today."

Others countered that Indians should be left alone to develop in natural, dignified ways that respected their unique culture. As the first post-revolutionary minister of education, Vasconcelos pushed for Indians to be taught Spanish so they would feel part of Mexican society. Vasconcelos won this round of the debate. Language instruction began.

The government's Indian policy took a decidedly pro-Indian turn during the administration of Lázaro Cárdenas (1934–40), who was part Tarascan Indian. He showed considerable sympathy for the Indians' fate. He proposed Mexicanizing the Indians while having respect for their traditions, especially their love for the land. He expropriated a lot of it and gave it to them. He formed a Department of Indian Affairs in 1936. In the late 1940s, the Instituto Nacional Indigenista (National Indian Institute) was created as a liaison between Indian and non-Indian Mexican society.

Modern presidents have continued the official concern about the Indian. President Luis Echeverría (1970–76), who considered himself a modern-day Lázaro Cárdenas, actively took up the cause of the Indian. To the chagrin of Mexico's upper classes, he redecorated Los Pinos, the Mexican White House, with "traditional" rugs, weavings, pottery, and paintings. He removed the European furnishings that had long been the style of the residence. Echeverría's successor, José López Portillo, showed a comparable concern for the Indians' plight, as did López Portillo's successor, Miguel de la Madrid. But despite all this official support and outreach, the number of Indians—defined as those who called themselves Indians—continued to shrink. About half the population at the time of the 1910 Revolution, Indians now account for only about 10 percent of Mexicans.

The political debate over what to do about the "Indian problem" rages on. Some anthropologists argue that the reservation-style life of some Indians is the equivalent of putting them in zoos. They are nothing more than guinea pigs for research conducted by light-skinned university professors, they charge. Leftist politicians, perhaps seeing the potential of all those millions of Indian votes, insist that cultural isolation is a ploy to block the "proletarization" of these poor masses. They favor integration of Indians into the economy in terms of language and jobs. A third wave of thought argues that Mexico should be recognized as a multiracial society that allows Indians to live as Indians, with autonomy over their lives and without cultural integration.

These are the arguments of the politicians and the experts. But the average Mexican seems to think very little about Indians, except to be glad that he or she is not one. It's not hard to see why. A visit to almost any Indian village in Oaxaca, Chiapas, or other states with heavy Indian populations is not likely to elicit a response of envy. Malnutrition, alcoholism, illiteracy, and many other serious social problems plague indigenous hamlets, many of which have been cut off from modern society because of lack of roads, electricity, or telephone service. Few have regular water service or indoor plumbing. Religion, a strange blend of Indian ceremony and Catholicism, dominates village Indians' lives. Superstition, suspicion, and belief in magic reign. Lack of educational facilities keeps members of Mexico's fifty remaining Indian groups ignorant about the rudiments of modern life. As a result, those who cling to Indian ways eke out a marginal agricultural existence. Some lives are even more precarious because of the repression by *caciques*, local strongmen who exploit Indians at every turn. Some use gangs of *pistoleros* (armed thugs) when flummery and fraud is not enough.

I found this to be the case when I visited San Bartolomé Quialana, a tiny Zapotec hamlet in the state of Oaxaca. All San Bartolomé's *jacals* ("huts") had dirt floors. None had electricity, sinks, or bathrooms. Only one person in this town of three thousand spoke Spanish. The rest spoke only a dialect of Zapotec. Drunks staggered down San Bartolomé's unpaved streets. Children looked malnourished. When Mexico celebrated *El Dia de La Raza* ("Race Day") on October 12 in place of Columbus Day, it was no cause of joy in San Bartolomé.

"We are the Jews of Mexico," said Josefina Martínez, a Zapotec who was given her Hispanic name when she was baptized. She had a simple explanation why the *ladinos* (non-Indian Mexicans) treated her and others in San Bartolomé so badly. "We remind them of what they were."

The future for Mexico's indigenous people appears no brighter than the present in San Bartolomé. Foolish government agricultural policies and greedy grabs for land by private business have made even subsistence living impossible for millions of Mexican Indians. Many have moved to big cities in search of jobs. This move into modern life has hardly been a formula for self-esteem. Indian women soon learn that if they are to be a success, if they are to be considered attractive to men, they must become *mestizos* in cultural outlook, if not in appearance. Influenced by television advertising and *telenovelas*, these women soon cut their long, beautiful hair and affect more "modern" styles. They begin wearing makeup and shed their traditional costumes for tight jeans and T-shirts. They become what they think is "Mexican." Indian men, many addicted to mezcal, pulche, or other Mexican moonshines since childhood, never fit in quite as well. Those not hindered by drink find their meager educations give them limited job opportunities. They dig ditches, sweep streets, sell trinkets on street corners, and perform the menial tasks that most Mexicans prefer not to.

*   *   *

Felicia had played evil characters almost exclusively in her movies and television shows. But I did not regard her as a "bad guy" on the issue of Indians. She is a woman of intelligence who is perfectly aware of her country's regrettable racial atmosphere. She has benefited from the idealization of the *güera* at the expense of the Indian and the *moreno*. But she does not condone such discrimination. She accepts it as fact. She would be considered beautiful in any society. She has no apologies for her beauty. She recognizes that blonds, particularly beautiful blonds, are a rare and desired commodity in Mexican show business, just as they are in Hollywood. Many women in the United States and elsewhere make themselves blonds because they think that's what men want. In a perfect world, there wouldn't be such an overemphasis on blondness. In a perfect world there would be racial equality. But the world is not perfect in Mexico, or anywhere else. Given Mexico's traditions and history, Felicia does not expect to see it become perfect anytime soon.

What I liked best about Felicia was that she was not blinded by her beauty as others were. She was happy to have it, but saw its traps. Maybe she picked up some of this un-Mexican thought from her time in American grammar and high schools or from living so close to the movie capital of the world. As a child she often read about Hollywood beauties who rose in fame like a Roman candle, only to sputter suddenly after they reached the top. Whatever the influence, Felicia, at the ripe old age of twenty-eight, was talking to me about what she wanted to do when the sharp edge of beauty had dulled a bit, when those who had been so quick to put her on a pedestal were willing to see her totter a bit and perhaps even fall. While she was still popular as a symbol of beauty, she said, she wanted to make a transition. She was looking for the sort of against-the-grain role that had changed the image of another blond beauty, Farah Fawcett, from a bubble-headed "Charlie's Angel" to a serious dramatic actress. She's already shown she can act against character by portraying women that Mexicans love to hate.

"People think that's the way I am," she said. "Evil. Wild at parties. But I'm not like that. Just the opposite."

Felicia does not drink or smoke. She designs many of her own clothes. She is something of a homebody. One of her best friends is her protective mother, with whom she lives in the San Jerónimo neighborhood of Mexico City. When she's not putting in fourteen-hour days filming *telenovelas,* she likes to relax with girlfriends. She rents videos of old Pedro Enfante or Dolores Del

Rio films from the golden age of Mexican movies. She is partial to Fred Astaire and Gene Kelly, too. She likes to cook up a storm when her friends come over to watch movies with her.

"I have a weakness for dessert," she said, although I saw no sign of it, looking at the black strapless harem-pants outfit she had poured herself into for our meeting.

Though her beauty could give her most any man she wants, Felicia has stayed single past an age when most Mexican women find themselves married. One reason is that she's been too busy with her career to get serious about marriage. Being single also plays better at the box office, she admitted. But the key reason is that she has modern ideas about marriage. At least they're modern for Mexico. Felicia likes her career and wants to continue it, doing more movies and perhaps even becoming a singer. She has tried a bit of club singing already. For many Mexican men, careers of any type are not acceptable activities for wives. In Felicia's view, Mexican men are protective of their wives, largely out of sexual insecurity. Fear of infidelity and jealousy drive men to order their wives to stay home, out of sight of other men. With a woman as beautiful as she, Felicia acknowledged, that urge might be even more intense.

"My work is very difficult," she said. "There are times when I work very late. I need someone who understands my work, who accepts what I do. Someone who is *simpático*."

The man Felicia wants must also know what he is and what he wants in life, she said. He should be strong but definitely not macho. It's not important that he be as handsome as she is beautiful, however. Beauty, said Felicia, has its limits.

"I'm more interested in what he is than how he looks," she said. "If he's handsome, that's great, of course. But I'm more interested in how he is with me."

She wants someone who loves her but not merely as a symbol of beauty. He must be a man, she said, who knows that being blond and blue-eyed is not enough, not even in Mexico.

· 19 ·

The *Feminista*

Even as a little girl, there was always something that made Rosa
María Ortega want to do more, to be more. It was not a common
attitude among little Mexican girls. At least it wasn't one many
Mexican girls talk about. Mexican girls, particularly girls from
poor families such as Rosa María's, are told that they are going to
be mothers and housewives. That's what they will be. They are
given some education. But few poor parents pay for more than
six years of grammar school. If there is just so much money in
the family budget for schooling, as is the case in so many Mexican homes, it goes for boys. The boys will need schooling, parents
tell their daughters, because they will be the ones to go to work.
That's what Rosa María's parents told her older sister, María Teresa. "Why do you want to go to school?" they asked. "You're just
going to get married. What do you need an education for?"

Some years later, they told Rosa María the same thing. But she
did not buy it. When she was told that she would have to quit
her studies when she finished grammar school, she sneaked out
of the house and defiantly signed herself up for high school. Maybe
because she was the baby of the family, her unwilling parents let
her continue.

Rosa María's sister was not so lucky. Seven years older than

Rosa María, she was given all the household chores to do. That meant cleaning up after Rosa María's four older brothers. As brothers will do in some Mexican families, they beat her when she did not iron something properly or when she forgot to make the beds. Rosa María's father, a construction worker, and her mother, who ran a small food shop, said nothing. By the age of sixteen, María Teresa had had enough. She got married, perhaps a little earlier than she had once wanted, and moved out. As her parents had predicted, she became a housewife and mother. She now has five children.

"I shall always remember the courage of my sister," said Rosa María of the violence that María Teresa had quietly suffered. "It made a very deep impression on me."

Rosa María was only nine years old when her sister moved out. She was too young to take over María Teresa's duties. She did some things around the house. Her brothers never beat her when they were displeased. "But I was always afraid that they would," she said.

Rosa María had wanted to go to the national university in Mexico City, where she was born and grew up. But she only made it through twelve years of school. That was twice as much education as the average Mexican gets, twice as much as her sister got. She said she feels privileged to have gone so far. But it wasn't as far as she wanted to go.

While still in high school, Rosa María met Juan José Castillo, who would become her husband. They fell in love. Modern ideas were floating about Mexico in the late 1970s when they met. Government forces had gunned down rioters in 1968 and 1971 to put down student protests. Students and others had fled Mexico to the United States and Europe. Later they brought back ideas of feminism and other isms that were changing the world. In 1973, Mexico, faced with staggering population growth, had begun encouraging women to use birth control. With unstated acquiescence from the government, abortions rose in number, even though abortion remained (and remains) illegal. The size of families was going down. Women, previously held hostage at home by six or seven children, were finding time to go out and meet people, to learn of the world. With some of these new thoughts in their heads, Juan and Rosa María talked of what kind of marriage they would have. Juan appeared the very model of a modern man. That made him an exceptional man for Mexico, where ideas of machismo often make it difficult for a man to be tender, considerate, or even fair with women. Juan talked about how they would both work. They would share the expenses of their new home. He said he'd help with the housework and with rearing the children they planned to have. Befitting this modern attitude, Juan and Rosa María moved in together without formally getting married. Fifteen percent of Mexican marriages are *unión libre,* or common-law ones. Usually people don't get married because they can't afford a marriage license or all the ceremonial rigmarole that goes with civil or church weddings. In Rosa María's case, not getting legally married was just a matter of principle.

"I loved him," she explained. "I wanted to live with him. That was all. To get married seemed a little *falso* ["phony"]."

Juan and Rosa María began their marriage in 1978. He was twenty. She was eighteen. They didn't have much money, so they moved in with his parents, as many young married couples in Mexico do. Juan and Rosa María were preoccupied with their studies. But there was still work to do around the house. Rosa María did her share of the cooking and cleaning. But Juan always seemed to have some excuse why he couldn't do his. It bothered Rosa María that Juan wasn't keeping the promises that they both had made before their marriage. But she kept quiet. She did the extra work. That was the way it was supposed to be, her mother-in-law told her. A woman's place, after all, is in the home, she said.

Family money grew tight. By 1980, Rosa María decided she had to quit school and go to work so she and Juan could meet expenses. It would only be for a while, she told herself. Then she would go back to school. She would become a college graduate. Juan, however, had other ideas. Gone was the Juan who had promised so much, who had seemed so egalitarian. Now he was acting very Mexican, very macho. He did not want her to work. What would his friends think, he said. They would say he was not a real man, because he could not support his new wife on his salary. His mother said the same thing. To show Rosa María that she could get by without working, Juan's mother began buying her dresses and other things. She told Rosa María she was *tonta* ("foolish") not to let her man take care of her. Juan had a different technique to discourage her working. He beat her.

Rosa María continued to work nonetheless, first as a department-store sales clerk and later in a variety of odd jobs. After a long day, she had little energy for housework. But she got no help from Juan, even after they rented their own apartment in 1984. Rosa María put in what Mexican women call a *doble jornada*, a "double day." She worked first at her job and then, for almost an equal time, at home. She cooked. She cleaned. She ironed. Later that year, her son, Carlos, was born. Rosa María quit her job to take care of the baby. She became a housewife for the first time. She had more time around the house. But in the early months after Carlos was born, she was feeling the fatigue that new mothers do. She found child care and housework very tiring. But still Juan refused to help out around the house. He said it was no work for a man. He became more demanding. Sometimes when Rosa María did not have the meals prepared on time, he beat her. With a baby to feed and clothe, Juan's salary proved inadequate. Rosa María set up a small repair business in their home, taking in broken appliances and other things to help make ends meet. She still had to care for the baby and take care of the house. But Juan continued to do nothing to help. The following year her daughter, Lluvia, was born. Things got worse. The marriage had not been going well. Rosa María was just too independent for Juan's tastes. He had made that clear. He had not only Rosa María's uppity ways to contend with. Now there were two more mouths to feed. Three months after Lluvia was born, Juan moved out. He moved in with another woman and has had a son by her.

Mexico has laws that say that Juan must support his two children by Rosa María. But like many Mexican laws designed to protect women, they mean a lot more in theory than they do in practice. When Rosa María recently discovered that Lluvia has a congenital eye condition that requires lots of antibiotics and a corrective operation, she went to see her estranged husband. She pleaded with Juan to give her money for their little girl. He said he had none to spare. He had a new family. He had other responsibilities, he said. Angry, Rosa María filed a legal complaint. The law was on her side, she had been told. But just before Juan was scheduled to appear before authorities to explain himself, he quit his job. At the hearing, he said he was unemployed and couldn't afford to pay anything. The authorities let him go. Rosa María didn't get a peso.

"I lived with that man for six years," said Rosa María. "It took me that long to find out who he really was."

Rosa María felt angry. She didn't know where to turn. She began searching for other remedies to get Juan to fulfill his obligations. In her search, she discovered a program that helps Mexican women learn about their legal rights. The Women's Program for Service, Development and Peace (Sedepac) offered Rosa María paralegal training as a *defensora popular*. A *defensora* helps battered, abandoned, or just poor women with legal problems. *Defensoras* go to police stations to help file complaints or to court to help present cases.

Rosa María took the *defensora* course and finished it in February 1987. She set out to help others while trying to solve her own problems. Her first case was typical of those that would come later. The woman had been beaten up by her husband and had been the victim of sexual violence. He had wanted to have sex. She had not. He beat her, then forced her. As far as the police were concerned, it was just a little disagreement between husband and wife. It's a man's right to make love to his wife, most Mexican police officers will tell you. Most police officers are men. That's not what the law says, Rosa María told the police. It was not perhaps what they wanted to hear. But thanks to *defensoras* like Rosa María, they are hearing it more and more every day.

Poor Mexican women—the majority of Mexican women—are hearing it more often, too. To most of them, it is a surprise. Most Mexican women have been told all their lives that they are inferior to men, that they must obey men. They feel ashamed about what has happened to them, be it rape or a beating by their husbands. They are stunned to find out it is a crime for their husbands to hurt them physically. Many feel regular beatings are just part of their lot in life. If their husband does not mistreat them, they think, then they are just so much luckier than the next woman.

These days, Rosa María's clients are poor Indian women of the Mazahua tribe who live in Mexico City. The government has given the women free space for a women's center in a small attic above La Merced, a large fruit and vegetable market in the heart of the capital. Every day they come to the center to weave dresses or shawls or to make yarn dolls that they sell in the streets. With the money, they support themselves as well as the center's social and educational activities, which include Rosa María's *defensora* work. No one makes very much. Rosa María gets a hundred thousand pesos a month (forty-five dollars), which is about half the wage the average Mexican makes.

The problems these women bring to Rosa María are typical of the ones that she encountered in her own marriage. Sometimes they are worse. Violence in the home is the most common complaint. Husbands verbally threaten their wives if they don't do what they are told. Others beat their wives. Some force their wives to have sex when their wives are not willing. Others complain they are verbally abused in the streets. Mexico has a tradition of *piropos,* clever but sexist sayings that Mexican men yell at passing women in hopes of annoying or attracting them. It's a little like the tendency of some construction workers in the United States to whistle at or tease women who pass their building sites. It's just a lot more widespread. "Rosita ["Little rose"], here is your gardener," is one *piropo* Rosa María might have heard. More generic piropos go: "What curves! And me without any brakes," or, "I wish I were a stamp so you could lick me with your little mouth." Sexual harassment at work is common too. Surveys done by feminists groups show that 95 percent of women in Mexico City have been subject to sexual harassment, about a quarter of it direct sexual propositions.

As a first step to ending such aggression, Rosa María tells women at the center that they have rights. In 1975, women were given equal rights under the law when a constitutional amendment was passed. They have the right to work, she tells them. They have the right to leave the house, despite what their husbands might say. They have a right to an education. If they are raped, they can file charges against the man who did it, even if he is a boyfriend or a husband.

Part of women's surprise at learning of such rights stems from the brainwashing they get in Mexican society. Women have had the right to vote since 1953. A woman has run for president. A woman has held the no. 2 post in Mexico's ruling political party. Women have been governors and senators and federal deputies. Hundreds of women run their own companies. But the reality of Mexican life is that it is male-dominated, male-run. Married men are entitled to have lovers. Married women are not. Adultery is against the law for both sexes. But a complaint by a woman against her philandering husband is generally not taken seriously by the police. If a husband chooses to file a complaint against his wife because she has cuckolded him, however, that is serious.

"For that," said Rosa María, "a woman can go to prison. However, the normal thing is not for a man to file charges. If his wife commits adultery, he will beat her."

Rape laws likewise require a woman to prove not only that she did not want to have sex with her violator but that she tried to prevent it. Police, judges, lawyers, and even doctors do not treat rape victims with the sensitivity and respect their condition warrants. It is not unlike the situation in the United States some years ago, before rape reform became widespread.

"By the time she gets through with the doctor and the police," said Rosa María, "a raped woman feels as if she's been raped two more times."

Much of this male attitude stems from the image men have created for women in Mexican society. A married woman is expected to be a wife and mother. Period. She is expected to emulate the pure, abnegated Virgin of Guadalupe, the patron saint of Mexico. In matters of sex, she is expected to be passive. If a man wants exciting, aggressive sex, he will get it from his mistress. Even widows are expected to show no sexual interest in other men, while no such expectation exists for widowers.

The situation was no different with Juan and Rosa María. Rosa María does not know if Juan had mistresses in their short marriage. Sometimes it takes a man a little longer to stray. But she does know that Juan did not appreciate her sexual advances. Rosa María tried to be more open, more experimental in her sexual relations with Juan. She wanted their lovemaking to be more interesting, more exciting, more loving.

"I tried new things with Juan," said Rosa María. "At first he liked it. He liked it very much. But a few days later, he reprimanded me. He said I had acted like a *puta* ["whore"]."

The virgin-wife image is passed down from father to son. It also goes from many mothers to daughters. With this sort of attitude ingrained in men and women, it is not surprising that many a loving relationship sours into suspicion and fear of betrayal. Out of fear of being cuckolded, men forbid their wives to go out of the house unescorted. They upbraid their wives if they talk with other men at parties. When they walk down the streets, they are vigilant for men who might flirt with their wives. When some man does, husbands blame their wives for encouraging it, as Juan sometimes did with Rosa María.

The experts will tell you this male insecurity is a legacy of Mexican history. When the Spanish conquerors came to Mexico, they came without their women. They took Indian women as concubines. The Indian men felt humiliated and betrayed. Modern Mexican men, 90 percent of whom have some Indian blood, retain that fear of humiliation and betrayal, the experts say. All this has given Mexico a unique brand of machismo, a cruel bravado that masks a fragile masculinity. Mexican men, under pressure from this tradition, often hurt and betray others before others can betray them. This insidious idea even invades the family.

The stereotype is that Mexican families are strong. Indeed, many are. Brothers and sisters play with each other and their cousins, but rarely with outsiders. Sons and daughters often live in their parents' homes, even after marriage. Those who want their own homes often build them next to or on the same block as their parents' house, sometimes with financial help from their parents. Mexican families stick together. They are insular, almost clannish. The family is all. But among Mexicans, there is another family stereotype, a much nastier one. In this stereotype, fathers and mothers still adore their children, whom they call *mi rey* ("my king") or *mi reina* ("my queen"). But the love is not so strong when it comes to man and wife. Among Mexicans, it's a dirty little secret that, after the bloom of honeymoon romance has faded, a husband often pits himself against his wife. Husbands, when they have become fathers, expect to be treated like a king when at home. But they spend an increasing amount of time outside the house, drinking or playing dominoes with friends or dallying with their mistresses. They rant and rave when their wives want to go out, secretly worrying about the possibility of wifely infidelity. Wives, feeling suffocated and spurned, smother their sons in motherly love in hopes of turning their male offspring—Daddy's pride and joy—against their fathers. Sons do worship their mothers. But despite mothers' efforts, sons, when they become husbands, start the cycle all over again. They become suspicious of and cruel toward their wives. This is the stereotype. It is not the case universally. Many Mexican couples who have traveled widely abroad or been university educated are fighting the stereotype with loving, sharing marriages. But as with so many stereotypes, this distressing image of Mexican married life springs from an undeniable, substantial reality. Just ask Rosa María.

Countering such attitudes will be a difficult task, Rosa María acknowledged. The male-dominated government encourages continued inferior treatment of women through nonenforcement or selective enforcement of rape, child support, adultery, abortion, and equal-rights laws. While it is no longer obligatory, most marriage ceremonies continue to include a reading of a letter by Mexican politician Melchor Ocampo, a practice that began in 1859. In part, it says: "The man, whose sexual attributes are principally courage and strength, should and will give protection, food and guidance to the woman. The woman, whose principal attributes are abnegation, beauty, compassion, perspicacity and tenderness, should and will give her husband obedience, pleasure, assistance, consolation and counsel, always treating him with the veneration due to the person that supports and defends her." Television commercials also portray a woman's role as exclusively a domestic one, with a side role of pleasure-giver for those women who aren't married. Movies portray the man as the one who knows best.

"I saw a terrible movie last week," said Rosa María. "It was called *Cuando Quiere un Mexicano* (When a Mexican Loves a Mexican). It was with Jorge Negrete. He played a *charro* [a type of Mexican cowboy] who is at first rejected by a beautiful Spanish woman. He tells her he loves her and wants to marry her. She refuses. He slaps her several times. And she changes her mind! What kind of message is that for women? Why should you want to marry someone who beats you?"

As I sat listening to Rosa María, a vibrant, beautiful, obviously intelligent woman, I couldn't help wondering why she had become what she had. Given the social forces loose in Mexico, she could have as easily become a quietly suffering, pliant wife. Half of Mexican households are headed by women like Rosa María, whose husbands have run out on them. Half. They quietly bear the burden of rearing abandoned children. What had made Rosa María so different from these quiet millions? From where did she get her outrage, her drive, her strength? I asked her if there was someone, some influence, that might explain it. Improbably, she said, it was a man. In high school, she had gotten interested in theater. Her theater teacher had encouraged her to continue her studies. She had talent for the theater, he said. She explained that she didn't know if her parents would let her finish high school, let alone be serious about theater.

"He told me," said Rosa María, " 'The theater is your responsibility. To finish school is your responsibility. You have the talent. You have a responsibility to use it. If your parents won't respect your talent, you have to respect it yourself.' "

Ironically, one of the roles that Rosa María played in that theater class was that of Marta, the youngest daughter of *The Children of Sánchez,* Oscar Lewis's 1961 study of poverty in Mexico. The nonfiction best-seller had been made into a play and later a movie. There were astounding parallels between Rosa María's life and Marta's, but important differences, too.

As a youngster, Marta, by her own description, was sort of a party girl. "Nothing tied me down," she told Lewis. "I could do what I wanted. I felt free." Like Rosa María, Marta had been the baby of the family. She had been allowed to get away with more than her brothers and sisters. But happiness was something for children. When Marta grew up, she encountered reality. And it was not a very happy one. About the time Lewis published his book, Marta had decided to flee her house in Tepito, a rough Mexico City neighborhood not far from the market where Rosa María now works. Marta wanted to escape her boyfriend, Crispin, who had beaten her regularly and had fooled around openly with other women. With little thought about where she was going, she grabbed the first bus out of town. It was headed for Acapulco. On the bus, she met Baltazar, a butcher whom she moved in with when the bus reached the end of the line.

While I was doing some stories on what had happened to the Children of Sánchez, I met Marta, whose real name, Berta Hernández, Lewis had changed to protect her. She is a plump, serious woman in her fifties. She had four kids by Crispin and seven more by Baltazar, whom she threw out of the house fifteen years ago. He had become an abusive drunk and had beaten her, just as Crispin had. She can't explain why she stayed with either one so long, except to say that that's what Mexican women of her generation were expected to do.

"A man who can't beat women isn't a man," she told me. "So goes the saying. Men still have three or four women [on the side].

That is the right. Women can't protest. They have to accept it . . . because the man is the boss. A woman's only real function is to have children and to take care of them until the end. A woman can't breathe. She has no life of her own when she's married."

One of Berta's sons has become a doctor. She has a daughter who is a computer programmer in New York. It is a remarkable achievement for an impoverished mother of eleven. But Berta's work is not yet done. She still has three school-age children to rear. She supports them by crocheting doilies and tablecloths that she takes to Tepito to sell once a month. She was making about fifty thousand pesos a month when I talked with her in late 1986, a little less than the minimum wage. It wasn't much money for a family of four, one of whom is Adrian, a teenager retarded since a childhood bout with meningitis.

Berta, who once dreamed of becoming a blond and falling madly in love, adores Adrian, an engaging, lumbering boy. But she also knows that Adrian's condition makes it unlikely she'll have any lovers ever again. It is something that weighs on her heavily.

"I haven't had any love life since my husband left," she said. "Who would live with the responsibility of taking care of my child hanging over his head?"

Berta is resigned to a simple, perhaps even sad, remainder of her life. But she is content to know that she has regained her dignity, her independence. She is free of the brutal men who once professed love for her. She takes solace in the Protestant religion, to which she has converted. She feels bitterness toward a Catholic Church that has given her sex little support. If Rosa María had been born more than half a century ago, as was the woman she once portrayed in a high school play, would Rosa María too have shared Berta's resentful view of life? If Berta had been born in 1960 like Rosa María, if she had heard the siren call of feminism, might she have had Rosa María's hope for the future? Two kindred spirits. Two different outlooks. But perhaps, in the end, the same fate.

Rosa said she felt more fortunate than Berta. But she couldn't be sure her future would be any happier. She had no guarantees she would ever be able to return to school. She didn't know if she'd ever make a decent salary. She did not know what she would do about Lluvia's eye operation. She had not thought much about the theater for a long time. With two children, would she too be denied a love life? Whatever her fate, she said, she would not accept it quietly.

"It is too late for that," she said. "All my life I have had ambitions. I have developed an idea of what I want in life. I cannot be satisfied with less."

There are professional feminists in Mexico. Maybe a thousand strong, they are mostly educated or upper-class women. They can be seen marching for this issue and that. They complain that their husbands won't help with housework. They write erudite screeds in journals and left-wing newspapers about the sexual injustice of Mexican society. They remark that men have no interest in hearing what women have to say about bullfighting, politics, or other supposedly exclusive intellectual preserves of men. They discuss whether Mexican women will ever get adequate day care or paid pregnancy leaves. Their issues are all valid. I cannot dispute a one. If these women were in the United States, they would be in the mainstream of feminist dialogue. But they are not in the United States. They are in Mexico. And in Mexico, it is Rosa María and women like her who are the real feminists, the frontline fighters for equal rights. Rosa María does not read *Fem* or other well-known feminist publications. She has nothing against them. She just doesn't have the money to buy them or the time to read them. She is busy struggling in the trenches against wife abuse, sexual violence, abandonment of children, institutionalized infidelity, and a host of other problems that make other feminist issues seem like fine tuning.

"We are going to work and struggle for an equal role for women, for equal power, for equal respect," Rosa María told me, sounding a bit like a soap-box speaker. "We will march in the streets if necessary. It won't be easy. It will take a lot of time. But we will succeed because we are doing it for our children."

· 20 ·

The *Expatriado*

In 1981, Roberto Contreras thought he had it made. Once the scion of a middle-class family in Mexico City, he had become the owner of five companies. One had a multimillion-dollar contract to supply drilling equipment to Pemex, the state-owned oil company. He was boss of five hundred employees. He was already worth ten million dollars. He was only forty-two years old.

Befitting his wealth, he had a sprawling, eight-thousand-square-foot home in one of the Mexico City's northwest suburbs. Among its amenities were three bedrooms for guests, a sauna, a covered swimming pool, and a separate apartment for his young, married son, Roberto Jr. Each bedroom had a walk-in closet and built-in cabinets for a color television and a videocassette recorder. Almost every room had an expensive imported stereo.

Contreras bought the best cars. He had a chauffeur. His house had two maids. He also had bodyguards. Bodyguards were not only for himself but to deal with the common threat of kidnapping that rich Mexican families faced. When it became clear that he had become rich enough to make his family a target of kidnappers, he had told his children: "If you are kidnapped, consider yourselves dead. I will get together all the money I can to track down those responsible. I'll kill them with my own hands. I'll pour salt in their wounds. But you'll be dead. That's just the reality."

His business with Pemex generated enough revenue so he could have a company jet. He used it for weekly trips between Mexico and Houston, Texas, where he had a partner in his oil-equipment business. He spent $30,000 a month on the jet, more than most Americans make in a year, more than many Mexicans make in a lifetime. He gave his wife jewelry for Christmas, usually $3,000 to $4,000 worth. He went to Las Vegas three times a year, sometimes dropping $5,000 or $6,000 at the tables. Twice a year he took his family to posh Mexican beach resorts, such as Ixtapa or Puerto Vallarta. Twice more a year, he went to Europe, usually doing a little business when he was not enjoying the sights of London, Paris, or some other capital. Switzerland was his favorite country. In early October, when the tourist crowds had thinned out, he'd rent a Mercedes-Benz. He and his wife would seek out intimate country inns where no reservations were required. Going from town to town, he'd push the Mercedes' accelerator down until the car hit his favorite speed—two hundred kilometers an hour. He felt like the king of the world. And why not? Mexico, his country, was on top of the heap, basking in the wealth of black gold—oil.

When vast reserves of oil were discovered in late 1976, Mexico suddenly became rich. In that heady atmosphere, Contreras thought Mexico might become a world economic power. When President José López Portillo had come to office in December 1976, he had said there was nowhere to go but up. Mexico was the future. Contreras believed him. He put every peso he had into Mexico.

In late 1981, however, the bubble began to burst. World oil prices began to fall. By February 1982, López Portillo devalued the peso from twenty-nine to the U.S. dollar to forty-six, just weeks after assuring everyone that he would defend the peso "like a dog." In March, with an eye toward upcoming presidential elections, López Portillo raised workers' salaries dramatically. All the experts said it was economic madness, a move that would create hyperinflation. Contreras decided to invest some of his money abroad.

With oil prices down, Pemex started a slow-pay policy for its suppliers, such as Contreras's main company, Repsafab. He eventually got paid in November, just before López's Portillo's successor, Miguel de la Madrid, took over. Contreras had his doubts about where things were going economically. But he still believed in Mexico. He had to. He had bought into the system.

A person can succeed in business in Mexico through talent. But talent is not enough. One also needed friends. When Contreras started in business, the government controlled about 70 percent of the economy, so friends in government were the best kind of friends. More important, one could not afford to have enemies.

That's what a man told Contreras shortly after it became apparent that Contreras's company would be a money-maker. The man said he had contacts at Pemex. For a fee, he said, he would handle any problems that Contreras had with the oil giant. He'd also prevent any problems from occurring. For his services, he said, he'd charge Contreras 5 percent of every supply contract he got from Pemex. Contreras knew what the man was offering. He was a front man for someone in Pemex who wanted a piece of Repsafab's action. Contreras tried the man out to see if he could deliver. He asked the man to open a few doors at Pemex's financial and purchasing offices. The man did. Contreras agreed to pay the 5 percent. In Mexico, he knew, there was really no other way.

Mexico's economic crisis continued. Devaluations became regular events. In 1983, the peso dropped from about 130 to the U.S. dollar to about 175. Contreras's contracts with Pemex required him to buy a lot of his raw materials from the United States, where he had to pay in dollars. But dollars now cost almost six times what they had in early 1982. Mexican contracts with Pemex did not typically have escalator clauses to cover such changed conditions. But during the López Portillo administration, Contreras and other business leaders had gotten a government commitment to make Pemex suppliers whole if inflation or devaluations cut into the value of their contracts. Contreras went to Pemex to explain that he needed more pesos so he could buy the necessary imported materials. He thought he was in a good bargaining position. He was an official of Canacintra, the national industrial chamber of commerce. He was the representative of the capital-goods industry. Moreover, he was just beginning a campaign to be elected president of Canacintra. He had run twice before, garnering 28 percent of the vote the first time, 40 percent the second. Victory seemed within his grasp.

He did not win, however. In retrospect, he says he was a bit naive about how brutal the Mexican government can be when it doesn't like someone, especially someone in business. Business holds a rather strange place in Mexican society. Officially, it is often the focal point of verbal attack by a government that still styles itself as "revolutionary" more than three quarters of a century after Mexico's last revolution began. Government-financed cartoonists regularly portray business owners as striped-pants entrepreneurs in silk top hats. The message is always the same: Business is out to exploit the worker. Public-school textbooks attack the avarice of capitalism and overlook the abuses of communism. Business is allowed little political legitimacy. Either it is lambasted for being the ally of the leading opposition party, National Action (PAN), or it is officially shut out of the affairs of the ruling Institutional Revolutionary Party (PRI). The PRI has three sectors—for peasants, workers, and bureaucrats. The latter also includes a few small-business owners. But big businesses can't apply. Privately, however, many of the most powerful business executives in Mexico—the owners of television stations, newspapers, and stock brokerages—are key allies of the PRI's top leaders. The government says little of this relationship. It takes political contributions from business and accepts their bribes. But any time that business tries to become more of an open part of political life within the PRI, party leaders usually side with the workers and the peasants, who always argue that business leaders, like the PAN, are counterrevolutionary. Business has to play along with this game because the government controls so much of the economy. One can't operate in business as an enemy of the government. Business executives make their little protests. Some contribute secretly to the PAN. Others inflate the amounts of invoices for needed imports and then get foreign currency at discount exchange rates under a government import program. They send fraudulent profits from this invoice scheme to secret bank accounts abroad. Few pay the income taxes they owe. Many keep two sets of books, one for the government, one for themselves. Others make cash deals with customers to hide income—and refuse to collect the 15-percent national sales tax. But, despite all these secret protests, businesses usually find they have to pay the government one way or another in the end. That's what Contreras found.

Contreras had been willing to play along with the government's all-businesses-are-bad charade. He had friends in the PRI. President de la Madrid's finance minister, Jesús Silva Herzog, was a buddy. Twice a week he played dominoes, the national passion of Mexico, with top officials of various government agencies. Officially enemies, privately friends, everyone winked. Everybody made money. Contreras knew there were corrupt officials in government. There were even a few thugs who would resort to violence to solve political problems. But he thought there were good guys, too, the sort of guys he played dominoes with. When he saw Mexico's economic situation worsening in 1983, he thought he could talk to such people about how to make things better. He had a good idea, he thought, about how to improve the economy. Surely men of reason, the sort of men he called friends inside the PRI, would at least listen, he thought. But he was wrong.

Contreras's idea, which he began to air in business speeches in late 1983, was hardly a radical one. But, as he would find out, it was considered treason by some in Mexico. As a capital-goods entrepreneur, Contreras knew that supply was exceeding de-. mand in his vital industry. Sales were in a slump. The key reason, Contreras felt, was the oversupply of products by a number of state-owned, white-elephant capital-goods companies. They were poorly managed financial disasters. In a market economy, they would never have survived. Mexico, of course, had a mixed economy, not a market one. But, he argued, if the government would give up a bit of its control of the economy by closing these businesses down or by selling them to more efficient private interests, the oversupply crisis in the capital-goods industry would end. Privatize. That was Contreras's message.

When some Mexican customs officials showed up at the Repsafab offices in January 1984 and said they were investigating allegations of smuggling, maybe Contreras should have suspected that the official reaction to his idea was not favorable. But he did not. His mind was on a meeting he and other business leaders were scheduled to have with President de la Madrid a few weeks later. The official reason for the meeting was to present the results of an important industry assembly held some time before. Contreras would make a major presentation. The meeting would also be an opportunity for de la Madrid to look Contreras over. Contreras was asking to become head of the most important chamber of commerce in the country. Someone who was not acceptable to Mexico's emperor-like president, Contreras knew, could not be elected.

At the meeting, Contreras made his "privatization" pitch. As is his custom, he was candid, even blunt. De la Madrid thanked him but was noncommittal. Ten days later, federal judicial police picked up Contreras's brother, who was one of Contreras's business partners in Repsafab. He was held for two days of interrogation about alleged attempts to bribe Pemex officials to get Pemex to pay what it owed Repsafab. The Contreras brothers had hired an agent to try and get the money owed. But, Contreras insists, they had authorized no bribes. A few days later, newspaper stories appeared in Mexico City saying that Contreras's company was involved in fraud and that Contreras had fled the country. The day the stories appeared, Contreras was in Mexico City giving a speech at a downtown hotel to a Canacintra group. Shortly after the stories, Canacintra members voted on who would be their new president. Contreras got 48 percent of the ballots. But he lost by thirteen votes to a candidate who was backed by de la Madrid's commerce minister.

"I'm sure I lost at least thirteen votes because of those phony stories," Contreras told me.

A few days later, the federal attorney general, Sergio García Ramírez, said his office had no proof of any fraud by Contreras or his company.

After the stories, Contreras's negotiations with Pemex came to a standstill. At the time, Contreras still didn't understand what was happening to him. He thought all his troubles would eventually pass. He believed in Mexico. He was trying to help. How could that be bad, he thought.

Contreras's troubles, however, mounted. The head of the customs team investigating Repsafab for smuggling demanded a large bribe to leave Contreras alone. The official admitted that he had not found any smuggling or other illegality. There were a few clerical errors in Repsafab's import paperwork, he noted. They would be enough to fabricate a charge of fraud unless Contreras paid the bribe.

Contreras refused. For half the amount asked, he said, "I could hire someone to kill you." That wasn't his style, however, he told the official, who suddenly seemed very alert about what Contreras was saying. Instead, Contreras offered to give the official a large commission—more than the bribe he wanted—if he could get Pemex to release the thirty million dollars that Contreras calculated Pemex owed him, given unexpected devaluations and inflation. The official, who had boasted of friends in Pemex and elsewhere in the government, warmed to the idea. But he returned a week later, saying he could do nothing. Contreras, he said, had powerful enemies in Pemex. One in particular, Contreras learned, had gotten the idea that Contreras was the source of information that police had used to arrest a top Pemex official for fraud in 1983.

Contreras, despondent at the buildup of all this bad news, finally asked a friend in June to talk with de la Madrid's energy minister, Francisco Labastida Ochoa. Contreras hoped the minister could get Pemex to give Contreras at least part of the money owed him. The friend met privately with Labastida Ochoa. He phoned Contreras late that night, after the meeting was over.

"I have something important to tell you," the friend said. "But I don't want to talk over the phone. Let's have lunch tomorrow."

At lunch, the friend revealed that the minister had pulled out a file, three inches thick, about Contreras and his views on reprivatization. The minister's advice was for Contreras to get out of the oil business and use what money he could scrape up to buy a cattle ranch or something unconnected with oil. When the friend pressed him as to why Contreras should do this, the minister said, "He has become an enemy of the system."

Contreras had about $250,000 in savings. He could have put it into Repsafab. At the rate the company was spending money, his quarter of a million dollars would have lasted three or four months. He might have declared bankruptcy. Legally one can go bankrupt in Mexico, but not politically. Because of the government's revolutionary rhetoric against business, corporate debts are usually treated the same as personal debts. If Contreras had closed down Repsafab and used his life savings to buy a cattle ranch, the banks—which the government had nationalized in 1982—would have eventually taken all he had. In July, Contreras decided that he had no real choice. He had to get out of Mexico.

He began looking for a house in the Houston area. He knew Houston. He had money there. Like a lot of nervous Mexicans, he had put some of his savings in the United States to protect its value from Mexico's ever-increasing devaluations. This outflow of funds, which economists call capital flight, exploded in volume in the late '70s and early '80s. The outflow got so bad in 1982 that President López Portillo publicly attacked such people as traitors, dubbing them *sacadólares* ("dollar removers"), even though what they did was not illegal. Between 1976 and 1985, Mexicans sent a mind-boggling fifty-three billion dollars out of the country, the most for any Third World country. It went out exactly when cash-strapped Mexico needed such funds the most. Contreras was a *sacadólar*. That's how I met him in 1986 while doing a story on the capital-flight phenomenon. He had sent a little more than a hundred thousand dollars to the United States between the late 1970s and mid-1984. He hoped to take an equal amount out when he moved his family to Texas. As far as he knew, it would be all the money he would have for his new start in a new country. His business funds—millions—were temporarily frozen. Workers at Repsafab, encouraged by pro-government union officials, had gone on strike and seized his factory because he hadn't paid them. He couldn't pay them because Pemex wouldn't pay him.

In August, Contreras made his final break with his homeland. He took the cash he had and left for good. He has lived in the Houston area ever since, bitter and substantially poorer. It took him a while to accept that he would have to start over. He kept hoping against hope that he could get his millions from Pemex or out of his investment in his factory. He had been rich and powerful in Mexico. In Texas, he did not want to admit that he was suddenly middle-class. He had no visa that would allow him to make a living. Without a job, his $250,000 nest egg would disappear quickly at Houston prices. He did have a car, a Cadillac Eldorado. He had bought it for business purposes in Houston. But he lost even that. It had been in his partner's name for insurance purposes. His partner had used the car's title to secure a loan. Shortly after Contreras moved to Houston, his partner defaulted on the loan. The bank repossessed the car.

Contreras bought a 1981 Oldsmobile to get around. It was quite a comedown from the luxury automobiles he had owned in recent years. He tried to get things going financially. But he found he had little motivation. "I had no reason to live," he said. A little more than a year later, he began experiencing chest pains. The doctor told him he was lucky he wasn't dead. His veins were badly clogged. A lifetime of rich food and all the recent stress in his life had made him a prime candidate for a heart attack, the doctor said. Contreras checked into a hospital. In November 1985 he had quadruple-bypass heart surgery.

As such operations sometimes do, the surgery gave Contreras a new outlook on life. He felt happy just to be alive. He began noticing his family more. They had all known he was depressed because of the setbacks in Mexico. They had never complained. His six children, three of them college students, worked hard in school, attempting to learn in a language that was not their own. They all got good grades. As Contreras put it: "They all did their jobs."

His wife had reason to be despondent. But she was not. She was brave, even though the wonderful, lavish life she had known in Mexico was gone, probably forever. She had regularly hosted twenty-five people for Sunday lunch in their large Mexican home. Now she rarely had more than a dozen for any meal, including the eight members of her family. Her 3,200-square-foot house in the Houston suburb of Sugarland was less than half the size of her old home. Most of her relatives had lived within a few blocks of her home in Mexico, as is the Mexican custom. In Texas, she had a few relatives scattered about. But most of her close family and best friends still lived in Mexico.

In Mexico, she had been a housewife, although a wealthy one. She had busied herself with family matters. She drove her kids to school, even though her husband provided a chauffeur. She went to the bank, shopped for food, and even helped her kids with their homework. That was a woman's job in Mexico. In Sugarland, errands didn't take a quarter of the time they had in the clogged pace and red tape of Mexico City. Her kids didn't seem to need her as much either. They were growing up rapidly. They seemed more independent, more self-confident with every day they spent in American classrooms.

Roberto suggested that his wife come to work at his new company. He had formed a firm to make bathroom and fireplace products out of Mexican marble waste. His wife had never worked in Mexico. But she gave it a try. She started out answering telephones. As she grew more confident, she did secretarial jobs, and later handled payables and receivables.

The family underwent a number of other changes. They had all had some English in school, so they didn't have to start from scratch in communicating in their new environment. But other differences were more difficult to adapt to. Money was the big thing. They weren't as rich as they had been before. Roberto Sr. had paid himself a salary of about $180,000 a year in Mexico. Now he had an official salary of $96,000. But his fledgling company could afford to pay him only half that. The rest went on its books as loans from him. At Christmas, he could only spend hundreds on jewelry for his wife rather than thousands. The family budget didn't allow for European trips. Instead, the family stayed in the country, visiting places such as Disney's Epcot Center, in Florida.

The Contreras kids found their friends were more diverse. In Mexico, they had only mixed with the rich kids of their class. Now they have friends from all sectors of Houston's white-black-Vietnamese-Chinese-Japanese melting pot. Luis, Jorge, Gerardo, and Alejandro found that school and life in general was more competitive in Texas than in Mexico. We talked about this after a wonderful dinner at the Contreras home in August 1987, when I went back to see them. The boys said they had to work harder to get what they wanted now. They found they were expected to do more for themselves, too. In Mexico, things had always been done for them. By their parents. By the authorities. By the maids. But they liked this new experience, they said.

Monica, the Contreras's only daughter, found she was treated better as a woman. She told me she felt for the first time as if her possibilities in life were limitless. Roberto Jr., the oldest of the Contreras children, had noticed similar changes in his wife, Claudia. "In Mexico," he said, "women are treated like dog meat. Men feel it is their duty to molest them. In Mexico, a professional working woman is a curiosity."

The family, always close, has grown even closer, Roberto Sr. thinks. In Mexico, because of three-hour lunches and, sometimes, late starts at the office, the family would be together only for dinner and on weekends. Given U.S. office hours and daylight saving time, he said, he now has evenings to bicycle with his kids and get to know them better. He exercises more, although not as much as he should, he said.

Some things have remained the same. Roberto Sr. still plays dominoes, although now it is only once a week. And instead of high government officials his partners are other *expatriados*, as expatriates as called in Spanish. Spanish is the lingua franca inside the Contreras home. Religion is still very important, too. There is a large crucifix on one of the dining-room walls. The family says grace before dinner. All eight ContRerases attend Mass each Sunday. But the Catholicism they have encountered at St. Theresa's Church in Sugarland is somewhat different from that they experienced all their lives in Mexico.

"In Mexico," said Roberto Sr., "they teach you that you came into the world to suffer. To be a Catholic in Mexico is to be God's servant, God's slave. You are here [on earth] to live and suffer. In the United States, you are the son of God, part of the chosen people. You can be proud. You have a large responsibility to share things with others. But your duty is to share, not to suffer. You can be happy. To share is your happiness."

Roberto Sr. also likes the give-and-take of U.S. Catholicism. As his fellow expatriates will readily tell you, Roberto has strong views on almost everything. Ever the conservative, he thinks the sanctuary movement is a lot of bunk. He has warned St. Theresa's pastor that the Catholic Church is being duped by Communists and Socialists.

Perhaps the most profound change the Contrerases have noticed is freedom. They feel they have more of it.

"Freedom is something you can't explain to Mexicans who haven't lived here. They'll say, 'Hell, Mexico is a free country. You can even drive drunk and fix everything with a little money.' That, to them, is freedom. But freedom is more than that. When you can start a company without interference from the government, when you can do whatever you want without questions from everyone so long as it is legal and moral, then you feel what freedom is."

The Contrerases have come to love and appreciate their lives in the United States. When Roberto Sr. got his green card in May 1987, he became a legal permanent resident of the United States. He is already worried about the fate of his new home.

"I think the Russians will kill us if they can," he said, already talking like the U.S. citizen he plans to become when he's eligible in 1992. "It is a principle of Lenin that the only way the Russian Revolution can survive is if everybody in the world is a Communist. The only way to deal with the Russians is with a big stick." He liked President Reagan's "cowboy" approach to foreign policy, even though he acknowledged that it had its dangers. He expressed fear that anyone less tough than Reagan with the Russians would cause El Salvador, Honduras, and maybe even the United States to fall to communism. Just in case enough Americans don't hear his message, the sort of message he once tried to spread in Mexico, Contreras said he plans to run for governor of Texas shortly after he becomes a citizen.

"I may fail, but I am going to try," he said.

He has instilled the same sort of positive drive in his kids, all obvious achievers. Monica is a good example. Less than two years after arriving in a new country, she was picked to give the keynote speech at her high school class's graduation ceremony. She gave a speech any American would have been proud to write. It began: "Life is a race, and the finish line is up to you. The issue is not whether you can succeed but whether you want to." Monica urged her classmates to want to. She quoted Martin Luther King, Jr., Enrico Caruso, and Jonathan Livingston Seagull, among others along the way. Whatever others might do, she said, she planned to succeed. "I have a dream, too," she concluded.

People such as the Contrerases are precisely the type of citizens Mexico cannot afford to lose, I thought as I left the house in Sugarland that night. They are skilled, educated, creative, and, yes, patriotic. Mexico can probably learn to do without the billions of dollars that Mexicans have sent to foreign bank accounts in a vote of no-confidence in the government. Mexico might even lure some of those billions back, as it had from time to time with new, promising economic plans. But human talent such as the Contrerases is something that Mexico has probably lost forever. Thanks to economic uncertainty and political repression, the statistics show that this alarming brain drain is on the rise.

•　•　•

In April 1988, Pemex officials got a court order that allowed them to seize the equipment that Contreras had held back at his Repsafab factory in protest of nonpayment. What little hope Contreras may have had about getting any money from Pemex vanished the day the equipment was grabbed. With his factory still in the hands of striking workers, there also didn't appear to be much chance he'd be able to sell Repsafab's buildings or the machinery inside. Somehow, though, Contreras told me, the thought of losing the millions he once had enjoyed was not as depressing as he once had thought it would be. He said he had probably had written off those riches the day he and his wife had started calculating Houston grocery prices in dollars instead of pesos. It was the day they had begun to think like Americans.

Contreras said he was too busy with a new business project to dwell on the loss of the money. He had persuaded the city of Brownsville, Texas, to back construction of a marble-manufacturing factory for him. The plant would make marble products on a large scale, just like the ones he'd been manufacturing in modest amounts since he had moved to Texas. If the city could sell enough industrial-revenue bonds, he said, he would be able to employ three hundred people and pay them seven million dollars in wages annually. He could have built the plant on the Mexican side, he said. There were thousands of profitable assembly and manufacturing plants along the border. It would have cost him less, he said. But, after all that he had been through, he said, it just wasn't worth the bother.

"You can't do business in a businesslike way in Mexico," he explained.

If he had built the plant in Mexico, it would have created the same three hundred jobs there, instead of in Brownsville. It would have generated about twenty-five million dollars in exports. The Mexican government, ironically now in the midst of "privatizing" many of its unprofitable state-owned industries as a means of streamlining its economy, has made exports the cornerstone of future economic programs. But now all Mexico will get from Contreras is two million dollars' worth of raw marble sales and no jobs at all.

Contreras is bitter about how the government treated him. He's made two visits to Mexico since moving to Texas. The authorities, who refer to Contreras as a gangster and a crook when outsiders ask about him, could have charged him with something if there had been a real basis for the allegations once voiced against him. But they did not. They seemed satisfied that they had just dirtied him up enough to destroy his credibility as a business and political leader.

Contreras still loves Mexico dearly. He would not move back there, however, even if a right-wing government somehow took over and offered him a cabinet post. But if his onetime homeland were threatened by a leftist revolution, he said, "I'd go back if I had to swim. I'd go back to help, to die if necessary. So would all my children. Then I'd come back here to live."

· Conclusion ·

In his best-selling book *Veil: The Secret Wars of the CIA, Washington Post* reporter Bob Woodward tells an interesting story about Mexico. When William Casey became director of the U.S. Central Intelligence Agency in 1981, the outgoing director of the U.S. Defense Intelligence Agency told Casey that he should be concerned about Mexico. Mexico, said the DIA chief, was plagued by guerrilla insurgencies, lack of federal government control of local areas, and urban poverty so extreme that an Ayatollah Khomeini–type figure could emerge to launch a revolution.

Casey kept this advice in mind. When the administration formulated its controversial policy to fund counterrevolutionaries to force Nicaragua's Sandinistas to make their country a democracy, Casey argued that one policy justification should be the protection of Mexico. Given what he regarded as its shaky political and economic conditions, Mexico, with its two-thousand-mile unguarded border with the United States, had to be saved from communism at all costs, he said.

In 1984, President Reagan's National Security Council expert on Latin America, Constantine Menges, told Casey that things in Mexico had gotten even worse. It was on the verge of chaos, if not revolution, he insisted. Mexico was strapped with a more than eighty-billion-dollar foreign debt, rampant corruption, and many other social problems. About the same time, an intelligence board that advises the president issued a top-secret report charging that the CIA wasn't paying enough attention to political instability in Mexico. This prompted Casey to order a CIA estimate of the Mexican situation. He picked his national intelligence officer for Latin America, John Horton, to head the project. Horton, who had been the CIA station chief in Mexico, picked another analyst, Brian Latell, to work up a draft report. Latell visited Mexico and wrote a report that listed the familiar items: urban and rural unrest, large foreign debt, enormous capital flight, and widespread corruption. Horton agreed with the facts in the draft but not with Latell's conclusions that Mexico was ripe to fall. Horton refashioned the report so that it concluded there was at best a 20 percent chance of a collapse in Mexico. A Horton footnote indicated that most U.S. intelligence didn't even support a number that high. Latell's mistake in making direr predictions, Horton told Casey, had been to assume that Mexicans would react the same way that Americans would to such conditions. Americans would revolt. Latell assumed Mexicans were about to do the same. It was an amateur's mistake.

After reading twenty chapters about Mexico's problems of poverty, illiteracy, income disparity, unemployment, malnutrition, crime, political repression, smuggling, massive foreign debt, bulging budget deficits, horrific environmental conditions, rural violence, corruption, religious fanaticism, racism, and weaknesses of the Mexican character, I hope that readers won't make the same amateur mistake. Mexicans are not Americans and never will be. Mexican poet Octavio Paz once wrote that the U.S.-Mexican border separates Mexicans and Americans from their absolute differences. Mexicans spring from a different history, a different tradition. They love their country as much as Americans love theirs. Just because Mexico has faults and weaknesses does not mean its people are ashamed of it or ready to overthrow their government. Mexicans may complain vehemently and often about the ineptness and corruptness of their leaders. But that does not mean that Mexico will soon go the way of Iran, or even the Philippines or Haiti. The glass may be half-empty in Mexico, but it is also half-full. There is joy and laughter and love of children. There is artistic talent and hard work. There is patience and, most of all, an ability to endure. *Aguantar* means to bear or endure, to put up with. That's what Mexicans do. They have suffered a lot through their Indian, colonial, and modern history. They have learned to put up with things that Americans and other foreigners have not. That does not make them inferior to those who would not stand for such things. One could argue that it sometimes makes them tougher. What is certain is that it makes them different.

That, I hope, is the principal conclusion that readers will take away from this book. Mexicans are different from you and me. Any attempt to deal with them as if they were the same would be shortsighted, maybe even disastrous. If Americans are going to deal with the Mexicans—and the numbers on trade, immigration, population, illegal drugs, and the environment show that we surely will—then we must deal with them on the basis of who they are. Mexicans, like any unique people, approach things differently from others because they look at life through a different prism. Mexicans place more emphasis on magic than on logic. They have more regard for fantasy than for truth. They laugh at death and sometimes show little respect for human life. They are resilient beyond explanation. Their humor is blacker than most. Mexicans can be exasperatingly fatalistic and uninterested in making their lot better. They drive visiting do-gooder reformers wild. They can be inspiringly heroic, like many of the people I have portrayed in these chapters.

Mexicans are the product of a singular past. History dealt Americans the Industrial Revolution, capitalism, and English democracy to help them form their character. Mexicans got the Counter-Reformation, feudalism, and the Spanish Inquisition. They are Castillians and Andalusians by way of Tenochtitlán and Chichén-Itzá.

I plan one day to return to Mexico with my adopted son, a native Mexican, when he is of an age to appreciate its reality. I hope, maybe a decade from now, that I can show him how things have gotten better. I hope that the vast potential I see in Mexico will at last be realized. Knowing what I do about the depth of corruption, the lack of proper political leadership, and the extent of poverty and ignorance, however, I fear that ten years may not be enough. I hope I am wrong. My son may not find that Mexico is that shining city on a hill. But I hope he will find that there are many things in Mexico he can respect and enjoy. I know, at least, that someone will show him that things there are different.

· **Afterword** ·

to the Paperback Edition

Carlos Salinas de Gotari, a short, balding technocrat, wasn't supposed to become a very impressive Mexican president. And few Mexicans expected when he took office in December 1988 that he would be able to parlay his razor-thin, questionable victory into anything approaching political popularity. But toward the end of his first year in office, that and a lot of other surprises had occurred on the Mexican scene.

Salinas, an intelligent, multilingual man with perhaps more to prove than most Mexican chief executives, lost no time in showing his countrymen and the world who was in charge. In January 1989, after a pitched gun battle, Mexican army troops arrested Joaquín Hernández Galicia, the supposedly untouchable chief of Mexico's oil workers' union, which had long had a corrupt stranglehold on the country's leading industry. The following month, perhaps to show he was no tool of the rich, Salinas had his men arrest Eduardo Legoretta, one of Mexico's leading financiers, for stock fraud. And in April, Salinas's police arrested Mexico's biggest drug dealer, Miguel Ángel Félix Gallardo, whom previous administrations had said they could not find, even though Gallardo had been living openly in Guadalajara.

On economic matters, Salinas stuck with the politically unpopular economic austerity plan that he had designed in 1987, when he was President Miguel de la Madrid's budget chief—and inflation was 159 percent. Vowing to keep wages and prices frozen and the peso at a slow but steady devaluation until at least March 1990, Salinas managed by the summer of 1989 to squeeze inflation to below 20 percent from its 1988 level of 51.7 percent.

His government also wangled a badly needed $3.6 billion loan from the International Monetary Fund. It topped that with a deal that rescheduled $54 billion of

Mexico's $107 billion foreign debt, a move that has the potential of cutting Mexico's crushing annual debt payment significantly.

Salinas's government, staying with de la Madrid's decision to have Mexico join the free-trade General Agreement on Tariffs and Trade (GATT), also made it easier for foreign investors to have 100 percent ownership of businesses they start in Mexico. Nervous Mexicans were persuaded to bring home more than $2 billion in hard currency they had squirreled away in foreign bank accounts, away from the vagaries of the Mexican economy.

On the political front, Salinas got a lot of good press—inside and outside Mexico—about his party's recognition of the July 1989 gubernatorial victory of the opposition right-wing National Action Party (PAN). It was the first governor's seat the opposition has been allowed to hold since Salinas's embattled Institutional Revolutionary Party (PRI) was formed in 1929.

He even improved relations with the United States, long the bogeyman-blamed for Mexico's principal woes. President Bush, pleased with Salinas's anti-corruption drive, sent five of his cabinet members to the first meeting of the U.S.-Mexican Binational Commission during Salinas's term. And in October 1989, a smiling Salinas signed a free-trade and investment agreement with the United States that should boost two-way trade between Mexico and its most important trading partner.

All in all, not a bad first year. But as any seasoned observer of Mexican politics will tell you, one year does not make a *sexenic,* as Mexicans call their president's six-year term. President de la Madrid had some flashy results in his first year. To show his determination to fight widespread official corruption, his police arrested Jorge Díaz Serrano, the former head of Pemex, Mexico's national oil company. And disgraced presidents José López Portillo and Luis Echeverría had people talking in their first years about how things were going to change at last. Things did change—but only for the worse. The question is: Will Salinas's administration be any different?

There are some worrisome signs that it won't be. While his party did recognize the PAN's gubernatorial victory in Baja, it stole, with a lot less fanfare, state legislative elections in Michoacán, home state of Cuauhtémoc Cárdenas, Salinas's principal rival in the July 1988 presidential election. Likewise, while the arrests of Hernández (affectionately known as La Quina), Legoretta, and Gallardo got some big fish off the streets, lots of low-level corruption continued. True to form, when Mexico City forced drivers to submit their cars for pollution tests, police didn't take long to establish a thriving business in bribes to let motorists go in spite of failing to have required emission-control stickers. Salinas himself showed some moral flaws by naming Miguel Nazar Haro, indicted in San Diego in 1981 as a major car thief, to the post of intelligence chief of the Mexico City police. The resulting uproar forced Nazar Haro to quit.

Other troublesome signs for Mexico's future remain immutable. Past birth rates dictate that one million new persons will join the Mexican work force each year; this will keep Mexico's unemployment and underemployment at alarming double-digit rates unless the economy grows significantly, which is unlikely. Reliance on oil is still out of balance. The arrest of La Quina makes restructuring that inefficient industry easier. But many of La Quina's henchmen remain in the union hierarchy. That $2 billion of vitally needed Mexican money brought back from abroad is just a drop in the bucket compared with what's still overseas—and likely to remain there because of a lack of public confidence built up over decades of government trickery and dishonesty. With red ink splashed all over his budgets, Salinas will also have a tough time reversing the abysmal social conditions of Mexicans, who continue to die from easily treatable diseases, such as diarrhea.

Political reform was easier. But then Salinas had no choice. With the bare majority his party won in the 1988 federal elections, one-party rule in Mexico ended. Salinas had to deal with the opposition, if only to line up help for any necessary constitutional changes, which require more than the 260 votes his party has in the lower house of the legislature. Reform was also in the PRI's interest, to show Mexicans it was responding to their desire for a more democratic form of government. Salinas did boot some party dinosaurs out of office, supposedly to signal a new direction. But the replacements were not liberal heretics. He released about four hundred political prisoners, but others remained in jail. The press is still told what to say. Salinas did the minimum to keep his party alive. But thanks to accurate foot marksmanship by opposition parties, the minimum has been enough.

The left has yet another new party. Cárdenas, who has a chance to win the 1994 presidential election, formed the Democratic Party of the Revolution (PRD) in May 1989, while maintaining lines of communication to the PRI. But neither the PRD, the PAN, nor any other opposition party is truly a national organization. No party but the PRI fielded candidates for every office in 1989. None but the PRI had poll watchers in every precinct to make sure the elections were honest. Such opposition disorganization, plus some good results in the economy, could pump new blood into the phoenix-like PRI, whose only real ideology is to do what's necessary to win. But things could just as easily go wrong. If and when Salinas decides to unfreeze prices and wages, Mexicans may vent pent-up expectations with startling raises and price hikes, rekindling hyperinflation. Oil prices, at the mercy of a fickle and glutted world oil market, could tumble, slashing Mexico's income by billions of dollars. That would be a disaster for a country whose hard-currency reserves—the money Mexico needs for foreign debt and import payments—dropped to an alarming level during Salinas's initial months in power.

I don't want to make things seem gloomier than they are in Mexico. Things were clearly better in the first year of the Salinas government than they were in the last year of Miguel de la Madrid's administration. But I want to caution against excessive rosiness. Despite all the surprising reforms that grabbed headlines in 1989, I haven't changed my mind about any basic conclusions I made in the hardcover edition of *The Mexicans.* I remain hopeful about Mexico but not optimistic.

· Notes ·

A Note on Notes

I did not intend this book to be a reference text on Mexico. By using the stories of people's lives to explain the vital and serious aspects of Mexico, I hoped to make the complexity of Mexico more accessible to the general reader.

For those who do want more detailed information about Mexico, however, I have included some amplifying notes on each chapter.

There is also an ample bibliography of books, in Spanish and English, that I found useful in getting to know Mexico.

One caveat on the numbers I use in the book and in the notes: Accurate, precise statistics are an elusive commodity in Mexico, as any foreign journalist or diplomat quickly discovers. I remember one political poll released before the 1988 presidential elections that illustrates the point. When each candidate's public support was added up, the figures totaled 121 percent.

I have tried as much as possible to use the most authoritative sources for numbers, such as the national census (prepared by the National Institute of Statistics, Geography and Information of the Ministry of Planning and Budget), the annual state-of-the-nation addresses by the president, and the annual economic reports by the Banco de Mexico, the central bank. Data on Mexico put out by the International Monetary Fund, the United Nations, the Pan-American Health Organization, the U.S. Department of Commerce, and the U.S. Drug Enforcement Agency are also reliable. The "Economic Trends Report" of the U.S. embassy in Mexico, put out periodically, is also an excellent source of economic data. The State Department's annual human-rights report, issued to Congress each February, is useful for political data. For the punctilious, all other sources might be treated with some skepticism, their data viewed as approximations rather than exact points on a graph chart.

The source of the people that I have profiled in this book was the people themselves. With few exceptions, all data on their lives came from tape-recorded interviews with the subjects.

Introduction

12. "I did not make my first trip to Mexico . . ." In the mid-1980s, the Mexican Ministry of Tourism reported that between four million and five million tourists visited Mexico each year, about 80 percent of whom were Americans. Such figures do not include the sixty million or so crossings made each year by Americans who did not go beyond a twenty-five-kilometer zone that runs parallel to the U.S.-Mexican border. These visits, usually made within a day, are mainly for shopping, dining, or auto-repair purposes rather than full-fledged vacations.

14. *The Mexicans* is a collection . . ." The minimum wage is set in pesos. Its value in dollars varies with the changing exchange rate between the peso and the U.S. dollar. The minimum wage has several levels, the highest of which is paid in Mexico City and a few developed states. During most of the 1980s, the minimum wage was the equivalent of about three dollars a day in Mexico City. Sometimes, depending on surprise devaluations, the minimum wage was slightly above or below this figure. In underdeveloped states, the minimum wage was less. In the last quarter of 1987, for example, the minimum wage was 5,625 pesos in Mexico City, when the peso was trading at between 1,650 to 2,250 to the dollar. In underdeveloped parts of Mexico the minimum wage was as little as 4,690 in the same quarter.

15. "That threat aside, Americans ought . . ." Figures on population are from the Instituto Nacional de Estadística, Geografía e Informática, Secretaría de Programación y Presupuesto.

15. "Mexico is the world's fifth largest producer of oil . . ." In 1987, Mexico produced about 2.541 million barrels of oil a day. It exported 1.345 million barrels of what it produced that year. In 1983, Pemex, the state-owned oil company, claimed Mexico had 57.1 billion barrels of oil in the ground (proven reserves), which ranked it fourth in the world behind Saudi Arabia, Kuwait, and the U.S.S.R.—and ahead of the United States. By 1987, that figure had dropped to 48 billion barrels, because of extraction and revised Pemex estimates of how much oil could really be recovered. Mexico's total proven hydrocarbon reserves (oil, natural gas, etc.) were about 70 billion barrels in 1987.

15. "Mexico is the no. 3 market for the United States . . ." The U.S. Department of Commerce estimated in 1987 that every ten-billion-dollars worth of U.S. exports created 193,000 jobs. U.S. exports to Mexico were $13.6 billion in 1985, $12.4 billion in 1986, and $14.6 billion in 1987. The United

States sells Mexico auto parts, electronic tubes, electrical switches, office machinery, and soybeans, among principal products. In dollar terms, about two thirds of what Mexico imports comes from the United States.

Mexico sold the United States $19.4 billion worth of goods in 1985, $17.6 billion in 1986, and $20.5 billion in 1987. Leading items were crude oil, coffee, automobile engines, and other auto parts. About 60 percent of what Mexico exports (in dollar terms) goes to the United States.

15. "Mexico is also the no. 1 U.S. source . . ." The U.S. Drug Enforcement Agency, which has a couple of dozen resident agents in Mexico, does not know how many tons of drugs actually make it into the United States from Mexico or other countries. Instead, the DEA uses figures on the amounts of drugs seized in the United States to make estimates of how much of a drug came from a particular country. On this basis, one third of all marijuana and heroin comes from Mexico. On the same basis, one third of all cocaine is transshipped from Mexico, which is used by Colombian, Peruvian, and other cocaine producers to refine the drug and arrange transportation to the United States.

Out of 601,708 immigrants legally allowed to enter the United States in 1986, 66,533 were Mexicans, a 9-percent increase over 1985, according to the U.S. Immigration and Naturalization Service. (The second largest national group was from the Philippines, at 52,558.) About 90 percent of all those illegal aliens detained by the border patrol are Mexicans.

16. "Mexico is the cultural homeland for the fastest . . ." The U.S. Hispanic population, 63 percent of which was of Mexican origin in 1987, grew by 30 percent between 1980 and late 1987, according to the U.S. Census Bureau. The rest of the population grew by only 6 percent. Illegals, most of them Mexican, accounted for 23 percent of the Hispanic increase, raising the total by 141,000 a year or a total of nearly a million by 1987. About nineteen million people in the United States called themselves Hispanic in 1987. Twelve million of them claimed Mexican origin. The birth rate for Hispanics—91 births for every 1,000 Hispanic women between 15 and 44 years of age—was also about 50 percent higher than for the rest of the population.

16. "The list goes on. Mexico City, the spy . . ." For a more detailed look at Soviet spying activities in Mexico, see John Barron's KGB: The Secret Work of Soviet Agents (Bantam, 1974).

For more details on the Mexican armed forces, one of the few Latin American military groups not to present a threat to the government, see The Modern Mexican Military: A Reassessment, edited by David Ronfeldt, Center for U.S.-Mexican Studies (University of California, 1984). Also see discussion of the military's role in politics in chapter 7, "The Priista."

Chapter 1: The Muchacha

22. "One reason why so many can afford . . ." The active work force in Mexico was 25.4 million persons in 1987. Forty percent of these workers made

the minimum wage, according to the National Minimum Wage Commission. Private economists have charged, however, that some of these workers, particularly those engaged in agriculture, made less because employers ignored the minimum-wage law. Some experts also insist that more than half of the work force makes the minimum wage or less. A 1983 national survey found that 21 percent of Mexican households (some with more than one worker) had someone who made the minimum wage or less. Fifty percent of all households with workers had someone making two times the minimum wage—six dollars a day—or less in 1983 (Instituto Nacional de Estadística, Geografía e Informática, *Encuesta Nacional de Ingreso-Gasto de los Hogares* 1983–84 [Resultados Preliminares], 1987, p. 19).

Mexico's gross domestic product was $143.1 billion in 1987, according to figures calculated by the Banco de Mexico and converted into dollars by the U.S. embassy in Mexico City. That was up from $127.23 billion in 1986 but still below the 1985 level of $176.8 billion. The rank in economic size is from the 1987 state-of-the-nation address of President Miguel de la Madrid.

23. "The Mexican constitution guarantees an adequate living . . ." Faustino Chena Perez, labor member of the National Minimum Wage Commission, argued repeatedly during the mid-1980s that even with three times the minimum wage, Mexicans would live in poverty. In late 1987, in the magazine *El Cotidiano,* Julio Boltvinik, of the Autonomous Metropolitan University of Mexico (UAM), issued a study showing that one could buy only 30 percent of the basics of life with the then-prevailing minimum wage. He, too, argued that workers needed about three times (3.3) the minimum wage just to subsist.

24. "All over the Mexico City area, the scene . . ." Figures on passenger round-trips and subway-bus capacity to handle them are from the Mexico City daily *La Jornada,* December 31, 1986, citing data from City Hall officials.

24. "The fare for the subway, fifty pesos a day . . ." In December 1987, the subway and Route 100 bus fares were increased yet again to a hundred pesos to raise revenues as part of a government emergency economic plan. To help riders cope with increased fares, the minimum wage was increased a combined total of 38 percent in December 1987 and January 1988. The government promised to index the minimum wage each month in 1988, based on price increases of a basic market basket. But it chose later to freeze wages and prices through August 1988 as part of a new economic rescue plan. Even with the 100 percent increase in subway fares in December 1987, the actual cost of providing subway and bus service was two-and-a-half times the new, higher fare, according to City Hall figures issued in April 1988. The government made up the difference through subsidies.

25. "Most Mexicans had the same problem . . ." In the view of some, the calculations by the Confederation of Mexican Workers (CTM) on loss of purchasing power were inflated for bargaining purposes in the periodic

negotiations between government and labor on the size of minimum-wage increases. But outside groups, such as the United Nations' Economic Commission on Latin America (CEPAL), made similar findings. In a 1987 study, CEPAL said mid-1987 minimum wages were the equivalent of 1963 minimum wages, after one stripped out the impact of inflation. Julio Boltvinik (see n. 2, above) found the same thing. Using a salary of 100 pesos in 1976 as a base, CEPAL found that although nominal salaries went up in the following decade, in real terms they actually went down. By the end of 1986, that 1976 salary of 100 pesos had fallen to a real value of 55.3 pesos, CEPAL found.

25. "With only two years of grammar school . . ." The nutrition figures are from the Mexican Association of Studies for the Defense of the Consumer (AMEDC), issued in October of 1987.

28. "Adelaida never had very much saved in a lump sum . . ." The figure on how much available credit the Mexican government used itself is from a study by the Morgan Guaranty Trust Co., published in the April–May issue of its newsletter, "World Financial Markets," pp. 4–5. In the 1982–83 period, the Mexican government took 82 percent of all new credit. That figure was reduced to 65.1 percent in 1984–85. In 1983, the government had 76.3 percent of all outstanding credit (year-end figure). In 1985, the figure was similar—72.5 percent, according to Morgan.

29. "The average person borrows only ten dollars from the *Monte* . . ." In 1985, according to *Monte de Piedad* figures, the average person pawned an item for 8,000 pesos. In 1986 it was 11,500. In 1987 it was almost 20,000.

29. "Other services in Ayotla were equally abysmal . . ." The 700,000 figure on irregular titles came from the Registro Publico de la Propriedad, whose officials were quoted in the Mexico City daily *El Financiero,* August 19, 1987.

31. "As for the phone, not having one . . ." The figure of 8 million private telephones (8.5 million as of May 1988) came from Joaquín Muñoz Izquierdo, director general of Telefonos de Mexico (Telmex), the state-owned phone company. As recently as 1982, Mexico had only 5.9 million private telephones. In 1988, there were also 35 million public telephones, which Telmex planned to increase to 70 million by the end of 1988. Digital phone service was scant in 1988, but Telmex officials insisted that 70 to 80 percent of Mexican phones would be digital by the end of the century, when Mexico was scheduled to have 70 million private phones. Mexico began free 800 service in 1988 for the first time but had not yet provided any regular cellular service for car phones. Despite all these grand plans, the federal attorney general for the consumer (Profeco), the government office in charge of consumer complaints of all kinds, reported in 1987 that Telmex led the list of companies—government or private—that Mexicans filed complaints about.

To avoid Telmex hook-up charges, many people who buy a home or rent an apartment usually keep the phone in the former owner's or tenant's name, rather than ask Telmex for a new listing. The Mexico City phone book is jokingly called the book of the dead.

31. "Ayotla also had no sewers . . ." The housing-shortage figure was issued by the Ministry of Urban Development and Ecology (SEDUE) in 1987. The figures on water, plumbing, and electricity are from the 1983 national survey of homes (*Encuesta Nacional de Ingreso-Gasto de los Hogares 1983–84*, p. 15–16).

33. "Adelaida has no illusions about completing . . ." The national educational level was a little less than the sixth grade, according to the September 1, 1987, state-of-the-nation address of President Miguel de la Madrid. That was up from 5.3 years in 1985 and 3.5 years of grammar school as recently as 1970. (In the United States, the comparable figure for 1987 was 12.6 years, meaning that the average American spent at least some time in college.)

The school expenditure figure was from Arturo Lomeli of the Mexican Association of Studies for the Defense of Consumers (AMEDC), who computed the expenses for the 1987–88 school year. Expenses ran as low as 7,000 pesos for kindergarten students to buy books, stationery, and the like, and as high as 60,000 pesos for high school students.

34. "Félix's dreams are even more restricted . . ." Eduardo Alonso Escarcega, of the Unified Movement of Retired Persons and Pensioners, estimated in 1987 that as much as 80 percent of Mexicans who were more than sixty years of age still worked because of the absence of an adequate social-security retirement system. According to the Pan-American Health Organization, Mexican social security covered only 45.1 percent of the population in 1984. Private pension plans covered others. But 18.4 percent of Mexicans had no coverage of any kind (Organización Panamericana de Salud, *Las Condiciones de Salud en las Américas 1981–84*, 1986, vol. 2, p. 190). In the 1980 Mexican national census, about 3.7 million persons were over the age of sixty, about 5 percent of the population at the time.

34. "Mexico has made great strides in reducing illiteracy . . ." The illiteracy figures are from the September 1, 1988, state-of-the-nation report by President de la Madrid.

Chapter 2: The *Junior*

40. "Journalist Guadalupe Loaeza wickedly chronicled . . ." Guadalupe Loaeza also writes a regular Saturday column on juniors and similar types in the Mexico City daily *La Jornada*. Her book, *Las Niñas Bien*, a collection of such columns, was published by Oceano in Mexico City in 1987.

42. "Mexico has its own rock stars . . ." Figures on Cablevision subscribers are from its parent company, Televisa, for the year 1987. Figures on satellite dishes are estimates from several satellite-dish companies in Mexico City for the same year.

43. "There are a few Horatio Alger success stories . . ." Income-disparity figures are from the Instituto Nacional de Estadística, Geografía e Informática, *Encuesta Nacional de Ingreso-Gasto de los Hogares 1983–84 (Resultados Preliminares)*, 1987, p. 22. For a detailed look at previous income figures, dating back to 1950, see James D. Cockcroft, *Mexico: Class Formation, Capital Accumulation and the State* (Monthly Review Press, 1983), p. 188. The richest 20 percent of Mexican households got 59.8 percent of the income in 1950 and 53.8 percent in 1983. The poorest 20 percent of households, on the other hand, saw their income share drop from 6.1 percent in 1950 to 4.14 percent in 1983—a one-third drop. The poorest 10 percent of households did even worse, dropping from a 2.7 percent share of income in 1950 to a mere 1.34 percent in 1983—a 50 percent decrease. The real winners were a growing middle class, especially the upper middle class. For example, the second richest 10 percent of the population got 10.8 percent of national income in 1950 but 17.09 percent in 1983—nearly a twofold increase.

44. "Gerardo's best friend already had to leave . . ." For a more detailed look at the nefarious deeds of Arturo Durazo, see chapter 12, "The *Policía.*"

Chapter 3: The *Tragafuego*

50. "Like a lot of government programs . . ." The "Employ Yourself" campaign was an idea of the National Publicity Council but was backed by the Mexican Ministry of Labor.

51. "The government was equally ineffective . . ." The definition of "employed" comes from the National Institute of Statistics, Geography and Information.

51. "Using more traditional definitions of unemployment . . ." Among the outside groups that put unemployment much higher than the government's figures were the United Nation's Economic Commission on Latin America (CEPAL). The quarterly "Economic Trends Report" of the U.S. embassy in Mexico City often did the same. A 1987 embassy report on labor conditions called the Mexican government's unemployment rate "grossly understated." In late 1987, both CEPAL and the embassy put national unemployment at 18 percent. Similar figures were issued by the Cámara Nacional de la Industria de Transformación (Canacintra), a business group, and by the Mexican Ministry of Planning and Budget.

52. "What had caused the unmanageable number of workers . . ." Two excellent sources of historical information on Mexico's population growth and its causes are Jorge Martínez Manautou, *The Demographic Revolution in Mexico*, 1970–1980, a 1982 publication of the Mexican Social Security Administration (IMSS); and Patricia M. Rowe, *Detailed Statistics on the Urban and Rural Population of Mexico: 1950 to 2010*, a 1982 publication of the International Demographic Data Center of the U.S. Bureau of the Census.

52. "The government's record of job creation . . ." In December 1986, the pro-government Mexican Confederation of Workers (CTM) said it had calculated that the administration of President Miguel de la Madrid had not generated a single job, in net terms, since it took over in December 1982. In fact, Fidel Valázquez, the CTM chief, said about 675,000 jobs had been lost. The figure for layoffs as a percentage of total unemployment was from the Ministry of Planning and Budget, issued in October of 1986.

52. "The government also wound up taking . . ." Morgan Guaranty Trust Co. estimated in 1986 that the government was taking about three quarters of available credit from Mexican banks for its own uses. It also estimated that Mexicans had sent fifty-three billion dollars out of Mexico to safer havens in the 1976–85 decade, the most for any Third World debtor nation. See chapter 20, "*The Expatriado.*"

   In 1987, Mexico sold $8.4-billion worth of oil exports. In the same year it paid $8.1 billion in interest on its then $106.3-billion foreign debt. Principal payments were an additional $4.7 billion, for a total debt payment of $12.8 billion—about 60 percent of the $20.6 billion it earned on all exports in 1987.

53. "To be fair to the government, one might . . ." Data on population growth and policies from Cortés on is from Martínez Manautou's book (n. 4, above).

54. "The population onslaught was being made worse . . ." Life expectancy figures for 1960 and 1980 are from Martínez Manautou. Current figures are from the Ministry of Planning and Budget.

55. "Mexico has one other thing going against it . . ." For more information on the impact of dropouts and truancy, see chapter 6, "The *Chavo.*"

55. "Not far from Los Pinos, where the president . . ." The figure for 2.5 million children working in Mexico City streets is from a July 1987 report in *El Financiero,* Mexico's leading business newspaper. Similar figures have been reported by the Pan-American Health Organization.

Chapter 4: The *Pollo*

59. "They know, too, the dangers. In Tijuana . . ." Frightening details of the trials and tribulations of illegal workers' border crossings can be found in Joseph Wambaugh's *Lines and Shadows* (Bantam, 1984), and in Ted Conover's *Coyotes* (Vintage Departures, 1987).

60. "Though Miguel made more in Dallas, he found . . ." Banco de México officials, using figures tallied from postal money orders and survey interviews with Mexicans returning from the United States, estimated in 1986 that at least one billion dollars was sent back annually to Mexico by those illegally working in the United States. Foreign tourism generally earns Mexico about two billion dollars a year. Tourism is the no. 2 source of hard currency, after oil exports, although income from in-bond assembly plants along the border is moving up fast.

61. "On the night of June 30, Miguel . . ."

On May 5, 1987, after years of wrangling in the U.S. Congress, a new immigration law, the Immigration Reform and Control Act (popularly called the Simpson-Rodino law) went into effect. Its main elements were:

— All illegal workers who had been living in the United States continuously since before January 1, 1982, and had no serious criminal record could apply to be given amnesty for all past immigration violations and to become permanent U.S. residents. Those eligible had one year from the May date to apply to the U.S. Immigration and Naturalization Service. Those who became U.S. residents are also eligible to become U.S. citizens.

— Illegals who did farm work have an easier time qualifying as residents under a "special agricultural workers" (SAW) program. Those who could prove they worked at least ninety days picking certain crops—mostly edible commodities—between May 1985 and May 1986 had the same amnesty, residency, and citizenship eligibility rights as other illegal workers. Those who had worked for the same period in previous seasons could become citizens even faster.

— If enough U.S. or legal foreign workers can't be found, the law permanently allows U.S. growers to apply to the U.S. Department of Agriculture for additional foreign workers, who can get temporary work permits to enter the country. U.S. employers other than growers can apply to the U.S. Department of Labor for similar workers.

— The law also provides fines and jail terms for employers who knowingly hire undocumented workers after November 6, 1986. The INS started out slowly, giving violators only warnings. Later would come the fines and, much later, jail terms. Almost all of the early focus of enforcement of the law was on factories, farms, and construction companies that had the potential for hiring large numbers of illegals—or a history of doing so. Little attention was paid to private homes, where hundreds of thousands of illegals are employed as maids or gardeners.

— The law also provided for a 50-percent increase in border-patrol and U.S. Immigration and Naturalization staff.

In fiscal 1986, a record year, about 1.9 million illegals were detained by U.S. Border Patrol agents after being caught trying to enter the United States without proper documents. Some of these people, however, were detained more than once, so it can't be said that 1.9 million persons tried to get in and failed. Most of those detained were Mexicans. In fact, so many trying to get in are Mexicans—usually about 90 percent—that all others are referred to in border-patrol jargon as OTMs—"other than Mexicans." In fiscal 1987, the first year of the strict new Simpson-Rodino immigration law, the border patrol made only 1.1 million apprehensions. Backers of the new immigration law said the lower figure showed that the law's new sanctions against employers was working to deter hiring of illegals. Critics of the law pointed out that hundreds of thousands of illegals stayed in the United States to apply for amnesty and permanent residency, as the new law permitted, rather than return home after the harvest or at Christmas, as was their usual custom. Thus, critics argued, there were fewer illegals returning to the United States in 1987 to be apprehended.

Figures on how many illegals live in the United States are also hard to pin down. In debates on the Simpson-Rodino act, legislators used figures ranging from three million to twelve million for the number of illegals living in the United States. It can be said that between the May 1987 initiation of the Simpson-Rodino law's amnesty–permanent residency program and the end of that program a year later, about 1.5 million illegals applied for amnesty under the principal program. A little more than 500,000 more applied under the special agricultural-workers program that operated for another six months.

68. "The numbers didn't make it seem the future . . ." At its worst, the Mexican population growth rate was 3.5 percent in 1970, a rate now being experienced by some African countries. In the time of President Luis Echeverría (1970–76), it was finally decided that such a rate was suicidal. A major program of birth control—education, sterilization, family-planning clinics—was implemented. By the time President Miguel de la Madrid took over in late 1982, the rate was down to 2.6 percent. By the time he left office in late 1988, it was under 2 percent. For more details on the impact of population growth, see chapter 3, "The *Tragafuego*," and chapter 10, "The *Pepenador*."

Chapter 5: The *Medico*

71. " 'I could use a few things . . .' " For some statistics on telephones in Mexico, see chapter 1, "The *Muchacha*," n. 10.

71. "Enrique said he could also use . . ." For more on pollution and other environmental problems of Mexico, see chapter 10, "The *Pepenador*."

72. "Maybe that was fitting . . ." For more on the importance of magic in Mexico, see chapter 17, "The *Mentalista*."

73. "I had first met Enrique . . ." In 1982 (the latest data available at publication), Mexico recorded 412,345 deaths. About one person in ten, or 35,271, died of infectious intestinal diseases, particularly diarrhea, according to the Instituto Nacional de Estadística, Geografía e Informática, in its *Información Estadística, Sector Salud y Seguridad Social,* cuaderno no. 5 (1986), p. 35. Among children under the age of four, the figures are even more disturbing. According to the Pan-American Health Organization, a World Health Organization affiliate, Mexico's rate of death by diarrhea-caused dehydration in 1982 was worse than that of all other countries in the Western Hemisphere save Ecuador, Guatemala, and Nicaragua, all of which were far less developed and whose data were for earlier (presumably worse) years (Organizacion Panamericana de la Salud, *Las Condiciones de Salud*

en las Americas, 1981–84 (1986, vol. 1, p. 50). After diarrhea and related diseases, the leading causes of death in 1982 were: pneumonia and influenza, diseases related to childbirth, non-auto accidents, and diabetes (*Información Estadística, Sector Salud y Seguridad Social*, (p. 35).

73. "When I went back to visit Enrique . . ." Respiratory diseases were also a major cause of death in 1982. Acute respiratory ailments are the no. 1 cause of hospital and clinic treatment. In 1984, there were 7,158,759 cases of acute respiratory infections reported to the Ministry of Health, accounting for 60 percent of all treatments that year. Diarrhea-type diseases were second, with 2,412,304 treatments in the same year (*Información Estadística, Sector Salud y Seguridad Social*, (p. 22).

74. " 'I don't include malnutrition . . .' " Ten percent of Mexicans die of hunger (not an official cause of death), and about 80 percent are malnourished to some extent, according to the National Nutrition Institute (INN). Acute malnutrition affects about half the population, according to a 1987 study by Autonomous Metropolitan University of Mexico (UAM) investigators Alberto Isunza Ogazón and José de Jesús Miranda. Malnutrition got worse after Mexico's economic crisis began in August 1982. Poor people, already living in bad conditions, saw their wages cut drastically in real terms as double- and then triple-digit inflation wracked the country. Many could no longer buy basic food items, such as meat and milk, which intensified their malnutrition. In October 1987, another report by UAM investigators indicated that Mexicans were consuming 75 percent less beef and 33 percent less milk than before the crisis, due to dwindling purchasing power. According to the Pan-American Health Organization, Mexicans' caloric intake dropped 18 percent between 1982 (when the crisis began) and 1984 (*Las Condiciones de Salud en las Americas*, vol. 2, p. 188).

75. "Enrique's patients—those with respiratory . . ." The World Health Organization estimated in early 1988 that 89 percent of all those living in the Mexico City area were suffering from a crisis it described as "psychological and very severely emotional." The problem is considered so severe in Mexico City that the government provides a free hot line that is manned by a group called Neurotics Anonymous, whose volunteers counsel stressed people by telephone. One result of stress-caused neurosis: alcoholism. Government officials estimate that about 6 percent of the population—and 15 percent of the work force—are alcoholics.

Causes of treatment are listed in *Información Estadística, Sector Salud y Seguridad Social*, p. 24.

Life expectancy for those born in the 1980–85 period was 65.7 years, up about 30 percent from life expectancy for those born in 1950–55, according to the Pan-American Health Organization, *Las Condiciones de Salud en las Americas*, vol. 1, p. 26. In his September 1, 1988, state-of-the-nation address, President de la Madrid said life expectancy had increased to 69 years.

In 1982, 33 out of every 1,000 Mexican babies born alive died in infancy. The leading cause of death was diarrhea. In comparisons made by the Pan-American Health Organization, Mexico's infant mortality rate of

33 per 1,000 (1982) ranked worse than every Latin American country for which data was available except El Salvador, Guatemala, Ecuador, and Paraguay (*Las Condiciones de Salud en las Americas*, vol. 1, 40, 420). Even some impoverished countries, such as Honduras, did better. The U.S. rate for that year was 11.5 per 1,000 babies. Between 1970 and 1982, Mexico did manage to cut its infant mortality rate in half, from 68.5 to 33.0 (Instituto Nacional de Estadística, Geografía e Informática, *Estadísticas Históricas de México*, vol. 1, p. 151). In his September 1, 1988, state-of-the-nation address, President de la Madrid said infant mortality had dropped to 23 per 1,000 registered births.

75. "Enrique's income reflected conditions . . ." To make Russian roulette with drugs an even more dangerous game, pharmacists or their helpers, who often play the role of ersatz doctor for the poor, recommend drugs that have been banned in the United States and other developed countries but are sold in Mexico.

77. "Enrique was right about that . . ." In per capita government expenditures on health, Mexico spends less than any country in the Western Hemisphere except Honduras, Bolivia, Peru, Paraguay, and Haiti (*Las Condiciones de Salud en las Americas*, vol. 1, p. 154). As a percentage of total government spending, health got only 1.29 percent of the budget in 1982. That was down dramatically from the 3.97 it got in 1978. In dollar terms, Mexico spent $8.16 a person in 1980 (latest figures). Brazil, its closest rival in economic size and population, spent $23.89 in the same year (*ibid.*, p. 210). As a percent of its gross domestic product, health spending dropped from 2.1 percent of GDP in 1978 to 1.6 percent in 1983 (*ibid.*, vol. 2, p. 191).

While comparative figures for other countries weren't made available, the Mexican Health Ministry announced in December 1987 that health spending had fallen 47.1 between 1982 and 1986, after adjusting for inflation.

In terms of hospital beds, Mexico had the lowest ratio of beds per 1,000 citizens of any Western Hemisphere country. In 1983, it had 0.77 beds per 1,000 people. The United States had 5.9 beds per 1,000 (*ibid.*, p. 161). In 1984, Mexico's number of beds per thousand dropped to 0.6, creating a deficit of 12,000 beds for people who needed them (*Ibid.*, p. 190). Figures were not available at publication, but the ratio must have worsened in 1985 because thousands of beds were destroyed in the September 1985 earthquakes in Mexico City. A massive hospital rebuilding commenced after the temblors.

Dr. Saul Rotberg Jankla, president of the 1987 National and International Congress of the Mexican Dental Association, said that even if all other causes of malnutrition were dealt with, Mexicans might continue to be malnourished because little is being done about their teeth. "They will suffer from malnutrition if they don't have teeth to eat [food] with," said Rotberg. He said Mexican kids under the age of fifteen typically have seven infected teeth—and few financial resources to have them fixed. His prescription: more preventive dentistry—a toothbrush, fluoride toothpaste, and a fluoride mouth rinse for every Mexican child.

77. "If the government wanted to increase health spending . . ." Part of Mexico's malnutrition problem stems from bad agricultural policies. In 1984, the National School of Biology estimated that as much as half of farm production is wasted because of bad handling, warehousing, or processing. Spoiled food, nonetheless, is sometimes sold to unsuspecting customers. For more on agricultural policies, see chapter 11, "The *Campesino.*"

In 1985, the Democratic Front for Unemployed Nurses and Doctors said the unemployment rate among physicians was 35.7 percent, and 30 percent for nurses. A key reason was uncontrolled medical-school registration. President Miguel de la Madrid's health minister, Guillermo Soberón, acknowledged in several speeches during de la Madrid's administration (1982–88) that unemployment among doctors had become acute at a time when one in five Mexicans had no access to medical care. He said medical schools, handcuffed by the revolutionary promise to provide schools for anyone who wanted an education, were turning out three to four times the number of doctors that Mexico needed.

Chapter 6: The *"Chavo"*

82. "I must admit that when . . ." The figure of 700,000 gang members for Mexico City is from Pablo Cabañas Diaz, professor of political and social science at the National Autonomous University of Mexico (UNAM). According to Cabañas, gangs in the capital began proliferating in Mexico City around the end of the 1970s in reaction to growing unemployment. Between 1979 and 1988, they increased in number by about 90 percent, according to a study by Cabañas. At a 1988 conference hosted by the Instituto de Estudios Económicos, Políticos y Sociales (IEPES), an arm of the ruling Institutional Revolutionary Party (PRI), invited gang members estimated that there were 30,000 gangs in Mexico City. Police said there were about 5,000.

86. "Mexico City, with a population . . ." In 1984, 1985, and 1986, there were 3,407, 3,562, and 3,519 intentional homicides respectively reported in Mexico City, according to the city attorney general's office. In 1987, police recorded 5,258 homicides and deaths caused by accident. The city attorney general's office did not make a breakout of intentional homicides for 1987, but officials told me they estimated the figure was in the 3,500 range as it had been the three previous years. Mexico City's 1988 population (without suburbs or outlying slums) was about ten million. In New York City, with a population of about eight million, there were 1,582 homicides in 1986 and 1,672 homicides in 1987, according to that city's police department.

Robbery was the most common form of crime in Mexico City. It accounted for about half of all reported crime, a proportion far larger than a decade before, according to the Mexico City attorney general's office. In 1984, 1985, 1986, and 1987, there were 72,606, 69,873, 92,021 and 101,557 robberies respectively. Of these robberies, 22,018, 21,527, and 29,809 were auto thefts in 1984, 1985, and 1986. No breakout was made for 1987 for auto theft, but officials estimated the figure had increased from 1986 to 1987. In New York City, there were 80,827 reported robberies in 1986 and 78,890 robberies in 1987, according to city police. There were 85,853 auto thefts in 1986 and 95,654 such thefts in 1987. One explanation for some of the difference is that New York had far more cars in those years than the estimated 2.5 million automobiles licensed in Mexico City.

Mexico does not keep comprehensive national figures on crime.

88. "This would-be bum, though . . ." A prize-winning video-film on the Los Mierdas Punk gang was made by Sara Minter, Gregorio Rocha, and Andrea Di Castro of Mexico City. It is called *Nadie es inocente* (No One is Innocent). A Mexican book, *Qué Transa con Las Bandas,* by Jorge García-Robles (Editorial Posada, 1987), also explores the lives and motivations of other Mexican street gangs.

90. "These kids, the future of Mexico . . ." According to a 1987 study by the Instituto Nacional del Consumidor, seven million kids who could have been in grammar or high school were not enrolled, mainly because the cost of books and other supplies was too much for their families to afford. Three and a half million Mexican kids live in the streets, according to a UNICEF study titled "Niños en la Calle" (Children in the Street). Twenty percent of the street kids engage in prostitution and half take drugs, the 1986 study found.

Chapter 7: The *Priista*

96. "The way Cárdenas saw it, sometime after . . ." When the government began keeping records again after the 1910 Revolution, it found that Mexico had about 11,000 grammar schools. By the 1980s, the number had grown to about eight times that. But that increase was only slightly greater than the growth of population, which went from 14 million to 80 million. During the same time, the number of houses grew from about 4 million to more than 12 million. A shortage of about 4.5 million houses still existed in 1988, however. Between 1931 and 1981, the number of Mexican deaths per year stabilized at about 400,000 persons, due to improved health services. But this exacerbated an out-of-control population growth. Infant mortality, a key health indicator, dropped from 223 deaths per 1,000 live births in 1922 to 33 deaths by 1982 (Instituto Nacional de Estadística, Geografía e Informática, *Estadísticas Históricas de México,* (1985), vol. 1, pp. 131–52). For more on health conditions in Mexico, see chapter 5, "The *Médico*." For more on income disparity, see chapter 2, "The *Junior*."

99. "De la Madrid had not been a politician . . ." Roderic A. Camp, of Central College in Pela, Iowa, has done excellent work on the backgrounds of Mexico's modern politicians. He has two books on the topic: *Mexico's Leaders: Their Education and Recruitment,* (University of Arizona Press, 1980), and *Mexican Political Biographies, 1935–75,* (University of Arizona Press, 1976).

99. "What the party had become in the 1980s . . ." An excellent summary of Mexican political history can be found in Martin C. Needler's *Mexican Politics: The Containment of Conflict* (Praeger 1982). Another account is found in Frank R. Brandenburg's *The Making of Modern Mexico* (Prentice-Hall, 1964).

100. "With the coming to power of Miguel Alemán . . ." Needler's book (see n. 3, above) is also an excellent source of how the PRI has resolved conflicts within the party.

102. "In saying that he wanted to be president . . ." The best Mexican account of how a president picks his successor is Daniel Cosío Villegas's *La Sucesión Presidencial* (Joaquín Mortiz, 1974). Also see Kenneth F. Johnson's *Mexican Democracy: A Critical View*, 3d ed. (Praeger, 1984), pp. 123–28.

103. "When the president makes known his choice . . ." The PRI won 84.13 percent of the presidential vote case in 1970, 92.27 percent in 1976 (when the leading opposition party, the National Action Party, boycotted the election), and 71.63 percent in 1982 (*Estadísticas Históricas de México*, vol. 1, p. 291).

108. "Cárdenas ran a frugal campaign . . ." The English-language weekly magazine *Mexico Journal* reported in April 1988 that an examination of one day's stories in fourteen Mexican newspapers showed that the PRI's candidate, Carlos Salinas de Gortari, got 13,838 lines of coverage. The PAN candidate, Manuel Clouthier, got 2,828. Herberto Castillo of the PMS got 2,817. Cárdenas got 2,127. Others on the left got a total of 2,075. Radio and television coverage was similarly weighted in Salinas's favor.

In March 1988, the Democratic Assembly for Effective Suffrage, a collection of opposition political leaders and prominent members of the public, estimated that Salinas was spending in a day what each of his opponents would spend in the entire campaign. In total, the assembly estimated that Salinas would spend two billion pesos, or about $800 million. Eighty percent of those funds would come from the public treasury, according to an assembly study.

108. "Despite such advantages, the PRI scheduled . . ." In the July 6, 1988, elections, the official results showed that Carlos Salinas of the PRI won 50.4 percent of the total, the lowest percentage in PRI history, Cuauhtémoc Cárdenas won 31.1 percent. Manuel Clouthier, the candidate of the National Action Party, won 17.1 percent.

Chapter 8: The *Panista*

111. "Sonorans, who have carved out . . ." There has been a rising chorus of political opposition across the northern tier of Mexican states. Baja California, Sonora, Chihuahua, Coahuila, Nuevo León, and Tamaulipas form an informal territory that many call "the border" or "Gringolandia." The latter name derives from the economic and democratic influences these states get from neighboring "gringo" (American) border states. Modern,

antigovernment thinking, spurred by U.S. influences, is one reason why these Mexican states have become more prosperous than the rest of Mexico. Another is the rise in the number of *maquiladora* ("in-bond") assembly plants that have sprung up on the border. These plants put together manufactured goods with U.S. parts and cheap Mexican labor. In an era of double-digit unemployment, thousands of out-of-work Mexicans have flocked to Mexico's north in search of jobs, swelling the political importance of this rebellious region.

112. " 'What impressed me was how . . .' " Sonorans are above average in many respects. Their illiteracy rate of 8.5 percent of the population was half the national rate recorded in the 1980 census. Twenty-five percent of Sonorans had more than six years of grammar school, compared with only 20 percent nationally, according to the census (Instituto Nacional de Estadística, Geografía e Informática, *Estadísticas Históricas de México*, vol. 1, pp. 91, 101; *X Censo General de Población y Vivienda, 1980*, pp. 51, 58).

112. "It would be a decade more . . ." The ruling PRI party has typically won 70 percent or more of the vote since it took power in 1929. Often its total was more than 90 percent. In the 1982 presidential elections, the PRI won 71.63 percent of the vote to the PAN's 16.41 percent. In order after the PAN were: the PSUM (Mexican Unified Socialist Party) with 3.65 percent, the PDM (Mexican Democratic Party) with 1.93 percent, the PRT (Revolutionary Workers Party) with 1.85 percent, the PPS (Popular Socialist Party) with 1.60 percent, the PST (Socialist Workers Party) with 1.52 percent, the PARM (Authentic Party of the Mexican Revolution) with 1.05 percent, and the PSD (Social Democratic Party) with 0.27 percent. Other candidates got the remaining .13 percent of the 22,539,279 votes cast that year. An astounding 4.5 percent of the ballots cast were annulled—about one million (*Estadísticas Históricas de México*, vol. 1, p. 291).

In the 1988 presidential elections, the PRI won 50.4 percent of the vote, the parties backing Cárdenas won 31.1 percent, and the PAN won 17.1 percent. The PDM and the PRT did not receive the required 1.5 percent of the vote and thus did not qualify to remain as legal political parties eligible for government subsidies and some of the chamber of deputy seats reserved for the opposition.

In this alphabet soup of parties, on the right is the PAN, which was formed in 1939 shortly after president Lázaro Cárdenas nationalized Mexico's oil fields, and the PDM, an extremely right-wing, pro-clerical, peasant-oriented party that grew out of the Cristero rebellion (1926–29), which was an armed protest against the antichurch provisions of the Mexican constitution. The PAN, which appeals to the urban business class, draws a sizable anti-PRI vote that has no ideological interest in the PAN.

The PSUM, formed in 1981, is a coalition of far-left parties that includes the old PCM or Mexican Communist Party, which was formed in 1919. The PMT is a Marxist party, led by well-known politician Herberto Castillo, who spent two-and-a-half years in jail for his involvement in the 1968 student uprisings in Mexico. In 1988, these two parties fused into a new party, the PMS or Mexican Socialist Party—but they chose not to use the

PSUM's hammer-and-sickle insignia. The PMS initially picked Castillo as its candidate, but he resigned. The PRT is a Trotskyite group that nominated human-rights activist Rosario Ibarra de la Piedra, a non-Trotskyite, as its presidential candidate in 1982 and 1988.

The PPS and the PARM, in recent years, have been fellow travelers of the PRI. In 1976 they backed the PRI's presidential nominee. In 1979, a PPS candidate became the first opposition member of the Mexican senate, an apparent payback for the PPS's good behavior. The PARM did not get the 1.5 percent of the vote in the 1982 presidential elections that it needed to be certified as a political party. Without certification, it was not entitled to all the financial goodies and free radio and television time that the PRI government provides the opposition. The PRI bent the law and allowed the PARM to be certified anyway. In the 1988 elections, the PARM backed Cuauhtémoc Cárdenas, the former PRI governor of Michoacán and the son of former President Lázaro Cárdenas (1934–40), as its candidate. Cárdenas, one of the founders of a rebel PRI group called the Democratic Current, quit the PRI after he was not made its nominee. He was also made the candidate of the PPS and the PST (Mexican Socialist Party), which renamed itself the PRCRN—the Cardenist Front for National Reconstruction. He put all of them under an umbrella group he called the FDN, the National Democratic Front. Later, the PMS also endorsed him.

113. "Notwithstanding all these publicity stunts . . ." In 1976, the PAN refused to field a presidential candidate against López Portillo in protest of antidemocratic conditions. Absenteeism got so bad during López Portillo's time that he changed the law so that opposition candidates, no matter how few votes they got, would divide up 100 of 400 seats in the chamber of deputies, the lower house of the national legislature. Votes were distributed proportionately, depending on what percentage of the vote each opposition party got. In 1987, the law was changed again to give the opposition a minimum of 150 of 500 deputy seats. The PRI-run government also provides subsidies to opposition political parties so they can campaign and run operations in non-election years. Despite all these political carrots, voter nonparticipation in national elections remains an acute problem.

116. "Since Sonoran Plutarco Elías Calles . . ." Officially, the PRI has never lost a presidential or governor's race. But in 1975, by some accounts, it unofficially lost the governor's race to a leftist candidate in the state of Nayarit. The PAN supposedly won the governor's post in the state of Yucatán in 1969.

Vote fraud was rampant in the presidential elections of 1940 and 1952. But while party leaders have since acknowledged that challengers' vote totals were reduced, it does not appear the challengers would have won the presidency if the vote had been honest. For more details, see Martin C. Needler, *Mexican Politics: The Containment of Conflict* (Praeger, 1982).

Chapter 9: *Fayuquero*

121. "Oscar Lewis told the early story . . ." The Sánchez family also figured in two other Lewis books, *Five Families: Mexican Case Studies in the Cul-*

ture of Poverty (Basic Books, 1959), and *A Death in the Sánchez Family* (Vintage, 1969).

121. "As a young man, he had drifted . . ." María was called Paula by Lewis in his book. The woman Luis had the affair with was called Graciela by Lewis.

122. "It was hardly a surprising choice . . ." The background on the word *"fayuca"* is from Jorge Mejía Prieto's *Así Habla El Mexicano: diccionario básico de mexicanismos* (Panorama Editorial, 1984), pp. 74–75.

122. "Over the years, Luis—and later . . ." Victor was called Alanes in *The Children of Sánchez.*

123. "That system is often described as mixed . . ." Two brief general histories of the Mexican economy can be found in *Mexico: A Country Study*, a handbook prepared by the Foreign Area Studies division of the American University (1985), published by the U.S. Government Printing Office, pp. 161–244; and Alan Riding's *Distant Neighbors: A Portrait of the Mexicans* (Knopf, 1984), pp. 134–156. A more scholarly treatment is found in Jorge I. Dominguez's *Mexico's Political Economy* (Sage Publications, 1982).

126. "Mexicans, led by the left wing of the PRI, have . . ." In early 1988, Mexico's three largest *paraestatales,* or state-owned industries, were: Petróleos Mexicanos (Pemex), the national oil company; Teléfonos de México (Telmex), the national phone company; and the Compañía Nacional de Subsistèncias Populares (Conasupo), which provides subsidized food items to the poor through a chain of supermarkets. These were also the three largest companies in Mexico in terms of sales, surpassing Chrysler de México and General Motors de México, the no. 4 and 5 companies, respectively. Also among the *paraestatales:* Aeroméxico and Mexicana de Aviación, the only national airlines; Diesel Nacional (Dina), a national truck and motor company; the Comisión Federal de Electricidad (CFE), a power company; Ferrocarriles Nacionales, the national railroad company; Inmecafe, the national coffee company; Azucar, S.A., a sugar company; Siderúrgica Lázaro Cárdenas–Las Truchas (Sicartsa), a steel complex in Michoacán; Pipsa, the national newsprint company; Fertimex, the national fertilizer company; and the Lotería Nacional, the national lottery. Of these, Pemex, Conasupo, the CFE, Azucar, S.A., and Sicartsa were the most important in terms of budget, accounting for 65 percent of the budget for parastatal companies, according to a 1988 report by the Ministry of Energy, Mines and Parastate Industries. In the spring of 1988, Aeroméxico declared bankruptcy, and Dina was slated to be sold to Chrysler and private Mexican investors.

127. "Oil is one business that could have been private . . ." At the end of 1983, de la Madrid's first full year in office, so-called oil exports (all foreign petroleum sales) were $16 billion out of that year's total export revenues of $22.3 billion. By 1987, oil exports had dropped to $8.5 billion out of a total of $20.6 billion. For some background on the oil industry, see George Grayson's *The Politics of Mexican Oil* (University of Pittsburgh Press, 1980),

and his *The United States and Mexico: Patterns of Influence* (Praeger, 1984), pp. 57–91.

127. "Revolutionary nationalism likewise called for . . ." For more on Mexican business's relationship with the ruling party, see chapter 20, "The *Expatriado*."

128. "With the 1970 election of Luis Echeverría . . ." One reason why Echeverría may not have chosen to raise taxes was the extent of tax fraud in Mexico. For more on that and on Mexico's tremendous problem with capital flight—money sent abroad by Mexicans seeking safer havens for their savings—see chapter 20, "The *Expatriado*."

131. "De la Madrid's progress in solving . . ." Unemployment, in single digits at the end of 1982, rose to 18 percent by 1988. The Centro de Estudios Económicos del Sector Privado, a private sector think tank, estimated in late 1987 that about six million Mexicans were engaged in the underground economy. Few paid any taxes on what they earned. The gross domestic product (GDP) went from $161.9 billion in 1982 to $143.1 billion in 1987. The decline is somewhat overstated in dollar terms, but clearly the country got poorer. The economy contracted in 1982 by 0.5 percent, contracted a further 5.3 percent in 1983, grew by 3.7 percent in 1984, grew by 2.7 percent in 1985, contracted 3.8 percent in 1986, and grew 1.4 percent in 1987. Mexicans' per capita share of GDP, a key indicator of how well they are doing economically, was $2,203 in 1982 but only $1,745 in 1987. Inflation was 98.8 percent in 1982, 80.8 percent in 1983, 59.2 percent in 1984, 63.7 percent in 1985, 105.7 percent in 1986, and 159.2 percent in 1987. The public-sector budget deficit as a percentage of GDP went from 17.6 percent in 1982 to 8.7 percent in 1983 to 15.9 percent by 1987. After nearly four decades of no trade surpluses, Mexico's surplus in 1982 was $6 billion. In 1987, it was $8.4 billion. The foreign debt, public and private, was about $85 billion at the end of 1982 and $106.3 billion at the end of 1987, about $14.4 billion of which was owed by private firms, and the rest by the government. Mexico's exports dropped from $21.2 billion in 1982 to $16 billion in 1986, largely due to a drop in world oil prices. They rebounded to $20.6 billion in 1987. Foreign-debt interest payments as a percentage of hard-cash merchandise export earnings went from 51 percent in 1983 to 39 percent in 1987, when interest payments were $8.1 billion. International reserves rose from $1.8 billion in 1982 to a record $15 billion in 1987. Foreign investment, which generally was less than 4 percent of total foreign-domestic investment, rose to about $20 billion in 1987, an 89 percent rise compared with 1982. Of this, 64.3 percent was U.S. investment, mostly in manufacturing. In 1987, non-oil exports were $12.1 billion compared with petroleum exports of $8.5 billion. Source: Banco de México, *Informe Anual*, 1982–87, and U.S. Embassy, *Economic Trends Reports*, 1982–88, which use mostly official Mexican sources and convert peso figures to U.S. dollars at prevailing exchange rates.

132. "When historians look back . . ." For every billion dollars of exports Mexico generates, it creates thirty thousand jobs, according to Alejandro Cruz of the National Foreign Trade Bank (Bancomex).

133. "In the short run, the government said, it hoped . . ." As an indication of the de la Madrid government's enthusiasm for GATT and the related opening up of the Mexican economy, it reduced maximum tariff levels on most goods to 20 percent—far below the 50-percent level required by the GATT treaty.

136. "While he waited for his new house . . ." For those interested, the story of what happened to the other Children of Sánchez is told in a series of stories I wrote in early 1987. The most complete accounts were published in the *San Jose* [California] *Mercury News* on January 18, 1987, p. 1, and in the English-language *Mexico City News* on February 4–6, 1987. A bit of what happened to Marta Sánchez, the youngest daughter of the family, is recounted in chapter 19, "The *Feminista*." In Lewis's book, Cristina is called Consuelo.

137. "Luis was skeptical whether . . ." In an April 1988 speech, Jorge Kawagi Gastine, president of the National Manufacturing Industry Chamber, told the National Foreign Trade Council that 150 companies accounted for 80 percent of all Mexico's exports.

Chapter 10: The *Pepenador*

139. "What little wind there is . . ." In 1988, there were 2.1 million automobiles and another 400,000 private vehicles (taxis, minibuses, etc.), and 30,000 factories in the Valley of Mexico, according to Luis Manuel Guerra, director of the Instituto Autónomo de Investigaciónes Ecológicas, a private Mexico City–based institute of environmental research. They put five million tons of polluted matter into the air that year. Cars accounted for 80 percent of the total, according to Guerra. At five million tons of pollutants, each of the valley's eighteen million residents in 1988 had more than 500 pounds of pollutants to call his very own. Environmentalists say breathing Mexico City's air is the equivalent of smoking two packs of cigarettes a day. Despite such figures, officials of the Federal Enviroment Ministry found in a 1986 report that "no causal relationship between the level of atmospheric pollutants [in Mexico City] and respiratory illness could be confirmed." Environmentalists insist that 50,000–60,000 persons each year in Mexico City would not have died had it not been for high pollution levels.

141. "Over the years, the *pepenadores* . . ." The size of the fortune supposedly accumulated by Gutiérrez, the king of the *pepenadores,* may seem fantastic. But it is quite conceivable if one considers that recycled trash in Mexico generates an estimated $600,000 a day, according to a study done by Guerra (see n. 1, above), based on information supplied by the public works department of Mexico City. Officials assumed a collected garbage figure of 12,500 tons a day for the Mexico City area in computing the figure.

144. "Don Pablo and the *pepenadores* did not win . . ." Open-air dumps re-

main in the suburbs of Mexico City, such as Nezahualcóyotl, which are under the jurisdiction of the state of Mexico.

145. "In March of 1987, Don Pablo's *pepenadores* . . ." City officials say about 11,000 tons of garbage are generated each day in Mexico City, which in 1988 had about 10 million of the 18 million residents in the valley. That's about a pound and a quarter of garbage per city resident. Twenty-five hundred tons a day was delivered to Los Prados de la Montaña—one ton for every *pepenador*. Including 300 clandestine city dumps and dumps in the suburbs, the 1988 figure for collected garbage in the valley was about 12,500 tons.

147. "The action against Santa Fe was a little surprising . . ." In Mexico City, thermal inversions occurred about two out of every three days in 1987. SEDUE, the Mexican Environment Ministry, has never issued figures to give citizens an idea of how polluted Mexico City air is compared with accepted international maximums for key pollutants. No figures are available for other major Mexican cities, because the government hasn't installed monitoring equipment elsewhere. In 1985, a study of Mexico City air done by the U.S. Environmental Protection Agency found that sulfur dioxide, ozone, and suspended particulates exceeded the maximums allowed by U.S. air-quality standards. Lead levels in blood were close to the maximum. As a result of the findings, the U.S. embassy in Mexico City was declared an unhealthy post. Employees were given bonus pay because it was assumed they would be sick more and wouldn't live as long.

A later study by Canada's Department of Health and Welfare found that Mexico City's levels of suspended particulates, sulfur dioxide, carbon monoxide, and lead were far beyond those permissible as maximums in Canada. For example, Canada allowed 70 units of suspended particulates per cubic meter. Mexico City had 389 units. Sulfur dioxide was 262 units, compared with Canada's maximum of 60 units. This study found that such levels could cause headaches, irritability, loss of memory, personality changes, damage to the digestive and respiratory systems, allergies, conjunctivitis, mental and physical retardation to children (through lead in the blood), hemorrhaging, and cancer.

In late 1987, Mexico's new environment minister, Manuel Camacho Solís, said that Mexico had made great environmental strides since he had taken over about two years before. Without giving comparative figures, he said lead levels in the Mexico City area had gone down by 6 tons, sulfur dioxide by 4 tons, suspended particulates by 7 tons, and sulfur dioxide by 200 tons. Ozone had gone way up, he admitted. In 1988, according to statistics of the environment ministry, lead, sulfur dioxide, and carbon monoxide were below international maximums. Other contaminants were still at pre-1986 levels. Ozone levels had gone out of sight. A 1988 study done by the Instituto Autónomo de Investigaciónes Ecológicas found that blood levels in Mexico City newborns were twenty micrograms per deciliter, which was twice the internationally accepted maximum for adults.

148. "The government told the public . . ." Pemex reduced lead levels in regular gasoline from an astoundingly high 3.5 grams per gallon to a rated

0.8 grams after the terrible thermal inversions of the winter of 1985–86. The new unleaded extra ("Extra Plus") is rated at 0.5 grams of lead per gallon. In June 1988, Pemex officials announced lead-free gasoline would be sufficiently available for new cars by 1989. They also promised to install controls at Pemex facilities to prevent significant pollution caused by leakage of gasoline fumes.

152. "While the enormity of environmental problems was greater . . ." In contrast, the government had gotten its act together on solving its problems of explosive population growth, which had contributed considerably to its problems of water and air pollution. See chapter 4, "The *Tragafuego*."

152. "With this type of attitude . . ." There were some minor victories for Mexican environmental groups. The new antipollution law of March 1988 was drafted in consultation with environmental groups. Environmentalists blocked a planned expansion of the Mexico City airport into the old lake bed of Lake Texcoco. They got the government to construct a nature preserve on the site instead. Under environmentalists' pressure, the government also constructed many "green lung" parks on sites of buildings damaged by the earthquakes that struck Mexico City in 1985. The daily pollution readings in Mexico City were an idea of environmental groups. At their suggestion, the government canceled plans for a series of dams along the Mexico-Guatemalan border that would have destroyed important Mayan ruins. The government created a sanctuary for the monarch butterfly, millions of which spend winter months in the state of Michoacán. It provided protection for endangered Mexican turtles. The number of environmental groups began to grow, too. In 1987, the Mexican Green Party was formed. It did not run candidates. But it went out on the stump during the 1988 presidential election to whip up interest in environmental issues—and specifically to try to block the opening of the Laguna Verde nuclear power plant.

Chapter 11: The *Campesino*

155. "The cause of the commotion was money . . ." *Ejido,* an organization that owns land farmed by peasants, derives from the Latin word "exitus," or exit, which once referred to the Indian lands that one found just outside the exits of Spanish colonial towns in Mexico. Such lands were used by Mexican Indians to grow corn, beans, and other traditional crops. In 1988, there were about 18,000 *ejidos* in Mexico. Fourteen thousand were of the type found around Independencia. On these, ejido members, known as *ejidatarios,* farmed individual plots and took profits from what their labors produced. But the *ejido* organization owned title to the land. *Ejidatarios* had only the right to farm certain plots, which right could be passed from father to son or from husband to wife as long as the land was farmed. Otherwise it would revert to the *ejido* for distribution to someone else. Some 4,000 of the 18,000 *ejidos* were farmed on a communal basis, with everyone working all the land that the *ejido* held title to. Mexican land-

reform laws also created a collective farm-land unit called a *colono,* which gave peasant farmers land that they would eventually have a chance to buy. When they did, it became private farm land, like half the farm land in Mexico. Collective farming also exists for pasture and forest land, and for cattle, shrimp, and similar agricultural operations.

157. "Farming is an expensive proposition . . ." A good overview of Mexican agricultural history can be found in *Mexico: A Country Study,* a 1985 U.S. Government Printing Office handbook prepared by the Foreign Area Studies division of the American University, pp. 208–33. A more scholarly and detailed treatment is contained in Steven E. Sanderson's *The Transformation of Mexican Agriculture: International Structure and the Politics of Rural Change* (Princeton University Press, 1986). David Ronfeldt also has done an excellent in-depth look at the history of Atencingo, an *ejido* in the state of Puebla, in *Atencingo: The Politics of Agrarian Struggle in a Mexican* Ejido (Stanford University Press, 1973).

158. "The revolution would change all that . . ." The data on how much land was distributed to peasants comes from the 1970 census. Data was collected during the 1980 census, but lack of funds has delayed its publication. In 1930, peasants working on *ejidos* and *colonos* had 10.9 percent of the land. Private farmers had the rest. By 1970, peasants had 49.9 percent of Mexico's farm land. Private farmers had 50.1 percent, according to the 1970 census. President Cárdenas distributed 17.6 million hectares of land to 808,000 *ejido* beneficiaries between 1935 and 1940.

159. "Peasants got non-arid land as well . . ." Of all the farms in Mexico, 22.8 percent are less than 1 hectare (2.471 acres); 42.8 percent are 1–5 hectares. An additional 22.4 percent are 5–10 hectares. Source: 1970 census. Even private farmers average only 31.1 acres, compared with 431 acres for U.S. farmers, according to the U.S. Department of Agriculture.

159. "There wasn't much good land to begin with . . ." Acreage and water figures are from the Mexican Ministry of Agriculture and Hydraulic Resources. In 1985, the latest figures available at publication, Mexican peasant and private farmers planted 17,163,343 hectares of land, 4.5 million of which had to be irrigated. Only 15,493,879 hectares of this land was harvested. If land planted with various types of nuts is included, the planted acreage for 1985 rises by 3,008,999 hectares and the harvested figure by 2,680,601 hectares.

160. "Credit was getting tighter . . ." López Portillo called his program SAM (*Sistema Alimentario Mexicano,* or "the Mexican Food System"). He increased guaranteed prices by 92 percent, after adjusting for inflation in the 1979–81 period. In 1980 he spent $2 billion on production subsidies, such as low-cost seed and fertilizer, and $1.5 billion on consumption subsidies, such as low-price food items in the supermarkets of Conasupo, the government food agency. In October 1983, de la Madrid created PRONAL (*Programa Nacional Alimentaria,* or "the National Food Program"). Less expensive than SAM, it focused on developing domestic food production, increasing food-processing productivity, and improving food marketing.

161. "The bizarre thing about this . . ." Mexico was expected to spend $280 million on dry milk in 1988, according to U.S. Department of Agriculture estimates.

162. "Likewise, more strawberries, broccoli . . ." U.S. agricultural exports to Mexico reached a peak of $2.7 billion in 1981. The worst economic crisis in modern Mexican history began in 1982, accompanied by the decreased ability of consumers to buy U.S. food imports. U.S. agricultural exports to Mexico dropped to $1.5 billion that year. The recent low point for such sales was in 1986, when U.S. agricultural exports hit $1.1 billion. They turned up in 1987 to $1.2 billion and were headed for $1.4 billion in 1988, according the USDA projections.

    Mexico in turn sold the United States only $1.1 billion in 1982. But in 1986, 1987, and 1988 it sold the United States an average of $2 billion in agricultural goods, according to USDA figures. It was more than any other country.

163. "It's not certain that the violence is over . . ." Amnesty International reported in 1985 that there were at least twenty-eight political killings in Chiapas between 1979 and 1985, most committed by *pistoleros* (armed gunmen) of local *caciques* (land bosses). Independent *campesino* organizations recorded about twenty more such killings between 1985 and mid-1988. A study by the Autonomous University of Chapingo reported that 525 *campesinos* were killed in Mexico between 1982 and the first half of 1985. Seventy percent of those killed came from Chiapas and neighboring Oaxaca state.

164. "Violence can also come at the hands . . ." Chiapas's celebrated Lacandon rain forest was a victim of this deforestation process. In 1970, it had nearly three million acres of virgin jungle. The year Abelardo Velasco died, it had only half that.

Chapter 12: The *Policia*

166. "The most common fear is police extortion . . ." In February 1988, the Mexico City police department instituted some reforms designed to reduce the amount of bribes that traffic police extracted from citizens. Some four thousand traffic cops were issued new, friendlier-looking light-blue uniforms, with white hats and gloves. Each officer was told to inform a citizen of the alleged violation and show the driver the traffic regulation in question. A blue book of traffic regulations was issued with the new uniforms. Fines went up substantially. But so did the amount of bribes. After several months of operation, little had changed except the uniforms.

167. "Tonio was a good source on Mexican cops . . ." Many police make only the minimum wage of about three dollars a day. Given the cost of living, that alone might prompt them to look to bribes to augment their income. But those assigned to motorcycles or squad cars often are forced to pay

maintenance on those vehicles out of their own pockets. Monthly repairs and parts can run more than their entire salaries. Police I talked with said they were willing to incur such maintenance payments and the hundred dollars or so it cost them to be assigned to vehicular duty because motorcycle and squad-car cops have more opportunities to demand bribes.

169. "The brunt of the morning rush hour . . ." Among the IDs Caro had on him were those of an agent of the security police of the Federal Interior (security) Ministry. Many other drug dealers were able to obtain similar police credentials. Pavón Reyes was later convicted for his involvement in drug trafficking. But his obstruction in the Camarena investigation, combined with other official foot-dragging, led the Reagan administration to launch Operation Intercept, a harassing border-inspection project that virtually shut down Mexican passenger and goods traffic to the United States until the de la Madrid government got moving on the Camarena case.

170. "We talked a bit about torture . . ." Details about police torture can be found in the annual human-rights reports of Amnesty International, The Americas Watch, and the U.S. State Department. In addition to techniques of near suffocation and electric shock, these reports note that Mexican police are regularly accused of "disappearing" political dissidents. In 1987, Amnesty International reported that about 450 persons remained "disappeared."

174. "Every modern Mexican president . . ." U.S. officials, using intercepts of electronic bank transfers to foreign banks and supportive intelligence, told me López Portillo's ill-gotten fortune might be as much as six billion dollars or as little as a billion. As a working estimate, they used the figure of three billion dollars, a figure López Portillo's spokesman said was preposterous. As for de la Madrid, if he took public funds illegally, he at least had the good taste not to flash them around. U.S. officials told me they had intercepted electronic bank transfers of millions of dollars that had been made in the name of a close de la Madrid associate. Opinion was divided in the U.S. intelligence community about whether this individual had acted on de la Madrid's behalf. There was no debate, however, that corruption had gone down dramatically in the economic-crisis atmosphere of de la Madrid's six-year term. As one cynic put it: "There was just less to steal."

175. "On closer examination, the program proved . . ." Interestingly, according to Joaquín Hernández Galicia, the head of the Mexican oil workers, Díaz Serrano had once suggested that the oil union buy a fleet of oil tankers so Pemex could throw a bunch of sweetheart deals toward the union's leaders, many of whom also had "inexplicable wealth." In an interview with the muckraking Mexico City magazine *Proceso,* the union leader, known to all as La Quina, complained that Díaz Serrano's successor, Ramón Beteta, had refused to honor the back-room deal, sticking the union with a lot of useless, rusting boats.

The controller general's office reviewed more than three thousand complaints about government corruption during the first five years of de la Madrid's administration, according to its 1987 report. In addition to Díaz

Serrano, about 350 low-level officials were convicted of corruption, as were the former heads of the national pawnshop and the federal airport system.

176. "No charges were ever brought . . ." A conservative lawyer, Ignacio Burgoa, did file embezzlement charges against López Portillo. But de la Madrid's attorney general, Sergio García Ramírez, found that there was no evidence to support them.

176. "The petition said nothing . . ." Durazo was secretly indicted by the Dade County grand jury. But rather than embarrass López Portillo, who was in the process of becoming the next president of Mexico, officials of the Gerald Ford administration promised to keep Durazo's name out of the indictment if López Portillo took care of Durazo. Durazo had been head of security at Mexico City's airport, a transshipment point for drugs. At the time of the indictment he was security chief of López Portillo's presidential campaign. López Portillo "took care" of Durazo by making him chief of police of Mexico City after he became president in December 1976.

177. "Durazo said González González . . ." González González's best-seller, *El Negro del Negro Durazo* (The Black Side of Blackie Durazo) (Posada, 1983), was made into a popular movie. Durazo was nicknamed El Negro because of his extremely dark skin.

180. "That was a laudable goal . . ." According to an April 1988 report by Seguros La Comercial, only 1,275,000 owners of Mexico's nearly six million cars carried insurance.

The problem of serious crime in Mexico, which is related to but different from corruption, is treated in chapter 6, "The *Chavo*." Incidents of rape and robbery by police in Mexican border towns are mentioned in chapter 4, "The *Pollo*." Rape by policemen is also dealt with in chapter 19, "The *Feminista*."

181. "All these bad examples . . ." For details on the life of a contraband seller and the government's efforts in the late 1980s to close down contraband sales, see chapter 9, "The *Fayucero*."

Chapter 13: The *Periodista*

184. "In many countries, 1968 was an extraordinary year . . ." A good account of the atmosphere in Mexico in 1968—and in a related violent time in 1971—is found in Octavio Paz's *The Other Mexico: Critique of the Pyramid* (Grove Press, 1972).

185. "Many of those who survived were jailed . . ." A thorough account of Scherer's election as editor and the events that followed is found in Manuel Becerra Acosta's book *Dos Poderes* (Grijalbo, 1984).

185. "His leftist rhetoric was taken . . ." A chilling account of the MAR's activities is found in John Barron's *KGB: The Secret Work of Soviet Secret Agents* (Bantam, 1974), pp. 312–48. The material also gives a good overview of how the Soviet Union uses Mexico as a springboard for its spying activities

in the United States with little interference from Mexican security services.

190. "Scherer also forbids *Proceso*'s reporters . . ." *Embute* comes from the verb *embutir,* which means to stuff something with something, as government stuffs envelopes (*sobres*) with cash for reporters on its bribe payroll.

190. "*Proceso* does not accept *gacetillas* either . . ." Within the journalism profession, *gacetillas* are so open a practice that newspapers publish a catalogue of prices for paid articles by size and location in the newspaper. In 1987, *Excélsior,* claiming a circulation of 200,000 copies daily, charged about 800,000 pesos for a *gacetilla* of 12.5 centimeters by 16.5 centimeters. Television has *gacetillas* too, which are read as if they were real news material.

193. "If a call from the government is not enough . . ." Listings of how many Mexican journalists have been murdered can be found in the annual human-rights reports of the U.S. State Department to the U.S. Congress, and in regular reports of human-rights groups such as Amnesty International and Freedom House.

194. "With all these restraints . . ." *Unomásuno*'s critical coverage might be expected. Some of the reporters who walked out of the July 8, 1976, meeting at *Excélsior* preferred to remain in newspaper work rather than become magazine journalists at *Proceso.* Manuel Becerra Acosta, whose late father was *Excelsior*'s editor for a brief period before Scherer took over, started *Unomásuno* with a group of ousted *Excélsior* reporters. In 1984, a group that felt *Unomásuno* wasn't being tough enough on the government left it and formed *La Jornada.*

According to industry sources, Mexicans buy about fifteen million comics a week, with a pass-on readership of five. Among the most popular are *La Familia Burrón, Vaquero, Lagrimas y Risas, El Libro Policiaco,* and *Memín Pingüín,* all of which come out weekly. Sales are down from a decade ago, when weekly sales were a mind-boggling sixty million—about one per Mexican per week. The key reason for the drop, say industry officials, has been the economic crisis and the loss of buying power it caused. Nationwide, Mexican newspapers claimed a circulation of 7.5 million in 1980, 4.5 million of which related to Mexico City newspapers. In a 1985 conversation, Roger Toll, then editor of the *Mexico City News,* told me that such figures are typically inflated, so newspapers can charge more for advertising. At the time, he said, based on private talks with other newspaper officials, *Excélsior* had a real daily circulation of about 120,000, about half what it claimed. *Unomásuno* had 15,000 to 18,000, considerably less than the figure it used for advertising fees. *La Jornada* had 15,000. The largest daily newspaper was the tabloid *La Prensa,* which, Toll said, had a circulation of about 250,000, just slightly less than it was claiming.

195. "This dampening effect on the circulation . . ." An excellent, detailed look at the government's co-optation of the media and Mexican intellectuals and its effect on society can be found in Roderic A. Camp's *Intellectuals and the State in Twentieth-Century Mexico* (University of Texas Press,

1985), especially pp. 177–207.

Camp notes that between 1934 and 1979, the Fondo de Cultura Económica published 2,992 books. Of its top ten best-sellers in that time, six were by Mexicans: *The Underdogs,* by Mariano Azuela; *Pedro Páramo* and *The Burning Lands,* by Juan Rulfo; *The Labyrinth of Solitude,* by Octavio Paz; *A Brief History of the Mexican Revolution,* by Jesús Silva Herzog; and *The Death of Artemio Cruz,* by Carlos Fuentes.

197. "Comic publishers argue . . ." The government has shown some awareness of the impact of comics. When it wants to promote a government policy such as birth control or a crackdown on tax evasion, it has used comic books to get the message out.

Chapter 14: The *Evangelista*

200. "I was in San Juanito . . ." Adelaida was the subject of chapter 1, a look at how Mexicans live on the minimum wage of three dollars a day. While this chapter focuses on the importance of religion in Mexican life—and the fervor that surrounds it—it also gives a glimpse of why millions of poor Mexicans in southern states, such as Oaxaca, fled their hometowns for brighter prospects in the big city.

200. "To a stranger, this might seem . . ." Mexican poet Octavio Paz has an excellent treatment of Mexicans' passion for fiestas in chapter 3 of *The Labyrinth of Solitude* (Grove Press, 1961), his classic study of the Mexican character.

201. "This sort of religious fervor . . ." When Spain's Catholic priests got millions of Indians to convert to Catholicism during the time of the conquest of Mexico, they didn't fully win the hearts and minds of Mexico's indigenous peoples. Indians were forced to destroy their pagan temples and build Catholic churches on the temple sites. Many Indians, however, clinging to old ways, hid images of their gods in the walls of the church. More than once, priests found supposed converts saying prayers in strange corners of the new edifices.

When I visited the Basilica of the Virgin of Guadalupe on the Virgin's feast day, outside on the massive plaza in front of the church, I saw half-naked Indian dancers recreating ritualistic pre-Hispanic religious dances as Mass was being said inside. Several of the people outside the church told me that, for them, the Virgin was a goddess, not the Mother of God. One said she was ranked higher in his mind than Jesus Christ.

203. "I wasn't really that surprised . . ." In the 1980 census, 89.4 percent of those surveyed said they were Catholics.

The antichurch provisions of the 1917 constitution are found in articles 3, 5, 24, 27, and 130.

203. "While that's what the law says . . ." Any good history of modern Mexico deals with the rise of the government's anticlerical attitude. Among the best in English are Frank R. Brandenburg's *The Making of Modern Mex-*

ico (Prentice-Hall, 1964); Frank Tannenbaum's *The Struggle for Peace and Bread* (Knopf, 1950); and Lesley Byrd Simpson's *Many Mexicos* (University of California Press, 1966).

204. "Many Mexican officials have had a schizophrenic . . ." While Catholic in private, many political leaders realize it is impossible to be so in public, notwithstanding Avila Camacho's profession of faith in 1940. For example, when President John F. Kennedy, a Catholic, came to Mexico in the early 1960s, he made a courtesy visit to the famed Basilica of the Virgin of Guadalupe in Mexico City. President Adolfo López Mateos (1958–64), his host, remained outside during Kennedy's inspection of the church.

In not-so-subtle fashion, the Catholic Church has allied itself with the National Action Party (PAN), a conservative, pro-religious group that is Mexico's leading opposition party. For whatever good it does, officials of the ruling Institutional Revolutionary Party (PRI) often warn voters that putting the PAN in power would mean a return to the domination of Mexico by the church, which once owned almost half the property in the country.

Archbishop Corripio frequently called for "respect for the vote" in the face of rampant vote fraud by loyalists of the PRI. He never mentioned the PRI by name or used the word "fraud."

205. "Father Octavio also had Melitón . . ." Protestant churches have made significant conversions in Mexico in recent years. In the 1980 census, 3.6 percent, or 2.4 million Mexicans, called themselves Protestants. That was more than double the 1.8 percent, or 876,879, who did so in the 1970 census. About 60 percent of Protestants are concentrated in six states—Mexico, Veracruz, Chiapas, Puebla, Tabasco, and Tamaulipas—as well as in Mexico City. In the early 1980s, the largest denominations were the National Baptist Church, the Seventh-Day Adventists, the Seventh-Day Baptist Church, the Church of Jesus Christ of Latter-Day Saints (Mormons), the Methodist Church, the National Presbyterian Church, and the Jehovah's Witnesses, according to the World Christian Encyclopedia.

206. " 'The Bible says all idols are an abomination . . .' " Feelings about the Virgin of Guadalupe run strong. When an exhibition at the Museum of Modern Art in January 1988 showed images of the Virgin with Marilyn Monroe's face, mobs stormed the museum and shut the exhibit down.

207. " 'It's difficult to be an *evangelista* . . .' " In late 1984, Dennis and Rose Carlson of Redding, California, and two of their friends, all Jehovah's Witnesses, were kidnapped in broad daylight in Guadalajara. They were never found. Their church insisted that the four had not been publicly proselytizing, which is against Mexican law. Some in Guadalajara, however, told police that the four had been seen going door to door to spread the word of their religion.

Chapter 15: The *Cómico*

211. "I met most of the characters . . ." The most famous study of the Mexican character is Octavio Paz's *The Labyrinth of Solitude* (Grove Press, 1961).

For a more up-to-date analysis of who Mexicans are, see Carlos Monsiváis's *Entrada Libre: Crónicas de la Sociedad que se Organiza* (Biblioteca Era, 1987), and *Escenas de Pudor y Liviandad* (Grijalbo, 1988). A wonderful fictional account of the character of rural Mexicans is found in Harriet Doerr's *Stones for Ibarra* (Penguin, 1985), which was made into a Hallmark Hall of Fame movie for television in 1988.

A more statistical approach to who Mexicans are and what they think can be found in *Cómo Somos los Mexicanos*, a 1987 collection of public-opinion polls published by the Centro de Estudios Educativos (CREA).

216. "This 'tremendous feeling of inferiority' . . ." For more on machismo, see chapter 16, "The *Maricón*."

218. "Negative names are part of a widespread cruelty . . ." Mexico's use of *"chingar"* is unique. In *The Labyrinth of Solitude* (p. 75), Paz details the meanings other countries give to *"chingar"* or its derivatives. They relate mostly to the dregs of a drink in a glass, the name for a tavern, or a shot of alcohol.

220. "This sort of black humor pervades Mexican culture . . ." In *Entrada Libre,* Monsiváis devotes an entire chapter to the San Juanico incident and the jokes it spawned (pp. 123–50).

Chapter 16: The *Maricón*

224. "Imbued with this new courage . . ." Ironically, Juan Jacobo taught, among others, the son of President Gustavo Díaz Ordaz, whose repressive acts against student protests in 1968 had sent Juan Jacobo and other gays out of Mexico, where they encountered ideas of gay liberation that were the seeds of the nascent Mexican gay movement of the late 1980s.

225. "When I met Juan Jacobo in June of 1987. . ." The first known case of AIDS in Mexico was reported in 1981, according to Gloria Ornelas Hall, director of Mexico's first AIDS information center, Conasida. The numbers at the beginning were small but began multiplying rapidly. Between late 1986 and mid-1987, about 100 active AIDS cases were reported, bringing the total to 500. One third of those 500 victims had died by mid-1987. By November 1, 1987, the number of active cases had risen to 866. By December 1, 1987, it was 1,043, although gay groups thought the actual number might be as high as 2,000. By July 1988 it was 1,656 and headed for 1,800 by the end of the year. Twenty-three of every 24 Mexican AIDS victims were men, a higher proportion than in the United States. Some cases were brought in by rich Mexicans who had relationships with gays in the United States or Europe while on vacation, according to Ornelas. Others were transmitted by undocumented Mexican workers, who, out of desperation for money, acted as male prostitutes for infected gays in the United States and then returned home to have sex with their wives.

228. "Rather bizarrely, persons who act . . ." The Octavio Paz quotations are from *The Labyrinth of Solitude* (Grove Press, 1961).

230. "Threats or violence can require stoicism . . ." Homosexuals in Mexico are called many things, the most common of which is *maricón*. Homosexuals themselves just call themselves gay. Activists such as Juan Jacobo also use the word *"joto,"* which is derived from a Mayan word, making the term uniquely Mexican. Sometimes, out of sheer audacity, Juan Jacobo likes to call himself a *puto,* which is a masculine form of *puta,* or "whore."

"It's a very beautiful, strong word," he told me. "I like it very much."

In turn, homosexuals have a name for straight people, referring to them as *bugas*.

232. "The government, which often pretends sex . . ." A spokesman for the Mexican Ministry of Health told me that by 1991 the number of active AIDS cases in Mexico could range between 20,000 and 30,000, based on the 500 active cases recorded in mid-1987. Alarmed by such figures, officials were seeking to cut the number of cases as much as possible through prevention—a tendency not regularly seen in fighting other diseases. One reason was the estimated cost to Mexicans for treating the disease. The typical seventy-two-day stay in a hospital for AIDS patients cost about fifteen million pesos (ten thousand dollars) in mid-1987, a crushing sum for the average Mexican, who makes about three dollars a day.

Among the actions taken by the government of President Miguel de la Madrid were strict controls imposed on the sale of blood. Prostitutes, homosexuals, and intravenous-needle users were found to be a large percentage of professional blood donors. Unfortunately, the government did not act until 1987, whereas gay groups had been warning since 1979 that blood in Mexico was infected with the AIDS virus. A new law also forced doctors to report all cases of AIDS. Previously many doctors had been hiding the existence of AIDS out of a desire not to embarrass their patients' families. The government also set up an AIDS information center in Mexico City. In its early weeks of operation in 1987, it was taking about 450 calls a day from worried citizens.

234. "This editorial line mirrored . . ." Mexico's pitiless yellow press joins in the police's game of presenting mincing, effeminate homosexuals as the norm. Through vicious cartoons and lurid, police-supplied photos, they create an image of gays as androgynous, unhappy, and weird.

Chapter 17: The *Mentalista*

235. "During my first weeks in Mexico . . ." The best source of information about magic and superstition is the Mexicans themselves. While professing not to believe in magic themselves, they will regale you with stories of what "other" Mexicans believe. For those who want something written, there is *A Guide to Mexican Witchcraft,* by William and Claudia Madsen, published by Minutiae Mexicana, 1972 (available in English and Spanish). There are also various works on the magic or superstitions of the various indigenous peoples of Mexico. One is *Magia, Mitos y Supersticiones entre los Mayas,* by Oswaldo Baqueiro López (Maldonado Editores, 1983). Some

brief treatment of other superstitions and of Mexicans' belief in magic can also be found in *The People's Guide to Mexico,* by Carl Franz (John Muir Publications, 1982). Magic is also a theme in many fictional works about Mexico, including Malcolm Lowry's *Under the Volcano* (Signet, 1974). Gary Jennings's novel *Aztec* (Avon, 1980), which contains a lot of good Indian scholarship hidden in a gory, sexy tale, is a good source of data about how the Aztecs viewed magic. I also found Oscar Lewis's *Children of Sánchez* (Vintage, 1961) an interesting source of the lower class's beliefs in magic and superstition.

243. "Maybe it's to be expected that Mexico . . ." In some cases, the Indian notions of magic and the next world have seeped into the principal religion of Mexico, Roman Catholicism. Indian beliefs in the return of the spirits of the dead, for example, have become part of celebrating All Saints' and All Souls' days, November 1 and 2. For more on this "folk Catholicism," see chapter 14, "The *Evangelista.*"

Chapter 18: The Güera

248. "In real life in Mexico, it's great . . ." Women who look Indian are discouraged from entering the Señorita México contest. Officials hold a separate beauty contest for Indian women, who do not become representatives of Mexico in international contests.

After the 1950 census, Mexico stopped recording who was Indian and who was not. In the 1980 census, officials did record who spoke indigenous languages. They found that 5.2 million people over the age of five said they did. Experts estimate that 8 million to 10 million Mexicans are Indians, defined as those who called themselves Indians. The state of Oaxaca had the largest percentage of Indians among its population—about 900,000 out of 2.3 million in 1980. Chiapas, with half that percentage, was the second most Indian state.

253. "I found it very sad . . ." For a basic overview of how Indians have been treated in Mexican history, see pp. 99–101 in *Mexico: A Country Study,* a 1985 handbook prepared by the Foreign Area Studies division of the American University and published by the U.S. Government Printing Office.

254. "Modern presidents have continued . . ." President de la Madrid's official policy on Indians was:

1. Design and implement a policy with the indigenous people.
2. Preserve their culture and traditions.
3. Slow down the process of reduction of the amount of Indian land.
4. Orient programs toward job training, production, and employment in accord with the nature of their resources and the traditions of their communities.

5. Increase the coverage of basic services.

6. Combat all forms of abuse by intermediaries.

7. Make real their individual guarantees and social rights.

Source: Instituto Nacional Indigenista, Documentos de Consulta, vol. 1, no. 1 (1984).

255. "These are the arguments of the politicians . . ." In Oaxaca, the most Indian state, 17 percent of children under five years of age had never eaten meat or drunk milk, according to the 1980 census. About half the 448,665 houses in the state had dirt floors. Only 45 percent had ready access to water, half of which was only available from sources outside the house. All these figures are worse than the national average recorded in the census. For more on *caciques, pistoleros,* and the other problems that Indians and other peasants encounter as farmers, see chapter 11, "The *Campesino.*"

256. "The future for Mexico's indigenous people . . ." For more details on what happened to one Indian woman who fled Oaxaca for the big city, see chapter 1, "The *Muchacha.*" Some further idea of life in an Indian village is given in chapter 14, "The *Evangelista.*" Mexican comedian Hector Suárez captured what happened to such Indians when they arrive in big cities. In the prize-winning film *El Milusos,* he portrayed a poor, uneducated peasant who becomes the target of con artists and unscrupulous employers after moving to Mexico City.

Chapter 19: The *Feminista*

260. "While still in high school . . ." A good history of the beginning of feminism in Mexico is *La Nueva Ola del Feminismo en México* (The New Wave of Feminism in Mexico), (Planeta, 1987), by Ana Lau Jaiven. It traces the rise of most professional feminist groups. A companion volume, *Mujeres en México: Una Historia Olvidada* (Women in Mexico: A Forgotten History) (Planeta, 1987), by Julia Tuñón Pablos, deals with unrecognized women's contributions to Mexican history.

According to the 1980 census, 16 percent, or 1,657,721 out of 10,245,394 marriages, were *unión libre,* or common-law marriages.

264. "The problems these women bring . . ." A 1987 study done by the National Autonomous University of Mexico, *Hostigamiento sexual en escenarios laborales* (Sexual Harassment in Work Settings), found that 95 percent of those women surveyed had been subject to sexual harassment. Seventy-eight of the harassers were married men. Twenty-three percent of the harassment involved sexual propositions.

264. "As a first step to ending such aggression . . ." Feminist groups estimate that there are about 180,000 rapes in Mexico each year, 20,000 of them committed in Mexico City. But only about a third of these rapes are reported to the police, either because women don't know how to do it, don't

think that what happened to them is a crime, or are ashamed of what happened to them.

264. "Part of women's surprise . . ." Rosario Ibarra de la Piedra, a leading human-rights activist, was the first woman to run for president in 1982. She ran for the PRT, the Revolutionary Workers Party, a Trotskyite group, although she herself is not a Trotskyite. Irma Cué de Duarte became secretary general of the Institutional Revolutionary Party (PRI) in 1984. President José López Portillo (1976–82) appointed Mexico's only woman cabinet member. But the woman, Rosa Luz Alégria, his tourism minister, was also his mistress. President Miguel de la Madrid had a woman in his subcabinet, Mexico City attorney general Victoria Adato de Ibarra. But she left in disgrace amid stories of prisoner torture by the attorney general's police. She was appointed to the Mexican supreme court, which got its first woman member in 1961.

Women elected to the senate or chamber of deputies tend to be pretty tame feminists. Senator Hilda Anderson de Rojas said in a 1987 interview that no woman could possibly become president of Mexico before the year 2000, a view shared by Federal Deputy María Emilia Farias Mackey. Farias went on to say: "We live in a man's political world and culture. We are not well organized as a political group. A Mexican woman is still not well received in politics."

La Asociación Mexicana de Mujeres Jefes de Empresa (the Mexican Association of Women Heads of Business) had only 400 members in 1987, 30 percent of whom were widows and 40 percent of whom were divorced. This reflected the small number of Mexican women who ran their own business or were professionals. In the 1980 census, 755,188 men said they ran their own business, while only 203,912 women did; 319,090 men listed themselves as professionals, while only 71,727 women did. Men technicians outnumbered women 3 to 2 in the same census. Women, on the other hand, outnumbered men 814,963 to 98,595 as domestics. Even in office work, men outnumbered women 1,112,478, to 870,730. This imbalance reflected the outnumbering of men over women in the active work force by 15,924,806 to 6,141,278.

Chapter 20: The Expatriado

273. "He did not win, however . . ." For more on the PRI and its relationship with business, see chapter 7, "The Priista."

Tax fraud reached such serious proportions that in 1986 the de la Madrid administration had to launch a special tax collection crackdown. According to the Mexican Finance Ministry, so few Mexicans paid income tax that such taxes provided only 39 percent of government revenues. To supplement such taxes, the government, several years before, had imposed a regressive 15 percent sales tax. In 1986, the sales tax accounted for 30 percent of government revenues, nearly as much as income taxes. As the pinch of Mexico's economic crisis tightened in the mid-1980s, however, many merchants evaded even this tax, increasingly resorting to cash deals in which no receipt was given.

277. "He began looking for a house . . ." A number of international agencies and banks have calculated the extent of capital flight from Mexico—the amount of money Mexicans sent out of the country to safer financial havens abroad. One of the most widely accepted figures was that done by the Morgan Guaranty Trust Co. in 1986. Morgan experts calculated that between the beginning of 1976, the year that President Luis Echeverría drastically devalued the peso, and the end of 1985, two-and-a-half years into Mexico's current economic crisis, Mexicans sent $53 billion out of the country. Venezuelans were second in capital flight in the same period with $30 billion. Argentines were third, with $26 billion. About a third of the Mexican $53 billion—some $17 billion—left after President López Portillo nationalized the Mexican banks in September 1982. Mexican central-bank officials insist that capital flight, while a serious problem, is overstated by studies such as the one Morgan did. Figures similar to Morgan's have been done by the World Bank and other international financial institutions.

The 1976 Echeverría devaluation and the 1982 López Portillo bank nationalization were the two biggest psychological shocks to the business community in recent times. Both events set off waves of expatriates and money to the United States and other countries. One group of twenty-five families that I encountered in La Jolla, California, had taken an astounding $125 million in savings with them when they left Mexico, most of them following the 1976 devaluation.

Without capital flight, Mexico would have had much less of an economic crisis. Because there wasn't enough money in Mexican banks for private and government borrowing, the government had to borrow abroad for development projects and to finance budget deficits. Morgan Guaranty officials estimate that if Mexico hadn't suffered capital flight, its 1986 foreign debt of about $100 billion would have been only $12 billion.

Even with just a fraction of those billions sent abroad, the Mexican government could have done economic wonders. Just $10 billion of that $53 billion was the equivalent of 7 percent of the gross national product in 1986, a year Mexico suffered a 4 percent reduction in GNP.

282. "People such as the Contrerases are precisely . . ." Figures on the extent of Mexico's brain drain can sometimes be elusive. Mexican experts such as Jorge Bustamonte of the Northern Border College in Tijuana regularly assert that anecdotal data show an increasing number of those immigrating to the United States are professional or technical people, almost all of whom had jobs in Mexico. Juan Casillas Garcia de León, executive general secretary of the National Association of Universities and Institutions of Superior Education (ANUIES), said in a 1988 interview that the number of Mexican academics leaving the country was on the rise because of the lure of better salaries and conditions abroad.

In the Houston area, where Roberto Contreras lives, market data shows that more Mexican professional and technical people have moved to the area in recent years. According to Telesurveys of Texas, Inc., more than a quarter of the Hispanics who moved to Harris County (Houston) between mid 1985 and mid-1986—80 percent of whom were Mexicans—were college graduates or had advanced degrees. That was double the percentage for long-term Hispanic residents of the area and double the percentage of non-Hispanic residents. Likewise, the percentage of Harris County Hispanics (mostly Mexicans) having incomes of $50,000 or more doubled after 1982, the year Mexico's economic crisis began.

· Bibliography ·

1. English

Barron, John, *KGB: The Secret Work of Soviet Secret Agents*, Bantam, 1974.

Brandenburg, Frank R., *The Making of Modern Mexico*, Prentice-Hall, 1964.

Camp, Roderic A., *Intellectuals and the State in Twentieth-Century Mexico*, University of Texas Press, 1985.

Cockcroft, James D., *Mexico: Class Formation, Capital Accumulation and the State*, Monthly Review Press, 1983.

Conover, Ted, *Coyotes*, Vintage Departures, 1987.

Domínguez, Jorge, ed., *Mexico's Political Economy: Challenges at Home and Abroad*, Sage Publications, 1982.

Erb, Richard, ed., *United States Relations with Mexico: Context and Content*, American Enterprise Institute, 1981.

Grayson, George, *The United States and Mexico: Patterns of Influence*, Praeger, 1984.

———, *The Politics of Mexican Oil*, University of Pittsburgh Press, 1980.

Instituto Nacional de Estadística, Geografía e Informática, *Mexico: A Synoptic View*, 1985.

Johnson, Kenneth F., *Mexican Democracy: A Critical View*, 3d ed., Praeger, 1984.

Katz, Friederich, *The Secret War in Mexico*, University of Chicago Press, 1981.

Lewis, Oscar, *Five Families: Mexican Case Studies in the Culture of Poverty*, Basic Books, 1959.

——, *A Death in the Sánchez Family*, Vintage, 1969.

——, *The Children of Sánchez*, Vintage, 1961.

Madsen, William and Claudia, *A Guide to Mexican Witchcraft*, Minutiae Mexicana, 1972 (also available in Spanish).

Martínez Manautou, Jorge, ed., *The Demographic Revolution in Mexico 1970–1980*, Mexican Institute of Social Security, 1982.

Needler, Martin C., *Mexican Politics: The Containment of Conflict*, Praeger, 1982.

——, *Politics and Society in Mexico*, University of New Mexico Press, 1971.

Paz, Octavio, *The Other Mexico: Critique of the Pyramid*, Grove Press, 1972.

——, *The Labyrinth of Solitude: Life and Thought in Mexico*, Grove Press, 1961.

Reynolds, Clark, ed., *U.S.-Mexico Relations: Economic and Social Aspects*, Stanford University Press, 1983.

Riding, Alan, *Distant Neighbors: A Portrait of the Mexicans*, Knopf, 1984.

Ronfeldt, David, ed., *The Modern Mexican Military: A Reassessment*, Center for U.S.-Mexican Studies, University of California, 1984.

——, *Atencingo: The Politics of Agrarian Struggle in a Mexican Ejido*, Stanford University Press, 1973.

Ross, Stanley, *Is the Mexican Revolution Dead?* Knopf, 1966.

Rudolph, James, ed. *Mexico: A Country Study*, prepared by Foreign Area Studies, The American University, U.S. Government Printing Office, 1985.

Sanders, Sol, *Mexico: Chaos on Our Doorstep*, Madison Books, 1986.

Sanderson, Steven E., *The Transformation of Mexican Agriculture: International Structure and the Politics of Rural Change*, Princeton University Press, 1986.

——, *The Struggle for Land in Sonora*, University of California Press, 1981.

Simpson, Lesley Byrd, *Many Mexicos*, University of California Press, 1966.

Tannenbaum, Frank, *The Struggle for Peace and Bread*, Knopf, 1950.

Tuchman, Barbara, *The Zimmerman Telegram*, Ballantine, 1966.

United States, Department of State, *Country Reports on Human Rights Practices*, 1983, 1984, 1985, 1986, 1987, U.S. Government Printing Office.

Wambaugh, Joseph, *Lines and Shadows*, Bantam, 1984.

2. Spanish

Banco de México, *Informe Anual*, 1984, 1985, 1986, 1987.

Baqueira López, Oswaldo, *Magia, Mitos y Supersticiones entre los Mayas*, Maldonado Editores, 1983.

Becerra Acosta, Manuel, *Dos Poderes*, Grijalbo, 1985.

Castañeda, Jorge, *Mexico: El Futuro en Juego*, Joaquín Mortiz, 1987.

Centro de Estudios Educativos (CREA), *Cómo Somos los Mexicanos*, 1987.

Colegio de México, *Historia General de México* (2 vols.), El Colegio de México, 1976.

Cosío Villegas, Daniel, *La Sucesión Presidencial*, Joaquín Mortiz, 1973.

——, *El Sistema Político Mexicano*, Joaquín Mortiz, 1972.

De la Madrid Hurtado, Miguel, *Informe Anual de Gobierno*, 1984, 1985, 1986, 1987, 1988.

García-Robles, Jorge, *Qué Transa con las Bandas?* Editorial Posada, 1987.

González Casanova, Pablo, ed., *México Ante la Crisis* (2 vols.), Siglo Veintiuno, 1985.

González de la Garza, Mauricio, *Carta a Miguel de la Madrid*, Posada, 1987.

González González, José, *El Negro del Negro Durazo*, Posada, 1983.

Instituto Nacional de Estadística, Geografía e Informática, *Encuestas en Hogares*, 1987.

——, *Comparaciones Internacionales México en el Mundo 1986*.

——, *10 Años de Indicadores Económicos y Sociales de México*, 1986.

——, *Información Estadística, Sector Salud y Seguridad Social*, 1986.

——, *Cuaderno de Información Oportuna*, 1985.

——, *Estadísticas Históricas de México* (2 vols.), 1985.

——, *Anuario Estadístico de los Estados Unidos Mexicanos 1983*.

——, *Encuesta Nacional de Ingreso-Gasto de los Hogares 1983–84*.

——, *X Censo General de Población y Vivienda, 1980*.

Krauze, Enrique, *Por Una Democracia Sin Adjetivos*, Joaquín Mortiz, 1986.

Lau Jaiven, Ana, *La Nueva Ola del Feminismo en México*, Planeta, 1987.

Loaeza, Guadalupe, *Las Niñas Bien*, Oceano, 1987.

Loret de Mola, Carlos, *Que La Nación Me Lo Demande*, Grijalbo, 1986.

Mejía Prieto, Jorge, *Así Habla El Mexicano*, Panorama Editorial, 1984.

Meyer, Lorenzo, ed., *México–Estados Unidos, 1982*, El Colegio de México, 1982.

Monsiváis, Carlos, *Entrada Libre: Crónicas de la Sociedad que se Organiza*, Biblioteca Era, 1987.

——, *Escenas de Pudor y Liviandad*, Grijalbo, 1988.

Ojeda, Mario, *Alcance y Limites de la Política Exterior de México*, El Colegio de México, 1976.

Organización Panamericana de la Salud, *Las Condiciones de Salud en las Américas 1981–84* (2 vols.), 1986.

——, *Las Condiciones de Salud en las Américas 1977–80*, 1982.

Partido Revolucionario Institucional, *Constitución Política de los Estados Unidos Mexicanos*, 1981.

Poder Ejecutivo Federal, *Programa Nacional de Ecologia 1984–1988*.

Scherer García, Julio, *Los Presidentes*, Grijalbo, 1986.

Tuñón Pablos, Julia, *Mujeres en México: Una Historia Olvidada*, Planeta, 1987.

Zaid, Gabriel, *La Economía Presidencial*, Vuelta, 1987.

3. Fiction

Sometimes fiction tells a reader as much, if not more, about a country as nonfiction works. Mexico has many fine novelists, including Carlos Fuentes, Juan Rulfo, Luis Spota, and Elena Poniatowska, whose works provide insightful details about the fabric of Mexican life. Non-Mexican writers, including Graham Greene, Malcolm Lowry, D. H. Lawrence, and the mysterious B. Traven, have also given the world an outsider's view of this hard-to-fathom country. Herein is a select reading list of novels in English about Mexico.

Azuela, Arturo, *Shadows of Silence*, University of Notre Dame Press, 1985.

Doerr, Harriet, *Stones for Ibarra*, Penguin, 1984.

Fuentes, Carlos, *The Old Gringo*, Farrar, Straus & Giroux, 1985.

——, *Terra Nostra*, Farrar, Straus & Giroux, 1976.

——, *The Death of Artemio Cruz*, Panther, 1974.

——, *Where the Air is Clear*, Farrar, Straus & Giroux, 1960.

Greene, Graham, *The Power and the Glory*, Penguin, 1971.

Jennings, Gary, *Aztec*, Avon, 1980.

Lawrence, D. H., *The Plumed Serpent*, Vintage, 1951.

Lowry, Malcolm, *Under the Volcano*, Signet, 1965.

Rulfo, Juan, *The Burning Plain and Other Stories*, University of Texas Press, 1967.

———, *Pedro Páramo*, Grove Press, 1959.

Somerlott, *Death of the Fifth Sun*, Viking, 1987.

B. Traven, *Government*, Allison & Busby, 1971.

———, *March to the Montería*, Allison & Busby, 1971.

———, *The Cotton-Pickers*, Allison & Busby, 1969.

———, *The Treasure of Sierra Madre*, Hill & Wang, 1963.

· Index ·

ABOUT THE AUTHOR

Patrick Oster grew up in the Chicago area, where he practiced law before taking up journalism as a career in 1973. He spent ten years in Washington, D.C., from the end of Watergate to the beginning of the second Reagan administration. He was Washington bureau chief for the *Chicago Sun-Times*. He covered the White House, the State Department, and the Pentagon, specializing in foreign affairs most of this time. He traveled to about fifty countries in the process.

In 1984, he became the Mexico City bureau chief for the Knight-Ridder newspaper chain. He has won awards from the Overseas Press Club and the Inter-American Press Foundation for his coverage of Mexico and Latin America. He and his wife and son now live in Belgium. This is his first book.